Louise Müller

Religion and Chieftaincy in Ghana

ANTHROPOLOGY OF RELIGION

RELIGIONSETHNOLOGIE

Band / Volume 2

LIT

Louise Müller

Religion and Chieftaincy in Ghana

An explanation of the persistence of a traditional political institution in West Africa

LIT

This book is printed on acid-free paper.

Bibliographic information published by the Deutsche Nationalbibliothek
The Deutsche Nationalbibliothek lists this publication in the Deutsche Nationalbibliografie; detailed bibliographic data are available in the Internet at http://dnb.d-nb.de.

ISBN 978-3-643-90360-0

A catalogue record for this book is available from the British Library

Klosbachstr. 107
CH-8032 Zürich
Tel. +41 (0) 44-251 75 05
Fax +41 (0) 44-251 75 06
E-Mail: zuerich@lit-verlag.ch
http://www.lit-verlag.ch

LIT VERLAG Dr. W. Hopf
Berlin 2013
Fresnostr. 2
D-48159 Münster
Tel. +49 (0) 2 51-62 03 20
Fax +49 (0) 2 51-23 19 72
E-Mail: lit@lit-verlag.de
http://www.lit-verlag.de

Distribution:
In Germany: LIT Verlag Fresnostr. 2, D-48159 Münster
Tel. +49 (0) 2 51-620 32 22, Fax +49 (0) 2 51-922 60 99, E-mail: vertrieb@lit-verlag.de

In Austria: Medienlogistik Pichler-ÖBZ, e-mail: mlo@medien-logistik.at
In Switzerland: B + M Buch- und Medienvertrieb, e-mail: order@buch-medien.ch
In the UK: Global Book Marketing, e-mail: mo@centralbooks.com
In North America: International Specialized Book Services, e-mail: orders@isbs.com
e-books are available at www.litwebshop.de

RELIGION AND CHIEFTAINCY IN GHANA

An explanation of the persistence of a traditional political institution in West Africa

Louise F. Müller

To my parents

Table of Contents

Acknowledgements

The author would like to thank James Cox, emeritus Professor of Religious Studies, and Paul Nugent, Professor of Comparative African History and Director of the Centre of African Studies at the University of Edinburgh, for their supervision of the thesis on which this monograph is based. She is also very grateful to Wim van Binsbergen, emeritus Professor of Intercultural Philosophy at the Erasmus University of Rotterdam, for supervising her MA thesis on Asante philosophy and for allowing her to participate in his Intercultural Philosophy research group at Leiden University/Erasmus University of Rotterdam. Furthermore, she is thankful to the Centre for non-Western Studies (CNWS) in Leiden for providing a visiting scholarship and academic support during her stay in the Netherlands. She is also grateful to David E. Skinner, Professor of History at Santa Clara University, for his comments on parts of her book. Furthermore, she would like to thank: Benedict Asante Kyei of the Language Centre of the University of Ghana for correcting her Twi, Richard Okine, Mine Geologist at Perseus Mining Ltd, Dr. Afe Adogame, Senior Lecturer in World Christianity and Religious Studies, Samuel Adu-Gyamfi, Postdoctoral Student at Kwame University of Science and Technology in Kumasi, Dr. Rosemary Amenga-Etego, Senior Lecturer at the University of Legon, Dr. Felix Ameka, Linguist at Leiden University Centre for Linguistics, Dr. Marloes van Amerom, Journalist and Editor at Kennislink, Alan Barnard, Professor of Anthropology of Southern Africa, Dr. Mary Catherine Burgess, Research Fellow at the University of Edinburgh, Jane Cameron, Researcher at London College of Fashion, Carolien Ceton, Editor in Chief of Groenlinks Magazine, Dr. BC Chew, Lecturer at the Technical University of Malaysia Melaka, Dr. Charles Coffie, Alumni of the University of Toronto, Associate Professor Michel Doortmont, University of Groningen, Dr. Wilhelmina Donkoh, Senior Lecturer at Kwame Nkrumah University of Science and Technology in Kumasi, Dr. Kofi Dorvlo, Linguist at the University of Legon, Dr. Setri Dzivenu, Lecturer in History at the University of Legon, Dr. Natalie Everts, Historian at Leiden University, Dr. Tom Fisher, Lecturer at Saint Augustine University of Tanzania, Dr. Julie Grant, Postdoctoral Research Fellow at the University of KwaZulu-Natal, Professor Robert Hefner, Professor at Boston University and Director of the Institute on Culture, Religion and World Affairs, Dr. Rania Hussein Khafaga, Lecturer in African Politics at the Center for African Studies at Addis Ababa University, Dr. Arkotong Longkumer, Lecturer in Religious Studies, Dr. Laura Mann, Postdoctoral Researcher at the University of Oxford, Dr. Andrew McFarlane, Researcher at the University of Edinburgh, Dr. Michael Ofori-Mensah, Alumni of the University of Edinburgh, Dr. Svetalana Milyaeva, Research Fellow in Sociology at Goldsmith University, Dr. Carys Moseley, Treasurer for the Society for the Study of Christian Ethics, Maggi Morrison, Researcher/Lecturer at University of Edinburgh, Maarten Mous, Professor in African languages, Dr. Julie Ndaya Tshiteku, Professor of the Anthropology of Religion and Research Methodology in the Social Sciences, Dr. Amy Niang, Lecturer in International Relations at the University of Witwatersrand, Dr. Maria Nita, Lecturer in Religious Studies at Weston College University Campus, Dr. Suzanne Owen, Senior Lecturer at Leeds Trinity University, Dr. Jan Platvoet, Convenor of the African Assocation for the Study of Religions, Dr. Lucia Siu, Assistant Professor in Sociology at Lingnan University, Elisabetta Spano, PhD student at the University of Edinburgh in African Studies, Dr. Paul Swanepoel, Lecturer in Criminal Law at the University of KwaZulu Natal, Dr. Piotrek Swiatkowski, Lecturer at Ethics, Corporate Social Responsibility and Sustainability at Avans Hogeschool, Dr. Menno Welling, Chairman and Managing Director at African Heritage Ltd, David Wilson, President of the Scottish Association of Spiritual Healers, and especially Dr. Meera Venkatachalam, Researcher/Historian at the University of Legon, for their academic support. The Prins Bernhard Cultuurfonds and the University of Edinburgh's College Award, for which she is also very appreciative, provided financial support for this book. Further, she would like to demonstrate her gratitude to the British Association for the Study of Religions (BASR) and the Africa-Europe Group for Interdisciplinary Studies (AEGIS) for giving her the opportunity to present papers and receive response on ideas from an international academic audience. Finally, she could never have written this book without the warmth of her family and the cooperation of her respondents. She is especially grateful to the contributions of two of her interviewees, Chief Brefo Gyededu Kotowko II and the Queen Mother Ama Serwah Nyarko. *Medaase paa*, thank you very much.

List of maps, symbols, photographs and schemes

Introduction

This book explains how Asante Indigenous Religion (AIR) constitutes an explanatory factor for the persistence of chieftaincy among the Asante people in Ghana.[1] Indigenous Religions are religions that regulate the relations of people with their social and natural environment: they further maintain those relationships by caring and sympathising for one another, through veneration, empathy, bonding, using the senses, and by creative and artistic expression such as dancing, making music, and making love. They are religions that place emphasis on the greeting of the bones or other parts of the body: the veneration of the ancestral spirits, the use of metaphors, axioms, proverbs, the sharing of myths about the origin of the world and the place of individual human beings and cultural groups in that wider world. Last but not least these religions share a philosophy of mind that celebrates the dominance of the right brain hemisphere over the left hemisphere of the brain. AIR is focussed on the right-brain invocation of spirits and the veneration of the royal ancestors or quasi-material guardians of the source of all life. Its adherents use metaphors and mytho-poeic language to express the state of their wellbeing and to explain their relationship with the inhabitants of the material and the social worlds. The *Adinkra* symbol of the ancestral crocodile (*nananom odenkyem*) is, for instance, a metaphor for the Akan wisdom that one should stick to one's own destiny (*nkrabea*) or divine function regardless of the environment (see 7.7 symbol 1). A crocodile differs from the fishes that surround him, and thus has a different destiny. The crocodile should therefore not start breathing in water as this will lead to his death. One's life (*obra bo*) should be in harmony with one's divine destiny by accepting and continuing one's own (cultural) identity despite societal change (Wright 2004:15,18-19). Like the ancestral crocodile, the determinacy of the Asante traditional authorities throughout Asante history goes hand in hand with their maintenance of their own cultural identity and of harmonious relationships with non-Asante indigenous religious believers, as well as, the continuation of these authorities' indigenous religious functions.

A central concept in this book is that of (Asante) Indigenous Religions. The author does acknowledge, however, that 'Indigenous Religions' (IRs) is a controversial term, both because of its colonial heritage – the term originates from

---

[1] The term 'Asante' means 'for the sake of war' (*ɛsa* means war and *nti* means for the sake of it). It refers to the common goal of the Asante union of fighting a war against the Denkyera, a superior power in the region on account of the gold trade with European nations and their control over significant gold producing states. The defeat of the Denkyera king by the union of states resulted in the foundation of the Asante nation (interview with Tweneboa Kodua, – the great grandchild of the late female warrior Nana Yaa Asantewaa). In the early nineteenth century, the Swiss (Basel) missionaries wrote down the Akan language. They tried to duplicate the name 'Asante' as they heard it, which resulted in their spelling of the word as 'Ashantee' and 'Shanty'. After Ghana gained independence in 1957, the new government commissioned the 'African Studies Centre' (ASC) at the University of Ghana, Legon, to rationalise and standardise the spellings of all traditional and historical names, which resulted in the word 'Asante' (www.scn.org/rdi/index.htm).

the encounter of European Christians with the religions of indigenous people – and because it implies that all religions of indigenous people worldwide resemble one another and therefore fit into a coherent category. The religions of these people are, of course, starkly different and might be more distinct from one another than similar. In fact, all religious categories contain divergent sects; Christianity is a popular example. If one emphasises the distinctions amongst all sects that fall under Christianity, one may wonder whether the general term 'Christianity' accurately characterise all of these practices. Within the context of this controversy, this book introduces AIR as one of the many IRs in the world with which it shares common attributes, such as its emphasis on the balance between body and mind, its focus on people and their natural environment and its adaptive and adoptive nature towards elements of World Religions, such as Christianity and Islam. By digging deep into the concept and the historical-anthropological reality of AIR, this book aims to contribute to current understandings of the nature of IRs in general. The category of IRs is not perfect, but as Lawrence Sullivan wrote, 'Any term used to think broadly about the human condition across cultures will be flimsy and loosely fitting, perhaps even ill-fitting. It helps in our task as interpreters to see the arbitrariness of the categories, for recognition that the arbitrariness lays bare our own prejudgements' (Sullivan 1991:31). This study of AIR as related to the persistence of Asante chieftaincy aims to enhance understanding of the conceptual history of IRs and to diminish Westerners' prejudgements towards them. It aims to challenge firstly, the resilient evolutionary idea that these religions are the relics of lower stages of human religious development and are therefore 'simple' and/or 'primitive', and secondly, the cultural primitivistic conception that indigenous people are able to be more emotional and self-expressive, because they are exempt from pressure of the social group, or that they are less in need of material wealth and more easily satisfied with life.

In addition to adding knowledge to Western notions of IRs, this book also addresses how the Asante traditional authorities, who are the representatives of the Asante Indigenous Religion have used that religion over the centuries to legitimate their chieftaincy institution. It aims to explain why the Asante chiefs and their female co-rulers did not cease to exist after Ghana gained independence. Like other former British colonies, such as Nigeria and Sierra Leone (but unlike Tanzania), the system of Indirect Rule gave these Ghanaian rulers a relatively autonomous sphere of chieftaincy decision-making, which has been the source of continuation of their influence and prestige in the postcolonial era. Whereas the chieftaincy institutions of the traditional authorities in most former French colonies were either despised (as in Guinea) because they remained the servants of higher authorities, like those in most former British colonies, such as Ghana, persisted, despite the reduction of those authorities' formal power.

In the precolonial period, the Asante traditional authorities were the rulers of one of the most powerful kingdoms in West Africa (comparable to the Oyo and Benin kingdoms in present day Nigeria, or the Kaabu kingdom in Senegambia) that exceeded the boundaries of present-day Ghana. In the colonial period the Asante kingdom ceased to exist, but its traditional rulers were incorporated in the colonial superstructure of Indirect Rule and continued to rule over their subjects. The institution of chieftaincy continued to exist despite the fact that in 1896 the Asante king (*Asantehene*) was exiled to Sierra Leone and, to further reduce his power, in 1900, he and his female co-ruler were sent to the remote Seychelles Islands. In the postcolonial period, the Asante chieftaincy institution and its traditional authorities were incorporated in the democratic republic of Ghana to deal with Asante traditional customs which were an integral part of AIR. It is the focus on religion that distinguishes this book from others, such as Rathbone (2000) and Austin (Austin 1988; 2007), that address the question of the salience of chieftaincy in Ghana.

Previously scholars who have focused on the economic, political, and juridical aspects of the persistence of chieftaincy in the past and the present all indicate that their focus has been somehow limited, because they lacked understanding of the Indigenous Religion that binds the chiefs to their subjects. The focus of this book is therefore on the enhancement of understanding of the Asante Indigenous Religion in its relation to chieftaincy in both historical and contemporary times. The main concentration is on the two indigenous religious functions of the Asante traditional authorities: those of mediation with (a) the beings of the spiritual world and (b) human beings regardless of their religious denominations in the social world. The traditional authorities perceive themselves as servants of the ancestral spirits, from whom they receive the divine power to rule by occupying a 'stool' (throne); in turn, they maintain a reciprocal relationship with them by venerating them and offering foods and drinks in exchange for care and the well-being of their community. Besides, since precolonial times, the traditional Asante authorities have also operated as religious peacekeepers as they have managed both religiously and socially to maintain a relationship of balanced tension between Asante indigenous practitioners, Muslims, and Christians within the society.

The author focuses on the indigenous religious roles of the Asante royal rulers, both male and female, to provide an explanation for the salience of Asante chieftaincy but acknowledges that their Indigenous Religion is not the only explanatory factor for this phenomenon. In fact, the Asante Indigenous Religion can only partly explain why the traditional political institution of the Asante people in Ghana did not cease to exist after the country gained independence in 1957. Explanatory factors of an economic, political and juridical nature, which other scholars have researched, therefore also receive attention in this book. The author takes into account that researchers from different academic fields analyse their data in contrasting ways and that people live within alternate, co-existing realities that require researchers to experience the same phenomenon from different perspectives.

To explain the aforementioned enigma of the Asante chieftaincy's longevity, this book will follow the two main indigenous religious roles of the Asante traditional authorities: those of (a) mediators and (b) peacekeepers.

(a) Once the Asante royal rulers occupy a stool (a throne), they mediate between beings of the spiritual world and the social world. They maintain their subjects' connection with ancestral spirits, and translate messages from the ancestral spirits for their subjects, who receive them via their spokesmen (*akyeame*) (Yankah 1995).
(b) The Asante traditional authorities maintain peaceful social and religious relationships with other groups of religious believers, mainly Christians and Muslims of various denominations.

This book, which addresses the 'persistence' of the Asante chieftaincy, focuses on the indigenous religious roles of the Asante traditional authorities in the precolonial (1701-1901), the colonial (1901-1957) and the postcolonial period (1957-2009). The synopsis is the result of a multi-method approach combining historical archival and oral historical research with fieldwork data.

Chapter I will elaborate on the point of departure, which is the theory that Asante Indigenous Religion (AIR) provides an explanation for the persistence of the Asante chieftaincy. It will provide further information about the special reasons why Ghana's traditional political institution remains after the colonial and postcolonial phases. To explain why chieftaincy remains, the chapter addresses the devastating effects of British colonial rule on the continuation of Africa's traditional political institutions. It then gives an overview of the economic, political, juridical and religious factors that drive the persistence of the Asante chieftaincy in Ghana. Thereafter, the author enhances scholarly understanding of the nature of AIR. This enhancement is followed by an elaboration of the relevance and novelty of the research on which this book is based. The author concludes Chapter I by introducing the key concepts in this book.

Chapter II details the research methodology used to collect the necessary historical and empirical data that underpin the questions that the author aims to answer. This chapter also contains a historical overview of the academic paradigms and ideas of scholars on the religions of indigenous people. It also discusses the sources of criticism that enable the reader to increase his or her understanding of the competing point of views, and interests and academic paradigms associated with previous authors who wrote on the Asante people. This book builds on but also differs from the works of previous contemporary scholars, like McCaskie and Wilks in that it does not makes use of philosophical frameworks that were created to analyse Western societies, such as that of Weber and his theory of ideal types or Gramsci and his school of historical materialism, to describe and analyse the Asante history. Instead, this book aims to present Asante religious and chieftaincy history by making use of the latest theories on Indigenous Religions, religious syncretism and the philosophy of spirit mediumship, which grew out of the necessity to enhance understanding of non-western societies and which are sensitive to the indigenous concepts of mediation. Furthermore, the book criticises the representation by missionary-oriented scholars of the spiritual world especially as related to female ancestral spirits that were left out of many of their scholarly works, which has had a negative impact on the position of the female rulers in Asante society. The author aims with this book to restore the significance of the female spirits and the female co-rulers in Asante history (or better 'her-story'). In contradiction to existing books on Asante chieftaincy, she therefore refers consistently to the ruling pair – the male ruler (*Asantehene*) and the female ruler (*Asantehemma*) – rather than mentioning only the male Asante ruler.

Furthermore, the author aims to increase insights into the actual historical-anthropological social reality by the use of these religious and philosophical theories, and of primary and secondary sources. The author admirers the scholars whom she cites and could not have written her book without their commendable contributions. Nevertheless, she felt that there is a lack of engagement by scholars of religion and philosophers with Asante history and a lack of engagement of Asante historians with the theoretical insights gained by philosophers and scholars of religion about the nature of African religions. She therefore decided to use her training in both historical anthropology and religious studies/philosophy to bridge between those academic fields of study and to enrich them with insights that were the result of academic cross-fertilisations.

Chapters III, IV, V and VI follow with historical and empirical data. In Chapter III, the author focuses on the two indigenous religious roles of the Asante traditional authorities in precolonial history. This chapter elaborates on the meaning of the religious artefacts, symbols and festivals that these authorities used to connect with and maintain the relationship with the spiritual beings. It also focuses on the way in which these authorities dealt with European Christian missionaries and Muslim leaders and their religious activities. To enhance understanding of the Asante traditional authorities' indigenous religious peacekeeping role in this period, the author introduces the model of religious syncretism by the German scholar of religion Ulrich Berner (Berner 2001; 2004). Chapter IV concentrates on the indigenous religious mediatory and peacekeeping roles of the two Asante kings and their female co-rulers who were ruling during the colonial period: the Asanthe *ahemfo* Prempeh I and II and the Asante *ahemma* Konadu Yaadom II and Ama Serwaa Nyaako. An elaboration of the continuity, discontinuity and change in these roles under colonial rule follows.

In Chapter V, the author attempts to reveal the nature of the indigenous religious mediatory and peacekeeping functions of the Asante traditional authorities in the postcolonial period. In relation to the traditional authorities' role of mediation, the postcolonial period intensifies the urgency of the question – even more than in the colonial period – of whether the rituals that the Asante royal rulers performed and the artefacts that they used were and are of a religious nature. Are they not merely cultural and invented traditions used by the traditional authorities for political purposes, to enhance/maintain the loyalty of their subjects after Ghana gained independence? To answer this question, the author digs deeper into the meaning and attributes of Indigenous Religions as well as focuses on the political situation in (post-) colonial Ghana. In this chapter, she returns to the theory of IRs in order to contribute to the Western, scholarly understanding of these religions. She looks at four Asante rituals and explains to what extent these rituals are of an indigenous religious nature: a royal pre-burial ritual, a pouring of libation ritual, a chief's installation ritual and the *Asanteman Adae Kese* festival. In Chapter VI she provides evidence for the persistence of the indigenous religious peacekeeping role of the Asante traditional authorities in present-day Ghana. Here, the author makes further use of Berner's models of religious syncretism to elaborate on the continuity, discontinuity and change in Asante society in terms of the social and religious relationship of the Asante traditional authorities with individuals who are not indigenous religious believers (especially Christians and Muslims).

To conclude, the objective of this book is to explain why Asante chieftaincy has persisted from the perspective of the study of the Asante people's religion. It provides a historical-anthropological overview of the indigenous religious roles of the Asante royal rulers in Ghana since the precolonial period until today. Furthermore, it enhances theoretical insight into the meaning and attributes of Indigenous Religions, especially that of the Asante, and it details the meaning of religious syncretism and spirit mediumship in an historical and empirical context.

Chapter I: Explanations of the persistence of Asante chieftaincy

If you want to walk fast, walk alone; if you want to walk far, walk with others – *se wo pese woka woho wo anamon tu mu a, womfa obi nka woho; na enso se wo tumi anantew adu akyiri a, wo hia obi aka woho.*

Asante proverb

1.1 Introduction

Contemporary Kumasi, the former capital of the Asante kingdom, is an interesting place. During the sacred days (*adae*) meant for the propitiation of the ancestral spirits, the streets are filled with royal servants (*nhenkwaa*) of the Asante king and the female royal state ruler, who is his senior. While some *nhenkwaa* are juggling with warrior shields, others are invoking the ancestral spirits on their drums (*ntumpane*). The *nhenkwaa* have all gathered around their king, Osei Tutu II, who is dancing in the middle of the audience, accompanied by his umbrella and sword bearers and his spokesmen (*akyeame*). The king is dressed in colourful silk *Kente* cloth, and on his chest a porcupine is embroidered – an ancient symbol of the Asante nation (*Asanteman*). His wrists are covered with bracelets of pure gold.

Apparently, the visual images and the artefacts used in today's *adae* celebrations are quite similar to those that British and Swiss visitors of Kumasi observed in the eighteenth and nineteenth centuries. These visitors include the merchant Thomas Bowdich, the British consul Joseph Dupuis and the Basel missionaries Friederich Ramseyer and Johannes Kühne. The question is, however, whether the meanings of these religious artefacts and events have remained the same or whether they are currently only used and organised to stimulate tourism in the Ashanti Region of Ghana. Is Asante Indigenous Religion a resilient religion or has it disappeared due to the many Islamic and Christian influences in Ghana? Another question is how and whether the development of Asante Indigenous Religion is related to the persistence of Asante chieftaincy. The salience of chieftaincy in former British colonies is not self-evident, as in many of these colonies – like Uganda and Tanzania – the process of decolonisation coincided with the clipping of the wings of the traditional rulers (Nugent 2004). To gain an understanding of chieftaincy and its persistence among the Asante in Ghana, unlike these other British former colonies, the author will elaborate on the indigenous religious roles of Asante chiefs and their female co-rulers throughout Asante history (see Chapters III, IV, V and VI). In the remaining sections of this chapter, however, she will provide an overview of the economic, political and juridical explanations for the salience of the Asante people's traditional political institution as formulated by historians, political scientists and anthropologists of law in Ghana Studies.

1.1.1 Political factors

In the precolonial period, the Asante traditional authorities had executive, legislative and judicial influence. They controlled all authority, and chieftaincy was the only political institution among the Asante people (*Asantefoɔ*). The relation of the chiefs and their female co-rulers, who were the office holders of that institution, along with their subjects (*nkoa*) is complicated. On the one hand, the Asante traditional authorities were chosen by the population and supervised by elders. This is why some scholars, such as Bamfo (2000), have depicted them as democratic precolonial rulers. Most non-Asante Akan scholars, however, perceive the Asante royal state rulers in the precolonial period as authoritarian leaders. They ruled by fear, i.e., by ritually killing slaves and war captives (*nnomum*) to accompany deceased Asante royal state rulers in their graves (Ramseyer, Kühne et al. 1875).[2] These were all methods used to suppress ordinary Asante subjects (*nkoa*). In 1844, the British Wesleyan Methodist missionary Thomas Birch Freeman wrote in his journal of his visit to the Asante kingdom:'The *Asantehene* [Kwaku Dua Panin] said: 'If I were to abolish human sacrifices, I should deprive myself of one of the most effective means of keeping the people in subjection' and under the influence of this feeling, he has confounded the sacrificing of hundreds and thousands of innocent victims, with the punishment of those who may have forfeited their lives on account of flagrant transgressions of their country's law' (Freeman 1844:164). Each *Asantehene* in this period had the exclusive right to execution as a way of exercising internal control of the Asante state; some Asante *ahemfo*, such as *Asantehene* Kofi Kakari, made extensive use of their rights, while others, such as *Asantehene* Osei Kwame, were less cruel (Wilks 1989 [first published in 1975]). The individual ruling styles of the various Asante *ahemfo* thus differed, but when an *Asante* royal state ruler fully misused his or her power in the eyes of the board of elders that controlled him or her, (s) he was usually dethroned or better destooled, such as *Asantehene* Osei Kwame.

In the colonial period, the following institutional changes were implemented: at the regional level, District and Assistant District Commissioners were appointed for the day-to-day administration of the 'Crown Colony of Ashanti' (see 7.5 map 3). The chiefs thereby became agents of the colonial administration, which made it more difficult for them to maintain good relationships with their subjects. On the one hand, they were still elected by their subjects for their office as moral-religious leaders, responsible for the people's social-economic wellbeing. On the other hand, under colonial rule, the traditional authorities were obliged to serve foreign rulers and British interests rather than those of their own subjects. As a consequence, there were also political reasons for the non-officeholders (*nkwankwaa*) to be disloyal to their traditional rulers and act in their own interests, a development that threatened the salience of chieftaincy

[2] In 1888 the Basel missionary Friedrich Ramseyer also took a photograph of the cutting of the ears and lips of an Asante thief, which was commonly practiced to evoke fear during the precolonial period (see: www.bmarchives.org/items/D.30.18.061).

(Rathbone 2000).

Nevertheless, the *nkwankwaa* were too divided and not organised enough to realise important changes. They rather collaborated with the traditional rulers, and on the 19th of September 1954, they formed a political movement – the National Liberation Movement (NLM) – that liberated itself from the Convention People's Party (CPP), which was driven by the *nkwankwaa* during the period of 1949-1951. The NLM consisted of traditional rulers, commoners, cacao farmers and intellectuals. The party's goals were to get access to gainful sectors of the economy, to increase the number of seats in the Asante Legislative Assembly to raise the price of cacao and finally to turn the Ashanti Region into a federation that would be permanently ruled separately from the rest of the Gold Coast (this had already been the case in the period between 1901 and 1946). The NLM received all the support of the royal state rulers Osei Agyeman Prempeh II, Konadu Yaadom II, and Ama Serwaa Nyaako, who called their subjects and other Asante royal rulers to support their movement on behalf of the ancestral spirits.[3] In fact, these royal state rulers used their religious power to gather political support. By making mention of a movement rather than a party, they believed that they could cross the sacred divide between chiefly statesmanship and party allegiances (Allman 1993).

Despite the tense relationship between the *Asantehene* (though not of the *Asantehemma*) and the *nkwankwaa,* the *Asantehene* also needed his subjects to reach his major goal of turning the Ashanti Region into a federation, which was preferable to it being swallowed by a central authority. The interests of the Asante royal state rulers and their subjects were largely interwoven. Only together they could operate as a political force, and so they did. It is exactly this collaborative effort that can provide a political explanation for the persistence of Asante chieftaincy in the last phase of the colonial period and thereafter. The main political rival of the NLM was the CPP, which was led by the politician Kwame Nkrumah, who later became the first president of Ghana. Unlike the NLM, which was only in favour of the destoolment of some individual traditional rulers, the aim of the CPP was to crush the traditional rulers and to get rid of the chieftaincy institution all together. The CPP received the support of the colonial government which, after the 1950s, changed its political policy in the whole of the Gold Coast colony from Indirect Rule non-interference in chiefly politics to self-government and the development of a democracy (Crook 1986).

The relationship between the NLM and the CPP was very tense. In 1956, the colonial officials feared a civil war over the question of federalism or central authority. The CPP tried to crush the traditional rulers by denying their former administrative and juridical roles and only recognising their customary function. Because of the bond of the traditional rulers with their people, the CPP did not succeed in fully clipping the traditional leaders' wings, as this would lead to increasing tension in the colony. Instead, with the help of the British Governor

---

[3] *Asantehemma* Ama Sewaa Nyaako was the second *Asantehemma* during the reign of *Asantehene* Osei Agyeman Prempeh II (1892-1931/35-70) and also reigned together with *Asantehene* Opoku Ware II (1919-70-99). She was a granddaughter of Afua Kobi Serwaa Ampem I.

(BG) Alan Clark, the CPP opted for the domestication of traditional rulers, and placed them under a form of 'Indirect Rule'. The CPP gave itself the authority to choose which traditional rulers could be deposed and destooled. Those traditional rulers who were against CPP ideology were removed from their offices. This policy also gave the CPP the opportunity to create new stools and appoint members of their party and the educated elite to these newly created positions for male royal rulers. This development further blurred the boundaries between traditional rulers and commoners, and ironically contributed to strengthened political unity between the traditional rulers and commoners, which resulted in the persistence of chieftaincy rather than the demise of the traditional political institution (Gocking 1994).

In 1960, in the postcolonial period of the First Republic (1957-1969) after Ghana had gained independence, the royal rulers depended on the government for their very existence. The CPP determined that chiefs had to be gazetted by the government to be allowed to fulfil their function, though female rulers were largely ignored. To eliminate rivals, the CPP then downgraded the status of those royal rulers who did not support their party. The deportation act enabled the CPP to get rid of all non-Ghanaian citizens, many of whom were Muslims. The Prevention Act also established that all other state enemies of Ghana, including Muslims, could be locked up in prison. At the time, the chiefs and their entourages were not yet integrated into the democratic socialistic government of independent Ghana; therefore, their voices were silenced. The CPP did not come to an agreement with the NLM, but had just suppressed the movement, which was to remain a source of contention between supporters of these two bodies throughout the postcolonial history of Ghana (Allman 1993).

Since Ghana gained independence in 1957 under the leadership of president Kwame Nkrumah, he and his CPP party members further attempted to enervate the authority of the chiefs. They perceived them as a stumbling block to the development of the Ghanaian state in the direction of modernity. The political power in the hands of Asante traditional authorities in postcolonial Ghana had thus gradually diminished in comparison with that of the precolonial and colonial periods. In the precolonial period, these Asante authorities had executive, legislative and judicial influence. In the colonial period, despite British control and Indirect Rule, the chiefs and their female co-rulers were permitted to rule over their subjects on their own but functioned under the political superstructure of the colonial state. In 1951, under the Local Government Ordinance, elective local councils replaced all Native and the traditional leaders further had to share their authority with politicians. Since the postcolonial period, there have been discussions about the role of chiefs and their female co-rulers in the public sphere. However, the position of traditional rulers as leaders alongside politicians only became permanent in postcolonial Ghana. This happened after 1956 when the CPP was clearly designated as the winner of that year's elections. In 1957, not more than one-third of all members of the local councils were chiefs, and the Local Government Act of 1961 banned all chiefs from local government. In 1969, the National House of Chiefs (NHC) was founded, with one third of the District Councils (DC) reserved for chiefs; further two of the chiefs of the Regional House of Chiefs (RHC) were appointed in the Regional Council (RC). In 1979, the Constitution ensured the one-third membership of the chiefs in the DC and allowed no more than two chiefs from the RHC as members of the RC. According the Constitution of 1992 (article 276-1), chiefs could not take place in active party politics. Since then, it has been debated whether chiefs should be involved in party politics at all, as their main function is to serve all people regardless of their religious and political affiliation. The chiefs' active participation in a political party could lose them the trust of their subjects. In postcolonial Ghana, the chiefs function in a dual political system consisting of Chieftaincy institutions (the NHC, the RHC and the TCs) and district Urban Councils (UCs). These Councils were based on the British model and replaced the Native Authorities, taking over most of their functions. Since 1994, the tasks of chiefs have been restricted to customary matters and to advising local government rulers on commoners suitable for occupying seats in the local councils. Since the colonial period, the political power of chiefs in government politics has diminished. Since the 1992 Constitution, a series of articles prevented chiefs from being elected as President, Vice-President, Speaker or Deputy Speaker of Parliament, and Minister or Deputy Minister of Parliament. By then, they had lost their active function in the legislative and top executive spheres of the state (Ray 1996).

Since the postcolonial period, the power of the chiefs and their female co-rulers over chieftaincy affairs has constantly increased, whereas due to the separation of state and chieftaincy affairs, their power in active state politics has been restrained. It is, however, exactly the separation of state and chieftaincy affairs that provides a political explanation for the salience of Asante chieftaincy.

1.1.2 Economic factors

In this section, the author will investigate to what extent the persistence of Asante chieftaincy can be explained by looking at the economic power of the Asante royal state rulers. She will concentrate on the development of economic power invested in these rulers from the precolonial up to the postcolonial periods, with a specific focus on the two main forms of their economic power, which they derived from their position vis-à-vis Asante stool land.

In the precolonial period, the Asante ruling pair was the 'custodian' of all farmland, which was believed to belong to the ancestral spirits. They gave out usufructural rights to their subjects to make use of ancestral land in exchange for a part of the surplus of the land and revenue on the mines and other land resources. The land itself could freely be used, except for the payment of drink money (*sika nsa*) which was a token sum of money that everyone had to pay to their traditional authorities (e.g., a bottle of schnapps). The drink money and these revenues went directly to the stool treasury. The chiefs, whose private money after their installation or enstoolment melts together with that of the stool treasury, were obliged to use the stool money for the benefit of the community with whom they had a reciprocal relationship. The stool wives, who were women belonging to the stool and were given to the chief after his instalment, used the subjects' gifts consisting of the surplus of the land to cook meals for all subjects. Everyone who felt hungry could come to the palace to eat and benefit from the tribute they paid to their traditional rulers for cultivating the land. The Asante subjects lived from the produce of the stool land that was cultivated by them on behalf of the Asante royal state rulers (Busia 1951:44-45; Jacquemot 2007:55-56).

The treasuries of the Asante traditional rulers were filled with money that they primarily received as custodians of the land. In Asante, there was no land market, because there was plenty of land, but labour was scarce. Instead, there was a market for slaves and pawns who helped the community to cultivate the land (Wolf 1982; Austin 2007; Kankpeyeng 2009). The Asante royal state rulers received their income from tributes of the land and tributes that had to be paid by traders and other strangers who wanted temporary access to the ancestral land. They also received an income through warfare and the tributes that defeated states had to pay to them. Other monies came to them from the gold mined by slaves and the collection and trading of kola nuts with the Muslims in exchange for slaves (Austin 1996). The neighbouring states also fell under the ownership of the ruling pair because the Asante had a tributary mode of production.[4] A tributary economic-political system is a way of managing foreign affairs in which the neighbouring or satellite states of a kingdom show their subservience to the king by bearing him tribute (Wolf 1982).

The first publication on the economic power of the Asante traditional authorities between 1807 and 1883 is of the historian Ivor Wilks (1989 [first published in 1975]). Wilks did heed the opinion that the Asante traditional rulers had near-total state dominance over the economic source of wealth in the Asante economy in this period. The end of the slave trade resulted in the creation of exorbitantly high taxes for Asante commoners as an alternative way to raise revenue. This was the reason for an organised *coupe d'état* of the *nkwankwaa* against the ruling duo Mensa Bonsu (1874-1883), and Afia Kobi Serwaa Ampem I (1859-1884) and the chieftaincy institution. In the 1990s, the historian Gareth Austin provided new insights in the economic Asante history of this period. His findings were that indeed that 'there was a large and often thriving state sector in the export-import trade; the state had a share in the production of marketable goods; the Asante traditional rulers had the largest concentration of slaves and slave descendants in the state; and inheritance taxes gave the state a powerful instrument for the appropriation of privately generated wealth. However, the private sector, too, was a major force in the extra-subsistence economy: an economy which included a lively domestic trade' (Austin 1996:29). Austin explains that commoners could also acquire wealth through both external and internal trade and

[4] For a full list of Asante kings and their female co-rulers, see: Akutsu, S. 1992. "The Demise and Enthronement of the *Asantehene*: Political Aspects of Asante kingship," *Ethnological Studies* 31: 503-534.

through production for both export and domestic markets. Commoners bought and used slaves in their household, and for gold mining and the kola industry, both of which relied heavily on slaves. The rebellion of the *nkwankwaa* in 1883 against the Asante ruling pair was caused by heavy taxes on commodities such as gold, and was therefore not the effect of a lack of opportunities to accumulate private wealth in a near-state-dominated economy. Instead, this opposition was a much more specific opposition towards those traditional rulers, including the ruling pair, who levied exorbitant taxes on their subjects. The resistance of the commoners against these specific exploitative royal rulers was organised with the help of the elders, to whom they uttered their complaints. In the precolonial period, an organised group of commoners who acted without and against the traditional rulers did not exist. Also, in the colonial period, the *nkwankwaa* were no force of their own but only in opposition against other forces, such as European firms in the cacao industry. Examples of the expression of the *nkwankwaa's* discontent with these firms are the cacao industry hold-ups of the 1930s. The National Liberation Movement (NLM) was also a mass movement that could not exist without the support of the Asante royal state rulers. The *nkwankwaa* were likewise not a separate status group that could mobilise themselves without these rulers. In fact, the *nkwankwaa* and these rulers were similar in their aim to convert their wealth into social status. Those *nkwankwaa* who got the chance were very willing to become rulers themselves (Austin 1996).

The increase of opportunities for Asante subjects to farm and trade cacao beans reduced the Asante royal state rulers' share of local wealth. In absolute terms, however, they benefited from the development of a capitalist mode of production. In this way, the economic and political positions of the Asante royal state rulers were probably strengthened more than they were weakened. In the 1920s and 1930s, the traditional rulers were the organising force behind four cacao hold ups (1927, 1930, 1934-1935, 1937-1938). In cooperation with the farmers' associations, they supported the interests of the farmers against European cacao firms. These farmers thereby invited the displeasure of the colonial rulers over them. This is what they would never have done if they had believed they did not attain the consent of the Asante royal state rulers. The hold ups themselves increased the popularity of these rulers among the commoners. It was exactly because of the commoners' support for these rulers that colonial officials could not coerce them during the last hold up in the period 1937-1938. The Chief Commissioner of Ashanti (CCA) was convinced that it would be unwise to force the traditional rulers to obey the colonial administration and thereby stop the hold ups. For the Asante royal state rulers, this would mean that they would act against their own economic interests and those of their subjects, which could undermine their authority and cause a serious setback to the development of Native Administrations (Austin 1988). The *nkwankwaa* supported the traditional authorities, because despite their improved opportunities to accumulate wealth, most capital in Asante society remained in the hands of those who had 'old money' and had already been able to accumulate capital in the precolonial period. These people were the Asante traditional authorities and the cacao brokers (*asikafo*) who, since the colonial period, were also allowed to operate inside the Ashanti Region. In the colonial period, the majority of the *nkwankwaa* remained economically dependent of these Asante authorities and wealthy Islamic cacao brokers and moneylenders. The social relationships in Asante society could therefore only really change if the cacao brokers, the *nkwankwaa,* and the traditional rulers united against the colonial regime and the European cacao-buying firms (Southall 1978; Austin 1996).

The phenomenon of the persistence of the economic power of the Asante royal state rulers in the colonial period can also be explained by looking at the income of the Asante *ahemfo* in precolonial and colonial Asante. In the precolonial period, 'the *Asantehene*' derived income from war booty, tribute paid by defeated or otherwise subordinated rulers; taxes on the income and wealth of the Asante population, ranging from market tolls and gold-mining rents to *awunnyadeɛ*, occasional labour service of all subjects (in war or public work); and the regular labour of the traditional rulers' servants' (Austin 1995:105). The Asante received slaves in the form of tributes of satellite states, and the Asante commoners had to pay very high rent – of one-third or even two-thirds – on gold dust winnings. Besides, all gold nuggets larger than a certain size were required by law to be sent to the *Asantehene*'s treasury, which would return part of its value in gold dust, to be divided between the local traditional rulers and the finder (Austin 1995). Death duties (*awunnyadeɛ*) were taxes that the family members of every deceased commoner had to pay to the Asante royal state rulers. The royal could be sure that a considerable amount of the wealth in the hands of their commoners would flow back to his treasury and enable the traditional rulers to remain economically most powerful. Wilks has suggested that *awunnyadeɛ* prevented commoners from the capability of accumulating private wealth, but Austin has argued that this seems unlikely. In Austen's view, part of the wealth of a person could already be transferred to his relatives before his death, such as in the form of a contribution to a son's marriage or as working capital for a long-distance trading expedition. The *awunnyadeɛ* also ended up in the treasury of paramount traditional rulers and sub rulers. Besides tax money that the commoners were obliged to pay, the Asante royal rulers also tried to persuade rich commoners to share part of their wealth with the state in exchange for social status (Austin 1996). The income of the Asante royal state rulers in the precolonial period was considerable, not in the last place because they had access to free labour, namely of pawns and slaves. These labourers were working without wages in the gold mines and the kola industry. When these export products declined, they successfully moved to the export of rubber and palm oil. In the colonial period, after the transition from palm and rubber to the cacao industry, the chiefs still received a considerable income from unpaid labour. It took until the period 1900-1916 before capitalist relationships developed in this industry alongside the existing structures of family and kinship unpaid labour. Until the twentieth century, the Asante royal state rulers thus got rich by the exploitation of slaves and commoners. They made sure that all those people who were subordinate to them remained both politically loyal as well as economically dependent. The royal state rulers maintained part of their economic and political power, because they looked after their own interests and those of their subjects in the cacao industry. In the period between 1894 and 1911, they retained their power, because they showed opposition to the proposals and rulings of the colonial government (the 1894 and 1897 bills) that declared all 'vacant' land property of the colonial state. Gold Coast merchants, lawyers and clergymen argued in support of their traditional rulers by claiming that there was no vacant stool land, because all land belonged to the community. The traditional rulers were thus clearly aware of the colonial government's attempts to claim the communities' and ancestral land. As a consequence, the colonial government did not succeed in gaining control over one of the traditional rulers' most profitable sources of income: the proceeds of their land. As a result of colonial rule, however, the question 'who' had to pay 'what' amount to make use of the land of the traditional authorities became more contested. The usufruct right to cultivate the royal (state) rulers' land traditionally came with lineage. Strangers or non-lineage members usually had to pay one-third of any product coming from the royal (state) rulers' territory (game, gold or forest products). In the colonial period, disputes arose about who had rights of lineage and who had the status of stranger and was therefore liable to pay tribute in exchange for the right to use land. Another often-heard dispute was about whether the tributes should be treated as personal income of the royal state rulers or as public revenue of the stool. As an effect of British colonisation, the right of access to land became dependent on the status of a person as 'stranger' or subject of a royal. Whereas subjects could freely make use of land, strangers had to pay to be allowed to cultivate a royal's land. The concept of stranger had to do with one's subordination to a royal's stool. The Asante thus also had to pay rent when they made use of the land of a traditional ruler to whom they did not belong. The colonial government tried to reduce the income of traditional rulers from stool land by reducing rent on this type of land from one third of the crop to one penny per bearing cacao tree, but due to subsequent falls in the producer price, the actual income of the traditional rulers was the same. Besides, cacao farms were mostly pledged and sometimes mortgaged in return for loans. Around the 1930s, the relations between labour and land changed. By then, wage labourers, who mostly came from the Asante hinterland, led to the introduction of a more favourable type of labour contract (share cropping rather than paying rent) (Austin 1987).

In summary, in the precolonial period, land was physically abundant and institutionally accessible, usually only for a token payment (the drinking money) or for free. Labour was relatively cheap, because the gold mining, kola and palm oil industries were family businesses. Later the Asante cacao farmers made use of family labour, and extra familiar labour was recruited in the form of slaves and human pawns. In the colonial period, the Asante traditional rulers came up with an innovation in land tenure and were prepared to lease (but rarely to sell) Asante land for one third of the (most often cacao) crop. Since the 1930s, this institutional change of colonial policies transformed the labour market from a mainly free market (familiar, slave and pawn) to a wage labour market. Besides, after 1914, the rapid growth of the cacao industry created a scarcity of Asante farmland for the cacao industry that could be leased by 'strangers'. After a period of severe exploitation of stranger leasers and labourers, the relationship of these strangers with the Asante royal rulers improved, and capitalist labour relationships emerged. The construction of wage labourers was less profitable for traditional rulers than that of free labour, but new income from the lease of Asante farm land, which used to be given out for free, compensated for their loss of income. In conclusion, the royal state rulers carried out a successful institutional transition from an industry mainly based on gold mining and the export of palm oil and kola to that of cacao crops (Austin 1995).

In the postcolonial period, though some Asante traditional rulers struggle for money, others still generate a good income out of their position as custodians of ancestral stool land. In Kumasi, the majority of the land is still in the hands of these Asante rulers. The *Asantehene* and the *Asantehemma* are in custody of most of the land in this town, which is their main source of leverage for power. The Ghanaian state only owns part of the Asante land. The Ghanaian state can force the Asante royal state rulers to lease land, for instance, to contractors who could help to develop the area if the state is not satisfied with their reason for refusal of such a lease; a method known as 'compulsory state land acquisition'. The Asante traditional rulers have thus lost some of their economic authority over their stool land, and they are often overpowered by the decisions of government leaders concerning the ancestral land (interview with Nana Brefo Gyededu Kotowko II, 23). On the other hand, the stool land, which is most of the land in Kumasi, is the most expensive land to lease in the whole Kumasi metropolis and its surroundings. The Asante traditional rulers lease out their land to strangers for exorbitantly high prices. Today, the precolonial-rooted symbolic drink money that used to be a symbolic gift to the traditional rulers in exchange for usufruct rights (e.g., schnapps) is currently equivalent to the price of the lease of the land. After the stool land is leased out, 25% of the revenue of their land goes to the stool, and 20% goes to the traditional rulers (Hammond 2001). These rulers manage land on behalf of the community. 'Strangers' are those people who do not belong to a stool and/or a traditional authority and have to pay a lot of money to lease land, whereas the royal rulers' subjects do not. As a consequence, there are many chieftaincy disputes over the question of the inheritance of usufruct rights of land as a result of one's belonging to a lineage. Conflicting stool histories often result in severe disputes over control and access to land (Berry 1997; 2009).

Besides the lease and revenue of stool land, the Asante traditional authorities generate income by court fees, the product of fines, royalties and the profits of marketing activities. Many traditional ruelrs also have forests, mines and income from NGOs. The *Asantehene* also received money for a huge development project of the World Bank (WB) (Jacquemot 2007). However, all together, for most Asante royal state rulers, this income is far less than the income their predecessors obtained from levying taxes during the precolonial and colonial periods.

To maintain a high social status, many Asante royal rulers have become educated and raise an income by accumulating private wealth through professions, such as being lawyers, businessmen or university professors. However, the persistence of Asante chieftaincy in the Kumasi metropolis cannot solely be explained by the economic and political factors analysed, so let us continue our exploration in other realms of influence.

1.1.3 Juridical factors

Since the precolonial period, the Asante traditional authorities have also obtained juridical power. They made judgments with regard to disputes between commoners and about matters of chieftaincy. The traditional legal system, which today is better known as a system based on 'customary law', grew out of a kinship system. On a micro level, when there were conflicts in the household of the core family (*efiefo*) it was the task of the male family head – who is the brother of the female family head – to solve them. In the extended family or the mother's lineage (*abusua*), which consists of a number of households (*efiefo*) with the same blood ties and descendents from a common ancestress, the family elders (the male *abusuapanin* and the female *obaapanin*) had the task of solving conflicts by listening to all those members of the *abusua* involved. In a village, the individual lineages formed wards (*abrono*) that consisted of freeborn subjects (*nkoa*), slaves (*nnkonkofo*), pawns (*nnwowa*) and war captives (*nnomum*). In those cases, where the conflicts were so severe that they could not be solved by the *oba panin*, the Asante commoners could go to either the village ruler (*odikro*), or the sub-ruler (*ahene* or *ahemma*) or the paramount or state ruler (*omanhene* or *omanhemma*). On the highest level, the ruling pair themselves dealt with problems in the Asante state court. The Asante royal rulers helped the non-royal rulers by mediating with the spirits, and by venerating all their ancestors (*anini nsamanfo*).

The Asante royal rulers also helped commoners by mediating between subjects, and conflicts were solved with the help of customary laws (interview with Osei Kwadwo, 26). The laws that these Asante judges had to comply with on all hierarchal levels were believed to be provided by the indigenous priest Anokye, who had helped the first ruling pair Osei Tutu I and Nyarko Kusi Amoa (1700-1750) to found the Asante nation in 1701 (interview with Tweneboa Kodua – the great grandchild of the late female warrior Nana Yaa Asantewaa, 21).[5] Priest Anokye was believed to have created 'Seventy-Seven Laws' with a divine origin.[6] In many recent studies by Ghanaian historians, such as those of Kwamena-

[5] The *Asantehemma* ruled together with the *Asantehene*, was co-ordinator and played a significant role in chosing the successor to the Stool. *Asantehemma* Nyarko Kusi Amoa was a full member and co-President of the governing body and she took part in all important decisions. She also exercised a supervisory authority over ordinary women. She was the mother of *Asantehene* Opoku Ware I (1720-1750) and the fourth *Asantehemma* Konadu Yaadom I (1778-1809).

[6] Some of the rules of priest Anokye are broad moral injunctions, while others form a sort of civil and criminal code. See for an overview of these laws: Lewin, T. J. 1978. *Asante Before the British: The*

Poh, the Priest Anokye is described as a real eighteenth-century historical figure, who came from Akuapem. Anokye did, however, not appear by name in any written historical source before the nineteenth century, but there is evidence of the existence of the descriptions of the earlier presence of indigenous priests (*akomfoɔ*) inside the royal Asante court (Owusu-Ansah 1991). Lentz remarks that in the oral traditions of the Sisala and the Dagara in Burkina Faso, the first settlers who were hunters (as was the case in Asante), erected an earth shrine to make an agreement with the bush spirits before settlement. The *akomfoɔ*, who were married to the *ɔbosom* of their shrine, thus pre-date the first settlers or royal state rulers (Lentz 2000). McCaskie suggests that the *ɔkɔmfoɔ* Anokye is a necessary element in the Asante interpretation of their history. In Asante Indigenous Religion magical explanations of phenomena are common. Anokye has been introduced by the Asante, because this priest could explain the otherwise magically unexplainable in historical events, such as the origin of the Golden Stool (*Sika Dwa Kofi*) which was believed to have come down from the sky (McCaskie 1986b). There is thus a difference between an *emic* and an *etic* explanation of the role of Anokye in Asante history. The author, who read *Asantehene* Prempeh I's history, believes that it was not Anokye but the *nsumankwahene*, the indigenous religious priest, who was also the *Asantehene*'s physician and the head of the Asante *Nkramofoɔ* who was involved in the myth of the foundation of the Asante nation in the second half of the eighteenth century. King Prempeh I namely mentions that the Golden Stool contained *suman,* which is the power that the *Nkramofoɔ* priests placed inside charms or amulets (Akyeampong 2003). Most likely, the myth of the Golden Stool was created in the period after the arrival of the Asante *Nkramofoɔ* upon invitation of *Asantehene* Osei Tutu Kwame, and is the result of the intermingling of the Asante *Nkramofoɔ* in Asante indigenous religious affairs.

According to a well-known Asante oral tradition, the task of the Asante state was to modify the Asante body of jural customs. The Asante distinguished between immemorial custom (*aman mmu*) (that which was not subject to fundamental change by legislative enactment) and jural custom (*aman bre*) (that which might be adjusted by a legislative act). In the eighteenth and nineteenth centuries, the task of the Asante state was to place lineage identity at its heart (jural corporateness). It would then assure that it would not undergo change by guarantying the inviolability of *aman mmu* (McCaskie 1999).

In the colonial period, the existing system of customary law, which the British referred to as 'Native law and court' or 'Native Tribunals', was not fundamentally reformed. By then, there were many plans to make fundamental changes, but for economic and political purposes, these plans were never fully realised. An aspect of the British policy of Indirect Rule was that the colonies should be self-financed, and as a result the costs of their administration, financing was kept to a minimum. Reforming the legal system was therefore not high on the

---

Prempean Years, 1875-1900. Lawrence: Regents Press of Kansas.See also Ramseyer, F. A., J. Kühne, et al. 1875. *Four Years in Ashantee*. London: James Nisbet and Co., 4,5 and 106.

agenda of the British colonisers. Besides, the British were afraid that the planned juridical reforms would set those traditional rulers who profited from the existing system against them (Lugard 1965; Rathbone 2000).

The legal system could thus not be reformed with British consent. Instead, the CPP decided to remove all those traditional rulers who were not members of their political party and to replace them with commoners who voted for the CPP. With the Chiefs (Recognition) Act of 1958, the ultimate determination of who could legally become or remain a chief was vested not in TCs but in the central Ghanaian Government. Only those chiefs who were recognised by the state as Gazetted could continue to carry out their function. Gazetted Asante chiefs were those who supported the CPP, and all other chiefs were thus juridically silenced (Rathbone 2000).

In the postcolonial period, during the Second Republic (1969-1972), the Third Republic (1979-1981) and the Fourth Republic (1981-current), the power of the state and Asante royal state rulers became more and more separated. The Constitution of 1969 (Articles 154 and 155) declared that the state of Ghana had the power and right to determine the status of a chief on the issues where he dealt with state affairs. In government-controlled development projects, the chiefs thus had to accept state sovereignty. All customary chieftaincy matters were, however, not controlled by the state. During the military National Redemption Council (NRC) government, the National House of Chiefs (NHC) was responsible for all changes of status of chiefs (in terms of enstoolments and destoolments). However, the state laid down rules of procedure in the operation of all Houses of Chiefs (HC) and in defining the jurisdiction of TCs. In 1979, during the Third Republic the Constitution changed again, and as a consequence, the state no longer had the power to determinate the status of chiefs. The chiefs who controlled the RHC and National House of Chiefs (NHC) systems received sovereignty over all chieftaincy affairs, including all decisions over their position. However, on certain legal matters, the Ghanaian state gave up certain aspects of its power, i.e., its sovereignty at the instigation of its 1979 Constitution makers. In the 1992 Constitution that was created during the Fourth Republic the position of the parliament became even more 'hands off'. It became prohibited for the parliament to have any role in the recognition of chiefs. Instead, the HC and the TCs were to determine the status of chiefs. The NHC was to continue to operate the register of chiefs, taking over the function from the government's Chieftaincy Secretary to publish their official recognition (gazetting the chiefs). Since the Second Republic, chieftaincy and government affairs thus became more separated powers.

1.1.4 New explanatory factors from the study of Asante Indigenous Religion

In the previous sections, the author has discussed the economic, political and juridical factors in the persistence of Asante chieftaincy. What binds the scholars who have provided an explanation for this phenomenon from their respective points of view is that they acknowledge that their explanation is atomic and one-sided. None of these scholars is therefore entirely satisfied with the outcome, and all of them come to the conclusion that there is an underlying, deeply rooted religious aspect of Asante chieftaincy that requires further study and could explain the institution's salience. The explanation of the religious aspects of Asante chieftaincy is, however, beyond the capacity of scholars in the academic fields of economy, politics or law. The political historian Rathbone for instance, ends his book with the remark that he can conclude that chieftaincy persisted after the colonial period because of the strong bond between chiefs and their subjects. This made it impossible for the CPP to crush the chiefs. Rathbone cannot, however, explain why the lives of the chiefs and their subjects were so intertwined that the latter remained loyal to their chiefs even after the emergence of a social status group, which was much less economically dependent on their chiefs. Rathbone believes that the answer for the enigma of the persistence of Asante chieftaincy should be found in the religious spheres. He ends his book with the remark: 'It would take a subtler scholar than myself and a very different research project to begin to unravel the deeper meanings that chieftaincy has for some Ghanaians. Some of these "deeper meanings" have been alluded to earlier. Chiefs continue to symbolise place, and Ghanaians can be deeply attached to their physical origins, the physical space of their families and their families' ancestors' (Rathbone 2000:164).

The author of this book has taken Rathbone's remark as her point of departure. She will concentrate on the relationship between Asante Indigenous Religion and the indigenous religious functions of Asante traditional rulers to account for the salience of Asante chieftaincy. In the opinion of Stoeltje, an anthropologist of law, chieftaincy has persisted because the Asante traditional authorities have dealt with legal issues that cannot be dealt with by British common law. Ghanaians namely do not feel connected to the content of those laws. Whereas British law is abstract and unconnected to Ghanaian community life, customary law solves issues that are about the daily-life rights of Ghanaians. They feel a sense of belonging to their community, being a member of the jural corpus, by the application of those laws (Rathbone 2000; Stoeltje 2006). Also, to gain an in-depth understanding of this feeling of belonging, it is necessary to study the religious site of the relationship between Ghanaian subjects and Asante traditional rulers.

Asante chieftaincy is an institution whose existence is dependent on the support of the subjects of their traditional rulers. The following Akan proverbs supports this view: *Nsuom nam firi nsuom a, Asante wu, ɔhene a ɔnni akyitaafoɔ no ɔnyɛ ɔhene bio*, meaning, 'A fish out of water dies; a king without followers ceases to exist' and *Nnipa na ema Ahennwa ye kesee*, meaning, 'It is people that make a royal's stool great'. Asante chieftaincy exists by virtue of its approval by the Asante population. The *Asantehemma*, who is the first Asante ancestress and the senior of the chief and who herself is chosen by her senior male or female lineage mates supported by a board of elders, has the main voice in the selection of a chief. Indigenous protocol also demands, however, that the Asante subjects approve the choice of the female royal ruler of their prospective chief. This raises the question about the role is of Asante chieftaincy and indigenous religious practices in the relationship of Asante traditional rulers and their subjects.

In this book, the author will explore this relationship in three ways by focusing on the two main religious functions of Asante royal rulers: those of mediation and peacekeeping. With regards to the first function, she will look at the possible way in which Asante Indigenous Religion (AIR) plays a role in the legitimacy of Asante chieftaincy. The author will also explore the way in which the Asante traditional authorities fulfil a need among the Asante population for an indigenous religious identity. With regard to the second function, the author will explore the role of AIR in the maintenance of harmonious social and religious relationships with Muslims and Christians in the Kumasi metropolis.

With regards to (1), the possible ways in which AIR legitimates Asante chieftaincy throughout Asante history, the author will focus on the role of Asante indigenous religious customs and material attributes. An example of such a custom that has played a role in the legitimation of Asante chieftaincy is the celebration of the *Odwira* festival. This festival was held in Kumasi since 1717 until its suspension in 1896. In 1985, the ruling pair Opoku Ware II (1970-1999) and Ama Serwaa Nyaako resumed the celebration of this festival, which by then had been transformed (McCaskie 1995:151). The last celebration with remnants of the precolonial *Odwira* festival took place in 2004 under the name *Asanteman Adae Kese*. In its cultural and religious meaning, the *Asanteman Adae Kese* 2004 festival was different from the precolonial *Odwira* festival, mainly because since the deportation of the Asante ruling pair Edward Agyeman Prempeh I, and Konadu Yaadom II in 1896, the autonomous Asante state ceased to exist. The resurrected version of the *Odwira* festival that has been held since 1985 is therefore deprived of the full range of the meanings it had in the eighteenth and nineteenth centuries. The question to be raised with regards to this festival is to what extent its continued existence is the result of its indigenous religious function in legitimatising chieftaincy, and to what extent its continuation should be explained by other factors, such as the capacity of rituals to attract tourists and the social and political function of organising a festival. Examples of material indigenous religious attributes that play a role in the legitimation of Asante chieftaincy are royal stools or seats, swords for the purpose of swearing oaths and the staff of the chief's spokesman (*akyeame poma*). It is, for instance, the royal ruler's connection with a royal stool in a stool room from which he or she derives his or her political and spiritual power. The stools are shrines that enable the Asante traditional rulers to distinguish themselves from other Asante. They provide a means by which to rule over ordinary Asante subjects.[7] They also enable the royal rulers to communicate with the ancestral spirits. The *akyeame poma* enable the male royal rulers to

[7] A stool is an indigenous religious material attribute and was never meant to be sat upon.

translate messages to their subjects on their behalf. These *akyeame* receive messages from these spirits – which are meant to help the living – of a religious, social or political nature. In the precolonial period, the ancestors could, for instance, instruct a royal to start a war with a neighbouring cultural group. The distance between royal rulers and their population contributed to their aura of sacredness. It was for this reason that many *akyeame* were hired to translate the ancestral war message for Asante soldiers (Yankah 1995:33-40). These days, a paramount traditional ruler can, for instance, use various *akyeame* to translate the ancestral message in order to prevent too many foreign investors from occupying their ancestral land. However, it is pertinent to query to what extent messages of the paramount ruler have an indigenous religious content today, and to what extent the procedure of making use of *akyeame* at the royal court is merely ceremonial. Another material object that helps to articulate the Asante royal rulers' sacredness is the ceremonial sword (*Mponponsuo*) that is used in oath-swearing rituals to symbolise Akan proverbs.[8] Others of these objects are *Adinkra* and *Kente* cloths and a palanquin. This is a U-shaped wooden structure, which looks like a coffin without a cover, in which the *Asantehene* is carried (and today also lower ranked male Asante royal rulers).[9] On the shoulders of four strong men, the palanquin goes up and down marching to the rhythm of great drums (*fɔntɔmfrɔms*). The *nhenkwaa* of the paramount chief carry these drums, alongside other attributes. The drummers (*akyerema*) beat their musical instruments with sticks to wake up the ancestors. The ruling pair's war shield bearers (*afonansaofo*) carry war shields, and their fan carriers (*kokosesefoo*) provide fans. The *nsumankwahene* carries a spiritually 'heavy' war deity that descended upon him in a pot on his head, which was believed to be the centre of all spiritual activity (Opoku 1970:14; McLeod 1981:91-92).

The Asante traditional authorities thus make use of customs and material objects to express their sacredness and to gain the consent of their subjects to legitimatise Asante chieftaincy. In this book, the question will be addressed to what extent these customs and objects were and are an expression of AIR throughout Asante history. It aims to contribute to the academic debate in religious studies of what IRs are composed.

To what extent is the ancient *Odwira* festival comparable to today's celebration of *Asanteman Adae Kese*? In 2004, the *Asanteman Adae Kese* festival attracted thousands of visitors from inside and outside Ghana, enough to fill the whole of the Kumasi football stadium (interview with Charles K. Coffie, 4). The popularity of this festival in today's Kumasi metropolis could serve as a piece of evidence for the resilience of AIR. It could, however, also be perceived as an expression of the cultural nationalism that emerged in Ghana at the eve of and after

---

[8] Chiefs and sub-chiefs make use of the following 'oath swords': *ahwe hwe baa*, *akrafona* and *Gyapatia* (PRAAD ARG 1/2/30/2/12a).

[9] These are silk and cotton traditional cloths that are locally woven by the Asante and originate from Bonwire, a village in the Ashanti Region or possibly Tekyiman.

the country gained independence in 1957.[10] Hence, it may be asked to what extent the present court life that represents elements of village life in the eighteenth century has its roots in the precolonial period. Colonial historical archives and missionary reports show that during the precolonial period, AIR overall had a much more violent character than in the colonial and postcolonial periods. In the precolonial period, various Asante *ahemfo* ruled by fear and used indigenous religious practices, such as the ritual killing of human beings and the cutting off of limbs of disobedient subjects, to create fear among the Asante population (Chapman 1844). Under colonial rule, the performance of such violent rituals was abolished. In all likelihood, there are also elements in the *Asanteman Adae Kese* celebration that date from the late colonial and postcolonial periods, at the time when, with the emergence of the modern state, the persistence of village life was threatened and people thought back with nostalgia about the precolonial era. New elements might have been added to precolonial indigenous religious practices, whereas other elements might have disappeared. The question is therefore whether festivals, such as *Odwira*, should currently still be regarded as expressions of AIR rather than as part of folklore and cultural practices meant to strike a sympathetic chord with politicians and African-American tourists.

The second aspect on which the author will focus is to what extent chieftaincy sustains the indigenous religious belief of the Asante in ancestral spirits and all other beings of the spiritual realm. Do the present-day Asante traditional authorities promote ideas about the sacredness of royal stools, or has the meaning of these stools completely been secularised? Do rites that surround chieftaincy these days have religious substance, or are they just a form of entertainment to please the Asante people? Is the Asante greeting custom a genuine demonstration of their respect for traditional authorities or is it merely a political performance? Does this custom refer to the importance of the royal rulers' indigenous religious functions? These questions address the extent of the legitimacy of Asante chieftaincy as provided by AIR in contemporary Ghana.

The third point, which the author will address in this book, is the role of Asante traditional authorities as indigenous religious peacekeepers, that is the social and religious relationship of these authorities with Christians and Muslims. The author will address the question to what extent AIR has been important for the maintenance of peaceful relationships with these religious believers and what role these relationships play in the persistence of Asante chieftaincy. Since the encounter with Islam in the eighteenth century, the Asante traditional authorities have a history of adapting and adopting Islamic and Christian elements to their IRs. Examples of Islamic religious elements in the latter religion are, for instance, the *Asantehene*'s warrior cloth (*bata kari kese*) or 'take away spirits' (*nsuman*). The author aims to increase insight into the degree in which these forms of syncretism have been part of a deliberate strategy of the Asante traditional authorities

[10] 'Cultural nationalism' can be seen as the aspect of social engineering, which is concerned with creating/ and strengthening a national consciousness. Forster, P. G. 1994. "Culture, Nationalism, and the Invention of Tradition in Malawi," *The Journal of Modern African Studies* 32(3): 477-497.

to promote cordiality with Islamic and Christian religious groups. In terms of social relationships, the Asante traditional authorities attend Islamic and Christian festivals to show their goodwill to these religious groups. They also invite Islamic and Christian religious leaders to attend important Asante indigenous religious festivals. On a Friday morning during the *Asanteman Adae Kese* festival, for instance, an indigenous priest (*ɔkɔmfoɔ*) pours libation for the ruling pair on the Durbar ground. Like any other Friday, though, the *Asantehene*'s imam also continues to pray and read from the Qur'an in the Great mosque in the old *zongo,* or the Muslim settlement in Kumasi. Afterwards, the ruling pair goes to the St. Cyprian's Anglican Cathedral, where they receive blessings from the bishops of both the Anglican and Roman Catholic Churches (interview with Charles Kingsley Coffie, 4). *Asanteman Adae Kese* is thus an indigenous religious festival that acknowledges the religious beliefs of indigenous practitioners, Muslims, and Christians.

On a meta-level, the author focuses on the role of AIR in the maintenance of the internal (by indigenous religious mediation) and external (by indigenous religious peacekeeping) order in Asante society. She will show how indigenous religious mediation has been used to regulate life in Asante society. Asante indigenous religious rituals, such as *Odwira,* and symbols, such as royal stools, were not only used to legitimate chieftaincy but also to create order within the Asante state. The adoption and adaptation of Islamic and Christian elements in AIR has been a way for the Asante royal rulers to regulate their social and religious relationships with Islamic and Christian religious groups. An Asante chief said: 'The key word in our traditional belief is "harmony". We do not only strive for a harmonious relationship between humans and spirits, but also for the achievement of peaceful social relationships' (interview with *Oboguhene* Owusu Asiama II, 12).

1.2 Indigenous Religions and Asante Indigenous Religion

Now that the economic, political, juridical and religious factors in the persistence of Asante chieftaincy have been broadly researched, it has become clear that none of them on their own provide a sufficient explanation for the persistence of chieftaincy. The political, economic and juridical roles of the Asante royal rulers have respectively been marginalised and diminished. Religiously, there has been certain continuity in their indigenous religious mediatory and peacekeeping roles. An explanation for the persistence of Asante chieftaincy seems therefore to lie in the sum of the economic, political, juridical and religious studies' factors. The religious factors will be explained with the help of theories and concepts that belong to the academic field of 'Indigenous Religions', which is a subfield in religious studies. A new concept from the field of religious studies will be applied to the field of African history; a discipline which previously made use of Western philosophers such as Weber and Gramsci to analyse Asante (religious) history. The relevance of the use of concepts from IRs is that, unlike the mentioned underlying philosophies in African history, they are not primarily derived from the Western political philosophical sciences, and can be applied to the study of non-Western religious phenomena. The application of the concept of IRs, a new subfield and abstraction in religious studies, is expected to increase the understanding of religion in Asante history and contemporary times.

Several academic debates are concerned with how to define 'Indigenous Religions' (IRs). Whereas some anthropologists continue to defend the point of view that originates within anthropology of the 1950s – that IRs do not exist and can therefore not be defined at all – other scholars of religion have created a list of essentialist attributes of IRs that deny regional variations of the phenomenon their uniqueness and do not take into account their historical transformations. Other scholars of religion, however, have attempted to move beyond the paradigm of cultural or romantic primitivism, evolutionism and essentialism and place IRs in their historical context by deducing generalisations about them from a number of historical studies in Indigenous Religions. Following is a list of attributes of IRs and African Indigenous Religions derived from historical and empirical studies of these religions. The aim of this book is to contribute to the study of (African) Indigenous Religions by describing the differences between the theory of these religions based on these generalisations and the actual Asante indigenous religious traditions in the historical and contemporary Asante society. According to the historian of religion MacDonald, the anthropologist ter Haar, and the empirical scientists Alola, Fisher and Cox, there are some significant attributes of IRs and African Indigenous Religions, which are presented as follows.

Indigenous Religions are:

(1). Religions that are rooted in particular landscapes and particular histories. Their members think with these mountains and these ancestors, with these plants and these animals. The emphasis is on the local and particular experience, in contrast to the universal and general that scientific thought abstracts from many particulars (MacDonald 2004). Cox mentions the significance of locality and the belonging or boundedness of spirits to a place as a minimum empirical characteristic of IRs (Cox 2007).
(2). Religions with a local creator God, associated with the sky that watches over the indigenous people (MacDonald 2004). According to Cox however, indigenous religious people and societies did not have a concept of God (Cox 2012).
(3). Religions in which illness is thought to result from damaged relationships in the community, and it is the task of the indigenous priest or priestess to identify the offence that has caused the tension of rupture in the relationship (MacDonald 2004).
(4). Marked by local discourses (e.g., about the environment and social disturbances) that begin with traditional tales of the relationship between spirits, people and land that do not provide answers but stimulate thought. Changes in these relationship can alter the telling of the tales (MacDonald 2004).
(5). Religions of whose believers hold the circle sacred, because of its infiniteness and whose believers hold that time is circular and life revolves around the generational cycle of birth, youth, maturity, and physical death, the return of the seasons, the cyclical movements of the moon, sun, stars and planets (Fisher 1997:43-44).

African Indigenous Religions are:

(1). The religions of kinship-based communities who especially venerate the ancestors of the ruling kin group (ter Haar, Moyo et al. 1992).
(2). Those that belong, in terms of modes of production, to African small-scale communities with food gathering (hunting and gatherers) and food producing (agrarian-metropolitan) societies (ter Haar, Moyo et al. 1992).
(3). 'Community religions', which means that their adherents are born in these religions and cannot be converted to them. By naming ceremonies, which take place around a week after they are born, they become a member of the religious community. Funeral rituals are the way to say farewell to a community member. These rituals are performed for all humans born into the community, making them all members of the community religion (ter Haar, Moyo et al. 1992).
(4). Marked by oral traditions and have no written scriptures (ter Haar, Moyo et al. 1992:38-42; Fisher 1997).
(5). Embedded in all other aspects of life (social, economic, political) and are therefore often invisible (ter Haar, Moyo et al. 1992).
(6). Religions that include the living as well as the non-living members of a community and are based on a reciprocal and harmonious relationship with the more powerful non-living (e.g., ancestors, deities) in the form of offerings (e.g., pouring of libation, slaughtered animals in exchange for a good harvest) (ter Haar, Moyo et al. 1992; MacDonald 2004).
(7). Complex and structured but not in their articulation in the daily life of their members.
(8). Non-proselytising (ter Haar, Moyo et al. 1992).
(9). Religions whose adherents are open minded towards other religions. New gods can easily be adapted to a pantheon of gods. Those gods who do not bring prosperity can easily be removed from any shrine or as objects of veneration (ter Haar, Moyo et al. 1992).
(10). Religions without a strong belief in life after dead. Many of these religions have protologies or myths of the origin of the world, but usually lack eschatologies or stories about the ending of the world (ter Haar, Moyo et al. 1992).
(11). Religions that share a belief in (a) ancestral spirits, nature spirits and human spirits, the latter of whom have a direct relationship with human beings; (b) human leaders that represent the spirits on earth; (c) and rituals that mark the transitions in the life of community members from the cradle to the grave, group consciousness, and the performance of rituals to reforge corporate life and maintain and re-establish a harmonious relationship with the spiritual beings (Alolo 2007).

In this book, the author describes and analyses Asante Indigenous Religion (AIR). She refers to Indigenous Religions (IRs) in capitals, because she feels that since all world religions are referred to in capitals, it would be a sign of disrespect not to use them in reference to IRs. She prefers to use the term 'Indigenous Religions' in the plural, because although Indigenous Religions worldwide have common attributes, there is such a wide range of them, that it does not make sense to place them all under one religion (IR), even though they have in common the veneration of ancestors, who are lower in hierarchy than the deities. All world religions, such as Christianity and Islam, also have common attributes, but in these religions, the word 'religion' is included to subscribe to the type of category. It is a convention in religious studies that Christianity and Islam embrace various types of Christian and Islamic beliefs, which makes it unnecessary to refer to these world religions in the plural. Due to the inclusion of the word 'religion' in the definition of 'Indigenous Religions', however, reference to the plural is necessary to emphasise the diversity of the religions included. Reference to 'IR' in the singular would emphasise their similarities and therefore their comparability. This is another reason to refer to 'Indigenous Religions' in the plural and to make the statement that these religions, which are not world religions, should be included in all religious studies text books that also discuss the world religions. The consequence of leaving out 'Indigenous Religions' from these text books, as Cox (2007) remarks, is that 'the majority of the religions worldwide would not be included in the academic study of religion'. The undesirability of this scenario becomes all the more clear once one realises that the 'modern' purpose of 'academia', which became well-known by a contribution of the seventeenth century philosopher Bacon (1905 [original 1609]) (1561-1626), is not only to 'transmit already gained knowledge to successive generations', but also 'to promote the continuous advancement of learning'. Indubitably, Bacon's contribution makes clear that excluding the study of the majority of the religions in the world is counterproductive to the further advancement of knowledge of religions.

The definition of IRs and Asante Indigenous Religion will enhance understanding of the contribution of IRs to the knowledge of religions and to the relevance of this study. In Cox's definition, the primary characteristic of IRs refers to its being bound to a location; participants in the region are native to a place, or, in Harvey and Thompson's (2005) words, 'they belong to it'. The single and overriding belief shared amongst IRs derives from a kinship-based world-view in which attention is directed towards ancestor spirits as the central figures in religious life and practice. As a result, IRs are restricted cosmologically because their spirit world is organised around lineage systems. Ancestors are known by name; they belong to a place just as their descendants do, and they are related to living communities as spirit conveyors of ancestral traditions.

Asante Indigenous Religion is presented in this book as a type of IRs that is adhered to by the Asante. The most important characteristic of IRs is that these religions are based on: (a) ancestral belief, (b) kinship, and (c) locality. The above mentioned attributes are also present in AIR, but most central to this religion was and is, the belief in the existence of a supreme consciousness or force that expresses itself in an infinite variety of transformations, such as the celestial bodies, atoms, plants, animals and human beings. The term that the Akan philosopher Gyekye used for this most important aspect of Akan belief is 'panpsychism' (Gyekye 1995). The Asante believed in a transcendental realm and living energies or spirits that affected the lives of human beings. The Asante priest Agyei said: 'I know that plants and trees are living spirits. If I take kola, I can communicate with these spirits during trance. The spirits of plants, for instance, appear as twin snakes and they are a source of passive knowledge' (interviews with *ɔkɔmfoɔ* Agyei, 2).

Besides panpsychism, an important aspect of AIR is also the Asante people's belief in a creator God (*Onyankopɔn* or 'The Shining One'), who was said to live in the sky and was associated with the wind. The creator God *Onyankopɔn* was an abstract god – possibly referring to the star Sirius B – who was believed to be powerful (*Otumfuo*) and eternal (*ɔdomankoma*). The god was born on a Saturday and had no specified gender (interviews with *ɔkɔmfoɔ* Agyei, 2).[11] Besides *Onyankopɔn*, the Asante believed in ancestors (*anini nsamanfo*) that they venerated as twin serpent spirits on Earth.[12] Initially, the names of the royal twin serpent ancestors were the female principle spirit (*Atoapoma-Odiawuono* or *Ngame*) who was the senior of the male principle spirit (*Nyame*). *Ngame* was personified as the Moon; she created the firmament with its stars and sun, and she was said to shoot life-giving rays into animals and human beings. *Ngame* and *Nyame,* providers of Oma Awia or Sun, were the male and female principles. However, they were gender free and were both the givers of life (*Atoapoma*) and the takers of life (*Odiawuono*) (Jeffries 1984; Graves 1992) (interviews with *ɔkɔmfoɔ* Agyei, 2). The Asante, in the pre-Christian period, had a shrine for the male principle energy and shrines for the female principle energy that were of equal ranking. The Asante believed that the serpent spirit and the serpent spiritess and their shrines comprised of life-giving energy (*ɔkra*) and life-taking energy (*sunsum*). The Asante believed that the life-force soul (*ɔkra*) was a spark of the Sun, born at the same time as the physical body, but had survived physical death as a spiritual entity. The *ɔkra* is an eternal soul that returns to the Sun after one passes away and reincarnates in another person's body. The *ɔkra* was believed to be entirely spiritual and its attributes were similar to the Egyptian conceptualisation of the soul of reincarnation (*ka*) in the Old Egyptian kingdom (Hart 1990). The pure *ɔkra* of a boy that had not yet reached adulthood was believed to be able to protect the Asante king against the evil of some spirits.[13] *Sunsum,* the quasi material and female Asante soul, is most likely derived from the Egyptian word *shemu* or shadow that finds its origin in the same period (Lane 2010 [first published in 1836]). The male and female energies did, in fact, also refer to the two halves of the human brain (the *anima* and the *animus*) (Jung 1982). The serpents might have represented these energies, because they look like the human brain and also had both life-giving (*ɔkra*) and life-taking (*sunsum*) attributes (interviews with *ɔkɔmfoɔ* Agyei, 2). Serpents have most likely been venerated for this reason by indigenous religious adherents worldwide, since the dawn of civilisation (Mundkur 1983). Recent archaeological research demonstrates that seventy thousand years ago, Afri-

[11] For additional evidence of the existence of the creator God *Onyankopɔn* in pre-Islamic and pre-Christian Ghana among the Akan, see Thompson, T. 1937 [first edition 1758]. *An Account of Two Missionary Voyages* London: Benj. Dod, rpt. by the Society for Promoting Christian Knowledge.For evidence of *Nyame* as an Akan guardian or ancestral spirit in the shrine cult of an Akan indigenous priest, see Kirby, J. P. 1993. "The Islamic Dialogue with African Traditional Religion: Divination and Health Care," *Social Science Medicine* 36(3): 237-247.

[12] Many references to the Asante veneration of the (twin) serpent and their egg food can be found, for instance, in the book of Bowdich. He observed the chiefs holding huge metal snakes in proverbs and oral traditions described by Yankah, and in one of the author's articles. Bowdich, T. E. 1819. *Mission from Cape Coast Castle to Ashantee: With a Descriptive Statistical Account of that Kingdom and Geographical Notices of Other Parts of the Interior of Africa.* London: John Murray., Yankah, K. 1995. *Speaking for The Chief: Okyeame and the Politics of Akan Royal Oratory.* Bloomington: Indiana University Press., Müller, L. F. 2010. "Dancing Golden Stools," *Fieldwork in Religion* 5(1): 31-5.

[13] See for a photograph of a soul boy: www.bmarchives.org. D.30.18.071.

cans in Botswana already venerated the snakes, because these animals can both kill their prey by using poison and heal those who are brought in contact with the antidote consisting of their poison mixed with its blood (Lawrence 1978; Coulson, Staurset et al. 2011). The Asante myth of origin says that the first Asante people were hunters and gatherers who lived in and came out of a cave in *Asantemanso* and were brought together by a snake (*onini*) (Rattray 1955 (first published in 1923):7-8; Shinnie and Shinnie 1995).

Another significant aspect of Asante Indigenous Religion is that the *Asantefoɔ* were believed to have come from the earth and receive the reincarnated soul (*ɔkra*) from their ancestors, which is why they buried their umbilical cord that connects them to their mother's womb at their place of birth. It is in that same earth where they wish to be buried after death (interview with Ama Framponee, 31). The Asante believe that the soul (*ɔkra*) allows them to enter the earthly world and affects their behaviour and their destiny (*nkrabea*). The celestial bodies, under whose influence children were born, were believed to have an effect on the characteristic of the child and to correspond with the seven days of the week. Sunday (Sun), Wednesday (Mercury) and Friday (Venus) were believed to be positive days associated with male energy, whereas Monday (Moon), Tuesday (Mars) and Saturday (Saturn) were believed to be negative days corresponding to female energy. The fact that the first Asante king, Osei Tutu I died on a Saturday strengthened the Asante in their belief in the energies of the planets and its relation to their ritual calendar (Bowdich 1819:226-227; Ramseyer, Kühne et al. 1875:269; de Marees 1912 [original edition 1602]-68, footnote 2). Those Asante whose names are Kwaku (male) or Akua (female) are, for instance, born under the influence of Mercury and are therefore believed to be children full of woe who trick others (Agyekum 2006). The spider god Kwaku Anansi, who is the leading figure in Asante folktales, was believed to be a half-god and half-human creature born on a Wednesday (Abarry 1991; Brookins 2003).

Besides believing in ancestral serpent spirits (*anini nsamanfo*), the Asante also believed in the lesser gods (*abosom*) in charms and amulets (*nsuman*), in individual spiritual powers (*sunsum*) inside animals and humans as well as inside natural objects such as trees, plants, rocks, mountains and hills. AIR was, however, not at all static, as the actual deities that were venerated depended on the Asante people's societal needs. The ancestors were continuously added to a growing number of deceased predecessors in the stool room – the ancestral burial place. The belief in these spirits was subject to changes that were caused, largely, by interreligious encounters and conversations.

The lesser gods (abosom)

Abosom exist in two forms. As spirits, they can take the form of natural phenomena, such as a tree, a river, a mountain, a lake, the ocean, a hill, etc., or they inspirit 'things' such as animal bones, balls, calabashes or brass pans (*yawa*). *Abosom* are believed to have protective spiritual power. The *abosom* that protect the *ntoro* or totem group and give their members similar attributes are water spirits, because water (*nsu*) symbolises fertility.

A 'thing' becomes valuable (*som-bo*) because of the *ɔbosom* that dwells inside it. *Abosom* are very important for the indigenous priests and priestesses who make use of them to foretell the future and heal people by letting these deities speak through their mouth: a practice which is known in academia as 'spirit possession', but which is in fact a form of mediumship.

Spiritual powerful animals (sasa moa) and plants

Some animals are believed to have spiritual power (*sasa moa*) whereas others do not (*sasa mmoa*). The sacred animals that should not be killed are elephant (*osono*), bongo (*otromo*, roan (*okuo*), waterbuck (*fusuo*), duiker (*otwe*), small antelope (*adowa*), black duiker (*ewuo*), yellow-backed duiker (*kwaduo*) (Sarpong 1971; Braffi 1992). In the vegetative kingdom, the following three trees that the Asante use for their carvings are believed to possess very vindictive spirits: *Tweneboa* or *Kudoa*, *Nyame dua* and *Sɛsɛ.* The root of the n.b. *Tweneboa* could turn itself into a serpent as a form of protection (Sarpong 1971).

Charms and Amulets (Nsuman)

Another source of natural or ritual power in AIR is known as *nsuman,* which is comprised of a diverse range of powers that are typically manifested in the form of physical charms or amulets. Charms are filled with passages from the Qur'an that are believed to be a cure for the believer. 'Amulets' are man-made objects that are believed to have special powers dwelling inside them that can satisfy various specific needs. Both charms and amulets can be regarded as 'take-away' miniature shrines. They are made up of little packages of wood and leaves, which are easy to carry and are a lower order of spirit operating through little objects, which can be good or bad. *Nsuman* are and have been produced by the Asante *Nkramofoɔ* (Owusu-Ansah 1991:117-119).

Witches (abayifoɔ)

Witches (*abayifoɔ*) are believed to be members of the *abusua* who either consciously or unconsciously, spiritually and/or physically, may harm other family members (Olsen 2003:236-237). The family aspect of witches made Geschiere remark that 'witchcraft is the dark side of kinship' (Geschiere 1997 [originally published in French in 1995]:11). These days, however, it is believed in Ghana that witches can also harm members outside the *abusua.*

Power

The Asante made and make a distinction between 'natural power' that is publicly accessible and political power that is only available to Asante royal rulers. Natural power dates from before the fifteenth century when most Asante were hunters and gatherers. The Asante believed that everything (the High God, lesser gods, spirits, ancestors, men, animals, plants, inanimate objects such as rivers and rocks) in the universe is inspirited and contains power. During their stay in Kumasi, the Basel missionaries Ramseyer and Kühne (1875:80) remarked, for instance, that 'the Asante king was not a little surprised, like the South Sea Islanders, that a piece of wood could speak'. The degree of inspiritedness of objects such as trees and stools is a subject of debate among Akan philosophers. In Wiredu's (1996:124) view, at least today the Asante believe that there are also objects that are not inspirited because the life-principle has left them. Therefore, according to Wiredu, 'dead wood is quintessentially dead'. According to Gyekye (1995:75-76), however, the Asante have continued to believe in a hierarchical order among entities in which natural objects, such as trees and rivers, are in fact lower than men, but because deities are dwelling inside these objects, they are actually higher than men and are therefore venerated by them. The Akan cosmologist Dr. Osei Agyeman, a retired lecturer in Akan cosmology at the Kwame Nkrumah University of Science and Technology in Kumasi, said: 'For human beings, and especially those trained in the maintenance of a good relationship with them – the traditional authorities, the *akyeame* and the *akomfoɔ* – it is important to be in a good relationship with higher entities or spiritual beings, because they are more powerful and can destroy all lower entities when they are dissatisfied with them. However, humans can also derive power from these higher entities and seek for their help' (interview with Dr. Osei Agyeman, 42).

Locality

According to Wiredu (1996:121-124), the concept of 'locality' is a very important characteristic of AIR. It helps to understand the nature of this religion. The Asante have a locative conception of existence that has cosmological implications. In Twi, which is the language of the Asante, there is no linguistic difference between 'being' and 'being in a place'. Consequently, to express that 'something is there', the Asante and other Akan say, *Biribi wo ho,* to say that 'something is', they use the same sentence. For the Asante, then, existence is always connected to a location. The cosmological implication of this is that the Supreme Being must have been part of the world He created rather than that He created that world out of nothing. According to the Twi language, without being in a place, the Supreme Being would not exist. This implies that when He created the world and all material entities in it, such as human beings, plants and stones, He was part of that empirical world. The Supreme Being and all entities of the spiritual world that He created, such as the ancestors and deities, are not fully immaterial, but quasi-material. These spirits are not visible to ordinary Asante who are not trained to see them and communicate with them. They are only occasionally tangible for these Asante. In terms of imagination, they are part of the empirical world, as they share the same material space as beings in that world.

1.3 Theoretical framework

This book aims to describe the interaction between changes in AIR and the mediatory and peacekeeping function of the Asante royal rulers in the precolonial, colonial and postcolonial periods in order to provide an explanation for the persistence of Asante chieftaincy. The 'indigenous religious mediatory function' of traditional authorities was, by the use of rituals, to create balance between the social and spiritual worlds within the Asante community, and this formed the main internal Asante policy. 'Indigenous religious peacekeeping' was the creation of a balance between the Asante community and non-Asante cultural communities and was meant to deal with the external Asante policy that was exercised by the Asante diplomatic service. In each historical period, there was also a tension between the two-mentioned Asante royal rulers' indigenous religious functions. Mediation with the spiritual world was meant to ritually control the society and went together with the exercise of coercive force by the use of weapons and violence. The Asante traditional authorities could, for instance, exercise the practice of the ritual killing of human beings at funerals and the practice of capital punishment of criminals (*akyere*) because of the military power at their disposal: the weapons in the Asante *ahemfo*'s palace, which symbolised the power over the peripheral tribute states. External ideologies, such as those advocated by European Christian missionaries (ECMs) and orthodox Muslims, threatened the persistence of internal peace of Asante society established by indigenous religious mediation. Both ECMs and orthodox Muslims condemned the practice of the ritual killing of human beings and consequently attempted to abolish the annual *Odwira* festival, which was of the uttermost importance for the legitimation of the Asante state. The abolishment of polygamy by the ECMs and the condemnation of the matrilineal descent system by orthodox Muslims endangered the persistence of the Asante state, which was based on the pride and pomp of chiefs, their many stool wives and the advisory role of the senior female rulers. In the opinion of indigenous religious peacekeepers, however, the penetration of beliefs on the syncretic level of taking elements from Islam and Christianity was a *conditio sine qua non* for the maintenance of diplomatic relationships with Europeans (Dutch, Danish, English) and Muslims in the Asante hinterland. Until the eighteenth century, the spokesmen (*akyeame*) of the Asante royal rulers used oral diplomatic skills to communicate with Christians and Muslims. In the nineteenth century, the Asante developed a bureaucratic apparatus including three Christian (Dutch, English and Danish) and one Muslim chancery. Christian missionaries and Muslim scholar (*ulama*) were appointed as permanent or temporary (by being kept hostage!) ambassadors in these chanceries because of the skills these religious leaders possessed and the potential contribution they could make to the culture of Asante diplomacy. The Asante diplomacy was one of many of the aspects of precolonial chieftaincy that survived the colonisation of Ghana in 1901 and the process of decolonisation. An aspect of Asante diplomacy from the foundation of the Asante kingdom in 1701 until today has been the high awareness of the Asante royal rulers of the potential negative effects of foreign religious influences for Asante society. The royal rulers have therefore aimed to limit these influences to the extent that their allowance has been beneficial for the exercise of Asante internal and foreign affairs, as will be elaborated in Chapters III, IV, V and VI.

1.4 The contemporary Kumasi metropolis, its demography and religions

To aid to the understanding of the indigenous religious functions of the Asante royal rulers in the contemporary Asante society, the author conducted long-term fieldwork in Kumasi, which is where the institution of chieftaincy has always been located. The following short history of Kumasi is meant to enhance insight in the urban contexts in which the Asante traditional rulers have operated. Kumasi was founded in 1701 on the location that was previously known as Kwaman; the capital of the Kwaman state. Kwaman grew out of the central market of the earliest Asante settlers, who were hunters for bush and especially for elephant meat (Kwamena-Poh 1973:131). Kumasi became the Asante kingdom's capital, and today it is the second largest city in Ghana after Accra, as well as the most important commercial and administrative centre in the Ashanti Region (see 7.5 maps 5, 6, 7). Because of trade and its huge open-air market, Kumasi has always been a place that attracted people from very distant places. The town therefore has a cosmopolitan outlook. The major cultural Akan group in the Kumasi metropolis is the Asante (see 7.5 maps 1 and 2), who have always been the largest and most influential historical Akan group in Kumasi and in Ghana (Ghana 2002).[14] The majority of the Asante live in Kumasi and the wider Ashanti Region, which is located in south central Ghana. They speak Twi and belong to the Eastern Akan cultural group, which consists of the Fante, the Akuapem, the Akyem, Akwamu, Bron, Wassa, Kwahu, Assin, Dɛnkyira, and Gomua. The Akan speak (and 30 percent of them also are also literate in) Fante, Twi, Akuapem, Dɛnkyira, Asen, Akyem Bosome, Kwahu, and Ahafo. In the Côte d'Ivoire live the Agni, Baulé, Nzima, Ahanta, Sanwi, Aowin, and Sefwi Western Akan groups (Ogot 1992:206). The Chakosi in northern Togo are also of Akan stock (Braffi 2002:8).

Since 1901, Kumasi has been the capital of the Ashanti Region. With its 1,170,270 inhabitants, Kumasi is the second-largest metropolis in contemporary Ghana and is also the administrative and commercial centre of the country (Ghana 2002). In terms of religion, the inhabitants of the Kumasi metropolis are

[14] The term 'cultural group' is also used in relation to the Asante and the Akan by Stoeltje, B. J. 2003. "Asante Queen Mothers: Precolonial Authority in a Postcolonial Society," *Research Review* 19(2): 1-19.

either Akan indigenous religious believers (0.3 percent or 3,511 inhabitants) and/or Muslims (16 percent or 187, 243 inhabitants) and/or Christians (78.8 percent or 922,173 inhabitants) (Ghana 2002). From these statistics, it looks as if the number of inhabitants of the Kumasi metropolis adhering to the Akan Indigenous Religions is very small. However, in the 1950s, Christensen (1959:269) already observed that 'many indigenous practitioners who claim to be Christians rarely if ever attend church services and continue to practice the IRs. Many who are active in the various Christian groups also often participate in ceremonies of the ancestors and nature deities and visit an indigenous priest or priestesses'. Because of Ghana's dual religious believers, Gifford (1998:63) thought that African Traditional Religion persists not as a separate 'African religion' but as enduring perceptions and habits within Christianity and Islam'. According to Dovlo (2004:47-48), this statement is not tenable. He believes that in today's Ghana, there are also people who practice an 'African Traditional Religion' – the term that they use to refer to African Indigenous Religions – even in urban communities as a separate religion. Since the 1990s, there has been a resurgence in the performance of rituals by traditional authorities in southern Ghana, who regard themselves as representatives of Asante Indigenous Religion. The history of the introduction of Islam and Christianity in Ghana demonstrates that 'for the Asante the adaptation of a new deity does not necessarily imply the negation of the old; it is rather to be regarded as an additive factor for protection against the uncertainties of life' (Christensen 1959:270). Of the author's respondents, eighteen of the fifty-six called themselves 'indigenous Christians'. In the official statistics, these people are classified as Christians, but when those of the respondents who called themselves 'indigenous Christians' were asked whether they attended church or read the Bible, only the minority of them answered positively. The majority of them said that despite their Christianity they were frequent visitors of one of the many Asante indigenous priests or priestesses. In addition to 'indigenous Christians', there are also Asante in the Kumasi metropolis who call themselves 'Christians' and who observe indigenous religious rituals but participate not as practitioners but out of a feeling of being socially obliged to continue participation in clan affairs.

By all means, the indigenous religious culture is a living religion in the Asante Region, including Kumasi. According to Baffour Domfeh Gyeabour I, who has been the administrator of all indigenous priest-healers in the Ashanti Region, there were 47 registered and licensed priest-healers in the Kumasi metropolis, of whom 98 percent worked full-time, which indicates that there was a high demand for their practice. 'Priest-healers are healers who are "called" by the spirits, whose treatments are spiritual, who treat mental and socio-psychological diseases, whose clients are most often residential and receive long-term help rather than on an *ad-hoc* basis, and who are not incorporated in the formal health system of Ghana' (Anyinam 1987). Besides, there were over two hundred and fifty other registered and licensed 'traditional practitioners': herbalists, whose treatments are 'non-spiritually based'; faith healers; and cult healers as well as a great number of non-licensed traditional practitioners. The metropolis had a healer-to-population ratio of 1:1373 for licensed and registered healers (Anyinam 1987; 1989). More recent sources indicated that there are still several licensed and registered indigenous priest-healers in Kumasi, but they are mainly consulted for indigenous religious advice of the *abosom* and minor psychosomatic or mental problems. In more serious cases of illness, most of the Asante go directly to one of the four services for psychiatric treatment in the metropolis (Anyinam 1987; Appiah-Poku, Laugharne et al. 2004:209). The fact that in less serious diseases the Asante combine modern and traditional health services provides no evidence for a decrease in their indigenous religious conviction. Among indigenous Asante, one looks for practical solutions to problems and attempts to find the best solution for each problem. As *ɔkɔmfoɔ* Agyei put it, 'I occasionally receive messages from the spirits to send my patients to a clinic or a hospital' (interviews with *ɔkɔmfoɔ* Agyei, 2).

With regard to the Islamic practitioners in Kumasi, the categorisation 'Muslim' is also more complicated than the statistics make it appear, because there is a category of Muslims who are in a sense also Asante indigenous practitioners. The so-called Asante *Nkramofoɔ* are Muslims who have become Asante through intermarriage and naturalisation and Asante who have become Muslims by conversion (interview with Asante *ɔkramoni* Al-Hajj Abdul Karim Sina, 14).[15] Although the Asante *Nkramofoɔ* are Muslims, their leader, the *nsumankwahene*, who himself is not a Muslim, is the head of the indigenous priests and priestesses and the Asante *Nkramofoɔ* herbalists in Asante as well as the leader of the long-settled Muslims. Many of these Muslims' non-herbal methods of medical treatment derive from medicine mentioned in the Qur'an (interview with Dr. Osei Agyeman, 42). There are thus a lot of similarities between the Islamic religion of the Asante *Nkramofoɔ*, who in a particular way make use of the Qur'an, and contemporary AIR. Since the eighteenth century, the Islam of Asante Muslims has been more interlinked with AIR than that of other Muslims in the Kumasi metropolis.

In conclusion, the official statistics of the Ghana statistical service do not take into account the complexity of the situation in terms of the religious beliefs of the inhabitants of the Kumasi metropolis. In practice, there is a lot more indigenous religious activity than the official statistics show. This is an important point in a book on the salience of Asante chieftaincy as related to the resilience of AIR, because the presumed relationship between the two phenomena is not the most obvious conclusion one would draw after studying the official statistics of the religious beliefs of this cultural group in the Kumasi metropolis. In these statistics this relationship remains invisible as they demonstrate that the majority of the population in Kumasi and surroundings is Christian, whereas the second larg-

[15] The Asante *Nkramofoɔ* were the first Muslims who settled in Kumasi as early as the beginning of the eighteenth century. The first Asante *Nkramofoɔ* were already converted to Islam before they came to Kumasi. Since the twentieth century, indigenous Asante who have been converted to Islam have also been called Asante *Nkramofoɔ*.

est group of believers in the metropolis consists of Muslims. These official statistics might have given the impression that IRs have died out. The historian Richard Rathbone (2000:2), also gives his impression when he remarked that 'Ghana is a modern state and its citizens are people whose belief is more informed by the Internet and MTV than by the shadows of the forgotten ancestors'. The author will, however, aim to demonstrate that AIR is a resilient and living religion and that the religious-political legitimation of chieftaincy is an underestimated factor in the salience of the Asante people's traditional political institution.

1.5 Summary

The persistence of Asante chieftaincy is a social phenomenon with many angles that can only be fully understood by increasing insight into its political, economic, juridical and religious studies' explanatory factors. The author has therefore first summarised the academic works of political and economic social scientists and anthropologists of law who have researched this topic and attempt to provide an explanation for this phenomenon from a different angle. She has indicated that all these scholars come to the conclusion that there are underlying but understudied religious factors, that could provide a deeper explanation of why Asante chieftaincy has persisted. Previous scholars could not conduct further research on the aspect of religion within the boundaries of their academic discipline. The objective of this book is therefore to focus on these religious aspects with the help of theoretical frameworks and concepts derived from religious studies, and Indigenous Religions in particular.

Chapter II: Historical anthropology in (indigenous) religious studies: some philosophical justification

You could count the amount of comparative historians in England on the fingers of both hands, if most of them had been amputated.

Evans-Pritchard 1962

2.1. Introduction

This book employs the methods of modern historical anthropology to examine the influence of religious factors in the persistence of Asante chieftaincy. Using an approach similar to that employed in works such as those of Nathan Wachtel (1992) and Alan Macfarlane (1970), the author aims to provides a holistic understanding of the religious functions of the Asante royal rulers by covering the period of time from the eighteenth century until today. Her historical and anthropological data are combined with conceptual frameworks that derive from scholars in indigenous religious studies (e.g. Cox, Olupona, Harvey, ter Haar, and Platvoet). This chapter will be devoted to a philosophical justification of her position as a historical anthropologist in the field of the study of IRs, a discussion of religious studies concepts and theories, and a discussion of her critical involvement with the historical and anthropological data that form the basis of her research. However, first of all, the author aims to answer the question of why the relationship between AIR and chieftaincy has not have been researched before. She will therefore intend to increase insight into the mainstream paradigms of the political sciences and religious studies and the socio-political circumstances under which these paradigms were shaped.

2.2. Historical background of Indigenous Religions and Chieftaincy as separate academic fields of study

Indigenous Religions and chieftaincy are separate academic fields of study that the author has combined in order to answer the question of why Asante chieftaincy persisted. The following short history aims to increase an understanding of the historical contexts of the two fields. ECMs and early anthropologists conducted the first studies of 'Asante Indigenous Religion' (AIR). They did not aim, however, to study the religion of Asante people as objective as possible. The main reason why in the eighteenth and nineteenth centuries European Christian churches sent their missionaries overseas was to convert non-Westerners to Christianity. The studies of many of these missionaries on the culture and belief of non-Westerners were therefore written in the tradition of 'preparatio evangelica'. This is the idea that God gave all human beings the cognitive capacity to embrace Christianity as a world faith. It was the task of these ECMs to enable non-Westerners to become familiar with Christianity by providing the Christian message in an understandable way. The study of non-Western cultures and religions was geared towards gaining just enough insight into these religions to be able to translate the Christian message in the language of non-westerners, and to adapt this message to the local cultural contexts. Some examples of studies among the Asante conducted in these traditions were: (a) Diego D'Azambuja's 'A report of the 1482 mission under the authority of King John II'. D'Azambuja was a Portuguese aristocratic mission leader and the founder of the slave fort Sao Jorge da Mina (St George's Castle in Elmina). He was sent to the Gold Coast to establish trade relations and to spread Christianity (Nathan 1904:34). In 1836 'The Religious Tract Society' published 'Missionary records: West Africa, London'. This society was founded in 1799 and a major British publisher of Christian literature which was intended initially for evangelism. Rev. T.B. Freeman's 'Journal of various visits to the kingdoms of Ashanti, Aku, and Dahomey in Western Africa' (London 1844) and John Beecham's, 'Ashantee and the Gold Coast', London 1841 were also published for evangelical purposes.[16] The Danish reverend Hans Christian Monrad's 'Bidrag til en skildring af Guinea-kysten og dens Indbyggere' (Copenhagen 1822), was equally meant to convert the indigenous population to Christianity. Monrad served as chaplain in the Danish settlements on the Gold Coast. The Basel missionaries Ramseyer (1842-1902) and Kühne (1840-1915) are similarly important sources in this genre.[17]

An Asante force, which had invaded Ewe territory, captured these Swiss missionaries and from December 1870, until the advance of a British military expedition in January 1874 they were held hostage in Kumasi. Ramseyer believed that his capture and suffering were part of a divine plan for him to bring Christianity to the Asante. An important German source is the report of the missionary André Riis (Yarak and Graves 1997:363). Finally, the Swiss-Ga missionary Carl Christian Reindorf (1966) (1834-1917) made a compilation of a large body of oral traditions that he had collected on the Gold Coast (Silverman and Owusu-Ansah 1989:330). Not only were these sources subjective because they were meant to convert Asante to Christianity, but also because precolonial missionary officials in Europe had few scruples about changing the wording of reports sent to them from overseas. Many presumed 'primary' sources of this time should therefore actually be treated as secondary sources (Jones 1991:174,197).

Such documents written by Western liberal missionaries who were convinced that God could reveal himself to Africans, (such as Geoffrey Parrinder (1954) (1910-2005) were not the only source for the study of AIR, as in the 1920s, anthropologists entered the field. Most well known in the anthropological tradition are the colonial ethnographies of the government anthropologist R.S.

[16] The Methodist missionary T.B. Freeman who visited Kumasi four times between the 1830s and the 1840s, was assisting Beecham in his work.

[17] Ramseyer and Kühne left a manuscript, two German editions, an English and a French translation.

Rattray (1955 (first published in 1923); 1959 [first published in 1927]) who was appointed in 1928.[18] Although anthropology in these years developed as an independent academic discipline, the products of this new anthropological school did not meet the standards of what contemporary scholars of religion would regard as objective research. Their main purpose was to serve the need of the colonial administration to justify the colonial enterprise by connecting it to the Christian ideology of helping the so-called 'savages' in the dark continent of Africa by enlightening them with knowledge of Western Judeo-Christian civilisation.

Thus both missionary and anthropological studies of AIR did not meet the requirements of objectivity in the current academic study of religion. During the years before Ghana gained independence, several 'academic' studies on IRs were written, which these days have been recognised as the result of the emergence of Ghanaian nationalism. The study of IRs of Africa, which due to the contributions of Parrinder at the time became known as 'African Traditional Religion' (ATR) (in the singular), continued to influence the growth of nationalism in Ghana and became an important part of the Religious Studies program in the University of Ghana (UG) in Legon. The politician Kwame Nkrumah, who played an important in the achievement of Ghana's independence, and who later became the nation's president, effectively made the study of the ATR program at Legon an 'African necessity' (Walls 2004:211). The study of ATR, which had been started by Parrinder at the University of Ibadan in Nigeria, fitted in well to Nkrumah's overall ideology of going back to the African roots and showing resistance towards anything connected to the former British colonisation of his country, such as European Christian Missionary education. The study of ATR in Legon was therefore highly politicised. The inclusion of political motives for studying ATR became even more prominent when Nkrumah's opponents also started to use the study of IRs in Ghana and the rest of Africa to gain power and strive for the countries' independence. Danquah and Busia were one of a few of a list of West African scholars of religion, who declared that 'in West Africa even a child knows of the omnipotence of the African God' (Okot p'Bitek 2011:12). Omnipotency was, however, never a characteristic of the withdrawn Akan creator God (*Onyankopɔn*).

The academic study of chieftaincy in Ghana, which became prominent in UG in Legon during the years of preparation for Ghana's independence, suffered from the same lack of objectivity due to the results of African nationalism. Both African and Western historians in Legon positioned themselves as anti-colonialists, whose aim was to get rid of the traditional authorities, because they believed that these authorities were conservative, anti-modern and collaborated

---

[18] For an extensive critique on the work of R.S Rattray see: Platvoet, J. G. 1982. *Comparing Religions, A Limitative Approach: An Analysis of Akan, Para-Creole, and IFO-Sananda Rites and Prayers*. The Hague and New York: Mouton Publishers.

with the colonial regime. From this background, these historians portrayed the institutions of chieftaincy in Ghana as leftovers of an archaic society that would soon disappear once Ghana had gained full independence from the British colonisers who occupied their country. Ironically enough, due to the colonisation of Ghana most of these historians were trained in the European historical tradition, which made their works highly Eurocentric. In order to free themselves from the political power of Ghana's Asante royal rulers, they compared their institutions with those of the ancient regimes in Europe. These regimes had to be dismantled by the organisation of revolutions (such as the French revolution). The aim of the majority of their historical studies was therefore to show that the Asante kingdom and other kingdoms in West Africa displayed parallels with the ancient regimes in Europe, as a justification for the wish to clip the wings of the traditional authorities. Even the well-known contribution of Wilks who wrote a political overview of Asante in the nineteenth century, betrays a political motive (1989 [first published in 1975]; Rathbone 2006:53-53).

This African nationalistic background of the study of both 'Indigenous Religions' and chieftaincy at the University of Legon clarifies why until very recently these two fields of study have not been integrated. In the department of African Studies at this university, researchers focused on chieftaincy. The religious aspects of chieftaincy were portrayed as superstitious belief and things that belonged to the past, in order to contrast the norms and values of the traditional authorities with the progressive aims and goals of the leaders of the new Ghanaian nation-state. The study of 'African Traditional Religion' (ATR) only fitted into the nation building project of African nationalistic leaders; it was to be a separate field of study, in which this religion could be portrayed as part of the pride of Africa; it was portrayed as having withstood the negative effects of European Christian missionary education on these religions, which threatened their persistence.

The author's initial research proposal (developed in 2004), which contained the idea of researching the relationship between Asante Indigenous Religion and Asante chieftaincy, derived from the discovered existence of a lack of integration of the two fields of studies. Rathbone, who in the introduction of his earlier work 'Nkrumah and the Chiefs' (2000) doubted the importance attributed to ancestral veneration in present-day Ghanaian society, later acknowledged the existence of a gap in the academic literature with regards to the study of chieftaincy in relation to African Traditional Religion. In 2006 Rathbone remarked that, 'there is virtually no mention of the significance of the otherworldly in what chieftaincy was or what chieftaincy did in that tradition', and that 'by the majority of the politicians and scholars in the period after independence until very recently chieftaincy was consistently regarded as essentially a political category' (Rathbone 2006:48-49). The multiple meanings and hence multiple roles of chieftaincy tended to be ignored in favour of an over-concentration upon chiefs as temporal rulers. There was also an avoidance of discussion about their wider roles as what Weber would have called 'authoritative alligators of values', as trustees of proximate heritage, and of their engagements with the otherworldly.

Outside Ghana and the rest of Africa, recent studies by social researchers such as the anthropologist Steegstra (2008), who wrote extensively on foreign development chiefs (*Nkosuɔhene koko /Nkosuɔhemaa koko*), reveal that African Studies departments in many Western Universities concentrate on development studies with a focus on Africa. From this background, researchers in these departments presume that the reason for the continuity of cultural values in relation to chieftaincy, such as respect for chiefs, lies outside Ghana.[19] They also believe that the traditional institution would have disappeared without the help of powerful institutions, such as the WB, NGOs, and the personal initiative of Westerners to become *Nkosuɔhene koko/Nkosuɔhemaa koko*. In the author's opinion, these studies have overemphasised the role of Western institutions and persons in the persistence of Asante chieftaincy in Ghana. In Kumasi, for instance, North Atlantic development chiefs or their female co-rulers are not taken seriously as traditional authorities but are rather seen as 'walking wallets', because they are eager to donate money for development projects in exchange for spectacular 'traditional' enstoolments, which are in actual fact an 'invention of tradition'. The latter is a term of Eric Hobsbawn and Terence Ranger used to mark those traditions that people invented to serve political goals and were not deeply rooted in history of the long durée. Colonial powers would often invent a 'tradition' that they could use to legitimise their own position. For example, a certain succession to a chief's office might be recognised by a colonial power as being traditional in order to favour his own candidates for the job. Often these inventions were based on some form of tradition, but were grossly exaggerated, distorted, or biased toward a particular interpretation. In the postcolonial period, the Asante traditional authorities equally invent traditions this time to get the financial resources of Westerners, who are willing to pay for these traditions in exchange for being enstooled (which is a form of enthronement) (Ranger 2002). The author believes that these development royal rulers for whom traditions are being invented are insignificant for the persistence of the religious function of the Asante traditional authorities and of chieftaincy. If development traditional rulers are not taken seriously as a traditional authority in a country, how can they be the cause of the persistence of a traditional African institution? With its 'Promoting Partnership for Traditional Authorities Project' (PPTAP), no doubt the World Bank (WB) has contributed to the transformation of traditional authorities into development authorities. But in itself this transformation does not

[19] The title was created by the late *Asantehene* Opoku Ware II in 1985, at the occasion of the 25th anniversary of his ascension to the Golden Stool Steegstra, M. 2008. "Development Encounters: Westerners and Chieftaincy in Southern Ghana," in J. Abbink and A. Van Dokkum. *Dilemmas of Development: Conflicts of Interest and their Solutions in Modernising Africa*. Leiden: African Studies Centre: 228-241.

explain why chieftaincy in Ghana has persisted: before the donation from, for instance, the WB grant to the *Asantehene,* the highest male traditional authority among the Asante in 2003, the respect accorded to institutions associated with Asante traditional authorities in Ghana were already there, and there were no signs that chieftaincy was about to disappear. The appearance of development chiefs might therefore have been the result of the persistence of chieftaincy in Ghana rather than its cause.

The 'academic' study of IRs and chieftaincy in Ghana has thus suffered from a lack of objectivity due to their emergence during the heydays of the preparations for Ghana's independence. This African nationalism has affected the institutionalisation of the mentioned academic fields of study. As a result, the study of IRs in Ghana as related to chieftaincy did not fit into Nkrumah's African nationalistic educational agenda. In many African Studies departments in Western countries, resulting from the connections between those departments with development studies, the focus regarding chieftaincy studies lies in the link of the institution of chieftaincy with the outside world. Not only in, but also outside Ghana there is thus a gap in the academic literature linking IRs and chieftaincy. The author aims to fill this gap by borrowing from the disciplines of history, anthropology, historical anthropology and religious studies and by employing historical anthropological methods within the discipline of religious studies. A short historical overview of these disciplines and their interwoveness will be provided in next section and aims to enhance understanding of the author's contribution of her historical-anthropological study to the field of indigenous religious studies and also to the Berner model of processes of religious syncretism.

2.3 Anthropology, history and historical anthropology

In this section, the author will increase understanding of the historical background of the disciplines of anthropology, history and historical anthropology.

The discipline of anthropology (anthropology literally means the study of human) has its roots in the natural sciences (polygenetics), humanities (biblical studies), and social sciences (developmental studies). In the nineteenth century, physical anthropology was dominant, and the idea of human evolution also affected the anthropology of religion. In those days, anthropologists did not conduct fieldwork, but made use of data collected by travellers, naturalists, colonial officials and/or missionaries to build theories while remaining in their offices. Today we refer to those nineteenth century Victorian scholars as 'armchair anthropologists'. An example of a British armchair anthropologist was E. B. Tylor, who used travellers' accounts to argue that religion in society went through evolutionary phases of social organisation (hunter-gather, feudal, capitalistic) as well as evolutionary phases of religious belief (from animism to polytheism to monotheism) (Stocking 1992). Modern anthropology distinguishes itself from nineteenth century armchair anthropology through its focus on long-term fieldwork and rejection of evolutionist ideas about the non-western so-called 'primitive mind'. Modern anthropology's functionalistic approach aims to reveal the function of rituals, objects, and symbols in societies in order to understand the structures or systems that regulate those societies. The father of modern anthropology was Malinowski; his discoveries about indigenous – or in his words 'primitive' – people marked the end of the Victorian anthropological train of thought. Malinowski was the first to argue that primitive people lived not in simple societies but in complex ones and that they were in fact just like modern people, but lived according to different societal rules. An anthropologist could learn to understand the mind-set and way of life of indigenous people by thoroughly studying those rules in the field, especially those rules related to the performing of rituals and those embedded in the exchange of gifts.

After Malinowski, anthropology was no longer text based (philological) but based on long-term empirical ethnographic fieldwork including participant observations (Malinowski 2006). Since the 1930s, his so-called functionalistic anthropological method became dominant in the British academic world. In the 1960s, however, the postmodern turn and the accompanying crisis of empiricism altered the course of anthropology. Many scholars no longer believe that it is possible to gain purely objective knowledge; they stress the influence of the researcher's perspective on the data due to ethnicity, sex, gender and status group. As a consequence, the modern anthropological tradition fell apart in various subtraditions, among them historical anthropology, which coalesced in the 1980s (Stocking 1992; Thomas 1996).

History means the study of the history of human beings. Until the end of the nineteenth century, historians thought that studying history was a useful occupation because they believed that there was a purpose hidden behind the chronology of historical events. These events were believed to be either part of a cycle or part of a set of progressive stages in the development of civilisations. The chronological outlook of philosophers of history and historians was thus either circular or linear. Examples of great circular philosophers of history are the Greek teleologian Aristotle and the Italian Vico while examples of linear philosophers of history are Hegel and Marx. These days, most historians no longer wish to be associated with the idea that there is an inner meaning in the study of history that could help to improve civilisation. In the current *zeitgeist* of postmodernism, the so-called speculative philosophy of history has come to an end, although Fukuyama, the most well known proclaimer of 'the end of history', is an example of a contemporary proponent of historical teleology. Today, most historians are practitioners of 'analytic history'; an approach that declares it is enough to study history for the sake of it and holds that, while bounded by the human mind, viable historical knowledge is that knowledge that is as objective and value free as possible. Most of today's analytical historians are, like most social anthropologists, affected by the postmodern turn, and acknowledge the impossibility of fully objective and value free historical knowledge. Self reflexivity is also a key word among contemporary analytical philosophers of history and historians, as it is believed that self-awareness and self-scrutinisation of one's own socio-historical position (either included in or excluded from the produced history) can improve the quality of that history as an objective and neutral source of knowledge (Lemon 2003).

Historians belong neither to the social sciences nor the humanities. They are betwixt and between the empirical scientists, who – unlike historians – can use their senses to gain understanding of their object of study, and the scholars in the humanities, who study aesthetic representations of the social world rather than that world itself. Every claim that historians belong to either the first or the second category of knowledge production has its own particular merits and blind spots. Not surprisingly, historians have been unable to develop a paradigmatic consensus about the main approach to their discipline and are therefore in a Kuhnan sense not a true discipline. This has resulted in a permanent division between adherents of the narrativistic historical tradition based in the humanities (e.g. *Historicism*) and those of the French Annales and German History of Societies (Gesellschaftgeschichte) based in the social sciences (van den Braembussche 1985).

The main characteristic of the historical discipline is that its object of study (the past) no longer exists. Historians therefore depend on sources about the past, which can be material (art objects, utensils) or immaterial (narratives, ideas), in order to reconstruct the past. Historians who align themselves with the social sciences believe that the main task of the historian is the reconstruction of past societies, whereas those aligned with the humanities are of the opinion that historians should reconstruct narratives about the past. The latter group of historians believes that the language that historians develop to create these narratives is so unique that the discipline of history should be an autonomous field of study that nevertheless borrows from literature. The former group finds this reasoning unconvincing, arguing that other disciplines like anthropology also make use of narrativistic and sometimes poetic language but do not distinguish themselves from other social sciences on that basis.

Historical anthropology grew out of the convergence of historical and anthropological approaches to knowledge production, and is particularly associated with the third generation of the Annales School of historical thought in the period 1968-1975. The Annales was of French origin but had followers in Western Europe and the USA. The historians of this School were international and interdisciplinary oriented. They aligned history with the social sciences and felt that knowledge of other social sciences, such as economy, geography, archaeology, sociology, and social anthropology, could help historians to reconstruct past societies (Vries 1991).

The aim of historians is to understand phenomena in the context of their time, which is not a static entity. History is progressive and thus emphasises change. Social anthropologists were concerned with understanding phenomena within the context of contemporary cultures and thus focused on one time frame. The social anthropologist E. E. Evans-Pritchard also influenced the scholars of the Annales. He attacked his anthropological functionalist predecessors, who believed that primitive people had no history. He also criticised the anthropologists Malinowski and Radcliffe-Brown for being overly static in their approach and praised the works of the Annales historians of his time, especially Bloch and Fevbre. Evans-Pritchard was of the opinion that the works of historians who wrote about past civilisations, such as works on the Carolingians could be useful to anthropologists in enhancing their understanding of what he called 'primitive societies'. He also thought that insights about past societies were vital to understanding the functions of phenomena in present societies, and opined that history makes anthropologists more aware of their contemporary context. Historians could benefit from the study of anthropological works because they offer first-hand descriptions of the lives of ordinary 'primitive' people that are analogous to the lives of people in the past. Evans-Pritchard also criticised history's focus on political events and neglect of the lives of ordinary people in past societies, who were, like 'primitive peoples', influenced by magic and witchcraft. According to Evans-Pritchard, historians could become more aware of the contexts that influence their own findings by studying the present, because every generation creates its own reconstructions of the past. Evans-Pritchard concluded his plea to conjoin the historical and anthropological disciplines by quoting the anthropologist Lévi-Strauss, who wrote 'the two disciplines are not different in aim, but only in orientation and are *indissociables*' (Lévi-Strauss 1958: 31 quoted in Pritchard 1962).

Institutionally, however, the indissociability of the two disciplines only became a fact in the 1980s. In this period, anthropology dared to give up its ahistorical approach, which followed a period of thinking of primitives as people without history and one of thinking of primitives as people in a lower evolutionary stage. The functionalists, who then fell into the trap of ignoring history all together, attacked the latter position. Historians were equally unprepared for historical anthropology before the 1980s, due to their engagement with colonial records (rather than oral history), political history, and later socio-economic history (rather than the history of ordinary people and their mentality). It was the shift to mental history that emphasised *longue durée* and encouraged the examination of the history of structural phenomena in past societies, creating objects of study held in common with anthropologists. Examples of these phenomena are rituals of birth, marriage, and death in the lives of common people (Thomas 1996).

2.4. Historical anthropology in (indigenous) religious studies

Religious studies is an academic discipline that has its roots in the nineteenth century linguistic tradition of the humanities. Today, scholars of religion also borrow theories and concepts from disciplines in the social sciences (such as sociology, psychology, history, and anthropology) and the natural sciences (such as cognitive sciences). The founding fathers of religious studies are the German Max Müller (1823-1900) and the Dutch Cornelis Petrus Tiele (1830-1902) (Waardenburg 1999).

Müller, who started his academic career as a linguist, is known as the father of the comparative study of religion. In his opinion, all higher knowledge was acquired by and rested on comparison. Müller believed that just as one could find the essence of a language by comparing that language with other languages, one could find the essence of a religion through the comparison of that religion (its myths, beliefs, and rituals) with other religions. Like the aforementioned anthropologist E.B. Tylor, Müller was part of the Victorian school of thought that viewed history as a progression towards European civilisation. He was a theorist who did not gather his own data, but made use of European scholars in the periphery of the British Empire (e.g. India and South Africa). These scholars, in turn, made use of local indigenous informants, who collected data for them on the religious beliefs of their people. At the end of his life Müller himself expressed concern about the reliability of the data that reached him, which formed the foundation of his theories on the progression of humanity from primitive to civilised religions. Before the data reached Müller, the European scholars had first categorised them, while Müller believed that he had received raw data. In addition, the local indigenous informants were not always reliable, as they brought their own interests to bear when participating in the chain of data collection (Chidester 2004).

Müller's comparative study of religion was thus not unproblematic, but has nevertheless – divorced from Müller's teleological oriented theory of the progression of humanity – remained a method in religious studies until today. Tiele embraced Müller's theory of comparison and classification, but was also a predecessor of the phenomenology of religion, a philosophical approach to the study of religion. He believed that an objective study of religion required the bracketing out of one's owns presumptions, presuppositions, and beliefs. Tiele was especially concerned with the psychological aspects of religion and believed that the essence of all religions was located in 'piety' or adoration (Molendijk 2005:123-142).

The aforementioned founders of religious studies refer to their methodologies as methods for the 'scientific' study of religion, but contemporary usage would say that these methodologies belong to the 'scholarly' humanities and not to the 'scientific' natural sciences or social sciences. Today, scholars of religion are drawing on more and more other fields of study to gain understanding of religious phenomena. History and anthropology are among these fields; it is therefore reasonable to use the methodology of historical anthropology if one's research question demands such an approach. Religious studies scholars are generally problem-oriented; i.e., the problem they are researching determines the type of data to be gathered. This book is concerned with the persistence of Asante chieftaincy, which refers to the condition of a phenomenon X (chieftaincy) from period Y (the past) to Z (the present). Because this research problem requires the gathering of data from both the past and present, historical anthropology proved the most useful methodology.

The author chose historical anthropology as her research methodology, but built up her theoretical framework by borrowing from theories in contemporary indigenous religious studies. Contemporary religious studies differ from previous studies of the religion of 'primitive' people, in that it aims to empirically and analytically study the religion of indigenous peoples as objectively as possible within the boundaries of human capabilities. It aims to do so without describing indigenous people from a position of belief in one's own superiority or portraying their religion in a romanticised way. Descriptions of the hard conditions in which the Asante people live and the cruelty of some of the Asante indigenous religious rituals are not left out of this book, rather the complexities of their society and religion are analysed as fully as possible. The processes of systematic religious syncretism in the model provided by religious scholar Berner has been used to enhance understanding of these complexities and their transformations over time.

2.4.1 The Berner model of syncretic processes

A model of syncretic processes is used in this book in order to explain the incorporation of elements of world religions into AIR. One aspect common to many IRs is that their adherents take a pragmatic attitude towards deities. Those deities who no longer serve a function for believers will no longer be venerated and therefore cease to exist. This is true not only for indigenous deities, but also for deities that are borrowed from IRs of neighbouring cultural groups or from world religions such as Christianity and Islam. IRs are thus very dynamic. As a consequence of this dynamism and the differing intensities of the encounters between Asante people and non-Asante believers, different processes of religious syncretism are applicable to different periods of Asante history. Berner's model runs from A1 to C5 and is designed to cover processes of religious syncretism and related processes. He thereby makes a distinction between two different levels of religious syncretism: elementary and systematic. According to Berner (2004:297) 'syncretism can be viewed as a process in the historical development of religion, which takes place on the system level where two systems enter into an association, which remains to be defined. It can also be a process on the elemental level, where the association concerns only elements, but not the entire associated systems'. On the element level, the determination of relations designates the proportional relationship of different elements, but does not eliminate the boundary separating them, so that they are preserved as members of a relation and remain recognizable to the adherents of the system concerned. On the system level, syncretism designates those processes where the boundary and thus the competitive relationship between the systems are eliminated. These processes can take a variety of different forms, some with relations on the element level or linked with syncretism on the element level.

The various forms that religious syncretism took in Asante chieftaincy history will be discussed in the chapters III, IV and VI of this book.

2.4.2 Spirit mediumship, health and power

Since the early twentieth century anthropologists of religion have discussed the religious experiences of spirit mediums in relation to mental health issues. In 1913 the Scottish anthropologist James Frazer wrote, for instance, 'the theory of inspiration and possession is commonly invoked to explain all abnormal mental states, particularly insanity or conditions of mind bordering on it. So these persons more or less crazed in their wits, and particularly hysterical or epileptic patients, are fort hat reason thought to be peculiarly favoured by the spirits and are therefore consulted as oracles, for wild and whirling words passing for the revelations of higher power whether a god or a ghost who considerately screens his too dazzling light under a thick veil of saying and mysterious ejaculations' (Frazer 1913:15). Today, leading psychiatrist like the Dutchman Dick Swaab are of the opinion that many significant figures in religious history, including apostle Paulus and spirit mediums in African (derived) cultures suffer from temporal lobe epilepsy and in between their attacks suffered from the *geschwindsyndrom*, which goes together with a feeling of euphoria, the idea of having a significant task to fulfil, a strong moral feeling, a lack of sense of humour, asexuality, depression and deep religiosity e.g. expressed in the form of religious revelations (Swaab 2011:347-350). The contemporary *etic* approach towards spirit mediumship in the field of cognitive science is thus still that religious specialists, who have experiences that are similar to those of psychiatric patients, are usually associated with spiritual mediatory roles. Swaab has much in common with the atheistic philosopher Daniel Dennet who believes that all mental experiences, including those of a religious nature, are the effect of internal brain processes. To Swaab and Dennet's understanding, the experience of God and near-death experiences are all the effect of certain stimuli in the brain that can be induced by electrical stimulation. Not surprisingly, Swaab's latest book has the provocative title 'We are our brain', and it includes a chapter with the heading 'There is nothing more between Heaven and Earth' (Swaab 2011).

Dennett shares Swaab's atheistic worldview and materialist philosophy of mind and has frequently compared the human brain with that of robots (Dennett 1991; Blume 1998). In the experience of apostle Paul and spirit mediums, however, the appearance of the spirits is not the result of internal brain processes but of the invocation of higher spiritual powers that come from outside the human brain. Swaab and Dennett argue that the experience of these powers is an aspect of the psychiatric disease of these religious icons, but they also confess that the academic knowledge of the functioning of the brain and its consciousness is still in its infancy (Dennett 1991; Swaab 2011). In this book the question that will be addressed is how the Asante spirit mediums have experienced their relationship with the spirits, focussing on power. Did and do the traditional authorities and the *akomfoɔ* believe that they submit themselves to higher powers outside themselves and did and do they perceive their relationship with the spirits of the deceased as a religious experience? Or were or are they in fact themselves unbelievers who perform rituals to legitimate their religious-political power, to receive a high social status within their societies and earn a considerable income by indoctrinating their subjects or clients with the Asante belief?

The question of whether spirit mediumship was and is perceived as a religious experience or an act, which is a secular performance, brings us to another *etic* explanation for spirit mediumship that is derived from the contemporary field of the anthropology of religion. Currently, spirit mediumship is often described in this academic field in terms of the centrality or marginalisation of power and power relations between dominated or subordinate groups within society. Janice Boddy, for instance, concludes that most contemporary anthropologists perceive spirit mediumship cults as a mode of resistance against cultural hegemonies. In her examples, spirit mediums, who were themselves marginalised, were consulted by subordinate groups in society, such as the clients of the *zar* in Northern Sudan (Boddy 1989; 1994).[20] Among the Asante, however, spirit mediumship was the profession of the traditional authorities, the religious specialists and their spokesmen (*akyeame*), who were subordinate to the royal rulers and advised them; these people were certainly not marginalised. In fact, the *akomfoɔ* and the *akyeame* helped the royal rulers in maintaining the *status quo* and in spreading the indigenous religious ideology that was the basis of the traditional rulers' religious-political power. At the same time, however, the *akomfoɔ* were dependent on the consent of their clients to carry out their profession as much as the royal rulers were dependent on that of their subjects. Rather than discussing the power relationship between the royal rulers and the *akomfoɔ* in terms of centrality of power or marginalisation or the one between the royal

[20] For more scholarly opinions on spirit mediumship see: Bourguignon, E. 1976. *Possession*. San Francisco: Chandler and Sharp., Holm, N. G. 1982. *Religious Ecstasy*. Uppsala: Almqvist and Wiksell., Lewis, I. M. 1989. *Ecstatic Religion: A study of Shamanism and Spirit Possesion*. London: Routledge., Friedson, S. M. 2009. *Remains of Ritual: Northern Gods in a Southern Land*. Chicago: University of Chicago Press.

rulers and the *akomfoɔ* and their subjects or clients in terms of domination and subordination, the author has chosen to include the voice of the spirits and the agency that is assigned to them in the *emic* Asante experience of spirit mediumship. The author aims to demonstrate, by including the spirits as independent agents in her historical-anthropological narrative, that the power relations in Asante society were to a certain extent reversible. The traditional authorities and the *akomfoɔ* were ruling but at the same time they were believed to be as prone to for the wraths of the spirits as their subjects or clients, and were embedded in a network of reciprocal relationships with humans and other-than-human beings.[21]

2.5 Historical and anthropological source discussion and the reconstruction of the Asante past

The indigenous religious functions of the Asante traditional authorities in this book are reconstructed with the help of both historical and anthropological sources on Asante history. As a researcher one should be as accurate as possible; therefore one needs to know how to interpret one's sources and be aware of their limitations. The next sections are critical analyses of the sources that were used to thematically reconstruct the precolonial, colonial and postcolonial Asante history.[22]

2.5.1 The precolonial Asante past

This section consists of an analysis of the historical and anthropological sources that were used to reconstruct the indigenous religious functions of the Asante royal rulers in the precolonial period, which has been reconstructed by the use of multiple sources: both written and oral historical and anthropological primary sources, as well as historical and archaeological secondary sources. The written primary sources can be divided in those from writers with religious and/or political motives (e.g. European Christian Missionaries and Islamic geographers and chroniclers) and those with commercial motives (e.g. travellers and merchants). The oral primary sources are oral traditions, which are passed on by 'men of memory'. The written secondary sources can be divided in those produced by archaeologists and historians. The author will now elaborate on the two types of sources and discuss their limitations. The problematic aspects of the eyewitness accounts of authors who visited the Asante people in the precolonial period whose writings had a religious aims, such as proselytisation, is that these

---

[21] For a recent historical anthropology of Anlo-Ewe spirit mediumship in Ghana that also includes the spirits' voices see: Venkatachalam, M. (2012). *Slavery in Memory*. Anthropology. London, SOAS. PhD.

[22] Müller, L. F. (2008). "The Reality of Spirits: A Historiography of the Akan Concept of Mind." *Quest: An African Journal of Philosophy* **XXII**(1-2): 163-185.

sources were most often highly coloured by those aims. As a historical anthropologist one should therefore be aware of the religious beliefs of these writers in order to interpret these sources as objectively as possible.

One should, for instance, be aware of the religious motives of the Islamic writers on the land of the black people of West Africa (the *bilad al-sudan*). Although the Islamic Mande-Dyula traders had traded with the Asante since the fifteenth century, they did not settle among them until the second half of the eighteenth century. The first Arabic sources on the Asante people are from that period, including the most important source, the *Kitabal-Ghanja* written by Umar Kunandi ibn and Umar Kamaghatay. This historical work dealt with the history of Gonja and the contacts of Muslim traders from this state with the Asante. Like other Arabic sources, the *Kitabal-Ghanja* was written for diplomatic reasons and had a political-religious overtone. Other important Islamic sources are 'the Arabic manuscript from the Guinea coast' and a series of letters exchanged between the Muslims in Kumasi and those in the northern provinces of Gonja, Mamprugu, and Dagbon (Silverman and Owusu-Ansah 1989). The Muslims, such as the Mande-Dyula traders or the Hausa, who came in contact with the Asante people, were instructed how to behave towards the Asante according to Islamic tradition. Much concern in these texts was given to the religiously proscribed attitude of Muslims towards these so-called infidels (the Asante), and strategies were explained for surviving in the land of unbelievers (*Dar-al-harb*) (Wilks 2000).

The first European who wrote about the people of the Gold Coast (currently known as present-day Ghana) was the Portuguese aristocrat Diego D'Azambuja. The Portuguese king John II sent him on the 11th of December, 1481 to the Gold Coast to look for gold and slaves and to spread Catholicism among the Gold Coast's indigenous population (Nathan 1904:34). When Diego D'Azambuja, through the medium of an interpreter, explained to the purpose of his expedition to Caramança (a corruption of Kwamina Ansa), he stated that the king of Portugal's first desire was to instruct this chief of Elmina, in the Christian faith (Ellis 1893:19). D'Azambuja's accounts of the Fante people, who like the Asante belong to the Akan, have thus been interpreted through the lens of a Catholic proselytiser.

The reports of the Swiss Presbyterians Friederich Ramseyer (1842-1902) and Johannes Kühne (1840-1915), who were captured by an Asante force that had invaded Ewe territory and held hostage in Kumasi, were also of a proselytising nature. In the forward to 'Four Years in Asante' (1875) the professor of theology and university preacher Theodore Christleib wrote: 'The south-west boundary of the Ashantee kingdom is opened, and not only this but the tribes there situate (Okwau and Dwaben) have expressed a wish for missionaries to come to them. Does not all this reveal the hand of God opening the gates to the messengers of His kingdom?' Needless to say, an objective account of the situation in the Asante kingdom would not include this rhetorical question that presumes that

God himself had opened up the Asante kingdom for Christian missionaries to bring the Gospel. Another sentence which is clearly not objective and demonstrates the aims and goals of the Swiss imperialists on the Gold Coast is as follows: 'Now that the weapons of our country have pierced the heart of Ashantee, and laid Coomassie in ruins, should not the Christian compassion and the vigorous faith of Englishmen seek to raise this unhappy nation from the dust; not to new death, but to true life in the light and liberty of the gospel?' (Ramseyer, Kühne et al. 1875:viii). Germany and Switzerland helped the British to campaign against Kumasi (Coomassie); missionaries were not only untroubled by the attack of ordinary Asante people, missionaries found this an excellent opportunity to familiarise the Asante with Christianity.

Not only the preface but also the main text of Ramseyer and Kühne is full of missionary language. For instance, they write that it was by God's grace that another missionary, Christaller, finished his translation of the Bible in Twi (Ramseyer, Kühne et al. 1875:156). When, following the burial of the wife of one of king Kofi Kakari's brothers, some human beings were killed to accompany her to and in the ancestral world (*asamando*), the authors compare this king to Satan and wrote: 'At such times the question would arise, what were we that we should attempt to do battle against this mighty bulwark of Satan? It almost seemed as if we heard his scornful laugh! But we sowed on in faith and hope, looking to God to preserve and fructify the seed' (Ramseyer, Kühne et al. 1875:169).

There are several other useful missionary sources. A Basel missionary who gives good insights into the life of the missionaries who lived among the Asante people and shows the complexities of the missionary discourse was André Riis (Yarak and Graves 1997). T. B. Freeman's 'Journals of various visits to the kingdoms of Ashanti, Aku, and Dahomi in western Africa' (1844) gives insight into the conversations between an Asante king (*Asantehene* Kwaku Dua Panin) and a missionary (of the WMMS – Wesleyan Methodist Missionary Society) who was sent to bring the gospel to the Asante people.

The primary sources of the precolonial period that European traders wrote for commercial purposes are often driven by a belief in the superiority of the Europeans over the Africans they encountered. One can find these ideas, for instance, in the earliest accounts of the Akan people, such as those of the Portuguese Duarte Pacheco Peirera (1937 (1505) as well as those of the German Fernandez' (1507). Both authors wrote works that radiate the spirit of the Renaissance. An example of a Dutch commercial primary source is that of the Chief Merchant Willem Bosman (1704 (translation 1705). Bosman visited the Gold Coast for the West-Indian Company (WIC) during the eighteenth century. He accuses the Fante of being 'unreliable, lazy and over-proud' and the British of the rival English Royal African Company (ERAC) of always being drunk (van den Heuvel 1981). The authors of these types of sources attempt to justify cruel practices towards indigenous African people by appealing to the business interests of their companies. About the practice of branding slaves Bosman wrote: 'Perhaps this branding of slaves comes across to you as a barbarian practice, but it is strictly necessary and we take care that they do not burn.' He also wrote: 'We have to say that when it comes to the neatness of the ship, we [the Dutch] surpass other Europeans. In our ships everything is clean and tidy in diametrical opposition to the situation among French, Portuguese and English slave ships where everything is untidy, dirty and smelly. Thereby the slaves on our ships receive three meals a day, which are of better quality than the meals that they would ever receive in their own country' (van den Heuvel 1981:9).[23]

A well-known British author who wrote about his visit to Kumasi is Thomas E. Bowdich (1819) who wrote 'A mission from Cape coast castle to Ashantee'. Bowdich was a scientist who was sent on a mission to West Africa to map the area, to establish a good relationship with Akan chiefs for the purpose of trade, and to explore the interior market. Over the course of his mission Bowdich describes the geography of the area, as well as the culture and religion ('superstition') of the people he encounters, including their language and music. From his writing it becomes clear that Bowdich was a scientist of the Victorian era, who clearly felt superior to the African people he encountered. In the report of his observations of the *Odwira* festival which is the most significant indigenous religious festival of the Asante people, he writes: 'I never felt so grateful for being born in a civilised country' (Bowdich 1819:275).

Bowdich clearly over-exaggerated the number of ritual killings of human beings that were performed during a funeral as part of this festival, because by emphasising on the uncivilised behaviour of the Asante people he could justify the colonial enterprise (Law 1985:53-60, 69-70). Also, in his descriptions of what he calls the 'primitive' Akan languages 'Fante' and 'Accra', he emphasises what these languages lack in comparison to the English language. He thus mainly describes the nature of these African languages in negative terms. Nevertheless, one can see the academic in Bowdich when one compares his descriptions of the indigenous people of West Africa with those of Hutchinson in the same book, who wrote that 'black men had the eyes of a thief, the paws of a tiger and the belly of a hog, for they were never satisfied' (Bowdich 1819:410). Other

[23] Other Dutch authors who wrote about the Akan people for commercial purposes are: Pieter de Marees' de Marees, P. 1912 [original edition 1602]. *Beschrijvinghe ende Historische Verhael van het Gout Koninekrijck van Gunea, Anders de Gout-Custe de Mina Genaemt Liggende in het Deel van Africa.* 's-Gravenhage: Nijhoff (Published by the Linschoten Society). Beschrijvinghe ende historische verhael van het Gout Koninekrijck van Gunea, anders de Gout-Custe de Mina genaemt liggende in het deel van Africa, and Olfert Dappers' Dapper, O. 1668. *Nauwkeuringe Beschrijvinge der Afrikaense Gewesten van Egypten, Barbaryen, Libyen, Biledulgerid, Negroslant, Guinea, Ethiopiën, Abyssinie.* Amsterdam: Jacob van Meurs., and also the unpublished works of the Dutch-speaking visitors of Kumasi: Willem Huydecoper in 1816-1817, Jacob Simons in 1831-32, Jacobus de Bruijn in 1836-1837, H.S. Pels in 1842 and David Mill Graves in 1857 Yarak, L. W. and D. M. Graves 1997. "A Dutch Embassy to Asante in 1857: the Journal of David Mill Graves," *History in Africa* 24: 363-380.

primary sources about the precolonial Asante history written by non-Akan people are those of Joseph Dupuis and Marie-Joseph Bonnat. Dupuis focused on the role of the Muslims in Kumasi (Dupuis 1824). Bonnat was a French trader, who mainly concentrated on the trade activities of the Asante during the reign of King Kofi Kakari (1867-1874) (Perrot and van Dantzig 1994).

Finally, there were also authors of West African origin who wrote about the Akan people in the precolonial period, such as the Fante lawyer Mensah Sarbah (1864-1910) and the Danish-Ga Basel missionary Carl Christian Reindorf (1834-1917). Sarbah is an example of a critical voice raised against the British's illegal confiscation of land in the Gold Coast (Sarbah 1968 (first published in 1904). Reindorf's work is of interest because he made a compilation of a large body of oral traditions that he had collected from across the Gold Coast (Silverman and Owusu-Ansah 1989:330). The problematic aspect of Reindorf's and Sarbah's sources is that they were so called 'black Englishmen'. They were indigenous intellectuals who were trained by Europeans and who therefore used a Western academic theoretical framework to express themselves. However, they had to use that same framework to break free from the Europeans and used their texts to create an African identity. Their sources therefore also lack objectivity, being infused with African nationalist ideology, a reaction to European colonialism (Korang 2004:90-144).

The Asante 'men of memory' who pass on oral history are the traditional rulers' representatives: their spokesmen (*akyeame*). The limitations of oral history are threefold. First, it is based on the memories of human beings, who are selective by nature. People tend to remember those events and historical facts that they find most interesting or pleasant. This implies that they suppress and forget those things that they find unpleasant or insignificant. Oral history is therefore not the best method to reconstruct the chronological order of events. It is a good method however, for discovering which events are of psychological interest to one's informants. A positive aspect of this method is also that the interviewer has direct contact with his source of information and can also pay attention to the interviewee's non-verbal communication. This makes it easier to gather information that is not highly coloured by the intentions of its author, as is often the case with written documents (Thompson 2000).

Secondly, the men of memory pass on history in order to legitimise the position of the traditional authorities. For this reason, the royal history of a cultural group is often a history of victorious events that celebrates the royal rulers of that group. The third problem with oral history is that historical events are often presented as if they occur in the present tense. For in the Asante philosophy of history there is no linearity in historical events. Instead, all historical events take place in the present and it is only the location of these events that is different from current events. In AIR, historical events are located in the realm of the ancestral spirits (*asamando*), which is believed to be a universe parallel to the social world (*wiase*). History is thus, in fact, 'presentism' and historical figures do not die but rather become part of the community of 'the living-dead', as Mbiti described the ancestors (Mbiti 1992 (First Published in 1969:83-91).[24] This Asante philosophy of history makes is very difficult for a historian who is trained in the North Atlantic world to reconstruct a linear history of the Asante past. In AIR, it is through the connection of the royal rulers with their ancestors – through objects such as stools – that they receive their religious and political power. The tradition in which royal rulers derive their power from their relationship with spiritual beings makes it impossible for Asante royal rulers to disconnect historical events from present times.

In conclusion, the aforementioned European primary sources are coloured by the missionary and/or commercial aims of their authors, while the oral histories are coloured by the royal's interests in specific versions of oral traditions. From a scholarly perspective, another limitation of these sources is that none of them were written purely for academic purposes and they therefore lack objectivity. The missionary sources are also untrustworthy because missionary officials in Europe often changed the reports of the European missionaries who were located overseas. The information that appeared in missionary journals and the writings that were presented as 'primary source' documents were thus in actual fact most often secondary sources (Jones 1986).

Significant archaeological secondary sources include those of Insoll (2003), Klein (1996), Boahen (1966) and Posnansky (1977). Archaeological sources are used to reveal changes in material culture, such as changes in house types, settlement patterns, diets, and funeral customs. The method that is used for this purpose is called carbon 14 or radiocarbon dating (C-14-dating). A positive aspect of this method is that it allows researchers to investigate material changes over long periods of time. However, a negative aspect is that this method has a probabilistic character especially when it comes to 'relatively' early history (Shott 1992). Historical secondary sources on the precolonial history of the Akan people are those of McCaskie (1983; 1986b; 1995; 1999), Wilks (1961; 1982; 1989 [first published in 1975]), Austin (1995; 1996), Baesjou (1979) and Yarak (1986; 1987; 1997). McCaskie has criticised Wilks' standard work on the Asante in the nineteenth century for using a Webern framework of analysis to describe the bureaucratisation of the Akan state, which would not fit accurately with the reality of the transformations in that state. According to McCaskie, too many Webern concepts were imposed on the Akan culture (McCaskie 1992). Most likely, McCaskie's analysis of Wilks is correct, although this does not safeguard his own work from the influences of Western philosophers. McCaskie uses a Gramscian theoretical framework to construct his

---

[24] For more on the philosophy of Mbiti see: Müller, L.F. (2004). "A Thematic Comparison between Four African Scholars Idowu, Mbiti, Okot p'Bitek, Appiah: What Do They Tell Us About the Existence of 'Truth' and a 'High God', And Why Is Their Work Significant ?" *Quest: An African Journal of Philosophy/ Revue Africaine de Philosophie* **18**(1-2): 109-125.

Asante history. Western philosophy has thus influenced the two best-known Asante historians. The main difference between the two scholars is that Wilks was influenced by the second generation of the historians of the Annales school of thought, whereas McCaskie places himself in a critical position towards both the second and the third generations of this school. With regard to the second generation, and especially related to Wilks, McCaskie remarked that they over concentrate on the compartmentalisation of disciplines and overemphasise the significance of political history. McCaskie accused Wilks of imposing Weber's analysis of the rationalisation and concomitant bureaucratisation of states on the Asante people. The Asante, argues McCaskie were illiterate, which makes Weber's analysis of the bureaucratisation ('bureau' meaning 'writing-desk') of states, irrelevant for the Asante as an analytical framework (McCaskie 1995:14-15). His critique on the Annales historians of the third school was that these historians did not study the history of cultural practice as such; they either reify it or isolate it from social, political and material reality. McCaskie found inspiration from the Annales historians Bloch and Lefebvre who were of the first generation of Annales historians. These historians, who were the founding fathers of the *histoire des mentalités,* were interdisciplinary, and made use of the disciplines of social and cultural anthropology, literary criticism, folklore and psychology to gain the insights necessary to write their histories of cultural practice (Vries 1991; McCaskie 1995:6-7). McCaskie, whose emphasis is on the role of religion in the legitimation of the Asante state, made use of the theory of the Italian scholar Gramsci who wrote extensively on the concept of 'cultural hegemony'. He describes the precolonial Asante history as characterised by cultural hegemony of the Asante over annexed states and the counter hegemony of the *akonkofoɔ* or educated Asante, who had different ideas on the accumulation of wealth, which they believed should *not* only be the privilege of the Asante state. The counter hegemony of the *akonkofoɔ* clashed with the hegemony of Asante royal rulers.

In the opinion of the author, the secondary sources of McCaskie (1995) and Wilks (1989 [first published in 1975]) on the precolonial Asante history are both a significant contribution to the field of Asante history (McCaskie 1995:12-19; Wilks 1995). McCaskie and Wilks have already extensively criticised one another's academic work, but nevertheless the author finds herself obliged to contribute to their discussion as a way of embedding her own point of view on the Asante history in the existing field of scholarship. The author agrees with McCaskie that Wilks use of Weber's archetype of 'legal authority' as a form of legitimate domination on the Asante to describe their precolonial history has led to a social construction that leaves out many aspects of that history including aspects of religion. McCaskie attacks Wilks on the basis of his analysis of the bureaucratisation of the Asante state, which would be appropriate for a society with a written culture but not the Asante oral society. In the author's point of view, this is not so much the problem: due to the Asante traditional rulers' invitation of

Muslim scholars with literary skills (the Asante *Nkramofoɔ*) meaning 'those who can read the Qur'an) at the royal court since the eighteenth century, the Asante state did indeed develop a bureaucratic apparatus. The point is, however, that the archetype of 'legal authority' does not cover this type of bureaucratic development, whereas Weber's ideal type of 'traditional authority' does. The Asante did and do not follow their laws because of the rationality of the content of those laws, but because of their ancestral source (The Seventy-Seven Laws that were created by the indigenous priest Anokye after he heard the voices of the ancestral spirits; his symbolic marital partners). Another sign that Wilks made a mistake in the archetype of authority he used to describe the Asante state is that unlike legal authorities the Asante royal rulers had and have *nhenkwaa* who are personal retainers rather than bureaucratic officials. As the already mentioned Akan proverb says: 'a fish out of water dies; a king without followers ceases to exist.' The author's opinion of the Asante royal rulers as traditional authorities rather than legal authorities is supported by more recent than Wilks studies on Asante traditional authorities in Africa with whom the Asante share many attributes.[25] Wilks' use of 'legal authority' as a Webern archetype inevitably led to the neglect of the religious source of the precolonial Asante state. The main interest that legal authorities have in religion is to maintain order, discipline and security; they are generally little inclined towards religion. Wilk's his description of the process of bureaucratisation of the state and the rationalisation of Asante society in Weber's terms thus automatically led to downplaying of the significance of the religious source of legitimation of the Asante state and of religion in general in Asante precolonial history. When it comes to the analysis of AIR, McCakie's use of Gramsci and is theory of cultural hegemony is, however, also problematic. Gramsci work falls in the Marxist tradition and Marx is known in religious studies as a highly reductionist philosopher on the matter of religion, as he reduced the phenomenon to a psychological state of being that was the result of an underlying mode of production (Benewick and Green 1992:89-92; Pals 1996:124-153). In the introduction of his doctoral thesis, Marx already said: 'Mit einem wort, ich hasse aller Goetter' (in one world, I hate all the gods) (Marx 1841 (1964):107).

Marx hated all the gods, because they did not recognise man's self-consciousness as the highest divinity. He was convinced that as a result of class struggle the economic basis of the masses would improve, which would eventually lead to the disappearance of religion, as it would no longer be necessary. Gramsci's concepts of hegemony and counter-hegemony are equally laden with the idea that religion is ideology rooted in the world of production (Femia 1975).

[25] See for instance: van Rouveroy van Nieuwaal, E. A. B. and R. van Dijk 1999. *African Chieftaincy in a New Socio-Political Landscape*. Münster and London and Piscataway, N.J.: Lit Verlag, Ray, D. I. and P. S. Reddy 2003. *Grassroots Governance? Chiefs in Africa and the Afro-Caribbean*. Alberta: University of Calgary Press.

Gramsci is thus also using a secular concept of religion. He is also using a political concept of agency, and refers initially to the factory councils and later to political parties as agents for political change (Schwarzmantel 2009). Gramsci's secularity in his concept of agency also makes the application of this Italian philosopher's theory on the Asante inappropriate to analyse the religious belief of the Asante people. Now, the main problem with agency is that it its awareness is non-perceptible and that it can only be understood from the insight (Guttenplan 1996:116-117). Nobody except for the Asante royal rulers in Asante history and in the contemporary society can know whether they were, as the Kenyan philosopher Mbiti claimed in relation to all Africans, 'notoriously religious'; an expression that the Kenyan philosopher Mbiti used to claim religion is central and underneath all other spheres of the life of all Africans (Mbiti 1992 (First Published in 1969):1). Whether one uses Western secular philosophers, like Weber or Gramsci, or whether one takes Mbiti as a point of departure is thus a matter of philosophical preference. With regards to the matter of agency, the author prefers to use Mbiti's philosophy, because she feels that with his concept of the living-dead he comes closest to the religious experience of the Asante people, who believe in the unity between the living and the deceased members that make up the *abusua* in the parallel and interconnected universes of the social and the spiritual worlds. In the opinion of the author, both Wilks and McCaskie do not sufficiently acknowledge the unity between the living and the dead in Asante society, which has significant consequences for the concept of agency. In AIR 'agency' is primarily in the hands of the spirits, who use the body of the representatives of the living (the chiefs, their female co-rulers and indigenous priests and priestesses) to mediate their messages to the social world. These representatives are either in case of the traditional rulers due to their connection to the stool (a religious object which serves as a shrine) or in case of the indigenous priest or priestess (*ɔkɔmfoɔ*) due to their extraordinary and trained mind receptive for the voices and visions of the spirits. In Asante society, those who are trained to be in connection with and partly in control of the spirits either with or without help of an object (of which the Portuguese wrongly referred to as 'fetish') were and are praised for their qualities. In the rationalised Western world the voices and visions of the gods that come from within us are silenced and those who still hear them are sent to psychiatric hospitals. The judgements of persons with hyper religious capacities are, however, culturally specific and in the experience of the Asante believers the spirits can be seen and heard by those who have the gift and patience to be trained for that purpose. The indigenous priests and priestesses and royal rulers have a high social status in Akan societies, because of their capacities to simultaneously 'see' the events in the social world and the spiritual world and to come to a mytho-poeic understanding of the meaning of their synchronicity.

2.5.2 The colonial Asante past

The colonial period of Asante history has been mainly described and analysed by British-trained anthropologists. The best knowns are the government anthropologist R. S. Rattray (1881-1938) and his successor Meyer Fortes (1906-1983). Their works, such as Rattray's (1955 (first published in 1923) 'Ashanti' and Fortes's (1950) 'African systems of kinship and marriage' were written according to the rules of the anthropological school of functionalism. Today these works are classics that serve as primary sources for current historians and historical anthropologists. Other primary sources of this period derive from Western liberal missionaries such as Parrinder, Ghanaian scholars such as K. A. Busia (1914-1978), J.B. Danquah (1895-1965), official documents of British administrators, and the book that *Asantehene* Edward Agyeman Prempeh I (Akyeampong 2003) (1888-1931) wrote in 1907 on the Asante history. Oral primary sources consist of those solicited from 'men of memory' as well as other individuals who remember events of colonial Asante history. Secondary sources from this period are those of British-trained scholars such as Allman and Parker (2005), Austin (1988) and Nugent (2004), as well as some Arabic scholars.

The limitation of the works of Rattray and Fortes is that they were trained as functionalist anthropologists. This focus makes them somewhat blind to the historical dimensions of life in the colonial period. These functionalist anthropologists were trained to concentrate on cultures as a whole and to gain understanding of the function of rituals, organisations, and laws in those cultures. In their effort to turn themselves away from the racial fallacies of evolutionism they also turned their back on the historical discipline, limiting themselves to the description and analysis of the function of specific cultural elements and societal unities. The work of functionalist anthropologists shows similarities with those of biologists who were trained to enhance understanding of the working of organisms in the body by describing the function of those organs for human beings as organic wholes. Another limitation of these works is that they were written for the benefit of the colonial enterprise in Africa without being critical about the anthropologists' role in that enterprise. The colonial government financed the fieldwork of these anthropologists because it helped them to gain geographical and cultural understanding of their empire in Africa and increase their control over the indigenous people. As a historian one should thus be aware of the lack of self-reflexivity of these classical functionalist anthropologists and their works.

Furthermore, this warning is relevant for the oeuvre of liberal theologians on the African continent such as Geoffrey Parrinder (1910-2005). He and other liberal theologians promoted the colonial enterprise out of the religious conviction that God was there for all races and could thus also reveal himself to Africans. Consequently, these theologians believed that it was their duty to bring the gospel to Africans and convert them to Christianity. The works of the aforementioned supporters of the colonial enterprise stand in deep contrast with those of

Ghanaian scholars such as K.A. Busia (1914-1978) and J.B. Danquah (1895-1965). These scholars worked towards independence and searched for an African identity, but were themselves – in terms of scholarly training – also products of the colonial enterprise. As a consequence they used their understanding of Western religions to argue that the religions of Ghanaians stood on equal footing with the Abrahamic religions (Judaism, Christianity and Islam). Like these religions, they portrayed AIR as a monotheistic religion that incorporated the belief in one male High God in the sky, overlooking the fact that AIRs venerated male and female ancestors as spirits on earth. Another flawed indigenous source that nevertheless provides an interesting perspective on Asante history is the work of *Asantehene* Edward Agyeman Prempeh I. King Prempeh's book is in fact a reconstruction of the Asante history of the precolonial period, but because of its official royal perspective it also reveals a lot about king Prempeh himself as well as his strategy of deploying aspects of precolonial life ways to re-legitimise his power once the British allowed him to return to Kumasi. Prempeh's history reveals the 'invention of tradition' as a strategic approach to precolonial history (Adjaye 1989). After Prempeh returned, he re-introduced the College of physicians (*Nsumanfiesu*), which included Arab scholars (Asante *Nkramofoɔ*), who reintroduced the use and production of Arabic historical sources such as the *Kitabal-Ghanja.* These sources were coloured by the diplomatic and religious interests of the Asante *Nkramofoɔ* as described in section 2.4. The secondary historical sources, such as those of Allman and Parker, also have their limitations. These authors aim to place anthropological studies in historical perspective. Meanwhile, however, they also heavily rely on these sources, and are therefore limited in their capacity to provide an alternative scope.

2.5.3 The postcolonial Asante past

The postcolonial period in Asante history has been reconstructed with the help of primary and secondary oral and written sources as well as participant observations resulting from over a year of fieldwork. The most significant sources for this period are the oral interviews that were conducted in Kumasi and adjacent villages in Ghana, and the participant observation in rituals. One unavoidable aspect of such qualitative research is that the researcher is the conduit for the research, introducing subjective biases. The aim of a qualitative researcher should be to be as 'objective' as possible within the limitations of human capacities. Some researchers, including the author, are of the opinion that one's research is more objective when one is aware of and shares the possible effects of the researcher's 'self' on the collected data.[26] The author will therefore add some

[26] One should be careful, however, that the amount of self reflexivity in the fieldworker's reports is in balance with the descriptions of the indigenous people he or she is researching, avoiding narcissistic narratives that tell more about the researcher than the indigenous people being researched. In other words, one should try to avoid what Margaret Mead called the 'Pompidou effect': showing the outside

self-reflexive comments on her gender, ethnicity, class, age, religion, and personality, thereby using the 'I' form, thereby emphasising the subjectivity of these comments.

I believe that my position as a woman encouraged my respondents to reveal their emotions to me more easily in the course of my research. When I addressed gender issues, female respondents had a tendency to focus on 'female' affairs. For example, I had conversations with the *Asantehemma* of Offinso, Ama Serwah Nyarko, about puberty rituals in Asante and the positive and negative effects of these rituals on girls' wellbeing, a conversation she might not have engaged in with a male interviewer. There were also women who spoke to me about the negative aspects of widowhood rituals, while declaring that they would not have talked about these aspects with male colleagues. When women talk to other women, even though they do not share the same cultural background, there is, I believe, a certain intimacy to the conversation that cannot occur in women's conversations with male researchers.

I believe that my ethnic position as a white European mostly worked to my advantage. A disadvantage of being an outsider is that, unlike an indigenous researcher, one does not speak the language fluently and one is not automatically embedded in local and national social networks that enable one to connect with key figures and relevant respondents (van Binsbergen 2003:125-155). It also means that there are time/space related limitations to the amount of data one can gather in the field, although today's Internet connections make it easier to reconnect to one's interviewees via Skype. However, a great advantage to being an outsider coming from the North Atlantic social realm is that one can share in the privileges and power of that part of the world. If, for instance, I had become ill, I could have had access to a relatively expensive hospital in Ghana, and during my stay I could afford to protect myself with anti-malaria pills that most local researchers cannot afford. My access to the online database of the University of Edinburgh in the field also gave me an advantage in terms of gaining access to local knowledge. In many instances, I prepared my interviews with the help of articles and books in that database, which I could download in handy pdf format on my laptop. This information helped me to get a better understanding of the situation in the field. It also prevented me from re-inventing the wheel by gathering already existing data. Another advantage that I enjoyed as an outsider was that I was very well treated. In Ghana white European or white American foreigners (singl. *oburoni,* pl. *aborofo*) are often treated better than the local population, as a result of both the Asante custom of showing great hospitability towards foreigners as well as the presumed positive effects of adding a white researcher to one's personal network. Ghanaians have a communitarian culture,

---

of a building/narrative to such an extent that the inside is no longer visible. It is for this reason that my reflections are not integrated into the rest of the narrative, but rather set out in this short separate section of the book.

and they believe therefore that if they treat a foreigner well, any other Ghanaian who travels to the North Atlantic part of the world will be treated well in return. Needless to say, many Ghanaians who have lived in Europe or the United States are very disappointed with their reception in that part of the world, and some of them who returned to Ghana asked me why 'Europeans treat Africans like monkeys'. I presume that following these bad experiences in the land of the white men (*aborofo*) Ghanaians will be less generous to white foreigners. My personal experiences were, however, very pleasant, as I received a very warm welcome.

In terms of my class background, I am a member of a somewhat privileged intellectual Dutch family and I carried out this research for the purpose of being rewarded with a doctoral degree in African Studies. During my studies I have experienced financial difficulties and have sometimes lived on the boundaries of exhaustion, juggling with time and various jobs, but still it was a privilege for me as a Dutch woman to be able to obtain a degree from a renowned university in the United Kingdom, and the hardships I put myself into were my own choice. I am thus in all aspects a fortunate woman and in terms of speech, gestures, and outlook I also make that impression – as I was told – on my Ghanaian interviewees. In terms of getting access, I certainly believe that my presentation as a 'privileged well educated white woman' has helped me. I hardly experienced problems in gaining access to the archives or the religious organisations and the Houses of Chiefs (HCs). Helping me to get access were the letters I carried with me from my supervisors, which were locally stamped and confirmed by distinguished university professors in Ghana who were their colleagues. Nevertheless, the reliability of those letters in the eyes of my interviewees also depended on my membership of a certain class of people in the Western world. A negative aspect of my privileged image was no doubt the fact that my most of my respondents (and especially male) believed that I was a very rich lady, despite the fact that I was dressed in clothes that from a Western perspective should tell the contrary. Many men believed that I would not be so mad as to spend a great deal of money to travel all the way to Ghana if there was no great financial reward waiting for me. They therefore presumed that I was making a lot of money gathering data and that I should compensate them as a result. Chiefs especially came to me with exorbitant financial demands; one asked me to pay ten thousand dollars for an exclusive interview, which of course put me off. My image thus came with the price of being treated by some Ghanaians as a walking wallet, whereas in actual fact I did not have much to live on. The inability and/or academic unwillingness to offer huge financial rewards to my respondents might have negatively affected the process of data collection. I believe it gave some of my respondents the feeling that I did not want to give them anything more than the compensation that I offered in order to offset the missed opportunity for work during the time they spent with me. However, I couldn't do otherwise because giving more than a token sum of money in exchange for data is bad academic practise, as it leads to the commodification of knowledge and negatively affects the reliability of the source. In short, my identity came with a certain amount of prestige and power that helped me to gain access but also came with financial expectations that I could not meet for personal and professional reasons. Being a woman in my early thirties produced another negative effect on the data because I had to deal with annoying marriage proposals from male respondents, who believed that as a white woman I must have travelled all the way to Africa because I would like the give birth to a mixed race child. They offered to marry me because they wanted to go to Europe (love never was an aspect of their way of reasoning) and get a European passport, so by offering me a child they hoped I would help them in exchange. My fake wedding ring did not help to change their minds, a situation that sometimes had a negative effect on my mood and may have put some informants off. When it comes to religion, I fall in the category of 'outsider outsiders', because I am neither Ghanaian nor religious. The positive aspect of this personal characteristic is that I have a relatively neutral, unbiased, and value free attitude towards any religion and any religious believer. Most likely, this attitude and my unthreatening personality (in the perception of the Asante and colleagues, family and friends back home) also helped me to easily gain access in the field.

My interview respondents consisted of: (1) the Asante traditional authorities and their subjects, (2) Muslim headmen and their subjects and (3) Christian church leaders and members. In all three categories, I included voices from above and below. I have, in other words, interviewed both the leading representatives of a particular religious or cultural group of people and their members or subjects. This dual perspective is intended to enhance the accuracy and reliability of my research. My interviews were conducted in English, Twi, Arabic, or Hausa. To interview my respondents in the latter three languages, I made use of three translators; two were indigenous Asante Twi speakers and one who was an indigenous Muslim Hausa and Arabic speaker who originally came from Lagos in Nigeria. For the interviews that were conducted in Twi, I was introduced to the respondents in their indigenous language in an attempt to create goodwill. I have learnt Asante Twi and can speak this language at a basic level.[27] The inhabitants of the Kumasi metropolis are not all Twi speaking, but I have concentrated on learning this language because the Akan (in particular the Asante, at 56.9 percent or 665,884 inhabitants) form the majority (77.7 percent or 909,300 inhabitants) of the city's community (Ghana 2002).

Other languages spoken in the Kumasi metropolis include African English (spoken in the villages only at a basic level); Arabic, spoken by most Muslim immigrants in the metropolis; Hausa; Ewe; and many other non-Akan indigenous languages. I made use of a translator, who was a native speaker of Arabic to interview the Muslim imam and headmen. The interview questions

[27] The Twi language consists of three dialects: Asante, Fante, and Akuapem, which are spoken by the corresponding cultural groups of the same names.

were semi-structured, an approach that ensures that the questions are not too fixed, but at the same time do not suffer from a lack of focus. I used themes to organise my questions. In the field and back home, I watched all my video interviews and listened to the tapes, transcribing the interview data myself. This was helpful as it required me to study each interview again and thus offered a firmer grasp on the data. My research had an exploratory character. All my interviews were face-to-face, except for a few in which I corresponded with my interviewees by e-mail. In total, I recorded, conducted, and analysed interviews with fifty-six respondents. This number of respondents limits my ability to perform statistical generalisation and to draw 'hard' statistical conclusions. It is possible however to perform qualitative generalisations, whose 'goal is not to produce a standardised set of results that any other careful researcher in the same situation or studying the same issues would have produced. Rather it is to produce a coherent and illuminating description of and perspective on a situation…' (Schofield 1993:202; van Binsbergen 2003:125-155). I also took to heart the wisdom of qualitative researchers who believe that it is their common task to build a mosaic in which all the pieces together will tell what social reality looks like (Bryman 1988).

I was involved in the following activities as a participant observer: (1) five pouring of libation rituals (two performed by a paramount chief, two performed by an indigenous priest and one during an *adae* performed at *Manhyia* palace, (2) three funeral rituals, one of which was a royal pre-burial ritual that I analysed extensively, (3) a puberty ritual (*bragro*), (4) a court case at Manhyia palace and (5) an Akuapem *Odwira* festival. In chapter V, I focus on the analysis on the Asante chieftaincy pouring of libation ritual and the pre-burial ritual of Nana Saaman Nantwi II, a deceased paramount chief who was the head of the household of the ruling pair Osei Tutu II and Afia Kobi Serwaa Ampem II. I visually recorded both of these rituals and analysed the images. In addition, I interacted intensively with the people involved in these activities. After each event, I transcribed short (semi-structured) conversations and recorded my impressions. I described the events and collected field documents such as brochures (e.g. the *Asanteman Adae Kese brochure*), newspapers (the *GNA*, *The Ghanaian Times*), and monthly magazines (e.g. *Enjoy Accra*). During my stay, the bi-weekly newspaper *Traditional Heritage* was launched, which helped me in finding out what was going on at the royal court in Kumasi.

2.6 Summary

In this chapter, the author explained how the research that resulted in this book was conducted according to the methodologies of historical anthropology as applied in the field of religious studies. She first defined the disciplines of history, anthropology, historical anthropology, and religious studies. She then introduced Berner's model of religious syncretic processes and outlined the way in which she applied these processes to the indigenous religious peacekeeping function of the Asante royal rulers. She next reflected upon the historical and anthropological sources that she used to reconstruct the Asante history of chieftaincy in this book. She outlined the limitations of each of these sources, relying on the wisdom that in a sense all sources are biased, and it is thus necessary for researchers to reveal those biases rather than pretend they can be nullified. In this book, oral traditions are used as both historical and anthropological sources. The author's point of departure is that these sources not only represent the present, but can also be used to enhance understanding of the past.

Chapter III: The indigenous religious mediatory and peacekeeping roles of the Asante traditional authorities in the precolonial period

Wo-to pampin a na wo-a-to kuro. – 'The fence (chief) protects the city from enemies'.

Asante proverb

3.1 Introduction

In this chapter, it is argued that the historical relationship between the indigenous religious mediatory and peacekeeping roles of the Asante traditional authorities in the precolonial period partially account for the persistence of Asante chieftaincy today. To gain understanding of the meaning of 'indigenous religious mediation' the author will study how the Asante state legitimised its position by ritual. Regarding the function of 'indigenous religious peacekeeping', she will study the introduction of Islam and Christianity into Asante society and provide an insight into the religious and social impact that these world religions had on Asante Indigenous Religion (AIR) and its believers. She will also study when and why the Asante traditional rulers incorporated Europeans and Muslims into their diplomatic service in their function as religious peacekeepers.

3.2 The Origin of Asante and the political structure of *Asanteman*

The Asante people have lived in the West African tropical forest as early as 930 ±130 Common Era (Klein 1996:254). They lived in caves and were organised into seven or eight matriclans. In the village *Asantemanso*, in the territorial division of Asumegya, twenty miles south of present-day Kumasi archaeologists have found evidence of house floors, faunal remains slag and pottery that dates back to the tenth century CE (Shinnie and Shinnie 1995:7-8).[28] *Asantemanso* also has a central significance in Asante myths of origin and early oral history to which the founders of Kumasi trace their origin. These Asante myths and oral history mention *Asantemanso*, because of the seven ancestors (five women and two men) that were believed to crawled 'out of a cave in the ground' in that village (McCaskie 1995:43; Shinnie and Shinnie 1995:7-8).

[28] It is necessary to make some reservations regarding this date. The investigation of the village of *Asantemanso* was part of an archaeological research project by Shinnie on the early Akan. The Carbon 14 (C-14 dating) method that was used to find out until what century the ancestors of the Asantes could be traced back. Shinnie presents this method as if it is very precise. J. Shott notices, however, that the method of C-14 has a probabilistic character especially when we are dealing with 'relatively' early history Shott, M. J. 1992. "Radiocarbon Dating as a Probabilistic Technique: the Childers Site and Late Woodland Occupation in the Ohio Valley," *American Antiquity* 57(2): 202-230.

The early Asante were hunters and gatherers, who believed in the power of spirits that were all around them. They believed that the Akan creator God *Onyankopɔng* had inspirited not only the Asante but also the trees, rivers and the animals in their environment. Boundaries between humans and animals were fluid and the belief in transformations from humans to animals was most common. Central to the early AIR was the veneration of serpent ancestral spirits. Early Asante myths note that initially the ancestral serpents lived on the Earth and were put in the Sky in a much later phase (Owusu-Ansah 1991; Brookins 2003). In the fifteenth and sixteenth centuries CE the Asante developed an agricultural society and their economy became part of the global trade in gold and slaves. The trade connections of the rulers of the Asante matriclans with the Islamic Northerners and European Christians on the Gold Coast provided them with a large number of slave labourers that they used to cultivate their farmland and to work in the gold mines. The Islamic Mande-Dyula traders, who the Asante traders encountered, were part of a large trade network that was controlled by so called Dyula (*Juula*) trade families that reached as far as Western Sudan. The Mande-Dyula traders had colonised Begho, an Akan city in today's Brong-Ahafo Region (see 7.5 map 5), which became a trading centre that supplied slaves from North of Kumasi, cloth and brassware to Asante traders in exchange for kola, palm nuts and gold (Wilks 1961). Since at least the fourteenth century, Muslims were fond of kola nuts (*colae semen*) that contains caffeine and functions as a stimulant and surrogate for alcohol, which their religion forbade them to consume (Blumenthal 2000). The gold from the Asante gold mines was brought back to Western Sudan from where it was transported by camels through the Trans-Saharan desert to Portugal and Spain and from there to other European countries where there was a shortage of gold. The gold that the Portuguese bought from the Dyula traders made them curious about the location of the gold mines. Soon after they discovered the gold entrepôts of the Western Sudan – and its trading link with the Asante people – they took the initiative to travel to the Gold Coast themselves. In 1471 the first Portuguese traders arrived at the Gold Coast and in 1482 they built the fort Elmina (Portuguese for 'the mine'). Until the 1650s, the Portuguese maintained a trade relationship with the Asante people and the Mande-Dyula traders: they sold them firearms and slaves obtained from Benin in exchange for gold (Russell-Wood 2009).

Since the fifteenth century the Asante thus traded in gold in exchange for firearms and slaves. The firearms were used for the protection of farmers and in wars with surrounding cultural groups. The slaves or free labourers were used to cultivate their farmland and to work in the gold mines to dig gold. The gold was used to buy more slaves from the Mande-Dyula traders, who collaborated with slave raiders in the non-centralised Northern states (e.g. Sisala and Grunshi) and the Portuguese (Wolf 1982; Kankpeyeng 2009). In 1660, with the help of firearms and of slaves, the Asante had developed a powerful agricultural society that consisted of a number of states or chiefdoms (*berɛmpon-doms*) that were ruled by male and female slaveholders (*omanhene* and *omanhenna*). The rulers of these *berɛmpon-doms* had one cultural enemy that was clearly stronger; the *Dɛnkyirahene* and the *Dɛnkyirahemmma* of the state (*oman*) Dɛnkyira south of Kumasi. To protect themselves against the Dɛnkyira rulers, those of the *berɛmpon-doms* of Mampon, Nsuta, Kokofu, Bekwai, Dwaben, Asumegya and Kwaman founded the Asante Confederacy (*Amantoonum*), a military union of states that initially were autonomous and had the same rights. Each state had its own paramount royal rulers, its own internal politics and celebrated its own religious festivals. In 1701, the states of the *Amantoonum* defeated their most powerful enemy Dɛnkyira capturing Jukwaa; the capital of that state. The so-called 'Battle of Feyiase' changed the political balance in the *Amantoonum* in favour of the *oyoko* clan of the Kwaman chiefdom. The military leaders (*nsafɔhene*) of the Confederacy, chose the successful general Osei Tutu I (1701-1718) as their first king, and Nyaako Kusi Amoa and Nkatia Ntim Abamo were to be the first female Asante rulers. Together with the king's relative and adviser priest (*ɔkɔmfoɔ*) Anokye, these royal rulers laid the foundation of the Asante nation (*Asanteman*) (Boahen 1975:16). The chiefdoms of *Amantoonum* became part of the Asante kingdom. After its foundation, the political structure of the chiefdoms remained the same but the position of the *Asantehene* and the Asante *ahemma* changed. Within the confederacy every Asante subject (*akoa*-male, *afana*-female, pl. *nkoa, nfana*) belonged the *abusua* that was headed by *abusua mpaninfo* (a male and female family head of the matrilineage). Asante subjects were all free Asante, but also enslaved persons of Akan origin. All servile labourers of other categories in the Asante kingdom, including war-captive (*nnomum*) foreigners, enslaved person of northern origins (*ɔdonkɔ*), slaves intended for sacrifice condemned criminals (*akyere*) and person pledged or given as security for the debt of a kin (*awowa*), were, however, not the subjects of the Asante royal rulers. The *abusua mpaninfo* were the first persons, who such categories of people could turn to help. Each Asante, however, also belonged to a small politico-economic unit and a so-called village head (*odikro*). The *odikro* dealt with those problems that could not be solved by the *abusua mpaninfo*. The *odikro* served under the divisional royal rulers (the *ɔhene* and *ɔhemma*), the paramount royal rulers (*omanhene* and *omanhemma*). After the birth of the Asante kingdom the paramount traditional rulers of Kwaman became the Asante king and his female co-ruler and they received a position of *primus-inter-pares* in relation to the *omanhene* and *omanhemma* of all other chiefdoms of the former Asante Confederacy (Platvoet 1979; Konadu 2010). Kumasi became the centre of Kwaman, which became the most significant chiefdom in the Asante kingdom. The city of Kumasi, meaning 'under the Kum' derived its name from the Kum tree of reception (*ogyedua*) that was – it was believed – planted by *ɔkɔmfoɔ* Anokye in 1701 (Ramseyer, Kühne et al. 1875). The 'death' of the *ogyedua* tree that was believed to be connected to the destiny of a nation, would bring misfortune (Platvoet 1985).

The Kumasi division of *Asanteman* was organised into nine (and, by the nineteenth century, ten) administrative-military units that the Asante royal rulers managed in addition to two councils presided over by them (Konadu 2010). The councils functioned as a court of justice and decision-making bodies: the 'Inner Council' or 'Kumasi Council', and the assembly of the Asante nation (*Asantemanhyiamu*). The court that belonged to the Kumasi Council dealt with cases of a civil nature. The *Asantemanhyiamu* dealt with serious offences against traditional rulers and other crimes committed by Asante subjects warranted the death penalty. Executions could only be proposed by the *Asantemanhyiamu* and took place once a year during the celebration of *Odwira*. In terms of decision-making, the Inner Council was a small deliberative body (*agyina*). The mode of decision-making of the *Asantemanhyiamu* was that of 'the great sitting down together' (*asetenakɛ*). In terms of membership, the only woman admitted to both councils was the *Asantehemma*. The 'Inner Council' further consisted of the male *Asante* royal rulers, as an attendant and four *ɔhene* councillors; the *Bantamahene*, the *Asafɔhene*, the *Gyaasewahene* and the *Adumhene*. The *Asantemanhyiamu*'s membership was on a territorial basis. It consisted of the Asante ruling pair again as an attendant, paramount chiefs (*amanhene*), senior Kumasi chiefs (*ahene*) and provincial rulers, such as the sovereign of Dagomba (Wilks 1989 [first published in 1975]:76, 392-416).

The *Asantemanhyiamu* usually gathered only once a year during the *Odwira* festival to discuss state matters. It could also be convened during state emergencies. It remained obligatory for the *amanhene* to gather once a year, but many of its members in fact chose not to exercise their right to attend other than the obligatory annual meeting. The dense forest in which Kumasi was located made it difficult for royal rulers to travel to Kumasi from remote places in the Asante kingdom. The paramount royal rulers of the chiefdoms other than Kwaman thus virtually abrogated responsibility to the members from Kumasi and those few of the *amanhene* who considered national politics to take precedence over their state (*oman*) affairs. In the early nineteenth century, this situation caused the Inner Council to take over more and more tasks of the *Asantemanhyiamu*. In structure the Inner Council of 1820 therefore differed considerably from the one in the eighteenth century. In that century, the Inner Council consisted of four councillors, two spokesmen (*akyeame*) and five other members, the so-called 'educated commoners'. In 1874, when the Inner Council had fully developed into the Council of Kumasi, membership was extended to incorporate members from the military and administrative elites of the capital. In 1888, in normal times, the size of the Council of Kumasi seemed to be fixed at about eighteen, the Asante ruling duo as attendant and some seventeen councillors (excluding the four initial councillors that made up the Inner Council). Besides this, the Council of Kumasi increasingly assumed the functions of central government and as a result became more and more into conflict with the *Asantemanhyiamu*. The conflict of the two councils, *Asantemanhyiamu* and Council of Kumasi, was 'never fully resolved'. However, at the end of the nineteenth century the conflict with respect to the functions of the two mentioned councils became less significant than that of other parties. For instance, some of these parties were in favour of fighting war with the British (the hawks), whereas others preferred to maintain relationships necessary for trade (the dovish) (Wilks 1989 [first published in 1975]:407-413).

The rapid growth of the Asante kingdom after its foundation and the development of its bureaucratic apparatus were unprecedented in the sub-region. The question that has puzzled many historians of West Africa, such as Daaku and Morgan, is how the Asante kingdom rose to such heights and how the Asante succeeded in conquering a territory that in the nineteenth century exceeded the area of present-day Ghana. The fact is that the Asante benefited from the continuation of their trade in gold with the Mande-Dyula middlemen who negotiated with the Muslims of the Asante hinterland, and the Europeans who were situated on the Gold Coast. After the Portuguese had left the Gold Coast in 1650, the Danish, the Dutch and the English developed an interest in the gold trade and also traded in ivory, hides, malaguetta pepper, beeswax and various tropical gums and dyewoods in exchange for firearms and textiles (Morgan 2009). The economic power behind the gold helped the loose Asante chiefdoms to develop them politically and to create the union or *Amantoonum* that was capable of defeating the initially more powerful state of Dɛnkyira. In 1701, directly after the foundation of the Asante kingdom, the Dutch traders of the West Indian Company (WIC) shifted their attention from trade with the rulers of Dɛnkyira to those of the Asante kingdom. They send David van Nyendael, a Dutch mulatto diplomat in the service of the Dutch WIC, on a journey to Kumasi to establish a peaceful trade relationship between the Dutch and the Asante. Nyendael died before he could submit a report on his mission and his report got lost, but he initiated a trading relationship that would last until the Dutch transferred their forts on the Coast to the British in 1872. In the eighteenth century all Europeans on the Gold Coast became more interested in the slave trade and firearms rather than the trade in gold. Since their occupation of several slave forts on the Gold Coast, such as Elmina Castle, in the 1650s, the Dutch only delivered firearms to those peoples with whom they had an established trading relationship: the Asante were most important of these (Konadu 2010). No doubt, the eighteenth century in Asante history was characterised by the increase in the purchase of firearms by the Asante royal rulers from mainly the Dutch in exchange for slaves, many of whom were war-captives (*domum*). The Asante military used the firearms to annex more areas and obtain more war-captives that were sold on as slaves, in exchange for firearms (Daaku 1972:240). For many years, Akan historians debated whether this 'slave-gun circle' was the cause of the remarkable rise of the Asante kingdom in the eighteenth and nineteenth centuries. Currently, there is a consensus among them that guns were indeed used to capture slaves and to perpetuate wars and slave raids, but that in most cases the importation of firearms went hand-in-hand with the militarisation of the Asante kingdom (Morgan 2009: 223-248). The question that remains to be answered is what attributes that were specific to Asante society that made this society flourish, while surrounding Akan and other cultural groups remained less developed in terms of politico-economic and military organisation.

The author will attempt to formulate an answer to this question by examining two indigenous religious functions of Asante royal rulers: those of mediators between their subjects and the spiritual beings and as peacekeepers between Asante believers, Christians and Muslims, in the social world.

To account for the process of state formation in the Asante history one should, however, not only focus on the Asante foreign affairs, but also on the internal policies of the Asante royal rulers in their relation to AIR. The Asante royal rulers believed that the spiritual forces were more powerful than those of human beings and that the demands of the spirits should be taken into account to prevent misfortune. The Asante believed that the ancestors were serpent spirits on Earth who would protect them and care for them as long as they venerated them by praying for them, by pouring libation with palm wine, by cooling down the spirits with animal or human blood.[29] They believed that the body (*honam*) was mortal, and a slave to destiny that was largely determined by the celestial bodies. The individual birth chart of a person was believed to be unchangeable, but the movements of the star could influence the direction of one's bodily destiny in the social world. The Asante believed that life-force soul (*ɔkra*), however, was eternal and would eventually join the spirit of the ancestors of one's *abusua*. The body determined the sex of a person, but never the soul, which was thought to be sexless. After one's death, the soul was thought to return to the sun god or the male principle and first male ancestral spirit (*Nyame*) or to the female principle or first female ancestral spirit (*Ngame*). These spirits were believed to be located in the world of the ancestors (*asamando*). It was believed that in the *asamando* none of the ancestral spirits had a body. The Asante therefore referred to the successors of *Nyame* and *Ngame* as ancestors without a sex differentiation. Sex differences were only added to a person after the bodily imprisonment of the internal *ɔkra* inside him or her, where it would remain until the departure of the *ɔkra* back to the Sun after one's death. The bodily life of a person was believed to be temporal and birth and death were just the beginning and ending of an awareness of the *ɔkra* that accompanied the quasi-material *sunsum* in the social world. Not surprisingly, these aspects of AIR meant that one's bodily appearance was not perceived as most significant. The Asante were aware of the temporality of all physical life and did not heavily fear nor ignore death. Servants and wives or husbands and the 'symbolic wives' (*akyeame*) or husbands of the

[29] A characteristic of blood is that it cools down quickly, which is why the Asante used blood to cool down the spirits and create and maintain a harmonious relationship with the spiritual beings (interview with Nana Ama Serwah Nyarko, 29).

Asante royal rulers accompanied them to their graves; slaves were sacrificed (*akyere*) repetitively to satisfy the ancestral spirits on sacred calendar days (*adae*). Clearly, the souls were more significant than the body and were believed to be separate entities that could live outside their bodily human host. The *sunsum* inspirited human beings during dreams, which gave the dreamer temporarily excess to a spiritual elsewhere that could enhance his or her insight in his past or help to predict the future. The *kra* connected a person to his ancestors, whose customs and wisdoms they inherited that they had gathered in past lives. The Asante built a society that put faith in the wisdom of the spiritual beings, who would inspirit them and advise them when and how to act. In war times, the Asante relied on the advices of these spirits and the belief in higher forces from outside transformed the Asante warriors in brave and proud soldiers, who could rapidly organise themselves in an *ad hoc* army to fight against their enemies. An Asante proverb goes 'Asante kotoko – if you kill a thousand, a thousand more will come', which referred to the remarkable trust of the Asante soldiers in their superiority in power and invincibility in the battlefield. Section 3.4 will look at the Asante and their relationship with the spirits with a specific focus on the servants of the Asante royal rulers in their mediatory roles (the *akyeame* and the Asante *Nkramofoɔ*) with their subject (*nkoa*) and their spiritual preparations on and during wars. Let us first examine the on the indigenous religious peacekeeping function of the Asante royal rulers.

Indigenous religious peacekeeping, which is one of the two main religious functions of the Asante royal rulers, developed in the second half of the eighteenth century. *Asantehene* Opoku Ware I (1720-1750) and his mother and female co-ruler Nyarko Kusi Amoa (1700-1750) annexed and incorporated twenty surrounding kingdoms and are still remembered as the great kingdom builders of the Asante (Tordoff 1962:401) (see 7.5 map 4).[30] An example of an Islamic kingdom that was annexed and incorporated in this period is Dagomba. A treaty with this kingdom compelled the *Dagombahene* Ya Na to take Islamic captives. He was to send two thousand prisoners to Kumasi each year. In 1772, Ya Na was captured in an Asante military campaign and ransomed for one thousand slaves (Konadu 2010). The Asante annexations thus increased the number of prisoners and slaves in their society that were used to cultivate the farmland, which resulted in a growth of the Asante population. Additionally, the annexed vassal states contributed substantially to the treasury of the Asante royal rulers, because of the high tributes they were obliged to pay to these rulers e.g. for the maintenance of the trade routes. Asante royal rulers served as leaders of the war captains and the tribute-collection service, though after the incorporation of

[30] Nana Nyarko, who was the first *Asantehemma*, was a full member and co-President of the governing body and took part in all important decisions. Nyaako was the mother of *Asantehene* Opoku Ware I and the fourth *Asantehemma* Konadu Yaadom I (1778-1809). The male rulers and female co-rulers were not appointed in the same year, because the first *Asantehemma* was appointed before the first *Asantehene* and was senior to him.

these neighbouring kingdoms as semi-autonomous vassal states these royal rulers were involved in the development of an *ad hoc* diplomatic service that was necessary to deal with the rulers of these vassal kingdoms and to regulate the Islamic Northerners of the Asante hinterland. Under *Asantehene* Kusi Oboadum (1750-1764) diplomatic negotiations with Muslims in and outside the Asante kingdom, were oral, and in the hands of those of the twelve spokesmen (*akyeame*) of the Asante royal rulers who dealt with the Northern districts. From *Asantehene* Osei Kwadwo (1764-1777) onwards, however, the Asante royal rulers invited literate Muslim scholars from Timbuktu (the so-called Asante *Nkramofoɔ*) to work at the royal court (*ahenfo*), and to support the *akyeame* in their diplomatic services. Since the 1840s, the Asante diplomatic service lost its *ad hoc* status and developed into four chanceries that were permanently involved in producing written documents whose content was orally transmitted by the *akyeame*, who were trained in the eloquence of speaking. On behalf of the royal rulers, the *akyeame* negotiated with the Muslims of the Asante hinterland, with the Danish, the Dutch and especially the British for commercial purposes and the prevention of wars. Under the reigns of the Asante royal rulers Kwaku Dua I (1834-1867) and Yaa Dufie (1824/33-1835), who was succeeded by Afia Kobi Serwaa Ampem I (1859-1884) and the ruling duo Kofi Kakari (1867-1874) and Afia Kobi Serwaa Ampem I members of the European Christian missions, such as the Methodist Minister Freeman and later the Basel missionaries Ramseyer and Kühne and were appointed as *ad hoc* diplomats to support the Asante chanceries (Adjaye 1985).

Asante diplomacy is important for the understanding of the peacekeeping function of the Asante royal rulers, because it was at the basis of the relationship of the Asante with Islamic and Christian foreigners, who in the preceding centuries became more and more part of their society. Most significantly, the Asante royal rulers primarily aimed to maintain a peaceful relationship with these foreigners. They were most interested in trade, and without peace the trade relationships were threatened. The peaceful mindedness of the Asante becomes, for instance, clear from the fact that they had no standing army, and only went to war after diplomatic negotiations had failed (Konadu 2010). Another piece of evidence is that various Asante royal rulers remarked that they did not intend to go to war, but now that they were in it, they had to turn the enemy into Asante prisoners-of-war (Owusu-Ansah 1991). The Asante councils consisted of various parties, and there were clear ideological differences between them. The Hawks believed it was easier to fight wars and increase the number of slaves, whereas the Dovish were more eager to maintain peaceful relationships to continue the trade in e.g. textiles and gold (Wilks 1989 [first published in 1975]). The purpose of most of the wars waged by the Asante was to guarantee the maintenance of open trade roads.

In the eighteenth century, *Asantehene* Opoku Ware I, for instance, fought a number of wars with the coastal states because the accessibility of the roads from Kumasi to Cape Coast were being threatened by these coastal states. In 1807, the Asante conflict with these states also led to conflict with the British, because of the involvement of the latter in trade with the coastal Fante people. Between 1811 and 1826, Fante revolts against their Asante overlords precipitated three separate military engagements between Asante forces and British troops. The Anglo-Asante relationships remained tense until in 1831 both parties signed a 'Treaty of Peace'. Among other issues, the treaty stipulated that the Asante government abrogated administrative responsibility over its former southern provinces: Accra, Adangme, Ahanta, Akuapem, Akwamu, Akyem, Aowin, Dɛnkyira, Fante, Sehwi, Twifo and Wassa. The British in turn, guaranteed Asante direct and unrestricted commercial access to the Gold Coast coastal ports. From a British point of view, the former southern provinces fell under British protection and became known as the British Protected Territory. However, from an Asante point of view, they had not relinquished their sovereignty over these areas as per the treaty, but only agreed to stop collecting tribute from the rulers of these states. The content of the peace treaty was not well defined, and the tensions between the British and the Asante were not really resolved by signing the treaty. Another problem was that some southern states (Akuapem, Akyem and Assin) had 'pro-Asante' interests, which also made it difficult for the British to exercise control over these states. Maclean was the architect of the 1831 treaty. After his retirement in 1843, the relationship between the Asante and the English deteriorated. In the 1850s, Maclean's successor Winniet took a harsh view of the Asante customs and emphasised the cruelty of their custom of ritually killing human beings. The British and the Asante soon began competing for influence over the coastal states. The points of conflicts involved were (a) the closure and maintenance of the southern trade routes, (b) the extradition of Asante citizens from British administrative territory (c) the restitution of fugitives and criminals (*akyere*) and (d) Asante government policy of maintaining political influence over its southern domains. An example of a conflict that involved point (a) and (c) between *Asantehene* Kwaku Dua Panin (1834-1867), and the *Asante ahemma* Nana Yaa Dufie (1833-1835) and Afia Sarpong (1835-1859) and Governor Winniet occurred after an Asante fugitive ran away to the British Protected Territory (Lewin 1978:41-53).[31] According to the Peace Treaty of 1831, the British were obliged to send back any Asante subject who looked for shelter in their Territory, to allow them to be convicted according to Asante law. Governor Winniet however, refused to give up any fugitive Asante. He used the argument that back in Asante territory a fugitive would become the victim of the ritual killing of human beings; a custom which was not in line with his or her Christian faith (Wilks 1989 [first published in 1975]:219). Most likely though, it also

[31] *Asantehemma* Afia Sapong was the daughter of *Asantehene* Osei Kwame. She was the second queen mother during the reign of *Asantehene* Kwaku Dua I and was succeeded by her only child *Asantehemma* Afua Kobi Serwaa Ampem I.

suited Winniet to depict the Asante royal rulers as ritual killers, as spreading a negative image of the Asante and not following their wishes made it easier for him to keep control over the southern states. In 1863, however, the Asante grew increasingly resentful of Winniet's behaviour. They invaded the British Protected Territory and recaptured the Asante fugitives. Anglo-Asante relationships remained tense and the Asante political councils were in conflict over how to manage the situation. *Asantehene* Kofi Kakari was initially hesitant to start a war, because as a member of the council that advocated peace, he believed that the state was essentially organised for the promotion of trade, which cannot be realised without peace. The council that advocated war, however, was in the majority, and consequently in late 1873 the Asante invaded the British Protected Territory once again. A bad omen concerning this invasion was that the famous general Asamoa Nkwanta had lost his war charm, that made him invincible, in the river Pra (McCaskie 1986b). The costs of the war, in terms of human casualties and materials, were so high that the members of the *Asantemanhyiamu* decided to withdraw from the coast. Subsequently, King Kakari and Afia Kobi Serwaa Ampem I hoped to enter into another peace treaty with the British when another bad omen crossed their path. On the 6th of January 1874, the ancient Kum tree in Kumasi's Great Market had been uprooted, which made the Asante royal rulers fear the worst for the destiny of their town (Ramseyer, Kühne et al. 1875; Platvoet 1985). The British, who were by now in competition with the French to increase their influence in West Africa, decided to invade Kumasi and to burn the city: this would alter the balance of power in their favour, and diminish the power of the Asante over the southern states (Lewin 1978:41-53; Wilks 1989 [first published in 1975]:492-509). On the 13th of February 1874, the Asante and the British signed the Treaty of Fomena and soon after, the Asante government agreed to pay a war indemnity and relinquished all political claims to the southern provinces, of which most became incorporated in the newly created Gold Coast Colony.

Between 1874 and 1881, the Asante royal rulers were occupied with rebuilding their nation after the devastating war of 1874, by implementing government reforms and strengthening government control over the remaining provinces and tributaries. Consequently, the seventy-five year old political debate in the Asante councils between whether to pursue peace or war lapsed temporarily. From 1881 onwards, however, the tensions between the two parties increased again in their decisions on how to deal with the British, and the war council made plans for another Anglo-Asante War. However, British intervention in Asante affairs increased, and in the mid-1880s, the British supported king Prempeh's movement to restore the monarchy. This way, the *Asantehene*'s movement hoped to improve their connection with the peace party and to curb the battle plans of the war party, thereby safeguarding the Anglo-Asante trade relationship (Lewin 1978:51-52). From 1874 onwards the British policy was focussed on weakening the Asante state in order to be able to colonise the Asante territory.

Then in 1891, the British official H.M. Hull invited *Asantehene* Edward Agyeman Prempeh I to place his kingdom under British protection. King Prempeh I, though, declined the offer, and attempted to resurrect the Asante nation (*Asantemanhyiamu*) to full power. He tried to dismiss the British consul office, who was placed in Asante by the British after the sack of Kumasi to restrict the power of the *Asantehene*. However, King Prempeh I made clear that he only appreciated maintaining a cordial trade relationship with the British. Nevertheless in 1896, the British government in London made the decision that an independent Asante was not in line with the concept of the British Empire. As a result, informally, the Asante kingdom ceased to exist: in January 1897, the British deported *Asantehene* Edward Agyeman Prempeh I to Sierra Leone. On the 28th March 1900 Governor St Frederick Mitchell Hodgson gathered all the chiefs and inhabitants of Kumasi to tell them that their king would not return and that the greatest power in Asante was the Queen of England (Wilks 1989 [first published in 1975]:660-661).

Then Hodgson made a great mistake, firstly by demanding that Kumasi officials surrender the Golden Stool (*Sika Dwa Kofi*), which was not only the symbol of Asante political sovereignty but also an object infused with religious power. Secondly by sitting on this royal sacred seat, he severely insulted the Asante: for not even their own rulers would ever sit on their kingdom's holiest religious object that symbolised their political and spiritual power. After the deportation of *Asantehene* Edward Agyeman Prempeh I, the colonial committee had appointed three experienced Asante to form the Native Committee of Administration (NCA).[32] 'In theory the jurisdiction of this triumvirate was confined to the capital and its villages, but in practice it maintained some of the attributes of a central government' (Wilks 1989 [first published in 1975]:659). Opoku Mensa, one of the three members of the triumvirate refused to reveal the location of the *Sika Dwa Kofi* to Hodgson, who then ordered his military attaché Captain C.H. Armitage to force the Asante to tell him were the Golden Stool was hidden. Many Asante knew that since Prempeh I's exile to the Seychelles Island, the Stool was hidden in the town of Bare to the North of Kumasi: but, because of their belief in the power of the Stool and their wish to remain an independent nation, nobody gave away its hiding place (Lewin 1978:219-220).

The incident surrounding the whereabouts of the Stool led to the outburst of the last Anglo-Asante uprising that was fought under the leadership of Yaa Asantewaa, the *omanhemma* of Ejisu. Yaa Asantewaa strove to ensure the safety of the *Sika Dwa Kofi* among the Asante, and for the kingdoms' independence. In 1900, however, as one of the descendants of Nana Yaa Asantewaa revealed, the Asante were betrayed by one of their own people, who revealed an important

[32] The names of these experienced men are Opoku Mensa, the *Gyasehene* from 1884 (the Gyase stool was created by *Asantehene* Opoku Ware I and its occupant is responsible for the *Asantehene*'s *nhenkwaa*, Kwaku Nantwi Kaakyera, who signed the Treaty of Fomena and Akapkade, who from 1877 sat in the council of elders.

Asante war strategy to the British, in exchange for a royal seat offered to him after the war (interview with Afua Tweneboa Kodua, 21). It was because of this betrayal along with the fact that the British were better armed than the Asante, which the Anglo-Asante War was won by the British.

By the 'Ashanti Administration Ordinance' of the 1st of January 1902, the Asante kingdom became known as the Crown Colony of Asante. The Metropolitan Region was divided mainly between the newly created central and southern provinces and the remaining territories of the former Asante kingdom, were assigned to the Western and Northern provinces. The new provinces were purely administrative units that were directly responsible to a Provincial Commissioner, and through him to the Chief Commissioner and the Governor of the Gold Coast in Accra. By mid-1905, the *Asantemanhyiamu* had disappeared and the Chief Commissioner of Asante, F.C. Fuller, decided that a resurrected Council of Kumasi should rule the Crown Colony of Asante. The members of this body were, for the majority, Dovish or adherents of a mercantilistic foreign policy, and they voted for peace for the purpose of trade and open roads. The Dovish voted for a break-up of the *Asantemanhyiamu*, of whom the majority of the adherents were Hawkish and an imperialistic foreign policy.

The new Council of Kumasi, which consisted of eighteenth members, equal to the extended Council of Kumasi of 1888, was structurally a continuation of the Kumasi Council in the preceding century. By the end of the nineteenth century, the members of the Council of Kumasi had taken over more and more functions of the *Asantemanhyiamu* and in practice ruled over the Asante kingdom. The members of the new Kumasi Council, on the contrary, were restricted by Fuller to deal with Greater Kumasi matters only. To prevent this new Kumasi Council from gaining back the full size of responsibilities of the initial *Asantemanhyiamu* and the late nineteenth century Kumasi Council, their task was limited to advising the CC on issues relating to Kumasi and its adjacent villages (Wilks 1989 [first published in 1975]:123, 403-407).

By the beginning of the twentieth century, the Asante kingdom had ceased to exist. It was under British direct rule, and the power of the Kumasi Council had been greatly diminished. The British, however, remained fearful towards the Asante; their supposedly cruel religious practices, such as the ritual killing of human beings, and their steadfast loyalty to the Asante king was particularly troubling. In order to diminish the political influence of the king on the Asante people, he was deported from Sierra Leone even further away to the Seychelles Islands. With the fall of the Asante kingdom, Asante chieftaincy, however, did not cease to exist, and the resurrection first of the *Asantemanhyiamu* and then of the Council of Kumasi indicates some of the resilience of this institution. The remaining sections in this chapter aim to make the link between the persistence of Asante chieftaincy and the indigenous religious functions of Asante royal rulers, in particular those of mediation and peacekeeping. These functions, however, cannot be fully understood without an explanation of the most significant indigenous religious symbols and customs that the Asante royal rulers used to legitimise their religious and their political power in the face of the introduction of non-Asante faiths, such as Islam and Christianity (see section 3.3 and 3.4).

3.3 The legitimation of *Asanteman*: the Golden Stool, the swearing of oaths and the *Odwira* festival

The Asante nation was founded in 1701, although its myth of origin is more recent. In the late eighteenth century, the increasing size of the Asante kingdom caused the Asante rulers to contemplate ways in which they could legitimatise the unity of the state. Since *Asantehene* Osei Kwadwo (1764-1777), Asante royal rulers invited Muslims (Asante *Nkramofoɔ*) to come to Kumasi, who were praised for their reading and writing skills and their superior knowledge of astronomy and of divination (Schildkrout 1970; Saad 1983). In the eighteenth century, the Asante *Nkramofoɔ* created the myth of *Nyame* as a monotheistic Islamic God with abstract attributes such as being omnipotent and omniscient. Additionally, Asante believers continued to venerate the ancestral spirits, who became nameless after this period. In the nineteenth century, the European Christian missionaries used *Nyame* to Christianise Asante Indigenous Religion, and since then, indigenous believers, Christians and Muslims venerated *Nyame*. The Islamisation brought an end to the veneration of the female principle *Ngame* who was turned into a nameless ancestress. This process had implications for the gender relations in Asante; it undermined the positions of the female Asante rulers.

In collaboration with the *nsumankwahene*, the Muslims also created the myth of the *Sika Dwa Kofi*, which they presented as a shrine for the *Asantehene* that was placed in the middle of the market space. The *Sika Dwa Kofi* is symbolic of creeping Islamisation of Asante society: it stood for the introduction of a male-dominated social order, and the curtailment of the freedom of women, who formerly owned market places. Not coincidentally, the *Sika Dwa Kofi* was born on a Friday, which is the birthday of the Prophet Mohammed. The Muslims initially propagated that it was *suman* that dwelled inside the Golden Stool. Later on, the Asante incorporated this Islamic tradition into AIR and did not refer to *suman,* but to the communal *sunsum* inside the *Sika Dwa Kofi*. Besides, they added a Silver Stool for the *Asantehemma*, which is known as the *ɔhemma Adwa* or *Dwete* Stool.[33] The Muslims not only used the myth of the Asante royal

[33] The presented history of the myth of the Golden Stool is based on the insight that *Nyame* was an Islamic word, that the Asante royal stools were first believed to contain *suman* rather than *sunsum*. Kirby, J. P. 1986. *God, Shrines, and Problem-Solving Among the Anufo of Northern Ghana*. Berlin: Dietrich Reimer Verlag., Owusu-Ansah, D. 1987. "Power and Prestige? Muslims in Nineteenth Century Kumasi," in E. Schildkrout. *The Golden Stool: Studies of the Asante Center and Periphery*. New York: Anthropological Papers of the American Museum of Natural History. 65: 80-92.

stools, the *Sika Dwa Kofi* and the *ɔhemma Adwa* to introduce *Nyame,* but also used these two as symbols of unity between the two rival houses from which the rulers (Osei Tutu I and Opoku Ware I) of the *oyoko* clan descended, who were one another's rivals (Wilks 1989 [first published in 1975]). Under the influence of Islam, the Asante elite ruled over their subjects by institutionalising myths within the community, and by fostering beliefs among their subjects in the legitimacy of their authority. The Asante elite was, although in a privileged position, part and parcel of these collective processes in the creation of legitimising myths. The establishment of power was achieved in a subtle and 'concealed' form. The messages of the elite were, so to say, 'hidden' in the rituals that were performed by their spokesmen (*akyeame*) on their behalf. Catharine Bell formulates it as follows:

> The strategies of ritualisation are particularly rooted in the body, specifically, the interaction of the social body within a symbolically constituted spatial and temporal environment. Essential to ritualisation is the circular production of a ritualised body that in turn produces ritualised practices. Ritualisation is embedded within the dynamics of the body defined within a symbolically structured environment. An important corollary to this is the fact that ritualisation is a particular 'mute' form of activity. It is designed to do what it does without bringing what it is doing across the threshold of discourse or systematic thinking (Bell 1992:93).

Rituals are a form of communication beyond the grasp of ordinary consciousness and articulation. The Asante royal rulers communicated the messages of the ancestral spirits to their spokesmen (*akyeame*), while being in an alternate stage of consciousness and their *akyeame* communicated them to their subjects in the form of proverbs and myths. The use of indirect communication was the Asante elite's way of preserving their 'sacredness' and of showing their respect for the ancestral spirits.

The myth of the *Sika Dwa Kofi* and the *ɔhemma Adwa* were meant to explain why the Asante royal rulers had sacred powers and therefore had a divine right to rule. According to the myth, the authority of the first *Asantehene*, Osei Tutu I, came from heaven in the form of a Golden Stool, which was a symbol of political authority, as it represented the soul of the *Asantefoɔ*. A famous priest called Anokye is said to have assisted Osei Tutu I spiritually in the destruction of the powerful state Dɛnkyira. Before, but especially after the victory over the Dɛnkyira royal rulers, an alliance of states was formed, amongst other things, by destroying all earlier regalia, such as the existing stools of the *ɔhene* who ruled over their own states, and by replacing them with the Golden Stool and the Silver Stool. Priest Anokye is said also to have helped *Asantehene* Osei Tutu to conquer Dɛnkyira by magic, and to have brought down from heaven the Golden Stool (McCaskie 1986b:318). The myth of the Golden Stool explains why Asante subjects should rely on the Asante royal rulers, who were the first settlers, as their sovereigns. The Asante subjects perceived their royal rulers as their supreme moral judge. The royal rulers were regarded as having inherited supernatural powers from their ancestors and were viewed as the 'owners' of the individual characters (*sunsum*) of their subjects that come together in the collective *sunsum* or power inside the Golden Stool.

The second symbol that Asante traditional authorities used to legitimatise their power was the swearing of an oath. The 'oath' was a sign of the relationship between the living and the dead. Every royal had to swear an oath before he could be enstooled. As part of his rite of passage of enstoolment, a prospective chief or his female co-ruler had to come to Kumasi to swear that they would give military help to the *Asantehene* when he needed it or would help the *Asantehemma* in providing support for the warriors. The religious meaning of the oath was that when its taker – the chief or his female co-ruler – would turn himself or herself against their paramount rulers, the *abosom* would kill them, *Sɛ woyɛ me dɔm da a, abosom nku wo* (Busia 1954:154; Rattray 1956 (first published in1929):103-104). Breaking the oath was both an offence against the spirits, and an open act of political rebellion and defiance. At first, the punishment that was exercised by the executioner of the Asante king for this type of open rebellion was death; later, in some cases, it was modified by permitting the offender 'to buy his head' and pay a penalty. Oaths apparently had the power to both protect and to kill. An Asante practice was to swear oaths during disputes. In the event that someone swore an oath and was lying, something similar would befall that person. The Great Oath of Asante was instituted by *Asantehene* Opoku Ware, the nephew of king Osei Tutu I, as a national pledge of allegiance, 'not only to assure the Asante that *Asantehene* Osei Tutu's spirit continued to guide the nation, but also to reunite and rekindle their fighting spirit and to achieve the purposes for which the Asante Union had been called into being' (Priestly and Wilks 1960:90-92; Fynn 1971:60).

Thirdly, since 1717, the Kumasi ruling elite made their sacredness visual by performing religious ceremonies such as the yearly *Odwira* festival.[34] The ancestors were venerated every twenty-one days by pouring libations of schnapps and the sacrificing of sheep, chickens or goats to cool down the spirits with their blood.[35] The merchant Thomas Bowdich observed the ritual killing of human beings for the veneration of the ancestral spirits and wrote:

> About a hundred persons, mostly culprits reserved are generally sacrificed, in different quarters of the town, at this custom. Several slaves were also sacrificed at Bantama (Bowdich 1819:279).

The whole Asante ritual calendar (*adaduanan*) started in between August and October and took forty-two days by which a year, comprising of 378 days, was

[34] *Dwira* means 'to cleanse'.

[35] There were two *adae* in every *adaduanan* cycle: (a) *awukudae* (the 'small' or Wednesday *adae*) which took place on day fifteen, also termed *kurudapaawukuo*; and (b) *akwasidae* (the 'big' or Sunday *adae*) which took place on day thirty three, also named *kurukwasie*.

divided into nine units of forty-two days.[36] The *adaduanan* consisted of four bad days (*da bone*) of which two were the *adae* (the great *adae* and the little *adae*). The *Odwira* festival was the ninth unit that marked the end of the year and the beginning of the new harvest.[37] Like the other *adae* it was an occasion to commemorate the death of all Asante royal rulers, to perform their mortuary rituals and to link the Asante royal rulers to the ancestral spirits (Gilbert 1994:103-104). The festival of *Odwira* had at least four functions. (1) It was held to celebrate the change from a primarily hunting and gathering community to one of agriculturalists, as well as an occasion to celebrate and later to remember the establishment of *Kwamen*; the first Asante village that later became known as Kumasi (Kwamena-Poh 1973:131). (2) It was an occasion to celebrate the New Year according to the Akan ritual calendar (*adaduanan*). During *Odwira*, the Asante cleaned their surroundings and quenched all fires to kindle new ones. (3) It was a time to recover relationships and to remember the deceased of the past year.

The festival symbolised the homecoming of the ancestors (*nsamanfoɔ*) who received mashed yam (*etɔ*). It honoured the first Asante hunters, who cleared the forest to cultivate the farmland. (4) It was also an occasion to thank the living for their contributions to *Asanteman* in the past year and for the renewal of the allegiance of the subjects, the royal household and the traditional authorities subordinate to the Asante royal state rulers.

At the beginning of the *Odwira* festival, the subjects of the Asante royal rulers symbolically threw away the yam of the past year and ate the yam of the new harvest but not before the Asante ruling duo had eaten first (Bowdich 1819; Gilbert 1994:108). The washing ritual and the distribution of new yam symbolised the rebirth of the Asante royal rulers by the renewed allegiance of their subjects. The *Odwira* festival was thus also meant to legitimatise *Asanteman* and to re-establish the power of the Asante royal rulers. During his mission to Kumasi in the period between the 1st of January 1838 and 1856, the Wesleyan missionary Freeman summarised the political significance of the *Odwira* festival as follows:

> It is a kind of annual parliament wherein, towards the latter end of the festival, all matters of political and judicial administration are discussed by the *Asantehene* and chiefs and their female co-rulers in Council, and where the latter answer all questions relating to their respective provinces, and are subjected to the consequences of appeals, form their local Judicial Courts, to the Supreme Court of the king in Council (Freeman 1886:8, quoted in Wilks 1989:389).

A recurring element in all Asante rites was the visit of the Asante royal rulers to the stool room, in which the stools of the former Asante royal rulers were placed.

---

[36] The forty-two (named) day cycle of the ritual Asante calendar combined the *nanson* cycle (six days in a week, originating from the Guan) with the *nawotwe* cycle (seven days in a week) (six times seven making forty-two). In the oral tradition the *adaduanan* was known as 'forty days' Bartle, P. F. W. 1978. "Forty Days: The Akan Calendar," *Africa: Journal of the International African Institute* 48(1): 80-84.

[37] *Odwira* means 'to purify', or 'to cleanse'.

It was believed that the spirit of the departed royal rulers resided in the stools that they had occupied during their lives as rulers.[38] In 1819 Bowdich observed the following stool room rite (*sokan hyire*):

> About twenty sheep are dipped, one sheep and one goat only are sacrificed at the time, to be killed in the palace in the afternoon, that their blood may be poured on the stools and doorposts (Bowdich 1819:280).

The stool room of Bantama, in which the blackened stools (*akonnwa tuntum*) of the deceased royal rulers were placed, served as the resting place of the Asante royal rulers, both male and female. The purpose of the rite of purification of the royal stools, the *Sika Dwa Kofi* and the *Dwete Stool*, during *Odwira* was to tell the Asante subjects that their kingdom would persist as long as these Asante rulers would continue to perform the stool rituals and would keep safe the stools. Human beings were ritually killed to remember the foundation of the Asante kingdom and the moment that the Asante royal rulers came to power. The ritual killing of human beings is a form of sacrifice that cannot be undone and therefore marks a clear beginning (Lambek 2007). In the morning of the 5th of February 1871, the Basel missionaries Ramseyer and Kühne made the following observations:

> The most dreadful of the Ashantee festivals, Bantama, or 'death wake', now approached. The king went early in the morning of February the fifth to Bantama, where the remains of his deceased predecessors were preserved in a long building, approached by a gallery, and partitioned into small cells, the entrances of which were hung with silken curtains. In these apartments reposed the skeletons of the kings, fastened together with gold wire, and placed in richly ornamented coffins, each being surrounded by what had given him most pleasure during his life. On this occasion every skeleton was placed on a chair in his cell to receive the royal visitor; who, on entering, offered it food; after which a band played the favourite melodies of the departed. The poor victim selected a sacrifice, with a knife thrust through his cheeks, was then dragged forward and slain, the king washing the skeleton with his blood. Thus was each cell visited in turn, sacrifice after sacrifice being offered, till evening closed ere the dreadful round was completed (Ramseyer, Kühne et al. 1875:117).

The fact that the indigenous religious rituals of the killing of human beings took place in 1871 is remarkable, because with the Anglo-Asante peace Treaty of 1844 these killings were officially abolished. In 1876, after debate in the Council of Kumasi and the central government (*Asantemanhyiamu*) the decision was taken – under pressure of the British – to cease carrying out mass executions on public occasions (Wilks 1989 [first published in 1975]). Nevertheless, the ritual killing of humans went on and became a resilient Asante ritual that was highly

---

[38] Royal paramount chiefs and sub-chiefs had their own stool rooms and their stools were also blackened after their death as a sign of honour. The stools of non-royals who became chiefs, however, were usually not blackened because they were not believed to play a role in ancestral veneration and ancestors were believed not to listen to them. Perbi, A. 1991. "Mobility in Pre-colonial Asante from a Historical Perspective," *Research Review* 7(1 and 2): 72-86.

feared by Asante subjects and European Christian missionaries, like Ramseyer and Kühne. In 1881, for instance, the then ruling *Asantehemma* had sacrificed a large number of girls and women to serve her sister, Yaw Affileh, in the ancestral world, who was also buried at Bantama (Ellis 1893:371).

Thus the myth of the *Asantehene*'s *Sika Dwa Kofi* and the *Asantehemma*'s *Dwete* Stool, the swearing of an oath and the *Odwira* festival legitimised the Asante state (*Asanteman*). Furthermore, the Asante royal rulers ruled by coercion and in subtle ways, by the procedure of the royals' elections and their indirect ritualised communication, gained consent of the population for the use of coercive force (McCaskie 1995). The Asante subjects were very afraid of the ritual killing practices of their royal rulers, but most victims of such killings were either war captives or slaves (*ɔdonkɔ*) raided at the Northern Asante hinterland (Cruickshank 1966 [1853]:242-246).

The concern of the Asante royal rulers with the legitimation of their authority and power was a matter of domestic politics. The persistence of their position as royal rulers was, however, not only dependent on the loyalty of their subjects but also on their relationship with the religious 'Other' in and outside the Asante kingdom. The next section analyses the foreign policy of the Asante royal rulers and their diplomatic negotiations with Muslims and Christians, whose religion formed a potential threat to the persistence of the Asante state.

3.4 The introduction of Islam and European Missionary Christianity in the Asante kingdom

This section is about the introduction of African Islam and European Missionary Christianity into the Asante kingdom. The focus is on the Kumasi area in the precolonial period in the Asante history. Islam was introduced into Kumasi in two different forms: (a) A moderate form of Islam known as 'the Suwarian tradition' that consisted of followers of Al-Hajj Salim Suwari, a learned cleric from the core Mali area who lived around 1500. Suwari had created a form of Islam that gave guidance to Muslims among 'pagans' (such as the Asante) who, because of their positions as guests in generally non-Muslim areas, could not afford to attempt to convert their hosts into Muslims (Robinson 2004:56) (b) An orthodox Islam in the tradition of Uthman dan Fodio that consisted of followers of this eighteenth century Hausa Muslim from Gobir, who in 1804 started an orthodox Muslim reform movement whose main goal was to reinvent the *Dar-al-Islam*. (Robinson 2004:139-152). Uthman dan Fodio is also known as the founder of the Sokoto Caliphate in northern Nigeria.

The Suwarian tradition was introduced in Kumasi in two strands. In the fifteenth century traders brought this religion to Kumasi, while in the nineteenth century, the educated Muslims at the Asante royal court (the Asante *Nkramofoɔ*) also spread it. In 1471, Portuguese traders reported that the Fante at the coast traded with the Islamic Mande-Dyula from the north of present-day Ghana

(Silverman and Owusu-Ansah 1989:326). The African Mande-Dyula came to the Akan zone for trade, not to impose orthodox Islamic religion upon the Fante, the Asante and other Akan cultural groups. Even the jihads, which Islamised Hausaland in the 1800s and Futa Toro, Segu and Masina in the 1850s and 1860s) did not significantly influence the Akan states. The Mande-Dyula merchants came from Daboya, Buipe, Begho and Bono-Manso (see 7.5 map 5), a town with a goldmine in the north of Kumasi, that in 1722-3 had been defeated by the southern Akan and had become a subject of the Asante kingdom. The inhabitants of these towns (*nkuro*) produced and distributed gold, for gold routes ran from Bono to Jenne, on the Niger bend. The Mande-Dyula traders from Bono carried the gold into Muslim Sudan and carried back salt, cloth, brass bowls and Islamic ideas into the Asante kingdom (Insoll 2003:334, 337). Further, Islam was introduced in this kingdom when, by the middle of the eighteenth century, the savanna kingdom of Gonja came directly under Asante control, bringing Dagomba and Mamprusi under its sphere of influence. Additionally, the rulers of the Asante kingdom had established diplomatic contacts with those of the Mossi kingdom of Wagadugu and the involvement of the Asante in the profitable trade of kola nuts also developed further contact with the Muslims. The literate Muslims (Asante *Nkramofoɔ*) that the ruling duo Osei Kwadwo (1764-1777) and Akua Afiyie invited in the eighteenth century to live at the royal court in Kumasi were also followers of Suwari.[39] The Asante *Nkramofoɔ* had received their religious education at the Sankoré teaching mosque, a centre of Islamic learning in Timbuktu. They worked for the Asante royal rulers as advisers in matters of trade and foreign affairs and as keepers of records and accounts in Arabic.[40] Another function of these literate Muslims was to 'perform religious services' for the protection of the Asante ruling pair with the help of talismans (*nsuman*) (Schildkrout 1970:256; Owusu-Ansah 1991:117-119). In fact, the greatest source of influence from the Asante royal rulers in Kumasi was the appeal of Islamic charms and Muslim prayers.

In 1819, the British Consul Dupuis (1824), who came to Kumasi for negotiations and stayed a full year in the town, observed that the ruling pairs' suc-

[39] *Asantehemma* Akua Afiyie succeeded *Asantehemma* Nana Nkatia Ntem Abamoo at an unknown time. Nana Nkatia Ntem Abamoo was *Asantehemma* during the reign of *Asantehene* Kosi Obodom (1750-1764). *Asantehemma* Akua Afiyie was the mother of *Asantehene* Osei Kwadwo (1764-1777) and of three daughters, who all became *Asantehemma*; Amma Serwaa, Adoma Akosua and Konadu Yaadom I.

[40] The Islamic learning centre in Timbuktu has sometimes been referred to as a university: fourteenth century medieval Timbuktu was indeed a collection of scholars and students living in a single community for the common purpose of religious teaching and learning. Intellectual influences came first from Morocco, and later (after 1500) especially from Egypt with Azhar in Cairo as a role model for the whole of the Islamic world. Hiskett, M. 1984. *The development of islam in West Africa*. London: Longman. The Moroccan conquest of Shonghai of 1528 brought a heavy toll to this centre of Muslim religious 'science'. Between 1528 and 1800 it stayed a local centre of Muslim religious scholarship, but it was certainly not the leading centre for the whole of the Sahel.

cessors *Asantehene* Osei Kwame (1777-1803) and *Asantehemma* Konadu Yaadom I (1778-1809) were also sympathetic towards Islam. They used Muslims to maintain a cordial diplomatic relationship with Islamised rulers north of the Asante kingdom, such as those of the Gonja and Mamprusi. Dupuis also observed that *Asantehene* Osei Bonsu (1803-1824) protected Islamic prisoners out of fear for displeasure of Allah (Dupuis 1824:99). He continued to associate with Muslim advisers who had a growing influence in Kumasi and developed a real chancery for the mentioned diplomatic services of the Asante *Nkramofoɔ*, whose records were kept in Arabic (Owusu-Ansah 1987:80; Adjaye 1996:136-138). At the same time, however, the Asante royal rulers made sure that the Muslims did not gain political power and they 'jealously guarded their constitutional rights, that prevented the Muslims from serving in any of the Kumasi legislative councils' (Owusu-Ansah 1987:80). 'The Muslims did not have to take an oath of allegiance to the Asante traditional rulers because of their belief in the Qur'an, but this banned them from membership in the council. Neither could the Muslims enjoy full privileges of sworn chiefs, such as the control of territories and land from which they derived revenue, which were the salient ingredients of political power in Asante' (Owusu-Ansah 1987:86).

As a result, the spread of Islam was effectively controlled. During the reign of the ruling pair Osei Bonsu's (1804-1824) and Ama Serwaa Nyaako (1819-1824/33) the Asante even established friendly relations with Ahmad B. Muhammad (Ahmadu Lobbo), a jihadist of Masina.[41] There is not much known about the jihadist Muhammad as the records about him were destroyed in the fire after the British sacked Kumasi in 1874. All the more radical Muslims who settled in Kumasi in the beginning of the nineteenth century came, however, from Hausaland. The best known of the Hausa Muslims was Sharif Ibrahim, a Borno (*ɛ-alim*). Ibrahim supported himself through the profitable business of manufacturing charms and amulets, objects that are integral to Africanised forms of Islam; he also offered prayers in return for gifts. Many Hausa leaders, such as Ibrahim were unpopular among other less radical Muslims in Kumasi, who were afraid that the influence of the more stringent Muslims would negatively affect the relationships between Asante royal rulers and Muslims (Hiskett 1984:131-135). The reason for the unpopularity of these radical Muslims was also related to their perception of AIR, as a pagan cult, which they believed, should be eradicated by converting the Asante to Islam. Orthodox Muslims had great problems with important elements of IRs such as the ritual killing of human beings and libation in honour of the ancestors.

---

[41] *Asantehemma* Nana Ama Sewaa ruled during the reigns of *Asantehene* Osei Tutu Kwame and perhaps also through that of *Asantehene* Osei Yaw Akoto. She acted as counsel and helped to maintain a balance between the Asante elite and the paramount chiefs. She was the mother of *Asantehene* Kwaku Dua I and *Asantehemma* Afia Sarpong.

Christians introduced their faith to the Asante through two main strands; European Missionary Christianity and African Christianity, the latter of which came into being in Asante during the 1920s (see section 4.3.2). In comparison to other West African cultures, such as the Yoruba, the Asante and other Akan groups were relatively hostile to Christianity and the rate of the uptake of this world religion in the Akan forest belt was notoriously slow (Peel 1987). The Basel Missionary Society (BMS) (BMS – currently the Presbyterian Church) and the Wesleyan Methodist Missionary Society (WMMS – currently the Methodist Church) began working amongst the Asante in 1828 and 1838 respectively. In the 1880s, the Society of the African Mission (SAM) or Roman Catholics also sent missionaries to Asante, as did the North German Missionary Society (NGMS). In 1880, the Roman Catholic missionaries August Moreau and Eugene Murat were welcomed in Kumasi by the then ruling *Asantehene* Mensa Bonsu (1874-1883). Moreau mentioned:

> One day I expressed my desire to visit Kumasi. I asked him [prince Boakye] whether the king would agree to see me or order to have my head cut off. The prince answered: 'The king would be very glad to see you, and be assured he will do you no harm.' This happened in the month of July 1881 and since then I have been waiting for the favourable moment to go to this Asante town (Report, the 16th of June 1882, in *AMA* 15/802.02.19.222).

The Society for the Propagation of the Gospel (SPG) which was a subsection of the Church of England (Anglican) was dormant during most of the nineteenth century (Buah 1980:130-138).[42] The Anglican Church itself appeared as a mission organisation known as The Church of England Mission (CEM). Neither the missionaries of the CEM nor the Anglican Church had much influence in Kumasi. In 1883, for instance, *Asantehene* Osei Bonsu wrote a letter to the Catholic priest Fr. A. Moreau to say that a Protestant minister who attempted to enter Kumasi was unwelcome. *Asantehene* Mensa Bonsu wrote: 'I do not refuse you [Moreau], and as for this minister [the Protestant Minister], never fear, he won't get in' (Groves 1955:189). However, in 1913, the CEM missionary G. W. Morrison succeeded in establishing an Anglican Church, a school and a chapel (Arhin, Afari-Gyan et al. 1992:55-57). Most missionaries started their activities on the Gold Coast and came only much later to Kumasi. The Methodist Church in Kumasi was founded in December 1841, and the Presbyterian Church in this town dates from 1869 (Ramseyer, Kühne et al. 1875:1-67). Rev. F. Andrew Ramseyer founded the latter who together with his colleague Rev. J.S. Kühne, his wife and young daughter, were taken from Anum and were sent to Kumasi as

[42] One of the few SPG missionaries who were, however, credited with taking the gospel to Kumasi was John Mills. In 1839 Mills held service with the then ruling *Asantehene* Kwaku Duah I. But when in 1841 the SGP proposed to send a man to Kumasi, the Governor at Cape Coast vetoed the plan on the grounds that too many versions of the Christian faith would confuse the Asante Williamson, S. G. and J. Bardsley 1953. *The Gold Coast: What of the Church?* London: Edinburgh House Press.

prisoners that same year. They stayed in Kumasi for four years, did much missionary work and established the Kumasi BMS station outside town. The British ransack of the city of Kumasi in 1874 resulted in the release of all BMS missionaries (Ramseyer, Kühne et al. 1875). Thereafter, the BMS was refused permission to settle in Asante and Ramseyer's presentation of the Twi Bible to the *Asantehene* was not well received. Although the king raised no objection to occasional visits of the BMS missionaries, such as that of Rev. Ramseyer in 1881, these were attempted: 'All to no purpose; king and nation hardened their hearts' (Huppenbauer 1905 [4th edition]:52-60). In 1896 Ramseyer came back to Kumasi. As a free person, along with his BMS colleague Perregaux, he was successful in converting many Asante to BM Christianity. The turmoil after the exile of the ruling pair Prempeh I and Konadu Yaadom II, however, made it impossible for them to establish a church for the new Christian members in the town (Arhin, Afari-Gyan et al. 1992:55-57). Most likely, the BMS was hindered by the fact that a soldier, Captain Armitage, accompanied them who the Asante believed was looking for the Golden Stool. Another negative aspect of the Basel Mission was that since 1885, under influence of the scientific revolution in Europe, the healing voice of God who had previously cured BMS believers from demonic spirits was gradually silenced. Whereas the new Basel missionaries in Ghana had been affected by the paradigm of scientific materialism, the Akan (non-Christian and the new converts to Christianity) continued to both fear and admire the religious power and *episteme* of their *abosom*. After 1885, the Basel missionaries had turned to biomedical rather than the combination of medicinal and spiritual healing, and as a result, they could no longer find the right spiritual connection with the Asante people. Consequently, the missionaries developed a problematic relationship with Asante Basel Christians, whom they forbid to consult the *akomfoɔ,* the trained professionals in spirit mediumship who the indigenous believers praised for their passive spiritual knowledge. Most of the newly converted Christians continued to believe in the healing powers of various spirits and continued to consult them; they were conditioned to being treated by the agency of unseen forces, deities, and God. Asante Christians, however, continued to invest legitimacy in the therapeutic abilities of their *abosom* long after conversion (Mohr 2009).

The Roman Catholics came to Kumasi in 1880, but only in 1905 did the James Anquanda, a jailor from Winneba, take the initiative to build a Roman Catholic Church. In 1910, Fr. Joseph Nuller, a Dutchman who was the first Roman Catholic resident missionary in Kumasi opened a missionary station there. In 1913, the first Roman Catholic Chapel was built (Kimble 1963: 153, footnote 6; Arhin, Afari-Gyan et al. 1992:55-57).

As we have seen, African Islam was introduced in the Asante kingdom in the fifteenth and eighteenth centuries in initially the moderate tradition of Suwari and then latterly in the radical tradition of Uthman dan Fodio. European missionary Christianity was introduced in the fifteenth, nineteenth and twentieth centuries. The mainstream Christian Churches that were established in the latter two centuries belonged to WMMS of the Wesleyan missionaries; the BMS of the Basel missionaries; the SPG of the Anglicans, and the Catholic SAM. Of all the missionaries who came to the Asante kingdom in the precolonial period, the Roman Catholics experienced the least resistance in bringing the gospel to the Asante due to their willingness to learn Twi and their respect for AIR.

3.5 The Asante traditional authorities and their indigenous religious mediatory function

The focus in the previous section was on three ways in which the Asante royal rulers legitimised their power. This section aims to enhance further understandings of the mediatory role of the Asante royal rulers. Their tasks as mediators were to guarantee the continuity of Asante society through intercession with the royal ancestral spirits (*anini nananom nsamanfo*) and to adhere to their demands. The central idea was that to create an atmosphere of spiritual peace and harmony, the Asante royal rulers had to promote serenity. Therefore carriers always accompanied the royal rulers by holding a large red and yellow umbrella (*kyiniɛ*) above their heads, continuously moving it up and down in the breeze providing protection against the sun. When the royal rulers sat down, the *kyiniɛ* created an atmosphere that cooled down the spirits, thereby stimulating the establishment and maintenance of peaceful relationships among all those who had gathered in the umbrella's shade. In the natural world, a shadow with similar attributes could be found under the tree of reception (*ogyedua*). This tree was planted in the centre of Kumasi that the Asante royal rulers used to gather under to perform rituals for the propitiation of the ancestral spirits. Each Asante semi-autonomous vassal state had an *ogyedua* in the city centre that symbolically represented the royal rulers and their forefathers. The city of Kumasi derived its name from the Kum tree of reception. Among the Asante, the destiny of each constituent nation was associated with the health of the tree of reception: spirits could cool down in the shade, and the deceased chiefs became associated with this tree (As the Asante say: 'A mighty tree has fallen' – *du pon kese atutu*) (Rattray 1959 [first published in 1927]: 107, note 1). The Kum tree is a *banyan* tree, which is in many cultures associated with the occult and the veneration of ancestors (e.g. in Ghana, India, Tahiti and Birma) (see 7.6.1 photograph 1). A specific characteristic of the *banyan* tree is that its roots seem to grow upwards, whereas their branches grow downwards. When viewed in water these trees symbolise the unity between the spiritual and the material worlds and the wholeness of the Universe.[43] In Hinduism, Buddhism and many Indigenous Religions

[43] An Asante proverb of the precolonial period that is still used by Asante women referring to the belief in the deception of sense data (and a bad marriage) is as follows: 'the ripening pepper fruit I thought would be sweeter; I hardly realised the more it ripens the spicier it gets'. Yankah, K. 1995. *Speaking*

of the world, the higher truth in this Universe cannot be found by studying the real world, which is deceptive (*maya* in Hinduism) but by gaining understanding of the spiritual world (Prabhupada 1984: 629). The Asante priests and priestesses also used *banyan* trees to invoke the *abosom*.[44]

The *kyiniɛ* and the *ogyedua* created the condition of coolness for the Asante royal rulers meant to maintain a peaceful connection with the spiritual beings (Platvoet 1985:174-200; McCaskie 1989:423-425). There were also some gendered differences in the acts of mediation with the spirits. The Asante chiefs partly connected in a manner to the inhabitants of the spiritual world, which was different from the Asante female co-rulers, whose tasks were dissimilar but complementary to those of the Asante chiefs. The Asante chiefs were the custodians of the farmland and had economic power, whereas the Asante female co-rulers did not have access to the profits of the surplus of the land (de Marees 1912 [original edition 1602]:116). Furthermore, the Asante chiefs were more involved in matters of war, whereas the Asante female co-rulers dealt with female affairs, like puberty rituals. The Asante female royal rulers were, however, the advisors of the Asante chiefs in both political affairs and matters of religion and were senior to them, thereby representing the first mythic female principle ancestral spirit (*Ngame*) who was superior and senior to the first male principle ancestral spirit (*Nyame*). Furthermore, the Asante female co-ruler not only held court, but also advised the Asante chief with juridical cases that were related to men. The Asante female co-rulers lived separately from the Asante chiefs but nearby the royal palace and had their own spokesmen (*akyeame*), body of councillors and orators, who were mostly female. Unlike the *akyeame* of the Asante chiefs, those of the Asante female co-rulers did not, however, use a staff. This so-called *akyeame poma* contained political messages for the Asante chief's host or enemy. Which was explained by the Asante chief's *akyeame* on diplomatic missions. An example is, for instance, the symbol of a snake head trapped in a bird's claws and the related proverb *Wosuo owo ti a, nea aka ye ahama* – 'If you hold the snake's head, the rest of it is mere thread', which may convey the message that 'If we succeed in capturing the chief, or general, your whole state is doomed to defeat'. Generally, Asante chiefs and male orators dominated the public domain. In this sphere, women had to remain silence or communicate indirectly e.g. through symbols on cloth (Yankah 1995).

The *Asante* ruling pair, the *omanhene*, *omanhemma*, *ahene*, *ahenna* and the *odikro* and the *obaa panin*, were the occupants of their sacred lineage stool. This occupation gave them access to a sacred space, an elsewhere, that provided them with strong spiritual powers due to their relationship with higher entities,

---

for The Chief: Okyeame and the Politics of Akan Royal Oratory. Bloomington: Indiana University Press.

[44] The Basel missionary Ramseyer took a photograph of a *banyan* tree that was used by indigenous priests and priestesses in front of the entrance of the Bantama mausoleum in Kumasi (see 7.6. photograph 1).

who were believed to be more powerful than human beings. Because of these powers derived from spirits, on all hierarchical levels the words of the chiefs and their female co-rulers were believed to be able to unleash deadly forces if communicated directly to their subjects or to foreigners. The Asante royal rulers therefore all communicated through an *akyeame*, who was there to sweeten their words and to stop those words from altering reality in a negative way. The Asante believed that words had magic potency and that the *akyeame* of the traditional rulers could break the power of their words by paraphrasing them or elaborating on their message. The *akyeame* speech should excel in eloquence but also in integrity and should maintain the authenticity of the royal rulers' words (Yankah 1995). As Yankah puts it: 'The royal oratory was a composite of the chief's words and the spokesperson's (*ɔkyeame*) verbal embroidery' (Yankah 1995:x). The *akyeame* were symbolically married with their chief or female co-ruler. They were the only one with direct communicative access to the Asante royal rulers in formal settings and were there to protect the audience against the power of their sacred words (Yankah 1995).

During indigenous religious rituals for the veneration of the ancestors, the Asante royal rulers invoked the ancestral spirits, whereas the *akyeame* poured libation and ritually killed animals or human beings. The British merchant Thomas Bowdich observed that Tuesday was the fetish day of the Asante traditional rulers; meaning those of the Asante rulers whose *abusua* ruled over the other *abusua* lineage groups. Similar as to his birthday (*kra da*), on which the Asante celebrated the renewal of their life-force, the soul (*ɔkra*), the *Asante* royal rulers sat on a special stool to offer fowls. The eating of these animals was taboo for the then ruling Asante royals (the *oyoko* clan). Slaves and children were also frequently offered to the stool (the fetish) in combination with ten ounces (*peredwans*) (Bowdich 1819:265-266).

The purpose of Asante royal rulers' veneration of the ancestors was to legitimatise their power by reminding the subjects constantly about the foundation of the Asante nation. Ritual is a common method for rulers in an illiterate society to keep their families' history alive. The presence of the communal ancestral spirit (*sunsum*) inside their royal stools was believed to link the Asante royal rulers to their ancestors. Also, by pouring libation and saying prayers, the rulers kept their history alive, and justified their claim to royal power. The reasons for the Asante rulers' legitimation of their position were twofold. First, they propagated that they should be the ones in power because they were the founders of the community, and also contributed significantly to the wellbeing of the community. Second, they believed their power was legitimised because they were in a better relationship with the ancestral spirits than ordinary people. What the Asante traditional authorities have in common with ordinary Asante subjects is that by birth they receive two souls: (*ɔkra*) and (*sunsum*). The *sunsum* enables them to sense the ancestral spirits and to communicate with them in dreams. Besides, their own *sunsum,* the Asante traditional authorities are also linked to the ancestors through a communal *sunsum* that contains the individual *sunsum* of all subjects of the Asante kingdom and resides in the Golden Stool (for male Asante rulers) and the Silver Stool (for female Asante rulers). This communal *sunsum*, which is similar to what Jung called the 'collective unconscious' is believed to dwell inside royal stools upon which the Asante traditional authorities sat and sit and which made and makes them more powerful. The higher the rank of a chief and his female co-ruler, the more spiritual power they were believed to receive from the communal *sunsum* inside his or her royal stool. The most powerful royal stool among the Asante are the *Sika Dwa Kofi* and the *Dwete* Stool, which are occupied by the *Asantehene* and the *Asantehemma*, which were and are at the apex of political and religious power (interview with *Oboguhene* Nana Owusu Asiama, 12). The royal stools were made of the *sɛsɛ* tree that was believed to be sacred: eggs and an animal such as a fowl was sacrificed to appease the tree spirit (Sarpong 1971). The spine of the stool represented a tree without branches, which symbolises stability and the rebirth of the royal ancestors (by the return of their spines). A similar reference to the ancestors can be found on the Djed pillar from the Tomb of Nefertiti (ca 1270 BCE) which bears the inscription 'direct you to Osiris-who returned your spines!' (Martin and Ronnberg 2011). The tree symbolism refers to a historical continuity between Egyptian and Sub-Saharan African kingship, but is also the result of South Asian and South East Asian cultures on West Africa (Seligman 1934; Wainwright 1949; Meyerowitz 1960).

One can compare the connection of royal rulers with the ritual object of their stools with the process of becoming enlightened in Buddhism, Hinduism or by practising Kundalini yoga. The connection with the stool or shrine opens the royal's 'third eye' or 'king's eye' (*ɔhene aniwa)* and enables him or her to enter into a stage of defocalised consciousness and a space of in-between-ness where spirits of the deceased and men meet. In that sacred space, the royal rulers can see more than ordinary people, who can only enter that same elsewhere with their quasi-material soul (*sunsum*) during dreams (Minkus 1980; Gyekye 1995). The mentioned parallels between these non-monotheistic world religions and the Asante Indigenous Religion are no coincidence, as West African cultures have been influenced by South Asian and South East Asian cultures as early as 15 thousand years before present (ka BP) and in more recent millennia (van Binsbergen 2012).

Because of the connection that the soul (*sunsum*) of a royal ruler has to make with the communal *sunsum* inside a royal stool, an extraordinary mind or potential for a strong third eye perspective is required for a royal to be appointed as a chief or female co-ruler. Such a mind-set, which implies an openness of the right brain hemisphere for the reception of non-empirical or active knowledge, enables the spirits to enter their body to communicate with them. The Asante say that the spirits are a source of 'passive' knowledge that the extraordinary minded could tap into after a demanding initiation ritual. After his or her enstoolment, which is a societal confirmation of their position and their access to spiritual power, he or she can reveal the higher truths of life, by their creative interpretation of the messages of the spirits. The Asante believe that nobody can know everything, but that a wise person (*anyansato*) is characterised by his ability not only to obtain active and passive knowledge (*nunya*), but also to come to a deeper sense of comprehension based on a large segment of experience. In potential the extraordinary minded could use his or her spirit-derived knowledge to do good or evil, because the spirits are ambivalent forces (interviews with *ɔkɔmfoɔ* Agyei, 2). The selection of the Asante royal rulers is therefore significant, because it is believed that this older woman (*aberewa*) is 'the epitome of eloquence' (Yankah 1995:70) and that she possesses the wisdom to choose an heir to the stool who is of good character. The female Asante ruler is the one 'who symbolises the physical reproduction of society and is believed to know genealogy' (Gilbert 1994:102). Because the female Asante royal ruler shares the blood (*mogya*) with the chief, she was believed to be most capable of making a judgement about the prospective chief's spirit and his qualities. A chief could therefore only be 'enstooled' (enthroned) after her weightiest judgement on the chief's suitability for the stool function in consultation with the elders and the subjects (*nkoa*).

The Asante ruling pair also communicated differently with the spirits in terms of their use of eloquent silence. Both male and female royal state rulers exercise a great amount of silence in the communication with their ancestors and their subjects. They communicated through their spokesmen (*akyeame*) who did and still do most of the talking at the palace. To keep a distance between themselves and their subjects they did not react to everything that the latter were saying. If the royal rulers speak, they speak indirectly and use maxims, proverbs and staffs with symbols to communicate. The *akyeame* can interpret the messages of the royal rulers by their knowledge of Asante culture and the societal context in which the royal rulers speak. More frequent than men, royal women made and make use of garment, such as *Adinkra* and *Kente* cloths, with symbolic messages (see more in section 5.2). The knowledge of the royal rulers of the divine is an intuitive form of knowledge and it is believed among the Asante that this type of knowledge is best communicated by using silence. The Asante female royal rulers were and are less trained in public speaking than the chiefs and like all women they were meant to keep silence in front of the chiefs. The female co-rulers of the chief therefore communicated even more indirectly with their (most often female) subjects through proverbs and sometimes songs (interview with Nana Prenhyia-Besease, 28).

The 'eloquent silences' and mytho-poeic language of the Asante royal rulers were thus central to pre-Christian and pre-Islamic practices of indigenous religious mediation. The royal rulers had a higher status than the indigenous religious priests and priestesses (*akomfoɔ*), who were their spiritual advisors (Yankah 1995). The *akomfoɔ* came from the Brong area that was part of the Asante kingdom and advised the royal rulers on the use of the Asante calendar (*adaduanan*).

Their specialised knowledge of this calendar was of use to the traditional authorities, because its bad days (*da bone*) that were preserved for the invocation of the ancestral spirits fell on another day every year (Bartle 1978). Dressed in red cloth (*koben*), the *akomfoɔ* who are the children of the *abosom*, first fell ill before receiving their gift of mediumship from their spiritual parents. Then, they received a period of years of professional training (*nkom-mu*) which lasted years overseen by professional *akomfoɔ*. During this training, they learned how to control the defocalised thought processes of the right brain hemisphere, and how to interpret the twisted and unrational messages of the *abosom* and the *onini (nananom) nsamanfo*. As in the case of the chiefs, an *akomfoɔ*'s ritual of initiation (in the *nsumankwaa* or the college of physicians) was a way to get consent among other *akomfoɔ* and Asante subjects for the access to spiritual knowledge and to obtain a position of power in society based on that knowledge. They inherited the gift of mediation and were 'called' by the *abosom*. After a wedding with them they were allowed to wear red cloth and became trained experts in invoking the *abosom* and the creation of natural charms, whose powers were believed to derive from these deities. They also learned ancient languages and songs to understand the various deities that landed upon their shoulders, and how to communicate with trees and rivers and with dwarfs (*mmoatia*) (interviews with *ɔkɔmfoɔ* Agyei, 2). Depending on their reputation, they had their own number of *akyeame*, who communicated the messages of the spirits to their audience and venerated the *abosom* by pouring libation, a form of prayer, and by cooling down the spirits with animal or human blood. The more reputable and spiritually powerful the *akomfoɔ* were, the higher was their number of *akyeame* (interview with Nana Ama Serwah Nyarko, 29). The *akomfoɔ* were also specialised in throwing and interpreting cowry shells to gain insight in and come to terms with the past and future of their clients, and with other forms of divination such as water gazing (Braffi 1992; Kirby 1993). Since the late eighteenth century, these *akomfoɔ* who worked at the Asante royal court, had received help from Islamic scholars from Timbuktu; the Asante *Nkramofoɔ*. The *Nkramofoɔ* Muslims were trained in the Sankoré teaching mosque in Timbuktu in geomantic astronomy that they used to determine the location of Mecca and to create an accurate calendar that included prayer times (Medupe, Warner et al. 2008). The ruling pair Osei Kwame (1777-1798) and Nana Kwaadu Yiadom I (1778-1809) were the first in a tradition of Asante rulers who recruited the *Nkramofoɔ* priests to become part of the *nsumankwaa,* or corps of *akomfoɔ* and physicians who made their knowledge of Islamic medicine and charms available for the protection of the Asante royal rulers and their kingdom. What distinguished the *Nkramofoɔ* priests from their Asante colleagues was the source of their knowledge of the divine. Whereas the *akomfoɔ* received their knowledge of a specific situation by going into trance, the *Nkramofoɔ* priests could read and write down phrases of the Qur'an. The latter used their skills to create charms and amulets that were filled with magic formulae deduced from this Holy Book. The Asante royal rulers were highly impressed with the skill of the Muslim priests, because they believed that the words inside the Qur'an were extremely powerful and could make them invincible. Consequently, the Asante royal rulers paid a significant amount of money to the Muslim priests to predict the future for protection with their talisman and charms derived from the Holy Script of the Qur'an (Owusu-Ansah 1987; 1991). The royal rulers believed that the Qur'an was a sacred object or fetish, like their Golden Stool, that contained spiritual power, which could kill those who would turn themselves against the words of the Qur'an. *Asantehene* Osei Tutu Kwame's (1804-1824) belief in the power of the Qur'anic script was, for instance, confirmed when he inquired from the head of the *Nkramofoɔ*, Muhammad al-Ghamba, what they did to establish peaceful relationships with foreigners. When Muhammad al-Ghamba answered that they then 'swear upon Qur'an', *Asantehene* Osei Tutu Kwame answered: 'That is good, because, if they keep evil in their heart, the book must kill them' (Dupuis 1824:159-161). For the *Asantehene* the effects of swearing an oath to the Qur'an were similar of swearing an oath to the spiritual power inside the Stool (the *suman*, which later became known as the communal *sunsum*). The Asante royal rulers often consulted their *akomfoɔ* as well as the *Nkramofoɔ* priests. In 1819, for instance, the ruling pair Osei Bonsu and Ama Serwaa Nyaako who were both Muslim enthusiasts first consulted an Asante indigenous priest, about several war issues. As usual the *ɔkɔmfoɔ* invoked the ancient state river god *Tano* (alias *Ta Kora*) to seek advice on when they should go to war (Rattray 1955 (first published in 1923):180, 181-191). The Asante believed that out of the 378 days there were only 150 or 160 days (the so-called 'good days') that were suitable to fight wars. The *ɔkɔmfoɔ*'s consultations of *Tano*, the old tutelary water spirit of Osei Bonsu's *oyoko abohyen* clan and *ntro* group, were supported by divinations from 'the flights of birds, track of particular beetles and insects, screeching of the turkey buzzard and dreams' (Dupuis 1824:213). Besides, however, these royal rulers also requested the *Nkramofoɔ* priests to pray for them at war and to protect them with the help of amulets that contained quotations of the Qur'an (*asuman*).[45] The British Consul Dupuis, who stayed in Kumasi in that year, commented that 'the Ashantees [Asante] without knowing the contents of the Koran [Qur'an] are equally persuaded that it is a volume of divine creation' (Dupuis 1824:247). In 1872, *Asantehene* Kofi Kakari summoned the Asante

[45] A charm, amulet or talisman is worn as a remedy or prophylaxis against evils, such as diseases and witchcraft; such amulets, consist or are composed of various things, such as feathers, hair or teeth of various animals, beads, scraps of leather or paper inscribed with mystic characters and tied around some limb or hung about the neck' Christaller, J. G. 1881. *A Dictionary of the Asante and Fante Language Called Tshi (Chwee,Twi), With a Grammatical Introduction and Appendices on the Geography of the Gold Coast and other Subjects*. Basel: Published for the Evangelical Missionary Society by Trüner and Co.

priests to his palace to discuss by foretelling him the future whether or not he should fight another war against the British. On the 26th of January that year:

> The priests were compensated for their efforts and received ten *peredwans*, twenty charges of salt, twenty pieces of cloth, twenty sheep, seventy bottles of rum and fifty slaves (Ramseyer, Kühne et al. 1875:208-209).

The prophecies of the Asante priests were thus highly regarded and the sum of their rewards formed a considerable part of the military budget of the Asante royal rulers. In addition, however, the royal rulers also spend *peredwans* to consult the Asante *Nkramofoɔ* at the royal court and to buy their *nsuman*. In December 1873 the Asante *Nkramofoɔ* also gave *Asantehene* Kofi Kakari religious advise, and he gave them a lot of gold to buy a Mohammedan charm from the north to keep away governor Wolseley who had planned to sack Kumasi (Wilks 1989 [first published in 1975]:239). The Asante *Nkramofoɔ* washed the king with Holy water (in Mande *nassi-ji*), which among Muslims is a way to protect the body and spirit of one who ingests it. A master of *batin* knowledge specially prepared the so-called writing water. The method, which involved washing Qur'anic verses from a tablet, and then washing the king with this water, was a way of establishing intimacy between Allah and the king. The Asante royal rulers also wore sandals with magic squares and invocations at the soles that were meant to call upon the powers of *Nyame* to protect them. Besides, the *Asantehene* Kofi Kakari wore a talisman wrapped around his ankles and on his sandal straps and footrest (*krokowa*) (Owusu-Ansah 1987). However, to find out what to do with 'the whites', the Asante royal rulers not only consulted the Asante *Nkramofoɔ* at the royal court, but also a Muslim priest of the Asante hinterland. On the 10th of February 1873, the Basel missionaries Ramseyer and Kühne reported that King Kakari sent a Muslim to the interior. The Dente oracle at Kratchi in the Bron region proceeded to inform him that: 'This war will not end to your advantage as long as you keep the white men, who are constantly crying to God, – prisoners; let them go, and you will conquer (Ramseyer, Kühne et al. 1875:210-211)'. The answer of the Dente oracle, who the Asante royal rulers often consulted on matters of warfare and security was, however, not to the satisfaction of King Kakari, who did not want to free the Basel missionaries. To the mind of Kakari, the answer of the Dente oracle was not the answer that one would expect from an oracle, because it was not multi-interpretable. Instead it was a clear message that he would only win the war against the British by releasing the Basel missionaries, who he needed as diplomats. King Kakari suspected that the Dente *bosomfo* had a political interest in preventing him to go to war, a decision that would negatively affect the Bron states, and ignored the advice of the oracle (Maier 1981:230). To be sure, he preferred to write a letter to the King of Bariba, north of Dahomey, 'asking for one fetish ointment made by one of his great fetishes, which had the reputation of possessing many virtues, amongst others that of misdirecting bullets, arrows and spears aimed at any individual smeared with it' (Lonsdale 1882:88-89). On the 6th of December 1873, King Kakari followed the advice of the *Nkramofoɔ* at his royal court and gave them ten *peredwans* for using sorcery to hinder the British from marching to the capital (Ramseyer, Kühne et al. 1875, 250). Precolonial Asante history demonstrates that the Asante royal rulers paid a great deal of attention to the consultation of traditional priests and priestesses, but not without critical judgment of their spiritual advises.

Since the late nineteenth century, the Asante royal rulers did not only seek the spiritual advice of the Asante *akomfoɔ* and the *Nkramofoɔ* but also from Christian missionaries. The ruling pair Kwaku Dua Panin (1838-1867) and Yaa Dufi, for instance, had long discussions with the mulatto Methodist missionary Rev. Thomas Birch Freeman on the matter of faith. Under influence of the Asante princes Nkwantabisa and Owusu-Ansa, who were educated and converted to Methodism in Britain under Maclean's guidance, the ruling duo allowed Freeman and his colleague Rev. Robert Brooking to begin work in Asante as they believed that Christianity would make them more powerful (Owusu-Mensa 1974; Wilks 1988). In November 1841 a small Methodist school and congregation were started in Kumasi and in the period 1840-1850 Prince Owusu Ansa became an active promoter of the Methodist domination up to late December 1862. His senior cousin Nkwantabisa had faded from the scene and Owusu Ansa became the main link between Asante and Methodist hopes in the Asante kingdom. Especially, after 1850, when the Asante-British diplomatic relations had become so troublesome that all European missionaries had left Kumasi and the rest of the Asante area to become active at the coast. From then on, Owusu-Ansa was left to carry on single-handedly his missionary work and it was not until 1852 that Rev. Timothy Laing arrived in Kumasi to help the prince with his religious task. In April 1853 Rev. Owusu-Ansa was stationed at Abakrampa, which was the capital of the Fante state of Abora, where he became a full-time Methodist minister in the Gold Coast District of the WMMS. In August 1854, Rev. Thomas Freeman who was the head of the Methodist Church on the Gold Coast appointed Owusu-Ansa 'superintendent of the Cape Coast schools.' After his years as a pioneer of converting Asante to Christianity, he became more involved in Asante-British diplomacy until his death in Cape Coast on the 13th of November 1884 (Owusu-Mensa 1974). Prince Owusu Ansa is a good example of an Asante royal who believed that the embrace of Christianity would not only enhance the spiritual power of the Asante but would also bring peace. In the next section, the author will elaborate upon the religious peacekeeping function of the Asante royal rulers in the precolonial period.

3.6 The Asante traditional authorities and their function as indigenous religious peacekeepers

In this section, the author's focus will be on the social relationship of the Asante traditional authorities with Islamic leaders, and on the extent to which those rulers adapted and adopted Islamic elements into AIR. Furthermore, it also aims to shed light upon the socio-religious relationships between the Asante traditional authorities and Christian leaders and their religion.

3.6.1 The Muslims

From the foundation of the Asante kingdom in 1701, there were three different groups of Muslims in Kumasi: the Mande-Dyula, the Asante *Nkramofoɔ* and orthodox Hausa Muslims. The first two categories were adherents of a moderate form of Islam, but the town also housed orthodox Hausa Muslims. The Mande-Dyula were a powerful trading family of Muslims who were the first link in a vast distributive network that extended northward from the goldfields to the greater entrepôts of the western Sudan and Sahel; this network further reached across the Sahara by caravan trails to the Mediterranean littoral, and so into Europe, the Middle East, and beyond (Wilks 2000:94). The Asante were dependent on the trade links of the Mande-Dyula families for obtaining kola nuts, which were used in various Asante indigenous rituals, but also, because of the trade in firearms that these Muslims obtained from the Asante, who bought them from the Dutch and the British at the coast (Kea 1971:209-210). The Asante tolerated Muslims in their capital for the purpose of trade. They allowed religious syncretism to occur between AIR and Islam only at an elementary level (Levtzion 1968:181-187; Insoll 2003). In terms of the Berner models that describe processes of religious syncretism, as introduced in Chapter II, the A1 model is most appropriate to describe the level of religious syncretism in Kumasi between the forms of Islam and AIR. A1 emphasises the unity of goals, the truth of the religions, and the possibility of testing different routes, with the latter eliminating the competitive relationship between religions (Berner 2004). In the eighteenth century, the Asante traditional authorities encouraged Muslims to settle in Kumasi. The Asante royal rulers hoped that the presence of an Islamic community in the Asante kingdom would encourage trade between the Asante people and the Mande-Dyula families. Furthermore, they hoped that they could make use of the diplomatic skills of the Asante *Nkramofoɔ,* who they invited to live at the royal court (*ahemfi*). At *ahemfi*, the *Nkramofoɔ* negotiated on behalf of the Asante royal rulers with Muslims in the Northern hinterlands and with the Europeans at the Coast first on an *ad hoc* basis and in the nineteenth century; the Asante *Nkramofoɔ* were members of the Arabic chancery under *ɔkramoni* Muhammad-al-Ghamba (Adjaye 1996:136-138). Being close to the Asante royal rulers, the *Nkramofoɔ* Muslims soon gained a considerable amount of political influence. The Asante *Nkramofoɔ* did not only function as diplomats but also became the recorders of historical and political events in the Asante kingdom, the authors of the chronology and dynastic annals of the Asante monarchs (Owusu-Ansah 1987).

In their function as indigenous religious peacekeepers, however, the ruling royals asked the Asante *Nkramofoɔ* to write peace settlements with Muslims of the Northern Asante hinterland. To prevent the ancient trade route from Kumasi through Bondoukou (the successor of Begho) and Kongo in the Middle Niger from falling into disuse, they for instance, came to an agreement with the Muslims of the north-west with whom the Asante were at war (Wilks 1961:14-29; Levtzion 1968:181-187).[46] Moreover, the strategy of the Asante royal rulers to maintain peaceful relationships with the Northerners by using Asante *Nkramofoɔ* diplomats was not unproblematic. In 1818 for instance, *ɔkramoni* Muhammad al-Ghamba, the head of the Arabic chancery, refused to carry out *Asantehene* Osei Bonsu's order to fight in the Asante-Gyaman War (1818-1819) against other Muslims. The Asante king felt scorned by al-Ghamba and declared that he would have put him to death had he not been a holy man (Wilks 1989 [first published in 1975]:268). Nevertheless, Osei Bonsu sent Asante boys to Al Ghamba's school, where by 1819 there were seventy pupils: Islamic tuition was the only formal literate education in a time that Christian education was discouraged, because the latter was believed to be a threat to the *status quo* (Dupuis 1824: 97,107 and ccxxiii; Owusu-Ansah 1991). At the same time, however, this Asante king was the patron of this school, and he made sure that it would not become too popular (Wilks 1961:20-21). The Asante boys were sent to that school as a sign of respect to the Muslim community, but not to promote the Islam of the Asante *Nkramofoɔ* in the Ashanti Region. The Asante royal rulers also demonstrated their respect to the Asante *Nkramofoɔ* by exempting them from bowing down to them, which was the appropriate behaviour that was expected from ordinary Asante subjects. The Asante rulers knew and respected the fact that the Islamic religion forbade the *Nkramofoɔ* to bow down to anyone else apart from God and that to disobey this aspect of the Islamic belief was considered a terrible sin by any Muslim.

The Asante ruling duo Osei Bonsu and Ama Serwaa Nyaako did thus not promote the Islam of the Asante *Nkramofoɔ* but they advocated living peacefully together, overall in respect of one another's religion. In turn, the Asante *Nkramofoɔ* did not attempt to convert Asante to their type of Islam. They accepted the authority of the Asante royal rulers and supported it insofar as it enabled them 'to follow their own way of life in accordance with the *sunna* of the

[46] The Kumasi – Bondoukou trade route was of vital importance for the economy of the Asante kingdom.

Prophet' (Wilks 2000:98).[47] Because of being so far away from 'the land of Islam' (*Dar-al-Islam*) referring to the part of the world governed by Muslims and the *shari'a*, the *Nkramofoɔ* often found themselves at the fringes of what was accepted with regards to their belief. They did, for instance, pray for the well being of the ruling pair and attended indigenous rituals such as the *Odwira* festival that included the ritual killing of human beings.[48] Overall, however, they kept a distance from Asante indigenous practitioners, for fear of backsliding (*ihmal*), and, were very much aware of the dangers, in terms of their belief, of living in 'the land of unbelievers' (*Dar-al-harb*) (Wilks 2000).

Under the ruling pair Osei Yaw Akoto (1824-1834) and Yaa Dufie (1824/33-1835) the relationship between the Asante royal rulers and the Asante *Nkramofoɔ* cooled down. The defeat of the Asante in the battle of Dodowa in 1826 against the Ga people of Katamanso made the royal rulers believe that they had lost the war, because the Asante *Nkramofoɔ* had used their magic against them. The Asante royal rulers therefore arrested many of these holy Muslim men on various charges of conspiracy and banned them from their palace (Owusu-Ansah 1987: interview with J.Agyeman-Duah, on the 6th of February 1984. Cited on p. 88). In 1829, the relationship between the Asante royal rulers and the *Nkramofoɔ* reached its lowest point after the king had executed the spokesman (*ɔkyeame*) Kwadwo Adusei Kyakye and many of his family members for planning a coup d'état. The Asante Kwadwo Adusei Kyakye had been a key figure in maintaining a good relationship with the Asante *Nkramofoɔ* and after his death many of these Muslims who as *nhenkwaa* had been part of the *gyaasewa* division of the Asante royal rulers left Kumasi. The Asante *Nkramofoɔ* continued to be barred from the Asante royal palace (*ahemfi*). The situation only changed in 1839 when under the reign of the ruling pair Kwaku Dua Panin (1834-1867) and *Asantehemma* Afia Sarpong (1835-1859), the *Nkramofoɔ* got involved in significant Asante politics. Nevertheless, these Asante royal rulers were also careful not to make the group of Asante *Nkramofoɔ* too powerful and when they established the Asante *Nkramo* Imamate in 1844 they deliberately did not recruit members of the remaining group of established Asante *Nkramofoɔ* in Kumasi. Instead, the Asante royal rulers invited the Asante imam Uthman Kamagatay, member of the Gbuipe Sakpare family form Daboya, whose Qur'an was copied in Buna, an important centre of Islamic scholarship to Kumasi. Under the reign of *Asantehene* Kwaku Dua Panin the Asante *Nkramofoɔ* were again allowed ac-

---

[47] A normative custom of the Prophet or of the early Muslim community, as set forth in the hadith (q.v.), which is the prophetic tradition; an account of what the Prophet said or did; second in authority to the Qur'an.

[48] Juula Muslims did not attempt to convert the Asante, nor were they fully passive towards the pagan religion of their rulers. They for instance tried to abolish the ritual killing of human beings by giving the example of sacrificing a sheep instead Levtzion, N. 1968. *Muslims and Chiefs in West Africa: A Study of Islam in the Middle Volta Basin in the Pre-Colonial Period*. Oxford: Clarendon Press.

cess to the compound of the palace to pray for the Asante royal rulers. By then, the Asante diplomatic apparatus was in the hands of the Asante princes Owusu Nkwantabisa and Owusu Ansa (Owusu-Ansah 1987; Wilks 1989 [first published in 1975]:316). Under the ruling pair Kofi Kakari (1867-1874) and Afia Kobi Serwaa Ampem I (1859-1884), the Asante *Nkramofoɔ* gained political influence and in 1873 they, for instance, advised the government to release the white missionaries in Kumasi, Bonnat, Kühne and the Ramseyers, as they did not believe that keeping those religious white men hostage would contribute to peace (Wilks 1989 [first published in 1975]:317).

The third group of Muslims that came to Kumasi in the precolonial period were the Hausa from the Sokoto Caliphate (currently known as northern Nigeria). Hausa Muslims were generally less welcomed by the Asante royal rulers to live and work in Kumasi, because of the orthodox form of Islam to which they adhered. After the 1830s these orthodox Muslims were restricted to Salaga and the markets north of the Volta (Lovejoy 1971:256-259). An exception is the case of Sharif Ibrahim, a Hausa Muslim who impressed the ruling duo Osei Bonsu and Ama Serwaa Nyaako with his 'great sanctity'. The Asante king asked Sharif Ibrahim to pray for an Asante victory in the campaign against Gyaman that was then being mounted, and also to accompany the armies in combat (Wilks 1961:27-28). Generally, regarding issues of religion there was less contact between the Asante royal rulers and the *Nkramofoɔ* than between these royal rulers and the Hausa Muslims, whose orthodox form of Islam was perceived by to be a threat to the Asante state. In 1803, *Asantehene* Osei Kwame (1777-1803) was, for instance, destooled to protect the Asante state. Osei Kwame had planned to become an orthodox Muslim and to make Islam the only religion of Asante society by 'his inclination to establish the Sharia as the civil code for the empire' (Wilks 1961:22). The kingmakers, and especially the *Asantehemma* Konadu Yaadom II , interpreted the *Asantehene*'s decision to convert to Islam as a threat to the community. They were afraid that it would mean that the *Odwira* festival would be prohibited because it contained, in the eyes of Muslims, pagan elements such as the ritual killing of human beings (Wilks 1966). In the eyes of the Asante royal rulers the prohibition of *Odwira* would weaken their position as this festival was organised yearly to venerate the royal ancestors and to legitimise the Asante state (McCaskie 1995:144-242). Islam continued to threaten the Asante royal rulers and AIR; sixty-six years later a British colonial official wrote that 'the fetish priests (the *akomfoɔ*) are beginning to lose their prestige, due to the spread of Islam, which already counts many adepts in Asante' (Hertz 1885:137 Cited in Wilks 1989, p. 318).

The main reason for the Asante royal rulers to adopt Islamic elements into their religion was to maintain a peaceful religious relationship with Muslims and to encourage their integration into Asante society. For this reason, the Muslims lived in multi-cultural and multi-religious communities in areas of Kumasi that were not distinct from other areas; they were also encouraged to speak Twi

(Schildkrout 1970:255; Robinson 2004:125). In a gesture of respect for Muslims the Asante royal rulers did not kill Islamic war captives, unlike other of their war captives and those avoiding persecution. As a result, Kumasi became the home of several Muslim refugees, such as *ɔkramoni* Muhammad-al-Ghamba, who had arrived in Kumasi in or shortly before 1807, to seek refuge from his relative, the ruler of Mamprusi (Wilks 1961:20). The *Asantehene* Osei Bonsu, who gave refuge to al-Ghama, also highly respected the fighting qualities of the Malinke Muslim cavalry. His bodyguard was a Malinke Muslim who seem to have been drawn from this cavalry (Wilks 1966).

In addition, the introduction of Islam and its accompanying patrilineal descent system threatened the continuation of the royal matrilineal system of descent. In the words of Dupuis 'the powerful chiefs in the capital feared, that the Moslem religion, which they well know levels all ranks and orders of men, and places them at the arbitrary discretion of the sovereign, might be introduced, whereby they would lose that ascendancy they now enjoy' (Dupuis 1824:245). Another restriction that the kingmakers might have put on the activities of Islamic religious leaders as part of a philosophy of accommodation and cooperation between Muslim and local non-Muslim communities, was on the building of spatially ostentatious mosques in and around Kumasi. Until at least the late 1840s, when the Asante royal rulers formed an official imamate in Kumasi, there is no record of such mosques in this town. This may be attributable to a deliberate Asante policy of preventing their construction in an effort to regulate the development of Islam. However, an explanation for the absence of these mosques may also lie in the ideology of the Suwarian tradition: many of the *Nkramofoɔ* in Kumasi believed that the building of mosques was unnecessary for the expression of their religious beliefs. The fact is that until at least the late 1840s there was no Friday mosque (*jami*) in Kumasi (Maier 1997:323-325). The building of mosques was more common among Hausa Muslims, who came to Kumasi at that time. Generally, because of the orthodox character of Hausa Islam, there was less syncretism between AIR and this form of Islam than that there was between the Asante Indigenous Religion and the Suwarian Islam of the *Nkramofoɔ*.

Examples of unaccepted forms of Hausa Islam by the Asante royal rulers were, for instance, the Hausa custom of male circumcision. The Asante royal rulers believed that the wholeness of the body was necessary for its transformation into an ancestral spirit, whereas this Islamic religious practice causes a mutilation of the body (Appiah 1990; McCaskie 2001:103-106). 'The practice of male circumcision was therefore prohibited as an "abominable thing" (*akyiwadeɛ*), for bodily incompleteness of any kind was deemed to be physically offensive and metaphysically dangerous' (McCaskie 2001:103). The prohibition of this practice by the Asante royal rulers did, however, not prevent Muslims from participating in the ritual of male circumcision; a practice that they find significant for the preservation of their Islamic identity in the land of the Asante infidels (*Dar-al-harb*).

A nineteenth century example of syncretism between AIR and the Suwarian tradition is, however, the capacity of Asante *akomfoɔ* to use Islamic forms of spiritual protection. McCaskie writes that 'by the first decade of the nineteenth century, Asante were familiar with writing in the form of letters, cabalistic formulae and quotations from the Qur'an' (McCaskie 1972:32). The Muslims bought amulets that contained Qur'anic quotations that served as charms to make their warrior clothes spiritually bulletproof. The Asante royal rulers copied this practice and wore vests that contained the protective powers of Islamic charms and amulets. These warrior cloths were known as *bata kari kese* and were believed to be 'war medicines' strong enough to kill all the inhabitants of the coast (Ramseyer, Kühne et al. 1875:241-250). In 1874, for instance, the ruling pair Osei Bonsu and Adoma Akosua wore *bata kari kese* during the Dwamen War to protect themselves against the evil spirits of the deceased enemies (Wilks 1989 [first published in 1975]; 1999).[49] Other forms of religious syncretism are evident: incorporation into the Twi language are words of expressions derived from the Muslims of Kumasi. The phrase such as small mosque (*Nyame dan*) and the expressions 'I will pray to God, I will go to the mosque' (*Me kɔ frɛ Nyame*) and 'to pray to God' (*Nyame fre*) all have Islamic origins (Christaller 1881). The duty of the Asante *Nkramofoɔ* to combine the Asante, the Christian and the Muslim calendars (Adjaye 1996:136-138) was also a form of religious syncretism.

3.6.2 The Christians

The focus of this section is the social and religious relationships between the Asante traditional authorities and Christian religious leaders in precolonial Asante. These relationships did not so much depend on the type of Christianity that was introduced in Asante but on British colonial politics. Because the European Christian Missionaries (ECMs) always joined forces with British colonial government servants, who aimed to bring civilisation to the Asante people, the Asante often perceived them as part of the same package (Bartels 1965:66-67). The Asante-Christian bond was thus controlled by the perceived trustworthiness in the eyes of the Asante royal rulers of the totality of the British colonial delegations that came to Kumasi. The Asante royal rulers who were in power during the visits of ECMs to Kumasi were respectively the royal state rulers Kwaku

[49] This is the war that *Asantehene* Osei Bonsu fought between 1811 and 1818 with the *Gyamanhene Adinkra*. The cause of the war was that *Adinkra* had illegally (as stated in the seventy-seven laws of *ɔkɔmfoɔ* Anokye in 1701) borrowed the idea of the Asante to make a replica of the Golden Stool, which was the symbol of the highest political authority. Wilks, I. 1989 [first published in 1975]. *Asante in the Nineteenth Century: The Structure and Evolution of a Political Order*. Cambridge: Cambridge University Press.

Dua Panin (1834-1867) and the female royal co-rulers Yaa Dufie (1824/33-35), and Afia Sarpong (1835-1859), and the ruling pair Kofi Kakari (1867-1874) and Afia Kobi Serwaa Ampem I (1867-1884), and the ruling duo Mensa Bonsu (1874-1883) who also ruled with Afia Kobi Serwaa Ampem I. After the reigns of these Asante royal rulers the relationship between the Asante and the British deteriorated. Since 1883, the Asante traditional rulers shifted their focus to internal politics as their kingdom became involved in a civil war. The situation only became better in 1894 with the enstoolments of the ruling pair Edward Agyeman Prempeh I and Konadu Yaadom II. Their policy was based on peace with the British for the purpose of trade.

Wilks (1989 [first published in 1975]) distinguishes two main political strategies of the Asante royal rulers who ruled in the nineteenth century. The policy of the majority of them, including the ruling pair Kwaku Dua Panin and Nana Afia Kobi Serwaa Ampem I, the *Asantehene* Mensa Bonsu and the still ruling pairs Afia Kobi Serwaa Ampem I, and the ruling duo Prempeh I and Konadu Yaadom II was to maintain peaceful political relationships with the British for the purpose of trade.[50] Others, such as the ruling duo Kofi Kakari and Afia Kobi Serwaa Ampem I, put emphasis on fighting wars. The latter Asante ruling pair aimed to control the Asante kingdom by imperialising tribute states and so created a buffer defence zone. The opinion of individual war or peace parties could be opposed to those of the Asante royal rulers; together with the parties they ruled the Asante state (*Asanteman*).

In relation to the reign of the above mentioned 'Dovish' (or peace oriented) and 'Hawkish' (or war oriented) Asante royal rulers and their parties, the author will discuss the relationship of the Asante royal rulers with religious leaders of the mainstream European Christian societies: the WMMS, the BMS, and the SAM. The Society for the Propagation of the Gospel (SPG) was dormant during most of the nineteenth century; the CEM was unsuccessful in entering Kumasi until 1913 and members of the North German Missionary Society (NGMS) never dared to come to the interior of the Asante kingdom until the 1890s.

Before the nineteenth century, none of the mentioned European Christian societies came to Kumasi. In order to reach the town, they would have had to travel through a dense forest, which would be a difficult trip with high costs and health risks. Because death rates among the Christian missionaries along the coast were very high, most of them simply did not make it as far as Kumasi. Besides, these missionaries who in the nineteenth century came to the interior often

[50] *Asantehemma* Nana Afia Kobi Serwaa Ampem I (1859-1884) reigned during the Asante *ahemfo* Kwaku Dua I, Kofi Kakari, Mensa Bonsu, and Kwaku Dua II. She was a full member and co-President of the governing body and she took part in important decisions. She was the mother of *Asantehene* Kofi Kakari and *Asantehene* Mensa Bonsu. *Asantehemma* Konadu Yaadom II (1917-1944) succeeded her mother *Asantehemma* Yaa Akyaa (1880-1917) and was followed on the post by her cousin Nana Ama Serwaa Nyakoo (1944-1977).

feared the Asante, because of their 'cruel customs', such as the ritual killing of human beings. Kumasi was therefore not an appropriate base for the first mission stations.

The ruling duo Kwaku Dua Panin (1834-1867) and Afia Kobi Serwaa Ampem I, however, welcomed Wesleyan and Basel missionaries to come, live and work in Kumasi, since they believed this was in the national interest of the Asante. In 1839, they welcomed the Wesleyan missionary T.B. Freeman to the royal court and gave him permission to hold in his presence, in the palace, a divine service, consisting of the singing of psalms and hymns, reading from the Bible and prayer (Unknown, the 25th of November 1961). In the same year, the Basel missionary A. Riis also came to Kumasi but after his experiences in the town, he was reluctant to work in the Asante kingdom (Reindorf 1966:288). Riis came back to Switzerland 'with the impression that he had to wait for better hints from the Lord' (Letter of 18 Dec. 1877, from the Rev. F. Ramseyer to Freeling, referring to the journey to Kumasi in 1839 by the Rev. A. Riis; CO/96/122). In 1841 Freeman came back to Kumasi along with his colleague, Robert Brookling and the two Asante princes Owusu Ansa and Nkwantabisa. The British in Kumasi hosted these princes, who were trained in the United Kingdom to become Wesleyan missionaries. Prince Ansa helped Freeman to start a small Wesleyan school and congregation and then returned to Kumasi leaving Rev Brookling in charge of the Kumasi mission (Reindorf 1966:230-231; Arhin, Afari-Gyan et al. 1992:55-57). In 1843, Freeman went back to the Asante kingdom and established a Mission station near Kumasi. In 1845, Freeman returned to Kumasi as General Superintendent of the WMMS on the Gold Coast. Despite all the courteous exchanges between Freeman and the *Asantehene* from 1839 onwards, the mission station had little success. Freeman, however, maintained faith in his mission to bring the Gospel to the Asante people and on the 4th of January 1842 he wrote about his meeting with the *Asantehene* Kwaku Dua Panin.

> We had a long conversation on Christianity, and civilisation: I pointed out the advantages resulting there from, and answered several important questions on these subjects. One objection, which had been raised in his mind respecting education, was, the danger of it making people rebellious; in which, I found, Apoko and other chiefs encouraged him. I told him, that in education, as well as in all other good things, there was a possibility of abuse; and that there would, doubtless, be a few unfavourable exceptions; but that, in general, it had a tendency to make the people more dutiful, and more obedient. He saw the propriety of my remarks, and said he would consult the Chiefs on the subject of sending their children to school. Thus far, all our negotiations are promising. O thou God of Mission! give thine own work success in his benighted land! (Freeman 1844:150-151).

The *Asantehene* allowed the missionaries to settle in Kumasi, because of missionary schools brought education to the Asante in diplomacy and preserved peaceful Anglo-Asante relationships. The Asante ruling pair were, however, also afraid of the introduction of Christianity into the Asante kingdom, because

Christians were opposed to and attempted to abolish the ritual killing of human beings. *Asantehene* Kwaku Dua Panin, however, perceived this ritual as 'the most effective means of keeping my [Kwaku Dua Panin's] people in subjection' (Freeman 1844:164). Then years later, Rev Laing reported that the *Asantehene* Kwaku Dua Panin did not encourage the Asante to become Christians. Many Asante were afraid to convert to Christianity, because their king did not support this religion, and, as a result they were afraid to expose themselves to his ire (Reindorf 1966: quotation 235).

In the period 1850-1876, the relationship between the Asante and the ECMs deteriorated and after 1850 all of them had left Kumasi. Prince Owusu Ansa was left to carry on his missionary work single-handedly and it was not until 1852 that Rev. Timothy Laing arrived in Kumasi to help him. In 1853 Prince Ansa left Kumasi to become a Wesleyan minister in the Gold Coast district (Owusu-Mensa 1974). From 1853 until the remainder of Kwaku Dua's reign, 'missionaries continued to be allowed into the capital, but their activities were carefully supervised: the government utilised their services as mediators with the British while at the same time minimising the impact they might have had upon metropolitan society' (Wilks 1989 [first published in 1975]:559). Between 1862 and 1879 for instance, the Wesleyan missionary J.S.Watts had an official appointment as councillor in the English chancery and helped the Asante government and the Asante royal rulers to compose letters to the British for diplomatic purposes. Because Watts was in an official and in a sensitive position he was prevented from engaging in private, unsanctioned correspondence, especially at a time when security decisions and preparations regarding war were being made, as they were in 1867 (Adjaye 1996:152-153). *Asantehene* Kofi Kakari had a more positive attitude towards ECMs than his predecessor Kwaku Dua Panin but was also pleased by the diplomatic skills of those missionaries and the possibility of using them as *ad hoc* chancery officials when the permanent members of the English chancery were away.[51] Ramseyer and Kühne were held captive in Kumasi for four years and during those years Kakari asked Ramseyer for example, to draft letters for him whenever necessary, which was something he could not ask his Asante subjects to do since they did not possess the right ambassadorial skills and fluency in the English language (Adjaye 1996:153-154). The ruling duo Kofi Kakari and Afia Kobi Serwaa Ampem I treated their prisoners well and they gave them a small allowance for living expenses and goods in

[51] The *ad hoc* ambassador represented the official who, without being a career diplomat, was appointed to a special mission. His appointment terminated with the conclusion of the mission. If he was a regular diplomatic office holder, he would revert to his former position at the end of his diplomatic assignment. While all career ambassadors were invariably Asantes, appointment as an ad hoc ambassador was not contingent upon Asante citizenship Adjaye, J. K. 1996. *Diplomacy and Diplomats in Nineteenth Century Asante*. Trenton and New York: Africa World Press.

the form of presents (Ramseyer, Kühne et al. 1875:73-74).[52] They also made time to hear the Gospel from them and they got the king's permission to establish a school with ten pupils near Kumasi, which they believed would be beneficial for the education of the youth.[53] Adu Bafo, the head of the war party, wanted the British to pay eight hundred *peredwans* for the release of the Basel missionaries, because he felt that the British had not kept to the Asante-British 'Treaty of Peace' of 1831 (Wilks 1989 [first published in 1975]:497-504).[54] The Asante ruling pair Kakari and Afia Kobi Serwaa Ampem I did, however not want to abandon the Asante custom of ritually killing human beings and like the *Asantehene*'s predecessor; Kwaku Dua Panin who also reigned together with Afia Kobi Serwaa Ampem I, they feared the effects of Christianity would put an end to their time-honoured customs.

The ruling pair Mensa Bonsu (1874-1883) and Afia Kobi Serwaa Ampem I also seem to have appreciated the diplomatic services of the Wesleyan missionaries and equally felt that Asante royal rulers should get involved in the introduction of Christianity. On the 10th of April 1876, the request of a Wesleyan missionary James Picot, for the re-establishment of a station in Kumasi became part of a debate between the peace and war parties in the Council of Kumasi. Mensa Bonsu indicated that the Wesleyans were welcome if, like Thomas Freeman, they 'helped the peace of the nation and the prosperity of trade' (MMA, London: Picot to Boyce, dd. Cape Coast, the 3rd of May 1876). The ruling Asante royal rulers, who were aware of the sensitivity of the topic among their subjects, remarked that missionary schooling was not a good idea. They believed that children had to work and that the customs of the Asante were not compatible with Christianity. The *Bantamahene*, a member of the peace party, added that polygamy and slavery could not and should not be abolished in Asante. The war party headed by Adu Bofo declared that they would never accept Christianity and would remain true to the ways of their forefathers. Bofo's intervention in the council proved decisive and consequently Picot's proposal was rejected (Wilks 1989 [first published in 1975]:518-519). Yet the missionary issue continued to polarise political opinion throughout the remainder of the nineteenth century. 'In March 1881, for example, the ruling Asante royal rulers bowed again to the

---

[52] On 25 May 1870, for instance, Ramseyer and his wife received from the king a couple of sheep, and an old pair of Dutch military shoes, accompanied by a pair of boots for Mrs. Ramseyer of English make, and the finest leather. They had been presented by the Wesleyan missionary Freeman in 1842, to the reigning sovereign, and inscribed on the soles in gilt letters were the following words-'To his Royal Highness, Quakoo Dooah, king of Ashantee, West Africa'.

[53] Ramseyer also attempted to open a Basel mission station and a school immediately in Kumasi. Unfortunately, the Basel Mission Home Committee did not grant this wish and he had to wait for some twenty years.

[54] In this Treaty the Asante and the British agreed that refugees from the Asante kingdom to the Fante coast and *vice versa* would be sent back for punishment under the law of the area where they came from. As a consequence of their Christian belief, the British, however, repeatedly refused to send back run away slaves whom they believed would be ritually killed once back in the Asante kingdom.

more liberal councillors and expressed their desire for the reestablishment of schools and a station in Kumasi' (Lewin 1978:67). Their response to Ramseyer's presentation of the Bible that year, and to other Wesleyan missionaries at earlier and later dates clearly indicates that the Asante royal rulers did not welcome these missionaries. An Asante chief repeated his king's answer to the missionaries in 1876 that:

> The Bible is not a book for us. God at the beginning gave the Bible to the White people, another book to the Cramos [Muslims] and the fetish to us. If God requires a human sacrifice or a sheep, he tells our fetishes and they tell us and we give them. We know God already ourselves, and we cannot do without human sacrifice...we will never embrace your religion, for it would make our people proud. It is your religion which has ruined the Fante country, weakened their power, and brought down the high man on a level with the low man (Findlay and Holdsworth 1921:175).

A factor that increased the difficulty for ECMs in bringing the Gospel to Asante was that Christianity was increasingly associated with colonisation and European culture and lifestyle. Their presence was consequently perceived to be a threat to the persistence of the Asante state, especially in the remote areas of the Asante kingdom which were semi-autonomous and fell under less of the Asante royal rulers' control (Lewin 1978:85-111; Wilks 1989 [first published in 1975]).

In 1880, unlike the protestant missionaries of the ECMs, the ruling duo Mensa Bonsu and Afia Kobi Serwaa Ampem I also welcomed the Catholic priests August Moreau and Eugene Murat of the SAM, who were the first Roman Catholics in Asante history to travel to Kumasi. In the tense years before the civil war of 1883 the Asante royal rulers welcomed these Catholic missionaries, but not their Protestant colleagues who were less sensitive to AIR. The Protestants condemned AIR and many Catholic practices, whereas the Roman Catholic cult of the saints was compatible with the Asante practices of ancestral veneration. The Roman Catholics therefore seemed much less of a threat to the persistence of the Asante religion and their chieftaincy institution. The Catholic priests, like Moreau, did their very best to learn Twi, the language of the Asante, even though until the Second Vatican Council, the Church's Latin liturgy of 1963, the Roman Catholics did not encourage much contextualisation of veneration into the local cultures (Fisher 1998:173-177). In correspondence to his SMA colleague Fr. Augustine Planque Moreau said:

> We must give continuous attention to the study of the language. The say it's a matter of six months. Once we know it we can think of spreading out and penetrating among the Ashantis (Letter to Fr. Planque, the 23rd of May 1880 in AMA 15/802.02.19.184).

Four months later Moreau wrote to Planque

> I hardly have time to write. I spend it all studying the language without which we will never be able to do anything in this country. Unfortunately, there are so many difficulties; fever and other distractions have taken up so much of my time that till now I have made only small progress (Letter to Fr. Planque, the 10th of September 1880 in AmA 15/802.02.19.184).

Of practical use to the Asante was Moreau's knowledge on healthcare, for which he received praise. Moreau:

> [...] Every time I passed the night in a village, I asked if there were any sick. In a short while I would be surrounded by dozens of individuals. A little medicine and ointment for the wounds were all they asked for, and I got the reputation of being a great doctor. On my return journey all who had already seen me did not fail to come and thank me. [...] I love the Ashanti's with all my missionary heart, and my greatest desire is to consecrate my life to them. Pray with me that the light may dawn over this great people (*Report*, the 16th of June 1882, in *AMA* 15/802.02 19.222).

Therefore, initially the ruling pair Mensa Bonsu and Afia Kobi Serwaa Ampem I welcomed Protestant missionaries of the Wesleyan and Basel Missionary Societies, because of their useful diplomatic skills. In 1880, when Asante-British relations became tenser, they only allowed Roman Catholic missionaries to enter Kumasi, because they were more understanding of Asante religious practitioners than their Protestant colleagues. By that time, the English chancery, which was part of the Asante diplomatic service, had educated several Asante to be proficient in English and to become familiar with British modes of diplomacy and knowledge of the Gold Coast and Asante affairs. Consequently, it was no longer necessary to ask the Christian missionaries, whose loyalty to the Asante royal rulers was often questionable, to fulfil the task of diplomats on an *ad hoc* basis.

Between 1883 and 1888, the Asante were plagued by a civil war. During that period the Asante government was highly unstable, and an interim government (*kwasafomanhyiamu*) ruled the kingdom (the 8th of March 1883 to the 28th of April 1884).[55] On the 26th of March 1888, *Asantehene* Edward Agyeman Prempeh I was elected to become *Asantehene* but not formally enthroned until six years later. In the eyes of the Asante he remained in this role until the 12th of May 1931. In practice, in 1897 the British deported Prempeh I to Sierra Leone together with Konadu Yaadom II. In 1901 they were sent even further away to the Seychelles Islands, only to return home in 1924 with the statuses of private citizens. The British re-enstooled *Asantehene* Prempeh I in 1924 as *Kumasihene* or paramount chief of Kumasi, and from a British point of view he remained in this position until 1931 (Adjaye 1989:223). Under John Owusu Ansa Jr., the son of John Owusu Ansa Sr., the Asante royal rulers developed a diplomatic service with Asante diplomats, who were well skilled and experienced in their negotiations with the British. These diplomats were not permanently working for Owusu Ansa, but came with him on diplomatic missions. The embassy to London of 1894-1895 was, for instance, composed of Owusu Ansa's brother Albert, Kwame Boaten, Kwaku Fokuo, Kwaku Nkrumah, Kwabena Bonna, Akyampon Daban and Kwadwo Tufuo, all of whom had a good reputation in the diplomatic

[55] The Asante ruling pair were Kwaku Dua II and Konadu Yaadom II (the 28th of April 1884 to the 11th of July 1884), Owusu Kofi (June 1884 to Nov 1884) Akyampon Panyin (Nov 1884 to 1887), Owusu Sekyere II (1887 to the 26th of March 1888).

service (Adjaye 1996:125). Consequently, the Asante royal rulers never had to make use of the Christian missionaries for their negotiations with the British. In the years before their departure, the Asante royal rulers were very reluctant to let in any of these missionaries; they feared an increase in the white men's (*aborofo*) influence on the religious ideas of their subjects would lead to the eventual fall of the Asante kingdom. In 1896, it became clear that their fear had become reality, when after arrival in London, the British refused to cooperate with the Asante mission, already having decided to send a military expedition to the Asante kingdom in order to annexate it and make Asante subservient to the British Crown (Adjaye 1996:124-131).

After the exile of the ruling pair Edward Agyeman Prempeh I and Konadu Yaadom II, the administration of the Kumasi state remained in the hands of Asante chiefs (Kwadwo 2000, 2nd edition). In consultation with these chiefs, the British welcomed the Christian missionaries in Kumasi and opened the city for their religious activity. Consequently, in 1899, the BMS had opened sixteen centres in the Asante kingdom, with a total of 164 church members and 451 scholars; the WMMS then had 1,500 church attendants and 675 scholars (in Sunday and day schools) in eight centres, and 7,600 Asante converts. Then in 1900, came the Asante revolt, in the course of which most of the churches were destroyed. However, in 1901, Rev. Frederick A. Lees, a Basel missionary, and John B. Baiden, Assistant African Minister, were given a cheerful welcome in Kumasi. They built a new mission station and at the end of 1902, there were thirty-two Asante converts. Since then the story of the Basel Asante mission was one of steady growth and development in the usual pattern of chapels, Sunday schools and day schools (Kimble 1963:153-154; Wyllie 1980:5-6).

In terms of the religious relationship between the Asante royal rulers and Christians, the royal rulers attempted, and to a certain extent succeeded, to limit the influence of Christianity on Asante society by only allowing the inclusion of elements of this religion. These limitations that were put on the acceptance of religious ideas in Asante society were part of the strategies of the royal rulers to protect the Asante kingdom from falling apart. An example of syncretism between AIR and Christianity on the element level is the coexistence of traditional and Christian marriage rituals. According to AIR a prospective husband should pay a 'knocking fee' (*abowmubodeɛ*), which symbolises the promise to marry a girl. Due to the influence of Christianity on Asante customary marriage rites, they came to include the giving of an engagement ring and a Bible, even in cases where parties were non-Christians. The *abowmubodeɛ,* the Bible and the ring were status symbols. As a result of Christian influences, many marriages also became monogamous, whereas traditionally they were polygamous. However, to secure offspring many Asante who had converted to Christianity married one wife but kept a number of concubines. Christianity also influenced the death rituals of the Asante. Traditionally, upon the death of a chief some citizens were killed with a view to their serving the deceased chief on the other side. The idea was that life in the spiritual world is a replica of life in the social world. Under the ruling pair Edward Agyeman Prempeh I, and Konadu Yaadom II, ritual killings of human beings were no longer carried out. Secondly, often in addition to indigenous religious rites, a church service was also held (Pobee and Mends 1977:6-8; Adjaye 1996).

Asante royal rulers attempted to put limitations on the influence of Christianity, because they were afraid it would negatively affect AIR and the persistence of Asante chieftaincy. The introduction by ECMs of monogamous marriages and the abolition of the custom of the ritual killing of human beings had a great impact on AIR and on the concomitant legitimatisation of *Asanteman*. After all, polygamy secured the sustenance of the royal lineage, and the Asante royal rulers used the ritual killing of human beings to keep people in subjugation. Christianity was also a threat to the Asante royal rulers, because the Christian missionaries undermined their authority. By introducing Christianity and European clothing they created Asante communities with 'modern' Asante identities, whose members distinguished themselves from the rest of Asante society and lived in separate parts of town (*sarem*). Instead of listening to the Asante royal rulers, the members of those communities now listened to the Christian missionaries, whose beliefs undermined kinship solidarity. In particular, the Wesleyan Christian congregations demonstrated a conscious opposition to the ancestral way of life and thought of the rest of the community. The great majority of these missionaries stemmed from Pietistic circles in the Wurttemberg Church in which the primary emphasis was laid on personal devotion to Christ and on experiential religion. The basic principle was to work together with Christ and spread the kingdom of God on earth, to bring individuals in touch with the saving grace of Christ and to build the converts into new Christian societies (Kimble 1963). The Basel missionaries showed little respect for the indigenous traditions and its practitioners. Referring to an Asante indigenous believer, the Basel missionary Ringwald for instance wrote: 'See this stupid man. He calls and receives no answer; he brings the fetish something and the fowls feed on it (Ringwald 1952:135).'

From the perspective of the Asante royal rulers, the foundation by Basel missionaries of separate Christian communities and their condemnation of AIR made these missionaries rivals for political and religious power in Asante society. Some Asante converted to Christianity to escape from the authority of the Asante royal rulers and the duties that derived from the regulations set during the foundation of the Asante kingdom, the so called Seventy-Seven Laws of *ɔkɔmfoɔ* Anokye.[56] Conversion to Christianity was especially attractive for

[56] One of *ɔkɔmfoɔ* Anokye's laws says that Thursday is a day of rest on which no one should farm. This aspect of AIR caused a clash with the religious belief of Christian missionaries who reserved Sunday as a day of rest. See for more on the laws of Anokye: Kyerematen, A. 1969. "The royal Stools of Ashanti," *Africa: Journal of the International African Institute* 39(1): 1-10.

groups within Asante society who fell outside the *jural corpus*, such as slaves, princes who could not become royal rulers, and barren women. The BMS attracted a lot of these Asante because they could offer them a higher social status; in the case of slaves, they could prevent them from being ritually killed. The Asante royal rulers were therefore especially reluctant to allow Basel missionaries to establish themselves in Asante society and spread their ideas (Middleton 1983:4-7; McCaskie 1995; Quartey 2007:149-157).

It has been argued that the Asante royal rulers were peacekeepers, who made use of AIR to maintain peace in both social and religious spheres with Islamic and Christian religious leaders and their followers. Christianity and Islam were internalised into Asante society in different ways: the former was only received for pragmatic reasons, namely to educate Asante to be able to work for the English chancery of the Asante diplomatic service. The Bible was not believed to bring any good to Asante society. Islam, on the contrary, was believed to increase the authority of the Asante royal rulers, who believed that the words that were written in the Qur'an were spiritually powerful. The Qur'an was incorporated into AIR as a ritual object (as the Portuguese said 'a fetish') that contained spiritual power and could protect those who were in touch with its content. The Asante royal rulers thus dealt with the Qur'an as if it was a shrine that contained spirit, like their royal stools.

3.7 Conclusion

Precolonial Asante was a mytho-poeic society. Spirits were believed to live on Earth in between the living, and to be tangible and sometimes visible. The relationship of the Asante royal rulers and *akɔmfoɔ* with the ancestral spirits or the *abosom* was established in flows of closure and flows of openness, connected to a sacred space, an elsewhere. Each Asante subject maintained a relationship with the spirits and their ancestors, but only those of the Asante royal rulers were collectively venerated. The Asante royal rulers and their *akɔmfoɔ* were praised for their extraordinary minds; their spiritual ability reached that space of in-betweenness where mediums and spirits meet, where ordinary Asante subjects could only reach in their dreams. Their spokesmen were admired for their use of eloquent silences, narratives, poems and proverbs and maxims, which they used to translate the message of the spirits to their audience. The Asante gave agency to the spirits and acted (e.g. during wars) according to their insights. In Asante eyes, their higher insights came from the spirits. The higher truths had their origin in the spiritual realm that was inhabited by beings that were believed to be more intelligent than humans and who were unhindered by the deceptiveness of the senses. The Islamic (*Nkramofoɔ*) priests, who combined their literary skill with enchanting oratory based on the script of the Qur'an were believed to possess powerful words with magic potency that could kill those who would turn themselves against Muslims; those who had sworn an oath upon the

Qur'an or used charms and amulets filled with magic formulae derived from this Holy Book could achieve invincibility. Since the eighteenth century, the *Nkramofoɔ* priests were most welcome in Kumasi at the Asante royal court as helpers in matters of religious mediation. Nevertheless, the Asante *Nkramofoɔ* lived in a semi-separated area of town (the *zongo*) under the authority of the Asante royal rulers. Orthodox Hausa Muslims had great difficulties with significant elements of AIR such as the killing of human beings and ancestral veneration. Besides, they felt obliged to convert the Asante infidels to Islam, which the Asante royal rulers perceived as a threat to the persistence of their kingdom.

In the nineteenth century, European Christian missionaries established themselves in Kumasi and succeeded in founding some churches and missionary schools and stations. The Bible, however, never became as popular as the Qur'an did in precolonial Asante as a Holy Book and a source of spiritual power. European Missionary Christianity was incompatible with the Asante indigenous belief in an elsewhere accessible by specialists in invoking spiritual beings and in foretelling future events with the belief that these beings could provide them with insights in the hidden affairs of the world. The Asante gave agency to the spirits and used their advice to make political decisions, such as the waging of wars. The Asante believed that human beings were in constant need of help of the spirits, and were dependent on them for their prosperity. The high fertility of women and a good harvest were believed to be the result of the fortunate agency of spiritual beings, caused by people's propitiation of the spirits. Asante society was therefore built on the principle of a relationship of reciprocity with the spiritual beings. Neglecting the wishes of those beings by not venerating them was deemed disastrous for the community in term of harvest and fertility. In the eyes of the Asante royal rulers, the persistence of chieftaincy was therefore believed to be dependent on the continuation of the maintenance of a good relationship with the spirits by venerating them during ritual calendar days (*adae*), by not breaking the oath of allegiance to the Golden Stool and by protecting that Stool against its destruction. Despite a number of bad omens, like the death of the Kum tree that was followed by the great fire in Kumasi, and the loss of the last significant Anglo-Asante war in 1900 the Asante royal rulers were convinced that the fall of their kingdom did not threaten the existence of their traditional political institution. As long as the Golden Stool was not destroyed, Asante chieftaincy was destined to persist.

The Asante royal rulers made use of the symbols of the Asante Indigenous Religion, such as the Golden Stool (*Sika Dwa Kofi*) to create unity. The Golden Stool symbolised the common source of spirituality and ancestral heritage, and legitimised the religious-political power of the Asante royal rulers, who were the first inhabitants of the ancestral land. Like the tree of reception (*ogyedua*) the *Sika Dwa Kofi* also symbolised a sacred space where the spirits could cool down and the spiritual energy could flow openly between the ancestors, the clans and individuals. The feeling of spiritual unity enabled the Asante subjects to work for a common goal and to maintain in a relationship of reciprocity to their chiefs, e.g. by paying tribute and rendering services for free, such as communal labour in exchange for protection and free meals at the palace. The Asante royal rulers expected reciprocity and loyalty of their subjects and the ancestral spiritual source of their power enabled them to gain consent among their subjects to rule by coercive force. The relationship of Asante subjects and chiefs with the spiritual beings was not only one of the principles of *do ut des* (*dan won a wo ama*), but also one of fear for the wraths of the spirits, who were believed to be superior to mankind. The Asante royal rulers felt responsible for maintaining a good relationship with the spirits and their subjects out of fear that the spiritual energy inside the stool would kill them. Their subjects feared for the spiritual power of the chiefs and especially the *Asantehene* who had the exclusive right to execute those of them who had been disobedient to one or more of the Seventy-Seven of Anokye's customary laws. The death penalty was also given to those captives or slaves who were obliged to serve in the Asante army and had demonstrated cowardice. In this political sphere of constant fear for spiritual forces and royal rulers, the Asante royal rulers nevertheless aimed to maintain peaceful relationships with their subjects, and the Muslims and Christians within their society. Religiously, they therefore allowed elements of Roman Catholicism and the Islam of the moderate Asante *Nkramofoɔ* into AIR. In terms of Berner's model of religious syncretism, the Asante precolonial period was characterised by a C2 process of elementary religious syncretism. In the C2 process, religious syncretism only occurred through the process of incorporating elements of other religions into AIR (Berner 2004). To control the extent in which Christians and Muslims could influence the religious basis of power of the Asante royal rulers, they were made to live in semi-separate areas in town and the Asante royal rulers restrained their commercial activities. Although represented by their rulers, the religious foreigners lived under the authority of the Asante royal rulers and were obliged to obey Anokye's customary laws. Nevertheless, the Asante royal rulers demonstrated their respect for the religious practices of Christians and Muslims. In relation to their peacekeeping function, the Asante royal rulers felt that Asante chieftaincy would persist as long as they succeeded in the control and protection of the spiritual source of their religious-political power. Their admiration for the literacy of the Asante *Nkramofoɔ*, the power of the magic formulae derived from the Qur'an, and their oratory skills convinced the Asante royal rulers that their connection with these Muslims would increase their spiritual power and would not cause a serious threat to the persistence of their political institution. The Muslims in Asante therefore remained foreigners and they were not represented in the Asante councils. Only a hand full of Asante was converted to Islam and mass conversion to Christianity did not take place before the foundation of the Crown Colony of Asante in 1902.

In conclusion, both during and at the end of the precolonial period the indigenous religious mediatory and peacekeeping function of the Asante royal rulers contributed positively to the persistence of Asante chieftaincy despite the fall of the Asante kingdom. In the next and following chapters, the author will attempt to answer the crucial question of to what extent the Asante traditional authorities continued to perform an indigenous religious mediatory and peace-keeping function in the Kumasi metropolis in the colonial (Chapter IV) and postcolonial periods (Chapters V and VI). The question that will be posed is if in these subsequent periods AIR remained the religious-political bases of power of the Asante royal rulers or whether Asante chieftaincy became an empty shell, an institution based on pride and pomp, meant for the entertainment of various external interest groups. If this latter scenario has become a reality, the earlier mentioned Asante rituals and the artefacts of the Asante royal rulers will have lost their religious meaning and will be dissociated from the Asante belief in the ancestors and the *abosom*, who inhabit the sacred but earthly space within the Asante universe.

Chapter IV: Indigenous religious mediation and peacekeeping in the colonial period

Nsuom nam firi nsuom a, ɔwu, ɔhene a ɔnni akyitaafoɔ no ɔnyɛ ɔhene bio – 'A fish out of water dies; a king without followers ceases to exist'.

Asante proverb

4.1. Introduction

In this chapter, the focus will be on how Asante royal rulers were able to engage in mediation and peacekeeping during the colonial period of Asante history (1901-1957). To gain an insight into these roles a short overview will be provided of the form of Asante chieftaincy in the Kumasi metropolis in this historical period. In the words of the mythical spider Kwaku Anansi, one can say that the colonial period was the time when 'Water' came in, which symbolises radical social change (Brookins 2003).[57]

4.2. The form of Asante chieftaincy in the colonial period

In the colonial period, two chieftaincy institutions developed in Asante: a resurrected Kumasi Council of Chiefs (KCC) – and the Asante Confederacy. The ruling pair Edward Agyeman Prempeh I and Konadu Yaadom II were the founders of the new KCC. King Prempeh I officially ruled between the 26th of March 1888 and the 12th of May 1931, but was deported by the British in 1896. The Asante Confederacy (*Amantoonum*) was founded under the decree of Prempeh II, who reigned between the 22nd of June 1931 and the 27th of May 1970, and his female co-rulers Konadu Yaadom II and her successor Ama Serwaa Nyaako.

In theory, from 1905, the politics of the British had implied that traditional Asante royal rulers would be able to continue to rule over the Kumasi metropolis in cooperation with a CCA who controlled the decisions of the Council of Kumasi. In practice, however, after the deportation of the ruling pair Prempeh I and Konadu Yaadom II, there was a power vacuum in Kumasi. The British filled these positions with chiefs who they enstooled as a reward for their collaboration with them during campaign against Asante (McCaskie 1986a:10-11). After the structural although not functional resurrection of the Council of Kumasi in 1905, the status of the Asante rulers depended on their membership of this Council. Consequently, some *omanhene* under the *Asantemanhyiamu* and the original Council of Kumasi, no longer maintained their political status. Other chiefs who

[57] For more on the persistence of Asante chieftaincy in colonial Ghana see: Müller, L.F. 2011b. "The Persistence of Asante Chieftaincy in the Colonial Period (1896-1957): Explanations For An Enigma." *Africana Studia* **14**(2): 61-85.

were hitherto not considered by their subjects were elevated to these newly-created positions by the British colonisers. Newly enstooled Asante chiefs filled many of the positions in the KCC and formed part of a highly self-consciously defined group of notables, capitalists and gentlemen (*akonkofoɔ*). The *akonkofoɔ* were neither necessarily literate nor Christian. They defended the individual right to accommodate and dispose of capital, and acquired their own cocoa farms; they invested their profits in buildings in Kumasi, and the other main towns in the Crown Colony of Asante that they then let to business firms for rental gains. They invested in buying chiefly stools whose purchase was also a way to maximise the opportunity for profit. Their 'this-worldly' aim of accumulating private wealth was to advance their power and prestige. They hoped to join the ancestors in the other-world by showing that they had played an important role in Asante society during their lives, prerequisites for becoming ancestral spirits. On the one hand, the *akonkofoɔ* appeared revolutionary in terms of shaking off the constraints of historical ideology surrounding accumulation, wealth and belief (based on exploitation); they were similar to the *asikafo* in 1888. On the other hand, they were adherents of AIR and did not oppose the meaning of indigenous religious symbols, such as the *Sika Dwa Kofi* and the *ɔhemma Dwa* or *Dwete* Stool (McCaskie 1986a:7-10).

Since 1905 the KCC kept busy with the administration of Kumasi and with questions of stool-land and their possession.[58] After the deportation of the ruling pair however, they could not curtail the governmental chaos in Kumasi (Tordoff 1965:152). The establishment of the KCC precipitated the end of central government in Kumasi, as the political chaos within administrative bodies made it impossible to rule over the whole of the Crown Colony of Asante from this town. Consequently, colonised Asante became divided into four different areas and members of the KCC ruled over only three of the four of these areas. This policy corresponded with the British *laissez-faire* approach, which they had used to rule over the Crown Colony of Asante since its foundation in 1902. The CCA 'was answerable to the Gold Coast Governor and was, except in major matters, subject to little interference from either Accra or London' (Tordoff 1968:155). The area that comprised Greater Kumasi, however, fell under the direct leadership of a CCA. The British preferred this form of leadership in relation to Kumasi because this town was believed to be most dangerous for a possible uprising of Asante (anti-colonial!) nationalism. The ruling duo, who was never officially destooled, invented the title of *Kumasihene* or paramount chief of Kumasi to make clear to their people that after their repatriation in 1924, they were no longer the rulers of the whole living area of the Asante people but merely the rulers of just one division (Kumasi). The title of *Kumasihene* had not existed before, because from the start of the foundation of the Asante union at the end of the seventeenth century, the rulers of Kumasi were known as the rul-

[58] 'Stool-land' is land that belongs to a chief's 'stool' or throne.

ing pair, since they ruled over the whole of the Asante kingdom and not only Kwaman and its capital Kumasi. Initially, the ruling pair of Kwaman had the same position as all other paramount *omanhene* and *omanhemma* in the Asante union, but from 1701 onwards, their position became *primus-inter-pares*, meaning one-among-many and was thus no longer equal to those of other *amanhene* and *amanhemma*. The title of *Kumasihene* was meant to imply, that the ruler of Kumasi was now as powerful as all other Asante *amanhene* and *amanhemma*.

The members of the KCC were divided about the desirability of the situation of direct rule of Kumasi by a CCA, and about the nature of British colonisation of Asante in general. Many traditional authorities were against British influence, and worked on the particulars of the Anglo-Asante peace treaties to bring back their royal duo from the Seychelles Islands to Kumasi to rule not only over Kumasi but also over the rest of the Asante Crown Colony. The newly enstooled Asante chiefs, on the other hand, who owed their position to the British, supported the British in diminishing the political and spiritual influence of the ruling duo in the colony.

In the meantime in the Seychelles Islands, the royal pair did everything to make sure that the British would allow them to return to the Cold Coast colony. In 1904, the exiled Asante royal rulers therefore became Christians. To prove that his conversion was sincere, the Asante king also opted to be monogamous.

> Prempeh's relocations [LM: his exiles to Sierra Leone and later the Seychelles Islands] impressed upon him the territorial scope of British influence and power. He became aware that only British goodwill could ensure his return to Asante. He decided on a policy of appeasement: he would demonstrate to the British government that he had become a loyal and 'civilised' subject (Akyeampong 1999:290).

Asantehene Agyeman Prempeh I divorced two of the three wives who were deported with him, as 'he discovered to his chagrin that polygamy ruled out his being confirmed as a Christian and partaking in the holy communion', and having more than one wife would militate against his desire to appear loyal and 'modern' to the British (Akyeampong 1999:296). His conversion to Christianity and his change of lifestyle were partly strategic and worked in his favour. On the 12th of May 1924 the ruling pair was informed via the officer in charge of political exiles that the Colonial Secretary (CS) had approved their repatriation to Kumasi as long as they would return as 'private' citizens and would reside within the political district of Kumasi. To some degree, an inner transformation had indeed occurred within the ruling duo, who due to missionary education had become 'modernised', and attempted to reconcile their understandings of AIR with Christianity. On his return to Kumasi, however, Agyeman Prempeh I became a different type of Christian from the one he was during his stay in the Seychelles Islands. Back home the king ceased being monogamous, he revived his royal harem, and took many wives and concubines (Akyeampong 1999:303-304). Prempeh I thereby restored an ancient Asante tradition of polygamy among Asante royal rulers, and argued that according to the Asante law – the *Asantehene* was 'allowed 3333 wives' (Bowdich 1819:289). The absence of Prempeh I in Kumasi had not resulted in the extinction of polygamy and the indigenous tradition continued to help to sustain the lineage and to satisfy the ancestral spirits. Prempeh I believed that he had been allowed to return to Kumasi because he had shown in the Seychelles Islands that he had modernised himself, and that he was loyal to the British and had adopted the British lifestyle. According to British sources, however, the ruling pair was repatriated at the initiative of the BG Sir Gordon Guggisberg who was in favour of the application to Asante of the principles of Indirect Rule.[59] Guggisberg hoped that his type of European colonial policy would improve the relationship between the rulers of former Kumasi villages (*odikro*), which was necessary because the foundation of the KCC had led to a deterioration of the relationship between subjects and their rulers. The villagers, who were placed under an *akonkofoɔ* chief and his female co-ruler, had often proved reluctant to serve Guggisberg, particularly when the Asante royal rulers in question owed their elevation to the administration. In many villages such as Offinso and Ejisu, the rulers and people were embittered at the removal of their traditional rulers and the elders. They – and many other Asante – resented the loss of their independence and the undermining of established customs and AIR. In 1926, Sir Gordon Guggisberg outlined a new policy, pledging that the Government would conduct the administration of the natives of the country through the 'proper native authorities'. 'By proper native authorities Guggisberg meant those authorities, which the Government recognised; to the Asante, however, this term referred to their traditional rulers. The two views could be reconciled only by restoring the *Amantoonum* and thereby the traditional pattern of allegiance' (Tordoff 1968:160).

However, since restoration of *Amantoonum* was not contemplated at this time, Indirect Rule made limited headway in Asante and none at all in the Kumasi Division, which was that part of the four areas in the Crown Colony of Asante that fell directly under the authority of the CCA. As a result, in November 1926, after two years of their return, the ruling pair who most Asante still regarded as their royal rulers, were given some official standing, as the British hoped that they would be able to restore order in the KD and so pave the way for the introduction of Indirect Rule.

The need for a restored Asante Confederacy became more urgent during the rule of H.S. Newlands, the CCA who had been 'appointed by the Accra government in November 1924' (Fortescue 1990:353). To Newlands it soon became clear that the Asante did not recognise any other stool than that of their traditional authorities, whom they believed to be the custodians of the land, which

[59] This was a type of European colonial policy as practiced in large parts of British India (see Princely states) and elsewhere in the British Empire (including Malaya), in which the traditional local power structure, or at least part of it, was incorporated into the colonial administrative structure.

belonged to the Asante people and the ancestral spirits. The Asante refused to pay direct tax to the British, as well as to the British created *akonkofoɔ* stools, which the Asante did not regard as legitimate. Newland therefore advised his superior, the BG Sir Shenton Thomas, that if Indirect Rule was to succeed in Asante, the Confederacy had to be restored. Sir Shenton Thomas investigated whether there was a basis for the restoration of *Amantoonum* in the Asante Colony. The outcome was that the majority of the Asante and Brong divisions (north of Kumasi, in the contemporary Brong-Ahafo Region) that originally fell under Asante rule were in favour of the restoration. This demonstrates that the majority of the Asante remained loyal to their traditional authorities, who were regarded as a link between people and ancestors; the newly appointed British chiefs had no spiritual stature and role. 'The guiding principle was to be that all chiefs should revert to their former pre-British allegiance so that all government-created chiefs would be reduced in status' (Tordoff 1968:164). On the 31st of January 1935, the foundation of the Asante Confederacy Council (ACC) was realised, and Osei Agyeman Prempeh II was enstooled as *Asantehene*, and Konadu Yaadom II (1917-1945) remained *Asantehemma* until her cousin *Asantehemma* Ama Serwaa Nyaako (1945-1977) replaced her. The ACC, although created as an instrument of Indirect Rule, was fashioned on the basis of the traditional view of members of the KCC. Nineteenth century Asante had enjoyed a confederate structure, and the *amanhene* were to possess autonomous jurisdiction except if they had voluntarily relinquished powers to the central government. These members probably made reference to the fact that the Asante kingdom grew out of a union of various states, which were equal in power. The British writer I. T. A Wallace-Johnson (1935) suggests that the term Asante Confederacy Council was wrong, as: (a) since the foundation of the Asante kingdom no Stool ever claimed equality with the Golden Stool and the Silver Stool. Instead the *Asantehene*, who occupied the Golden Stool and the *Asantehemma* who occupied the Silver Stool had a *primus-inter-pares* position, which means that all other *amanhene* and *amanhemma* were subservient to them. (b) many Asante traditional authorities, so far, including the *Mamponghene* and *Mamponghemma*, through family allegiance, willingly submitted themselves to the supreme power of the ruling duo. Others were, however, subdued by conquest. Thus Asante was nothing other than a monarchy for the ruling pair. Consequently, at the first session of the Confederacy Council in June 1935, the representatives of the *Mamponhene* (or paramount chief of Mampong) expressed his rejection of the position of the colonial Government, which decreed that the ruling duo was only allowed to interfere in the stool affairs of the Kumasi Division (KD) and not in the four divisions comprising the Crown Colony of Asante. They added that the ruling pair became the overlord of all the stools in Asante and as such it was unconstitutional for him to be told not to have a voice in matters affecting stools (Wallace-Johnson 1935). It was not until 1946, however, that members of the ACC, who attempted to legitimate the authority of that body, began to argue explicitly for its institutional continuity with the *Asantemanhyiamu* of the nineteenth century. After 1946 the resurrection of the *Asantemanhyiamu,* the body maintained an important point on the agenda of the ACC throughout the colonial period (Wilks 1989 [first published in 1975]:412-413). Resistance against the restoration of *Amantoonum* came from two groups: (a) the *akonkofoɔ* chiefs and their female co-rulers and (b) the *nkwankwaa.* The *akonkofoɔ* rulers had a realistic fear that they would lose their status as (paramount) chiefs and paramount female co-rulers. The *nkwankwaa,* who had organised themselves in the Friends of Asante Freedom Society (FAFS), campaigned against restoration, because 'they did not want any state, except as a tool for individual advancement' (McCaskie 1986b:19). Most likely they were afraid that, equivalent to the situation in the 1880s, the restoration of the *Amantoonum* would lead to the return of a strong centralised state. However, the *nkwankwaa* made few Christian converts and 'early in January 1935 the Secretary of State turned down a petition against restoration submitted by the Society, and the Ashanti Confederacy was restored at the end of that month' (Tordoff 1968:165).

In the same year Osei Agyeman Prempeh II, was officially recognised as *Asantehene* and ruled together with *Asantehemma* Konadu Yaadom II, while the Kumasi traditional authorities resumed their traditional role as Kumasi divisional elders and national advisers. Some villages (*odikro*) now fell into the hands of different rulers, a policy that created winners and losers among the various paramount traditional authorities. All British 'government-created' *amanhene* lost their paramount statuses. The *amantoo* (the states of the first Asante Confederacy that was founded in 1666) and the Brong States renewed their oath (*ntam kese*) to the Golden Stool and the Silver Stool under the original traditional authorities.

4.3. The indigenous religious mediatory role of the Asante ruling pairs Edward Agyeman Prempeh I and Konadu Yaadom II, and Osei Agyeman Prempeh II and his female co-rulers

The restored Council of Kumasi affected the indigenous religious mediatory functions of the Asante traditional authorities considerably. In the colonial period, the Asante royal rulers, called upon *Nyame* and *Asase Ya* the Supreme Being and the spirit of the Earth respectively. Anokye's customary laws demanded that *Asase Ya* was venerated on a Thursday (*Yaa*). This law prevented the Asante from going to the farm on this day and so protected the agricultural land from exploitation. Under British colonialism and Christian influences, *Asase Ya* became known as the female Earth goddess. The colonial government anthropologist Rattray wrote: '*Nyame*, the Supreme Being, whose position, except in so far as it is shared by *Asase Ya*, the Earth goddess is undoubtedly at the head of the Ashanti pantheon (Rattray 1959 [first published in 1927]:359). In the colonial period the Asante royal rulers' *akyeame* mentioned first *Nyame* and then *Asase Ya* and their exploits were recalled and celebrated. The *akyeame* were thus still in service of the royal rulers and after the British had deported the ruling pair Edward Agyeman Prempeh I and Konadu Yaadom II, many other Asante did not stop showing allegiance to these royal rulers as if they were never officially deposed. In 1924, the ruling pair was repatriated to Kumasi but not as a traditional authority but as private citizens, which is why some Asante felt that their loyalty should lie with the CCA. Other Asante, however, had never ceased believing that the Asante ruling duo Prempeh I, and Konadu Yaadom II were their *Asantehene* and *Asantehemma* and they continued to assign their loyalty to them and to respect them as religious rulers. The inhabitants of Kumasi (*Kumasifoɔ*) are categorised into five different groups of Asante people: (a) the *akonkofoɔ* and the Asante educated elite (b) the *nkwankwaa*, and (c) the *nhenkwaa*. Amongst the *Kumasifoɔ* there were: (d) those who turned against the ruling pair, and (e) those in favours of these Asante traditional authorities. For each group of people, the author will also study the political and/or religious reasons that have influenced their attitudes towards chieftaincy and its role in AIR during this period.

On the 12th of May 1931 *Asantehene* Edward Agyeman Prempeh I died. On the 22nd of June the same year, Kwame Kyeretwie was enstooled and known, until his death on the 27th of May 1970, as *Asantehene* Osei Agyeman Prempeh II who ruled together with *Asantehemma* Konadu Yaadom II (1917-1944), who was later succeeded by *Asantehemma* Ama Serwaa Nyaako (1944-1977). On the 24th of April 1933, the British restored the Asante Confederacy, an event that Agyeman Prempeh I, and Konadu Yaadom II could only have dreamt of. Osei Agyeman Prempeh II and Ama Sewa Nyaako were the first rulers of the new semi-autonomous Asante government. As an *Asantehene* rather than a *Kumasihene,* Prempeh II had a lot more to say about the Asante people than his predecessors. Nevertheless, Osei Agyeman Prempeh II and his female co-rulers equally had to deal with a complex society of people of whom some were more in favour of his personal policies than others. Under colonial rule their power as Asante ruling pair was much less self-evident as for the Asante royal rulers, who were ruling in the precolonial period of the Asante history. Osei Agyeman Prempeh II and his female co-rulers, for instance, lacked many of the suppressive methods that the precolonial Asante *ahemfo* could use to keep the Asante commoners under their control, such as the monopoly on carrying out the death sentence and ordering the ritual killing of human beings (Dupuis 1824; McCaskie 1989).

Social classes such as the *akonkofoɔ* and the *nkwankwaa* were better organised and more vocal during the reign of Prempeh II and his female co-rulers, mainly on account of their ability to accumulate private capital through the new industries of the colonial period. Prior to their reign, these sections of society were constantly in conflict with the Asante royal rulers, because they did not agree with the level of tax they had to pay to them. They were also resentful of opportunities at the disposal of the privileged traditional elites. In addition, they also adhered to an alternative interpretation of AIR that did not accord the traditional elites a pivotal position. Besides, Asante society became more multi-religious as various groups of Muslims and Christians had become established than in the late eighteenth and nineteenth centuries. Finally, the Asante royal rulers had to deal with increasing unrest in Asante society as a result of the increasing dissatisfaction of forces that turned themselves against the colonial regime; these anti-colonial forces gradually metamorphosed into political parties. These royal rulers thus did not rule in an easy period of the Asante history, and continued to carry out their indigenous religious function as mediators and peace-keepers to keep control over their subjects. This section will be on the relations of *Asantehene* Edward Agyeman Prempeh I, and *Asantehemma* Konadu Yaadom II with their rivals and adherents, to further illustrate how chieftaincy persisted.

The Asante traditional authorities had not ceased to follow AIR in the colonial period. During the reign of Osei Agyeman Prempeh II, traditional authorities generally looked positively towards some neo-indigenous religious movements in the Ashanti Region, such as *Tigare*, which protected spinsters and prostitutes against witchcraft accusations. As unmarried women, these people did not comply with the Christian and indigenous norms, which made the ideal victim of these accusations (Allman 1996; Müller and Venkatachalam 2013).

The *Tigare* cult, which was active in the Ashanti Region between 1946 and 1948, was reported to have originated in French territory (from Ypala near Wa) and had a branch at Adadientem near Ejisum in Asante. In 1946 the Commissioner of the Gold Coast Police (CGCP) recommended that all these movements, of which *Tigare* was believed to be the most harmful, should be abolished. Letters written by the Asante royal rulers that were included in the report of the ruling DC reveal that they made a clear distinction between neo-indigenous religious movements that in their eyes were harmful for the community and those that were beneficial since they protected their subjects against miscarriages, epilepsy and the other evil caused by witches. *Tigare* was perceived to be one of the movements that the Asante traditional authorities did not want to abolish. Consequently, the CGCP suggested that perhaps the time had come when the Asante Confederacy Council (ACC) and the Joint Provincial Council (JPC) could be asked to take steps to bar certain fetishes by licensing some and forbidding all those that were unlicensed (Criminal Investigation Division, The Gold Coast Police Accra, the 27th of June 1946, 6/1/40 – 'Fetishes' (0014) 1944-1948). Unlike their earlier attempts to suppress all neo-indigenous religious movements, the British colonial officers now recognised the importance for the Asante community of healing powers of some of those cult leaders who had great knowledge of traditional medicine. In fact they had not much choice, because under the changing regime from direct to indirect rule, an increasing number of Asante traditional authorities started to write petitions to the Colonial Officers to request them to be able to keep these forms of veneration in their villages. The leaders of these movements were praised and admired for their healing powers and skills to eradicate witchcraft. The British, who could not rule without the Asante royal rulers, could not afford to displease them and they looked for other solutions rather than the earlier strategy of the suppression of those movements. The incapacity of the British to control these indigenous religious activities in the Ashanti Region shows the resilience of AIR, which evolved to offer a place of protection for single women and prostitutes outside the male-dominated social order against witchcraft accusations. Witchcraft, arguably, was the result of firstly the introduction of Christianity and modernity, and secondly of the introduction of new Islamic movements, such as the Alhus-Sunnah wal-Jama'ah body and Wahhabi organisations. These Islamic reform movements turned themselves against moderate Muslims, who believed in the possibility of communication with the spirits of deceased persons and dream visions (Mittermaier 2011). In their role as indigenous religious peacekeepers Osei Agyeman Prempeh II, Konadu Yaadom II and Ama Serwaa Nyaako dealt with (d) these Christians, and (e) these Muslims. To mediate between beings of the spiritual and the social world, their challenge was to maintain a peaceful relationship with (a) the educated Asante elite and (b) the *nkwankwaa.*

4.3.1. The *akonkofoɔ* and the educated Asante elite

The Asante kingdom grew out of a union of states (*oman*) whose rulers (*abrempomma*) aimed to defend themselves better against their mutual enemy, the *Dɛnkyirahene*. The rulers were slave owners, who had built their state with the help of slaves, who worked for them on their farms and in the gold mines in their states. The *abrempomma* had equal rights, but due to its central position in the slave trade with the Europeans at the coast the Asante gained more wealth than the surrounding states and became more powerful (Arhin 1978). In 1701 the Asante kingdom was founded and the Asante royal rulers achieved the position of *primus-inter-pares* among the *abrempomma.* The Asante royal rulers used AIR symbols to Asantenise the surrounding cultural groups and keep them under control by seeking consent among the subjects of these states which were now part of the Asante kingdom for the use of coercive force; a ruling strategy that McCaskie (1995) has described as 'cultural hegemony'. At the end of the nineteenth century, however, due to the emerging rubber and timber industry the *abrempomma* managed to accumulate private wealth (Dumett 2009). They began to demonstrate their discontent with the hegemony of the Asante royal rulers and especially their policy that prevented non-royal rulers from accumulating wealth. The ruling royal rulers managed to suppress the *abrempomma* as serious contenders for power. However, due to their involvement in the rubber, the timber and especially the cocoa industries of the late nineteenth and twentieth centuries, the rich *akonkofoɔ* managed to accumulate private wealth. In 1901, they establish a highly self-conscious group that developed an alternative vision on the accumulation of capital, which according to them, should not be the preserve of solely the Asante royal rulers (McCaskie 1986a; Hunt 1990). In Gramscian terms, one can speak of the *akonkofoɔ*'s 'counter-hegemony', a concept that the author will now elaborate on.

The Asante traditional authorities were fearful that huge sums of private capital in the hands of ordinary Asante, such as the *akonkofoɔ,* would threaten the persistence of the Asante state. It would enable non-royal rulers to gain economic power, and therefore to compete with chiefs for political power or to sell arms to political rivals of the Asante (Arhin 1986:25-31). In the eighteenth century only traditional authorities (the 'Asante merchant princes'), were involved in large trade and trade organisations (Arhin 1986; McCaskie 1986a; Dumett 2009). In the 1880s and 1890s, the *akonkofoɔ* accumulated private wealth by fleeing to the coast and by trading with Europeans as rubber brokers, moneylenders and dealers in gold. This made them politically influential and enabled them to question the enrichment of the Asante royal rulers at the cost of ordinary Asante taxpayers and to organise themselves against them (McCaskie 1981:125-154). To understand the mediatory function of the Asante royal rulers, it is important to analyse whether the *akonkofoɔ*, who became influential in Asante society under early colonial rule, were only economic or also religious dissidents.

The *akonkofoɔ* behaved like big men or chiefs and were not reluctant to show off their wealth by buying big mansions and wheel charts. They were impressed by the culture of their British colonial rulers, dressed like Westerners and formed their own associations; although they were illiterate, as a consequence of their travels as traders and their contact with the Europeans, they were the purveyors of new ideas. They were in favour of the Western education for their children that the ECMs provided, even though many of them were neither literate nor Christian (Arhin 1986; McCaskie 1986a).

A sign that the *akonkofoɔ* favoured AIR is that with the support of colonial rulers, they managed to buy chieftaincy positions to achieve personhood, a prerequisite of becoming ancestral spirits (McCaskie 1986a; Wiredu 1998:306-317). The *akonkofoɔ* also demonstrated that in religious terms they did not stand against the old establishment of the Asante royal rulers when they joined in the agitation for the return of *Asantehene* Agyeman Prempeh I to Kumasi, and when they contributed to the fee for Fante politician J.E. Casely Hayford to write a petition to the British government to permit the return of their king (Arhin 1986). The opposition of the *akonkofoɔ* to the royal rulers was limited to the economic regulations that prevented them from accumulating private wealth. In religious issues, despite their modern Western lifestyle, the royal rulers remained adherents of AIR and generally they supported the Asante traditional authorities and their *nhenkwaa* in continuing their religious mediatory role. The economic point of conflict between the Asante royal rulers and the *akonkofoɔ* was also a conflict about AIR. The *akonkofoɔ* did not want to pay tribute and bought chieftaincy positions in the hope that this would turn them into significant ancestral spirits. Asante royal rulers felt their refusal to pay tribute was a sign of disrespect to the ancestors, just as buying land was also a sign of disregard for the land and the soil as a spiritess, as Asante deities could not be bought and sold (Rattray 1956 (first published in1929):347; McCaskie 1986a). The disagreement about this aspect of AIR demonstrates the blurred boundary between religious, economic and political matters in Asante society. The *akonkofoɔ* and the Asante traditional authorities also had different economic and political interests that were legitimised with the help of AIR. We have little information, however, on whether the *akonkofoɔ* were adherents of AIR (see Chapter II for the discussion on 'agency'). Most likely, the behaviour of the *akonkofoɔ* was the result of a combination of economic, political and indigenous religious factors.

The Asante educated elite slotted into the societal position occupied by the *akonkofoɔ*. They aimed at promoting national unity, and at improving the living conditions of the Asante population (Tordoff 1965). The elite distinguished themselves on the basis of literacy and the use of the English language during meetings, and they dressed like Europeans (Arhin 1986). In 1916 they founded the Asante Kotoko Society (AKS) that aimed to guide the Asante into modernity. In the 1940s, the members of this society split up and joined two opposing political parties; either the United Gold Coast Convention (UGCC) that promoted traditional rule, or the CPP that had a different agenda (Brempong 2000). The Asante educated elite were divided into a group of Christian women who were adherents of AIR, and Christians who despised the religion of their ancestors (Akyeampong 2003:45-47). As a consequence, these conflicts within Asante Christians affected the ways in which the Asante royal rulers exercised their religious mediatory role.

4.3.2. The *nkwankwaa*

Besides the *akonkofoɔ* and the *nhenkwaa*, there was a group of Asante living in Kumasi and its adjacent villages known as the *nkwankwaa* ('young men and women' or 'non-office holders'), such as lawyers, shopkeepers, petty traders, public letter writers, clerks, schoolteachers and artisans (Boahen 1975:103). The *nkwankwaa* are sometimes referred to as 'young men', a term that refers to their fresh ideas about modernity, individuality, gender relations and the accumulation of wealth, which – like the *akonkofoɔ* – they believed should not be a privilege of the traditional authorities (Allman 1990:263-279; Chazan, Lewis et al. 1999:269). The *nkwankwaa* were both the subjects of and political dissidents of the Asante royal rulers. Under the ruling pair Mensa Bonsu and Afia Kobi Serwaa Ampem I, the *nkwankwaa* and the *akonkofoɔ* had petitioned together against any restoration of the historical fiscal powers of the state, which was symbolised by the Golden Elephant Tail (*Sika Mmra*). Between 1896 and 1921, the *nkwankwaa* also showed signs of disloyalty to the *Sika Dwa Kofi*, when this sacred object was hidden successively in the villages of Bare Tonto Kokoben, Wawase and Aboabogya, under leadership of the *Gyaasewahene* Kwabena Asubonten. In 1921, a road gang unearthed the *Sika Dwa Kofi* and it was subsequently stripped of its gold by a group of individuals who were later apprehended, brought to trial and variously punished. The anthropologist Rattray described this event in his memorandum as an act of desecration of the *Sika Dwa Kofi.* He described the stool as exclusively religious, 'a shrine' embodying 'the soul of the Ashanti people'; it was a 'symbol of Ashanti nationality', something that through hallowed custom and belief engendered the objective and consensual virtues of 'obedience', 'respect', and 'great loyalty' (Rattray 1955 (first published in 1923):292-293).

According to McCaskie (1986a:14-16), this incident involving the Golden Stool was not the doing of religious dissidents. He argues that the *nkwankwaa* acted out of economic and political reasons to repudiate the controlling authority represented by the *Sika Dwa Kofi*. To the *nkwankwaa* the state was the enemy and 'stripping the *Sika Dwa Kofi,* was a literal stripping of the extractive power of the precolonial state'. The *nkwankwaa* did not disagree with the perception of the Kumasi royal elite that the *Sika Dwa Kofi* was a sacred object, but they did not wish to accept it as a symbol of the highest political power. In 1930, the *nkwankwaa* were particularly outraged by news that the *Kumasihene* Agyeman Prempeh I and Konadu Yaadom II, and his sub-chiefs and female sub co-rulers were considering a law that would require that a percentage of a deceased person's property should be given to the *Kumasihene* and these other royal rulers. 'After discussions with the "Chief Commissioner", the ruling pair dropped the issue' (Allman 1990:269). On the 24th of September 1921 the stool carrier Kwasi Nsenie Agya confessed that he and other *nkwankwaa* were guilty of stripping the *Sika Dwa Kofi* from its gold. Agya remarked:

> While we were sharing Dwantua [Kwadwo Dwantua] said, he is a stool carrier [*nkonnwasoani*] and that only the wood in it [the Golden Stool] is important but the gold about it is nothing (Harper 1921: quoted in McCaskie 1986:16).

According to McCaskie (1983; 1986a) the fact that Agya, who worked for a chief, made a clear distinction between the wooden core inside of the *Sika Dwa Kofi* that he believed to be inspirited, and its golden covering, indicates that the *nkwankwaa* did not stand against the Asante royal rulers for indigenous religious reasons and believed in the equality of male and female leaders. The *nkwankwaa* remained supporters of AIR, despite their flirtations with modernity, individuality and more equal social relations (Chazan, Lewis et al. 1999:100-102). Politically, however, the *nkwankwaa* were rivals of these authorities, just like the *akonkofoɔ*.

To politically undermine these authorities, the *nkwankwaa* were becoming involved in the foundation of a number of neo-indigenous religious movements such as *Bere-Kunde* and *Aberewa-Manguro*, which eventually became a rival force in Asante indigenous religious matters (Debrunner 1959:125-154). Between 1907 and the 1950s, the *nkwankwaa*-led movements mushroomed in the Gold Coast and became very popular, because they used the local IRs as a format, so that its Asante believers would feel familiar with these new movements and protect them against the effects of witchcraft (*bayi*) (Dovlo 2004). *Aberewa-Manguro*, which like all neo-indigenous religious movements, refers to the female and male serpent spirits, had been established in Asante around 1907. It was the property of the *nkwankwaa* and was viewed with hostility by senior officeholders who saw it as an alternative locus of authority, and deeply threatening to their position, since some *nkwankwaa* pledged their loyalty to *Aberewa-Manguro* in direct opposition to obedience to office holders. Additionally, *Aberewa-Manguro* threatened the legitimacy of their office, because its leaders took advantage of the need of many Asante women for security by offering protection against witchcraft accusations, threats, such as adultery, envy, theft, cursing, the bearing of false witness, poisoning and barrenness (McCaskie 1981:138-141). As a result, some of the traditional rulers attempted to abolish the *nkwankwaa* and their organisations (Tordoff 1965).

The urgent need for protection was caused by an increase in the degree of insecurity in Asante society, due to – among other reasons – the effects of the attempts of ECMs to convert them, which went together with the supporters of a different, modern lifestyle – and Fernando Po's introduction of cacao in 1879. Cocoa affected the Asante, because it brought the possibility of the accumulation of private capital. In the precolonial Asante kingdom, almost all capital had been in the hands of the state. The Asante royal rulers were in charge of the treasury and gave office holders the chance to prove themselves as successful rulers by lending them money for which they had to pay 'rent'. This contributed to the state's enrichment. After the death of each Asante chief all his wealth went back into the state's treasury (Wilks 1979). In the precolonial state, the traditional rulers had thus a monopoly on the accumulation of wealth, which precipitated the growth of *ɔdomankoma;* a neo-indigenous religious cult, whose members attempted to accumulate private wealth. The adherents of this cult in due course made an effort to destool the then ruling *Asantehene* Osei Bonsu. This Asante king did not in any sense tolerate the accumulation of private wealth, and consequently, he executed several of *ɔdomankoma*'s members, which contributed to his prosperity. However, king Osei Bonsu's cruelty and greed led to the increasing dissatisfaction with his regime which eventually caused his destoolment (McCaskie 1981:129-138).

The *ɔdomankoma* cult attracted many single Asante women because it offered the possibility of accumulating private wealth in Asante society, which was new to them. Prior to this period, the state had the monopoly on the accumulation of capital. The cocoa boom provided opportunities for the individual for the accumulation of wealth. But the societal consensus was that witches must have caused the accumulation of wealth, or women who did not want to be fully economically dependent on their husbands or partners. Also, it was believed that rich subjects' accumulation of wealth must have caused the impoverishment of others. Precolonial witchcraft movements, such as *ɔdomankoma* and colonial ones such as *Aberewa-Manguro* that could catch witches – who were in the majority rich people – were popular because they were believed to be able to get rid of people's poverty. A side effect of the introduction of cocoa as a mono-cash crop in Ghana and the resulting possibility of the accumulation of private wealth was also that it caused trouble in many Asante families. The increase of wealth among some family members and the impoverishment of others resulted in strained relations between them. Again, witches were believed to be the cause of these tensions that were in fact caused by the suppression of the *anima* in the Asante psyche that came with the increased influence of Christianity over the Asante people. On both the macro-level, which caused increased stratification in the society, and micro-level, which caused increased income differences and tensions within the conjugal family, witches were believed to be operating. They therefore needed to be eradicated and neo-indigenous religious movements flourished in Asante until 1950.[60] Thereby the colonial officers removed the last possibility for Asante women to escape from their suppression by chiefs and the male-dominated social order that had developed under colonial rule.

Although Fuller's opinion was most likely not purely objective, it made clear that the British were keener on cooperation with the Asante chiefs than the leaders of neo-indigenous religious shrines in Asante. The latter challenged the power of the Asante royal rulers who fell under the authority of the CCA. In terms of religion, the policy of the British was 'not to interfere with the natives' religious affairs' (F.C. Fuller, the 6th of August 1908, 1/30/1/6 – 'Chief Fetish Priest *Aberewa-Manwuro*' (2/07) 1907-1908). An exception was made, however, for those cases where the practices of neo-indigenous religious movements should be regarded as criminal. The British strategy was thus to control the indigenous religious practices of the Asante by the application of laws. During the period of direct rule over the Kumasi Division (1901-1935) and Indirect Rule

[60] The movements included *Tigare* (which became the most famous), *Bere-Kune*, *Senyakapo, Nana Tongo, Kankamea, Blekete*, *Kwasi-Kukuro*, and *Kwaku-Firi* shrines. See for more on the male spirits only. Field, M. J. 1940. "Some New Shrines of the Gold Coast and Their Significance," *Africa: Journal of the International African Institute* 13(2): 138-149., Debrunner, H., W. 1959. *Witchcraft in Ghana: A Study on the Belief in Destructive Witches and its Effects on the Akan Tribes*. Accra: Waterville Publishing House. After 1950 witchcraft movements became unpopular, whereas prophets, such as Sampson Oppong, increased in popularity and developed mass movements, which became the forerunners of the Independent Churches in Ghana Miller, N. N. and E. P. Skinner 1968. "The Political Survival of Traditional Leadership: the 'Paradox' of Rural Leadership: a Comment," *The Journal of Modern African Studies* 6(2): 183-201.

over the remaining divisions in the 'Crown Colony of Asante', this strategy resulted in a policy to suppress those neo-indigenous religious movements that in the eyes of the British were regarded as illegal forms of worship. In fact, some of these religious practices were actually supported by the local Asante royal rulers, who believed in the power of the anti-witchcraft medicine (*aduro*) that were provided by these movements. The latter reveals that those colonial Asante royal rulers had continued to believe in the power of *anini-nananom nsamanfo* and maintained their spiritual function. In this period the British, however, regarded AIR in the working of those medicines as 'superstition', and as a result, they proscribed many neo-indigenous religious movements, such as *Aberewa-Manguro*, which became forbidden in 1908. The British feared that this movement could develop into a mass movement, which – after being underground for some years – indeed became a reality in the 1920s (McCaskie 1981:138-141; Olsen 2003:249-250).

Aberewa-Manguro (male-female spirits) and other of these indigenous religious movements were thus politically threatening for both the Asante traditional authorities and the colonial government, because they ran against the psychological suppression and economic independency of women. Once these movements gained in popularity they also became rivals to the traditional authorities. They legitimised themselves by making use of symbols and laws that went together with AIR, such as the swearing of an oath and the creation of a list of life rules within the cult, which was also done by Priest Anokye during the eighteenth century (the so-called 'Seventy-Seven Laws of Anokye') (Olsen 2003).

To sum up, the *nkwankwaa* were political rivals of the ruling pair Prempeh I, and Konadu Yaadom II and the other paramount and sub Asante traditional authorities. With the neo-indigenous religious movements, they were able to establish themselves as rivals in the spiritual realm. They made a clear distinction between the political and the religious function of the *Sika Dwa Kofi*, which shows that they found it important to let people know that they did not disagree with its indigenous religious meaning. However, they then used these and other Asante indigenous religious symbols to create neo-indigenous religious movements that for the Asante traditional authorities were a rivalling force in the spiritual realm. The decline in popularity of the *tete abosom* under the reign of Agyeman Prempeh I was caused by the increase of the popularity of these witch-catching deities that belonged to the neo-indigenous religious shrines (Silverman 1987). The Asante traditional authorities believed that the large number of the followers of the neo-indigenous religious shrines and the *abosommerafoo* undermined the Asante institution of chieftaincy and weakened their role as religious mediators.

In 1949, the *nkwankwaa*, who had continued to strive for political power since the 1880s and hoped to gain economic power through this engagement, played a key role in the founding of the CPP, a party that would win the elections at the eve of independence with Nkrumah as its helm. Under the leadership of people like the debt collector and newspaper reporter, Krobo Edusei, the *nkwankwaa* came into a series of confrontations with the Asante ruling pair. The key *loci* of conflict were land rights in building land and the income to be gained from that. The *nkwankwaa* attacked the chiefly authorities by challenging their rights to land and their accumulation of wealth from the use of that land. They accused the *Asantehene* and his associates of profiting from the building boom in Kumasi, by their access and control over land (McCaskie 2001:219).

In 1953, the *nkwankwaa* saw a drop in the percentage of their seats in the new Legislative Assembly, of five percent, compared to that of 1951 in the Asante Council. In 1954, the government passed an amendment to the Cocoa Duty and Development Funds Bill that fixed the price of cacao far under the average price on the world market. This was a decision meant to diminish the wealth of the *nkwankwaa*, many of whom were involved in the cocoa business. The *nkwankwaa* drew the conclusion that the party was not going to help them achieve their goal. Therefore, they broke with the CPP and sided with the Asante traditional authorities. Initially, some of these authorities felt that the *nkwankwaa* had betrayed them, because only shortly after the British colonial rulers had restored the *Amantoonum* they had attempted to destool the ruling duo Osei Agyeman Prempeh II and Konadu Yaadom II, in an act supported by powerful paramount chiefs, such as the *Dadeasoabahene, Bantamahene, Akyempemhene* and *Adumhene*, who did not stand to benefit from the Confederacy's restoration (McCaskie 2001:219). Eventually, those traditional authorities sympathetic to the Asante royal rulers joined the latter and the *nkwankwaa* in their struggle against the CPP for pragmatic reasons: the *nkwankwaa* were the only group in Asante society that could mobilise the masses of Asante farmers and other Asante subjects that were dissatisfied with Nkrumah's decision to lower the cocoa prices. In a successful effort toward reconciliation with the chiefs, the *nkwankwaa* coupled their demand for a higher cocoa price with Asante autonomy within a federated Gold Coast. They called for the preservation of the chieftaincy, and positioned themselves as defenders of the 'sacred' (in their eyes) Asante institution of chieftaincy. The *nkwankwaa* knew how to make pragmatic use of cultural nationalistic feelings of ordinary Asante to reach their goals; in their fight against the low cocoa prices they used slogans such as 'We have the warrior spirit of our great Ancestors within us' (Baffoe 1954). They believed that they needed the chiefs to ideologically legitimise their movement against Nkrumah, because these chiefs would bring 'the support of the spirits and ancestors of the entire nation' (Allman 1990:272). Allman holds the view that the *nkwankwaa's* use of these words in quotations should be perceived as expressions of cultural nationalism that enabled the *nkwankwaa* to mobilise a mass of Asante people against the CPP. The *nkwankwaa* made use of the creatively reintroduced symbols of AIR some with help of the British to reach their political goals. However, in the opinion of this author, the *nkwankwaa*'s use of reintroduced AIR expressions and symbols cannot be explained only by referring to their political instrumentality.[61] First, McCaskie (1986a) makes the point that in 1921, the *nkwankwaa* were not political enemies of the ruling pair but also indigenous believers who did not oppose the religious meaning of the *Sika Dwa Kofi* and the *ɔhemma Adwa.* Second, McCaskie informs us that in 1874, when the former Asante kingdom became a protectorate of the Gold Coast government, the open celebration of the *Odwira* festival was suspended at the level of the state. Lewin (1978:105) makes clear that during this period, in several divisions on a village level, the chiefs, the female co-rulers and Asante commoners continued the celebration of the ritual days (*adae*), such as in North Ashanti (e.g. Wenchi). Since the *adae* had been the most significant ritual celebrations during the colonial period, in postcolonial Ghana the *Odwira* festival transformed into the *Asanteman Adae Kese* celebration, which included the old elements of the *Odwira* festival and new Islamic and Christian elements (interview with Osei Kwadwo, 26). The *nkwankwaa* adhered to AIR which, like all IRs is pragmatic and seeks to incorporate useful aspects of other religions and ideas (Platvoet 1992). According to Cox (1998) 'indigenous religious believers are tolerant of the religions and ideas of other people and often borrow and incorporate aspects of them into their own belief and practices'. After the 1950s, neo-indigenous religious shrines became unpopular and the *nkwankwaa* helped the Asante traditional authorities to spread their cultural national ideology based on AIR. Under the reign of the ruling pair, despite cultural nationalism, the *nkwankwaa* did not cease to be indigenous believers and they remained loyal in religious terms to the Asante traditional authorities, which had a positive effect on the religious mediatory role held by these authorities.

4.3.3 The *nhenkwaa*

In the precolonial period the *nhenkwaa* were a political and economic subelite, who participated in the royal administrative system. Some *nhenkwaa* (*ɔbosomkwaa*) served a deity (*ɔbosom*) and were appointed to help in the performance of religious rituals of the paramount traditional rulers during the ritual calendar days (*adae*) (McCaskie 1986a). Many of the Asante *Nkramofoɔ* were also part of the *nhenkwaa*, but they will be discussed in a separate section of this chapter. In the nineteenth century, when the Asante chanceries became less dependent on Christian and Islamic diplomats (a fact that enhanced the reliability of the Asante diplomatic service), the *nhenkwaa* became part of those chanceries and specialised in dealing with issues in relation to the English, Danish and

---

[61] Ranger further describes the practices of African traditional authorities under British colonial rule to invent traditional customs as a colonial strategy of controlling their subjects Ranger, T. O. 2002. "The Invention of Tradition in Colonial Africa," in E. J. Hobsbawm and T. O. Ranger. *The Invention of Tradition*. Cambridge: Cambridge University Press: 211-263.

Dutch or the Islamic hinterland north of Kumasi (Adjaye 1990). Furthermore, they had jobs that were meant to increase the well-being of the royal rulers, such as those of sword bearer, palanquin carrier and cook (McCaskie 1986a:10-17). The *nhenkwaa* obtained land grants with settled bondsmen and exercised judicial authority over them. Sources of income for them were benefits from the state in the form of shares in war booty and commission on tribute, tax and levy collection, shares in judicial fees, extortions in the judicial process and trading capital.

In the colonial period, these royal servants remained loyal to the Asante traditional authorities, from whom they derived their social status. After the deportation of the ruling pair Agyeman Prempeh I and Konadu Yaadom II in 1896, many of the *nhenkwaa* had left Kumasi as under the British colonial authorities and they had become jobless.[62] But, loyal as always, when the ruling pair returned to Kumasi in 1924, some of their steadfast supporters also moved back to Kumasi from its surrounding villages (Akyeampong 1999:297-298). Although under the ruling pair the offices of the *nhenkwaa* were not officially reinstalled, the *Kumasihene* offered many of them jobs at the palace and for them life seemed to continue as if their 'king' had never been exiled from Kumasi.[63]

The *nhenkwaa* no longer worked in the ruling pair's diplomatic service which was suppressed under colonial rule, but they continued their jobs as servants of royal households and the maintenance of religious practices, such as the pouring of libation and the celebration of the *adae* rituals that went together with the veneration of the ancestors and the honouring of the land (Akyeampong 2003). They also continued the celebration of the *Odwira* festival on a local level, although openly on a state level its celebration was suspended until 1985 as it was perceived to be a threat to the colonial authorities (Lewin 1978; McCaskie 1995). The British decision to postpone the celebration of *Odwira* after the foundation of the Crown Colony of Asante in 1902 demonstrates that it was still perceived as the main way to legitimise the Asante traditional political institution. The presence of this British perception of the meaning of *Odwira* shows that there were clear limitations to the extent to which they managed to control the private religious lives of the Asante and especially women, for whom AIR was very important. Because of the continuation of AIR practices during the period of the ruling pair's exile, such as the quiet performance of the *adae* rituals, the indigenous religious mediatory function of the Asante traditional authorities did not cease to exist. The continuation of the celebration of Asante indigenous religious days and rituals was due to the attitude of many British officials who did not wish to interfere with the religious affairs of the Asante. An

---

62 These authorities were: the District Commissioner (DC), the Provincial Commissioner (PC), the Chief Commissioner (CC) and the Governor.

63 Because Prempeh I was never officially destooled before his deportation, in the eyes of the Asante, he remained their king. He returned in 1924 as *Kumasihene.* After his deportation, exile and return, the British did not recognise him any longer as Asantehene, a situation that remained the case until his death in 1931.

exception was made for those rituals that the British judged as criminal, such as those of the neo-indigenous religious movements. On the 3rd of August 1908, F.C. Fuller, the CCA, wrote to the BG:

> The people have their religion and they have their innumerable fetishes, alright, nobody will forbid these, but the *Aberewa-Manguro* practices are no religion or cult but simply a devilish way to suck on the people money by taking advantage of their superstition and stupidity (F.C. Fuller to his Excellency the Governor, Kumasi, the 3th of August 1908, 1/30/1/6 – 'Chief fetish Priest Aberewa' (2/07) 1907-1908).

The quotation shows that F.C. Fuller made a clear distinction between IRs that were represented by the Asante traditional authorities, with their acceptable practices, and other cult practices. Secondly, during the period of the ruling pair's exile, many Asante refused to live under the colonial order and remained loyal to the ruling pair. In the Seychelles, the ruling pair continued to celebrate the *adae* when possible since the stools of the Asante ancestors were absent. Libations, however, continued to be poured and the Sunday (*akwasidae*), and was even marked by church attendance. The persistence of the *adae* celebration in the Seychelles was very important for the ruling pair, as it was also a celebration of their genealogy, which means that 'to abrogate it is the equivalent of genealogical erasure or social death' (Akyeampong 1999:295). With the help of the *adae* celebration, the ruling pair maintained their social – but not their legal status – as *Asantehene* and *Asantehemma* for their people exiled in the Seychelles, but also for the Asante back in Kumasi who continued to perceive them as their traditional leaders. This turned out to be the case from Governor Sir Shenton, who in 1924 wrote that:

> In the eyes of the government he [LM: Agyeman Prempeh I and Konadu Yaadom II] returned as a private citizen…in the eyes of Ashanti it was their *Asantehene* who had come back to them. The Golden Stool had once more an occupant and the people had once more their supreme spiritual head (Governor Sir Shenton, 1924).

Even though officially the Asante traditional authorities returned home as private citizens, their people embraced them as the ruling pair and demonstrated their loyalty to them as the representatives of the Golden Stool and the Silver Stool. Many chiefs (*amanhene*) took the oath of allegiance to the *Asantehene* and celebrated the *adae* festival during their absence.

Under the Asante traditional authorities the *nhenkwaa* thus showed themselves to be in favour of these leaders and committed to the restoration of Asante indigenous religious elements. They had remained loyal to their royal rulers and perceived them as the representatives of the ancestral spirits, who are the rightful owners of the land. In imitation of the *nhenkwaa*, many other Asante subjects (*nkoa*) also embraced the indigenous way of life. They continued to perceive their royal rulers and other of the Asante traditional authorities as mediators between the social and the spiritual worlds. These leaders never ceased to exist for them.

The Asante royal rulers Osei Agyeman Prempeh II, and Konadu Yaadom II and later Ama Serwaa Nyarko also had *nhenkwaa*, but their loyalty to the Asante royal rulers was more derived from a working relationship than from a religious conviction. Under these royal state rulers the libations and sacrifices offered by them at the *adae* and *Odwira* ceremonies and festivals had lost their full significance, especially for the increasing number of their Christian subjects. Some of these Christianised Asante no longer believed that the crops would fail or that misfortune would befall the cultural group if the sacrifices to the ancestors were not performed. Institutional Christianity challenged the traditional authorities' religious position and repudiated their spiritual headship. The religious lives of many Asante under these royal state rulers were no longer revolved solely around AIR. Many of them adhered a syncretic form of AIR and Islam or Christianity thereby venerating the male and female serpent spirits through the connection with the traditional authorities on equal footing (Danquah 1952; McCaskie 2001:194-200).

4.4. The indigenous religious peacekeeping role of Agyeman Prempeh I and Osei Agyeman Prempeh II and their female co-rulers

In this section the focus will be on the efforts of the ruling pair Agyeman Prempeh I and Konadu Yaadom II and the royal state rulers Prempeh II and Konadu Yaadom II, who was succeeded by *Asantehemma* Ama Serwaa Nyaako, and in particular their maintenance of peaceful relationships with: (d) groups of Muslims, and (e) groups of Christians.

4.4.1. The Muslims

Before the deportation of the Asante royal state rulers to the Seychelles, a friendship had emerged between them and the Asante *ɔkramoni* Almami Samori, who was hostile to the British (Wilks 1989 [first published in 1975]:318). In 1924, the Asante traditional authorities resumed their negotiations with Suwarian Muslims and orthodox Muslims in their society. From the early nineteenth century, Muslims lived in a 'spatially circumscribed' neighbourhood of Kumasi, known as the old Kumasi settlement, which was not a distinct area in town for Muslims only (see 7.5 map 6). The Asante *Nkramofoɔ* were kept physically close to the traditional authorities place of power (Maier 1997:333). The relationship of these authorities with the Asante *Nkramofoɔ* remained cordial and the authorities had been impressed by their religious skills. The Asante *Nkramofoɔ* were also the medical advisors of the ruling pair and they healed the king's children (Recorded by Agyeman-Duah 1972). In April 1928, Agyeman

Prempeh I expressed his wish to the District Commissioner (DC) of Kumasi to revive the defunct *nsumanfiesu*. Between 1844 and 1896, the *nsumanfiesu* headed by the *nsumankwahene* had been responsible for the physical and spiritual welfare amongst the Asante royal rulers. The Asante *Nkramofoɔ* occasionally provided the ruling pair with talismans and religious maxims, as they had regularly done to their predecessors (Eastern Provincial Commissioner's Diary, April 1928, NAG, Accra).

The attitude of the ruling pair toward orthodox Muslims in Kumasi was more problematic. In 1926, after king Prempeh I had become *Kumasihene*, his policy regarding these Muslims and other foreigners was not one of encouragement of their entrepreneurship. He was disturbed that many of the nice 'storey buildings' in Kumasi were the property of orthodox Muslims from up North and from Syria (Akyeampong 1999:299-300). For foreigners renting a plot of land, building storey buildings or houses on it and being landlords were one of the few options for investment used to display their wealth, as the land was in hands of Kumasi's royal elite (Schildkrout 1970:256-257). The ruling pair, however, preferred these buildings to be in the hands of the Asante, and the display of wealth ran against their conservative opinion that 'was very much in line with old Asante state concerns: innovation must strengthen the state and maintain the *status quo*' (Akyeampong 1999:299-300). In practice this meant that the ruling duo attempted to keep Kumasi closed to what they believed to be harmful foreign influences and tried to prevent orthodox Muslims from entering.

The traditional authorities remained ambivalent about orthodox Muslims of the Kumasi settlement who had not shown any loyalty to them during their exile and had instead openly supported the CCAs. The Muslims of the Kumasi settlement, especially the Hausa, had profited from British colonisation, because in 1927, the British appointed their headman, the Sarkin *Zongo*, as the 'chief' of all Muslims. The British thus made the Muslims more important in relation to the Asante rulers. Under the rule of the Asante royal rulers in the eighteenth and nineteenth centuries, the Muslim 'headmen' in the settlement had not been recognised by the Asante rulers as 'chiefs'. In the same year, in addition to the status of traditional authorities, the British gave the Sarkin *Zongo* his own civil tribunal in which issues concerning the inhabitants of the settlement and issues concerning the Asante were tried under Muslim law. The British gave the Sarkin *Zongo* much power, because they profited from his ability to keep the settlement a peaceful place (Schildkrout 1978:88-89).

The Sarkin *Zongo* was respected by the British as a leader of all Muslims because 'he performed numerous services for all the inhabitants of the Muslim settlements that the administration would otherwise have had to undertake' (Schildkrout 1970:260). The British increased the importance of Hausa Muslims in relation to the Asante rulers, as the former had not had any traditional authorities in the precolonial period (Akyeampong 1999). For the British the recognition of a *primus-inter-pares* authority in the settlement, like the Sarkin *Zongo*, was necessary: for after 1896, when the Asante power was broken, northern soldiers recruited by the British and northern traders and labourers came to Kumasi in large numbers (Schildkrout 1978:69). This meant that several measures had to be taken by a clear overall authority to maintain order. The lives of the people of the Muslim settlements had always been dependent on local authorities – first the Asante royal rulers, then from 1901 the CCA, and from 1927 the Sarkin *Zongo* (Schildkrout 1970:258-260). As true loyalists to the British, who ruled over the Crown Colony of Asante from 1902, Muslims and also other inhabitants of the Muslim settlements were not a group of people from which the ruling pair could expect much sympathy and find supporters. The ruling duo did not, however, put any restrictions on their religious freedom. The Muslims were allowed to build mosques anywhere in the Kumasi metropolis: as a result, small mosques and European missionary churches could be found next to each other (interview with Al-Hajj Sheikh Zakuruka, 17).

The Asante royal state rulers Osei Agyeman Prempeh II and Konadu Yaadom II and Ama Serwaa Nyaako continued the cordial relationship between the Asante traditional rulers on all hierarchical levels and the Asante *Nkramofoɔ* that had been so characteristic from the eighteenth century. Under their reign, the restored *nsumanfiesu* remained intact even though the demand for *asuman* decreased. Furthermore, these Asante royal state rulers improved the relationship with the Hausa Muslims and political power shifted from the traditional authorities to the political parties, which could only organise themselves by using the existing political structures of the regional chieftaincy institution (Schildkrout 1978:214-220).

After 1951, the Gold Coast was divided into constituencies that were set up without strict regard to traditional affiliation but using population consideration, which meant that people under paramount Asante traditional authorities could be made to incorporate people of another traditional area and elect someone to represent them in parliament. Political parties were formed and the party, which won the majority seats in parliament, became the ruling party, and exercised power over and above that of the king. Nevertheless, the parties were dependent on the support of the traditional authorities, and in 1956, for instance, it was only with the help of these authorities that the NLM formed into a proper political party (Allman 1990). In 1958, the MAP and the NLM, among other political parties, were united in the United Party (UP) in a mutual struggle against Nkrumah's CPP. The UP stood for the promotion of traditional values, Asante or Muslim, and the preservation of chieftaincy, which ideologically bound the Asante and many inhabitants of the settlement together. Some Muslim headmen continued to support the CPP, but the majority of these headmen and subjects joined the UP (Schildkrout 1978:214-220). The traditional authorities' continuation of the custom to welcome Asante *Nkramofoɔ* to live at Manhyia palace and their agreement to fuse their political party with that of the orthodox Muslims is evidence of the religious peacekeeping role of the Asante royal state rulers.

4.4.2. The Christians

Initially, until their deportation in 1896, the ruling pair Agyeman Prempeh I, and Konadu Yaadom II prevented ECMs from settling in Kumasi. In the Seychelles in 1909, they were baptised into the Anglican Church, which was the state Church of England, and they encouraged all other Asante people in the Islands to become Anglicans, while they also continued to celebrate the *adae* and to perform rituals for the ancestral spirits. In 1908, the Roman Catholic Church received land in Kumasi from the royals to build clinics, schools and hospitals. In 1924 they allowed the building of a Wesleyan secondary school and two teaching training colleges of the Basel Mission. The Wesleyans attributed their growth in adherents to their contact with the evangelist Samuel Oppong, who preached in the Ashanti Region between 1920 and 1926 (Kimble 1963:165). Oppong was the disciple of an educated prophet from Liberia, known as Prophet Harris (1850-1929); an African spirit Baptist who was very successful in gaining adherents for the Christian belief. For example, without any Western missionary financial support, Prophet Harris baptised 120,000 West Africans into Christianity in two years. Philip Quacoe (1741-1816), a fellow Anglican African preacher who was trained in Britain for the Gold Coast and depended on Western missionary finance and control, preached for nine years and only converted fifty-two persons. Samson Oppong, who believed that he had heard the voice of God, was a converted indigenous priest who burned the material attributes (fetishes) that he had used in his pre-Christian existence and started preaching the Gospel. Equal to Harris and the European Christian missionaries, Oppong's aim was to attack the beliefs and practices of African indigenous religious practitioners and to replace the African Indigenous Religions with the Christian gospel. Both Harris and Oppong were also encouraged by the Methodist Church to join them. Under Oppong's influence, in less than two years, around ten thousand of Asante people converted to Methodist Christianity including some Asante traditional authorities and *akomfoɔ*, who then proceeded to burn Asante indigenous religious objects. However, Prophet Harris and his disciples Samuel Oppong and also John Swatson also challenged the European Christian missionaries by baptizing Africans who had not received any instructions in the Christian faith. They offered healing services and gave space to the visions and dreams of ordinary Africans by both rejecting the African Indigenous Religions and the form of Christianity that was brought to Africa by European missionaries. Like African prophets in other African countries in this period, who also positioned themselves between the African indigenous priests and the European Christian missionaries, Harris and his disciples became the founders of an indigenous form of Christianity in Africa and the predecessors of the Pentecostal-Charismatic Churches (PCC) on the continent. The leaders of these indigenous Christian churches attempted to make a complete break with their

African indigenous religious past, especially by rejecting the female ancestral serpent spirit (e.g. *Ngame among the Asante*) and to replace her with a male God that was believed to be stronger and superior to that female spirit, and to preach against those aspects of their African Indigenous Religion (such as ancestral veneration, the veneration of objects or fetish and the ritual killing of human beings) that they found were not compatible with their indigenous Christian faith. Despite the rejection of these indigenous Christians of the African Indigenous Religions, most European missionaries perceived this form of indigenous Christianity as religion that was deeply and overly embedded in the African indigenous religious traditions (Shank 1980; Meyer 1998; Chidester 2000; Amanor 2011).

The Wesleyan Methodist Missionary Society

Asantehene Prempeh I was the first literate Asante ruler and a great proponent of missionary education. In 1907, after his education in the Seychelles Islands, he encouraged his nephew and successor Agyeman Prempeh II, to enrol at the Kumasi Wesleyan Methodist School. Prempeh II, who appreciated his Methodist education, encouraged missionaries to open schools in the Ashanti Region (interview with the royal anthropologist C.K. Coffie, 4). The Asante rulers Prempeh I and Prempeh II were thus both literate and proponents of missionary education. However, none of them were Methodists. The opening of the Methodist schools and those of the other missionaries of mainstream Christianity (the Presbyterians, Anglicans and Roman Catholics) were merely a reaction to the fact that in the Seychelles Islands, King Prempeh had become an Anglican and since then had promoted all forms of Christianity and Christian education in Kumasi (Debrunner 1967). The Asante kings mentioned and their female co-rulers both had cordial relationships with the Methodists, and supported their Synods by donating to the building of a Methodist school in Kumasi, while also supporting the establishment of Wesley College in this town (Manhyia Archives Group 1/15/2 1929-1947).

The Basel Missionary Society

In the Yaa Asantewaa uprising of 1900, all missionary personnel disappeared, buildings were destroyed and the converted slaves were re-enslaved. After the uprising, the Basel missionaries, including Ramseyer, therefore had to start all over again to bring the Gospel to Kumasi. For many reasons, however, the numbers of Asante converts remained low in comparison to other areas of the Gold Coast in which the Basel Mission was active (Kwamena Poh 1974; Mohr 2009). Ramseyer and his wife had always had a cordial relationship with the traditional authorities, such as King Kakari and Prince Owusu Ansa. They lived under one roof with an indigenous priest and they had showed their respect for the *adae* (Akuamoah 2007). Nevertheless, the general attitude of the Basel Mission was one of intolerance towards attributes of AIR, such as polygamy , the matrilineal system of inheritance and the veneration of the ancestors during the *adae* (Agyeman 1978). As a result, those Asante who were converts of the Basel Mission came into conflict with the Asante royal rulers, who in line with customary law, encouraged them to perform indigenous religious services. In 1912, the relationship between the traditional authorities and the European Christian missions (the Basel Mission, but also the Wesleyan and the Roman Catholic Missions) became so disturbed that the colonial government decided in a committee with the CCA that the Asante rulers needed to distinguish indigenous rituals from ceremonial services. The Christian converts were then obliged to obey their rulers but should be exempted from attending their religious rituals (Harper Mss. Brit. Emp. S. 344. Box 2/5. 1920. Colonial Reports: Ashanti 905). Despite this law, the relationship of the Asante converts with the traditional rulers remained troublesome, because their conversion and the hard work as cocoa farmers and craftsmen had increased their material wealth and independence from chiefly authority (Miller 1990). Many young Asante men converted to Christianity to escape from the gerontocratic traditional society that obliged them to obey the traditional rulers, and e.g. work for free in communal labour projects, while for women, the church offered an escape from the pawnship slave marriages that the chiefs used as a way to keep control over the reproductive capacities of women (Allman 1996).

In 1917, the Basel missionaries, of whom most were German citizens, were forced to leave the Gold Coast after they were suspected of serving German interests. In the period 1918-1925, the African Churches that were built under the Basel Mission became practically autonomous under the guidance of the Scottish Presbyterian Mission. In 1926, one year after the return of the Basel missionaries, the African Churches became known as the Presbyterian Church of the Gold Coast. Until 1972, the Presbyterians remained fierce proponents of monogamy, which remained a source of conflict between them and the Asante royal rulers (Agyeman 1978).

The Anglican Church

In the precolonial period, the Anglican Church had grown by local self-appointed prophets. In the colonial period it remained in the hands of lay organisations, such as, for instance, 'the Guild of the Good Shepherd'. The successes booked by the Society for the Propagation of the Gospel (SPG) in the early colonial years in terms of conversion of the Asante were, little and activities ceased in 1904. In 1913, the SPG sent the missionary G.E. Morrison to Kumasi, who was assigned to work in this town between 1913 and 1920. Unlike all other SPG centres of veneration in the present day Ashanti Region, Kumasi had a residential priest. He worked, however, on his own and there was nobody to take over his work after him. In addition, after his resignation the post remained vacant for three years. This situation shows that missionary leadership of the SPG in Kumasi was relatively strong in comparison with the rest of the Asante area but certainly had its limitations. With one missionary and a considerable gap between the resignation of the one missionary and his successor, the SPG could not exert full control and provide leadership in detail. In this gap period, the SPG was mainly in the hands of indigenous church leaders. Due to the small amount of missionaries per centre of veneration, the indigenous influence in the missionary work was considerable. In 1902, simultaneously with the beginning of Anglican services, an Anglican school was set up with the support of chieftaincy funds. The traditional authorities were interested in schooling, but due to a shortage of Anglican missionaries and the unattractiveness of the Gold Coast as a location in comparison to others, the SPG could hardly get any missionaries who were willing to teach. As a result, the Anglicans were very unsuccessful in their mission despite their cordial connections with the Asante royal rulers and their tolerance towards AIR (Jenkins 1974; 1974). The Anglican Church, being a mainly African Church, allowed many Asante indigenous religious elements in the practice of the Anglican religion, such as dancing and the participation of its members in traditional rituals (Akyeampong 1999). Unlike the Basel Mission, the Anglicans did not have strict control on the marriages of their members and could not prevent them from practising polygamy (Jenkins 1974).

The Anglican Church was also the church of the British royal rulers, and to demonstrate their sympathy to the British in the hope to be able to return to Kumasi, the ruling pair Prempeh I and his female co-ruler Konadu Yaadom II had encouraged their entire family and their subjects to convert to Anglican Christianity during period of exile on the Seychelles. The Asante king was himself involved in the process of conversion and he became an Anglican in name and behaviour. In 1904 the royal rulers were baptised at St Paul's Church in Mahe, and on the 23rd of December 1921, they were confirmed (Sargent April 1960). After their repatriation from the Seychelles in 1924, they attended church services in the St. Cyprian Anglican Church in Kumasi that was founded in 1913, and allowed the Anglican missionaries to do their work (Boahen 1975:86; Akyeampong 1999:280-282). Since the 1920s, in reaction to the rise of Anglo-Catholic expansion in England, the Anglican Church in Kumasi became Anglo-Catholic. The Anglo-Catholics could afford to send more missionaries and to provide them with a better education and qualifications to teach at the Anglican school. The Anglo-Catholics were more successful in converting Asante people to Christianity and many of its converts were eager to become better educated and gain material wealth (Jenkins 1974).

The Anglo-Catholics were more under the control of foreign missionaries, which after the installation of Agyeman Prempeh I in Kumasi in 1926 as *Kumasihene* caused a break in their connection with the Asante royal rulers. King Prempeh I ceased to be a communicant of the St. Cyprian Anglican Church and attempted to restore as many precolonial rooted Asante indigenous religious symbols and objects as possible.[64] Prempeh I promoted Christian education because he believed it was important for future generations of Asante in the modern society, but he also restored the harem with stool wives, invested in the restoration of the royal mausoleum at Bantama and of the Golden Stool after its desecrations by the *nkwankwaa* in 1921. Restoring the harem and other indigenous religious customs and symbols disappointed and worried some of the *akonkofoɔ* who had helped the ruling pair to come back to Kumasi and had hoped to bring back a modern leader. Yet, for the Asante royal rulers, restoring the harem was the only option, because otherwise, they would have lost important connections with the royal Asante families and the *nhenkwaa* that were their important indigenous religious traditions (Arhin 1986:51-55). The ruling duo felt that the restoration of the whole Asante institution of chieftaincy would not be realised during their lifetimes, and that they would reign over their people under colonial rule. To bind the Asante indigenous believers to them without being subversive to the British, whom they feared would send them back to the Seychelles Islands, they disposed the Golden Stool, the most important symbol of political power in the eyes of Asante indigenous believers, to the church of the coloniser (Akyeampong 1999:304-305; 2003:51-55).

The Roman Catholics

In terms of the incorporation of Christianity in AIR, *Asantehene* Osei Agyeman Prempeh II, and the Asante *ahemma* Konadu Yaadom II, and Ama Serwaa Nyaako continued the project that their predecessors had started. They encouraged their subjects to become Roman Catholics rather than to be associated with the church of the coloniser. In 1967, they offered a piece of land for the foundation of the St. Hubert's seminary in Kumasi. The belief of the traditional authorities in Roman Catholicism did not prevent them from remaining Asante indigenous religious believers, and also believing in Jesus as Nana, '*the Great and Greatest Ancestor*' (interview with Peter Sarpong, 11). When king Prempeh II spoke the Lord's Prayer he never closed his eyes as no Asante indigenous religious believer is expected to do. He doubted whether there was a Heaven (*Onyankopɔng Kurom*) but at the same time uttered a deep fear for the Hell fire (*Obonsam Kurom*). Despite their Roman Catholic background the ruling authorities followed the royal protocol by visiting the stool room at Bantama to honour their ancestors – the departed Asante royal rulers – during *akwasidae* (Anti 1996:178-180).

A development in the history of the Roman Catholic Church that has stimulated interreligious dialogue is the transition stage from Vatican I (1869 –

[64] An example of an indigenous religious symbol is the *Aya Kɛseɛ*; a huge brass pan that stood in the shadow of the *banyan* tree in front of the Bantama royal mausoleum (see 7.6. photograph 1).

1960) to Vatican II (1962–1965). In the latter period, the Roman Catholic Church was much more tolerant toward the incorporation of elements of IRs into Roman Catholicism. The ruling authorities were pioneers in finding common elements in Catholicism and AIR. Their positive attitude toward religious syncretism throughout the colonial period is evidence for the continuity of their religious peacekeeping role.

4.5 Conclusion

In this chapter, the author provided insights into the relationship between the continuation of the indigenous religious mediatory and peacekeeping roles of the Asante royal rulers Prempeh I, Prempeh II, Konadu Yaadom II and Ama Serwaa Nyaako, and the persistence of chieftaincy in the colonial period. Asante chieftaincy in this period took many forms. Under the ruling duo Prempeh I, and Konadu Yaadom II, the institution became known as the Council of Kumasi, which was a transformed form of the precolonial Kumasi Council. Under Prempeh II, and his female co-rulers, the Asante's traditional political institution took the form of a 'resurrected' Asante Confederacy. In this period, the Asante traditional state rulers and all other Asante traditional authorities maintained their indigenous religious mediatory and peacekeeping responsibilities, and Asante chieftaincy persisted. These responsibilities were to legitimise their institution with the help of symbols derived from the Asante religion and to regulate the relationship with Europeans and Muslims. The *akonkofoɔ*, the *nkwankwaa* and the *nhenkwaa* maintained loyalty to their royal rulers and continued to believe in their sacredness. As religious peacekeepers, Prempeh I and Konadu Yaadom II prolonged cordial relationships with the Muslims and Christians, despite the rebellion of orthodox Christian converts, by providing them with religious freedom, e.g. to allow the Muslims to build mosques and Qur'anic schools and the European Christian missionaries to build churches and schools. Prempeh II and the Asante state *ahemma* continued to carry out their indigenous religious mediatory and peacekeeping functions. Under their reign, the *nkwankwaa* regarded the Asante institution of chieftaincy as a sacred institution and the Asante royal rulers maintained a relatively cordial relationship with the Christians and Muslims in the Kumasi metropolis. These traditional rulers converted to Catholicism and were co-founders of the United Party (UP), a body that united the interests of Asante political lobbies with those of the Muslims in Kumasi.

It should be remarked that in comparison with the precolonial period, during the colonial phase the significance of the Asante royal rulers' indigenous religious mediatory role had diminished. As an effect of the influence of the spread of Islam and of Christianity and of colonialism, the number of *Kumasifoɔ* who believed in the nineteenth century rooted *tete abosom* and ancestral spirits had been reduced. Since the end of the nineteenth century, the *akomfoɔ* therefore decreased in popularity except for the *akomfoɔ* and the witch-catching deities (*abosommerafoɔ*) of the neo-indigenous religious shrines, which increased in popularity throughout the colonial period. Also, in the precolonial period Asante of royal descent, who were either educated and/or wealthy, occupied most stools. This change in the occupation of an Asante stool meant a diminishment of the importance of the lineage and its celebration by the performance of indigenous religious rituals (*adae*), which negatively affected the indigenous religious mediatory role of the Asante royal rulers. Besides the membership of a royal family, the possession of elitist qualifications became important as a basis for a right to rule. The royal rulers' indigenous religious peacekeeping role, on the other hand, increased in importance due to the increase of numbers of Christians and Muslims into Asante society. Their peacekeeping role was to lead the Asante community into modernity by linking it with the several Christian traditions brought by European missionaries and with the Islamic traditions, while safeguarding the essentials of the indigenous religious value system. In terms of Berner's processes of systematic religious syncretism, the colonial period is characterised by a transition from a C2 to an A1 process. The A1 process emphasises the unity of the goal, the truth of the religions, and the possibility of testing different routes, the latter eliminating the competitive relationship between religions.

Chapter V: The Asante traditional authorities and their indigenous religious mediatory role in today's Kumasi Metropolis

Onipa wu a na onwu – 'One who passes away is never really gone'.

Asante proverb

5.1. Introduction

The aim of this chapter is to investigate the continuation of the indigenous religious mediatory function of the Asante traditional authorities in post-colonial Ghana to explain the phenomenon of the persistence of Asante chieftaincy in this period. Currently, it is no longer self-evident that the rituals that the Asante royal rulers perform are of an indigenous religious nature. Some rituals, such as those being performed at the yearly *Yaa Asantewaa* festival in Ejisu, do not have any roots in AIR. They are not meant to venerate the ancestral spirits and are only being performed to entertain tourists. To draw conclusions on a possible connection between the continuation of indigenous religious royal mediation and the salience of Asante chieftaincy the author's focus in this chapter will be on testing the presence of 'indigenous religious elements' in the following four Asante rituals that were performed in the Ashanti Region in the period between 2004 and 2006: (a) a pre-burial ritual of a deceased paramount chief (b) two private pouring of libation ceremonies of Asante royal rulers (c) the *rite of passage* of enstoolment of a chief, and (d) an *Asanteman Adae Kese* celebration.

The chosen religious rituals are all related and performed in a chronological order, since they form part of the Akan *adaduanan* ritual calendar. An introductory remark is that there happens to be a clear distinction between the official relationship between the 'Asante Indigenous Religion' and 'Asante chieftaincy's persistence' and their connection in actual practice, which is why each of the four rituals will be discussed in relation to these two factors.

5.2. The Asante royal pre-burial ritual of *Saamanhene* Nantwi II and its indigenous religious attributes

The pre-burial ritual of the paramount chief Saaman Nantwi II took place on the 5th and the 6th of March 2006. Nana Saaman Nantwi II was the head of all the *nhenkwaa* of the Asante royal rulers and responsible for the organisation of the palace and the preparation of the king's food. In the eighteenth century, the *nhenkwaa* were all part of a specific division, which was a military or administrative unity that was created to effectively rule over the Asante kingdom. Those divisions have continued to exist up to today. The *Saamanhene* had four *fekuo* in Kumasi under him: the *gyase*, the *ankobea*, the *manwere* and the *nkosuo* people

(Odotei and Hagan 2002:73). In this section, the *Saamanhene*'s funeral ritual, as observed by the author, will be described in the context of the theory of IRs. The main question posed is whether or one should regard the current Asante royal funeral rituals, such as the one of Nana Saaman Nantwi II, as an expression and legitimation of AIR.

Asante funeral celebrations consist of at least four phases. (i) the preparation for after-life, (ii) pre-burial mourning, (iii) the burial and (iv) post-burial mourning (Nketia 1963:58-59). Only close relatives of the deceased obtain permission to observe ritual (i). The preparations for after-life include all rites in connection with the washing of the corpse, the dressing of the body and the pouring of libations. The actual burial (iii) took place in Sawua, the chief's birth village. The postburial mourning ritual (iv) took place after three months before the relatives had gathered enough money to make the proper funeral arrangements to bury their deceased chief. Meanwhile, the body was kept in a mortuary. For the purpose of in-depth analysis, the author has divided the preburial rituals of Nana Saaman Nantwi II into eight events that took place in chronological order (see scheme 1).

Events during the pre-burial ritual
(1). The announcement of the pre-burial rite by the firing of musketry.
(2). Public mourning and dancing on the rhythm of a gong-gong (*dawuro*) and various African drums.
(3). A laying-in-state (*ahodae*) ceremony.
(4). The last expressions of care and respect for the deceased by shaking hands with the *abusua*.
(5). Performances of the musicians of the Manhyia Kete *NnwokorƆ* group and *adowa* dancing
(6). The drinking of palm wine (*nsa fufuo*) and eating of kola nuts.
(7). A gift giving ritual (*adosoa*).
(8). The *akƆm* dance of an indigenous priest (*ƆkƆmfoƆ*).

Scheme 1: events during *Saamanhene* Nantwi II's pre-burial ritual

Early in the morning, the pre-burial ritual of the *Saamanhene* started with the fire of musketry, a generic display of Asante pride and pomp (*ayisɛm*), which in this case announced the death of the paramount chief. His *nhenkwaa* used gunpowder (*atuduro*) that was fired from a local gun (*atuo*) and to drive away evil spirits the *nhenkwaa* used locally made incense (*agyi*). The musketry ritual was followed by a performance of ten of the *Saamanhene*'s 'symbolic wives', who were hired for the task of public mourning and mimic-dancing (*adowa*) (see 7.6.1 photograph 3). The hired mourners wore black cloth (*kuntunkuni*) and red cloth and wept bitterly as an expression of sympathy for the deceased. Black and red are the two colours of the cloth that are worn during all funeral ceremonies and which symbolise the bond between the deceased and the living members of the *abusua*. The colour black in Asante context symbolises maturity, as spiritual potency, energy and communion get darker when they mature (interview with Kwaku Amoako-Attah Fosu, 39). The colour black also symbolises transitions of the soul through death or reincarnation (Bartle 1982). 'Red' is associated with blood and symbolises serious commitment, spiritual power, sacrifice and struggle (interview with Kwaku Amoako-Attah Fosu, 39). More generally it stands for fecundity, passion, danger, defilement, seriousness and dirt (Bartle 1982).

'Public mourning' and *adowa* dancing are meant to invoke ancestral spirits to guide the deceased to the ancestral world (*asamando*). Men only dance during the public mourning event, because normally they must demonstrate their bereavement in a different way. An Asante maxim goes 'wailing, does not make you a man' (Nketia 1955:8). The mimic dance is a stylised, symbolic employment of gestures and movements of the body in tune with the rhythm of African musical instruments. Its main function is to alleviate sorrows and loneliness. The Asante like to dance their sorrows away and to chase away death. Music, such as that made by drums, is generally not designed to add to the sadness of the occasion but rather to provide an outlet for emotion, or to be a means of expressing sympathy and goodwill to the living (*ateasefoɔ*) or 'as a means of making a commentary on the event of death' (Nketia 1963:65). Men who dance at the pre-burial rites of a chief usually hold key positions in the family or in the royal palace (interview with Nana *Maabahene*, 28). Mimic dancers always perform on the rhythm of a *dawuro* and various African drums, such as the 'talking drums'; the *fɔntɔnfrɔm,* the *dono* and the *atumpan,* all of which are used to invoke ancestral spirits. During the *Saamanhene*'s pre-burial ritual, two men in red cloth (*koben*) who played a gong-gong (*dawuro*) accompanied a handful of male mimic dancers. Another four men who were also dressed in red played the drums in a funeral band. Family members of the bereaved usually wear black cloth, whereas all other visitors of the pre-burial ritual should wear red cloth.

'At funerals, bereaved relations are usually not the makers of music, but it is their duty to initiate music-making by verbally informing all friends of the deceased and fellow music-makers or fellow members of a particular association to which the deceased belonged' (Nketia 1963:60). Two men used a huge talking drum (*fɔntɔnfrɔm*) that is either beaten when resting on the ground, such as at the *Saamanhene*'s funeral, or when on the heads of two carriers. The *fɔntɔnfrɔm* can only be used during burial rituals of a royal (interview with *Maabahene*, in conversation with *Maabahene* and Nana Prenhyia, 28). 'Rank or prestige may also be reflected in the details of rites and in the intensity of celebration' (Nketia 1963:58). The *fɔntɔnfrɔm* drums are talking drums and their special function is to drum proverbs or sayings. Rattray (1959 [first published in 1927]:285) remarks regarding the *fɔntɔnfrɔm* that 'their dress is made of silk; they are commonly decorated with skulls of famous enemies; a newly made pair of *fɔntɔnfrɔm* may have a dog sacrificed upon them'. During the ceremony, one man used a *dono*, which is a small drum with a tight membrane at either end in the form of an hourglass. This drum is also called the 'armpit drum', because it changes tone when the drummer squeezes it under the left arm. Another man used a drum (*atumpan*) that is an instrument of prayer and mediation with the sacred order of the deities and the ancestors. The *ntumpane* produces two types of sounds – 'the low or masculine pitch of the tonal language and the high or feminine pitch' (Fisher 1998:34). With these two tones the instrument 'is capable of reproducing proverbs, statements and instructions' (Aning 1968:14). By drumming, the drummer (*ɔkyerɛma*) summarises the myth of creation along with the court crier and the executioner, and he represents the stages of creation and life. *ɔdomankoma* (the Shining One) created the *ɛsɛn* (town crier), then *ɔkyerɛma;* and lastly *Kwawu Kwabrafo* (death)' (Opoku 1978:22).

The drummer uses his drums to invoke the ancestral spirits to ask for their blessings for a successful burial, so that the soul of the deceased can enter the world of *nsamanfoɔ*. Before he can use his drums for this task, the *ɔkyerɛma* has to 'warm up' the drums. He addresses the drum parts and their spirits such as the cedar tree (the source of the wood), and the elephant whose hide forms the membrane over the head and the fibres in the strings and the pegs. He calls upon a dark blue bird (*kokokyianaka*), which is the drummers' totem or patron animal. Then he calls upon *Nyame* and *Asase Ya,* which are the Supreme Being and the Spirit of the Earth whose exploits are recalled and celebrated. The *ɔkɔmfoɔ* referred to the Spirit of the Earth as *Asase Ya*, in contradiction to postcolonial missionary oriented scholars, like Pobee, who currently refer to her as 'Mother Earth' (Pobee 1976; Pobee and Mends 1977). Thereby, these missionary oriented scholars implicitly provide this local spirit of the Earth with abstract and universal attributes, just like they did with the male ancestral spirit *Nyame*. An Asante proverb that alludes to the non-existence of the Mother Goddess in the pre-Christianised AIR goes 'We are all the children of *Onyankopɔn*, and none of us are the children of the Earth' (interviews with *ɔkɔmfoɔ* Agyei, 2). In the missionary-oriented academic literature, however, the sky god *Nyame* is much higher ranked than *Asase Ya,* thereby further undermining the equality in the relationship between men and women in line with Christianity.

When the drummer beats his drum he receives messages from the ancestors and it is through the deep rumbling of the drum that the ancestors speak. Concerning the initiation of the drum and their warming up ceremony, one of the drummers at the funeral that the author spoke to, said: 'These days, we do not sacrifice animals to initiate our drums, neither do we warm them up like in previous times. However, we still use drums to invoke the ancestral spirits'. From the *Saamanhene*'s pre-burial event, one can therefore conclude that ancestral veneration is still a significant aspect of this ritual.

During the 'laying-in-state' (*ahodae*) ceremony the author observed that *Adinkra* symbols were present on the curtains and on the cloth (*ntiamu ntoma* under the body of the deceased paramount chief) (see 7.6.1 photograph 2). The word *Adinkra* (*di nkra*) could be an inversion of the word *nkradie*, which means 'to part, to be separated, to leave one another or say good-bye' and implies a message that a soul (*ɔkra*) takes along when leaving the earth. 'Only humans or spirits who can bear or realise intelligence, possess 'kra' (Wright 1987:24; Willis

1998). *Adinkra* cloth was traditionally only worn by the royal and spiritual leaders for mourning during funeral and burial rites. *Adinkra* symbols often go together with Akan proverbs and can be found again in the form of brass, gold weight figures and other artistic expressions of the Asante, such as brass rings. *Adinkra* symbols have been local to the Asante since the nineteenth century and could also have been named after the *ɔhene* of Gyaman, which was a kingdom in eastern Ivory Coast that was founded in the early eighteenth century, and consisted of all those inhabitants that submission to the Asante *ahenfo*. The Asante fought several wars with the *Gyamanhene* and the overwhelmingly non-Akan majority of his subjects until they conquered the Gyaman state in the period 1739-1740. Only in 1875 did Gyaman recover its independence, as a consequence of the British victory of 1873-1874; the confrontation between Asante and Gyaman came to an end only when the Asante became paralysed by internal strife in 1884 (Terray 1987). In 1811 the *Gyamanehene* Kofi *Adinkra* was believed to wear vermillion *kobene* to mark his defeat: he was then captured and taken to Kumasi after his creation of a copy of the *Sika Dwa Kofi*, thereby challenging the *Asantehene*'s claim to sovereignty over Gyaman (Polakoff 1982:88, 92; Wilks 1989 [first published in 1975]:271).

The *abusua* of Nana Saaman Nantwi II used *Adinkra* symbols to express their feelings towards him. An *Adinkra* symbol representing palm wine (*nsa*) was on one of the white curtains behind the bed on which the paramount chief was laying in state (Rattray 1959 [first published in 1927]:265). 1.  '*Nsa* comes from a design of this name found on *nsa* cloths', and refers to the palm wine that is given to the ancestral spirits during (i) the preparations made for the after-life and (iii) the actual burial ritual. Both are private occasions. *Nsa* is thus associated with the invocation of ancestral spirits.

2.  The *Adinkra* symbol, which is known as a 'state ceremonial swords' (*afona*) goes together with the Akan proverb 'the retiring great warrior always has a royal sword of rest', *Akofena kunim koa, wobo afena kye no safɔhene*. This symbol and proverb refer to the reason why the *amanhene* and *amanhemma* are always laid in state accompanied by a couple of *afona*. These swords not only help them to survive in the world of the *nsamanfoɔ*, but also provide a way for traditional rulers to say 'goodbye'. With the installation of a paramount chief, all *ahene* swear an oath to this royal prior to swearing an oath to the ruling pair. Now that the chief 'has gone to the village' (has passed away) the swords are displayed for the sub-royal rulers to speak their last words with which they show their allegiance to the deceased who are in the process of being transformed into ancestral spirits. During the actual burial ritual, all the swords will go with the Asante traditional authorities to be buried together with the body in the coffin.

The following *Adinkra* symbol 3. , which is a sign of hope, is known as: 'O God, everything which is above, permit my hand to touch it', *Nyame, biribi wo soro ma no me ka me nsa.* This emblem, which originates from at least the colonial period, was stamped on paper and hung above the lintel of a door in the palace. 'The ruling pair used to touch this lintel, then his forehead and breast, repeating these words three times' (Rattray 1959 [first published in 1927]:266).

Hope is necessary for the completion of the journey that a deceased ruler shall have to make in order to reach the world of the royal ancestral spirits (*asamando*): not all subjects nor all Asante rulers automatically become ancestral spirits. Chief Brefo explained that 'those persons who have behaved asocial during their life because might end up as vagrant spirits (*ɔsaman twɛn-twɛn*), whereas those who are infertile (*tofo*) or disabled might never reach the ancestral world' (interview with Nana Brefo Gyededu Kotowko II, 23). The three mentioned *Adinkra* symbols refer to 'the invocation of ancestral spirits', and demonstrate the significance of ancestral veneration during the *Saamanhene*'s preburial ritual. 'Locality' is also an indigenous religious characteristic of this ritual: *Adinkra* symbols are created locally and in its religious interpretations the Asante make reference to local spirits.

Another way for the Asante to express aspects of their AIR is by making use of *Kente* cloths. These are silk and cotton traditional cloths that the Asante weave locally, a practice which initially originated from the Asante hinterland (Rattray 1959 [first published in 1927]:220; Lamb 1975:104-110). The *Kente* cloth came from Bonwire, a village in the Ashanti Region, or possibly Tekyiman that is located in the Brong Ahafo Region of contemporary Ghana (Warren 1974; Ross 1998; Spencer 1998). The names of the various *Kente* cloths refer to Akan proverbs and *Adinkra* symbols. Each cloth consists of strips that are about three to four inches wide, with different patterns and symbolic meanings. Woven strips sewn together form one *Kente* cloth; a cloth is typically ten to twelve feet in length and five to six feet in width (Magee 2005:593). *Kente* weaving is believed to be a gift of *Onyankopɔn* and the loom on which *Kente* cloth is woven is perceived as a divine instrument. Before the weavers start weaving a *Kente* cloth, they use kola nuts, which induce nerve system stimulation, to go into trance and to pour libation to *Onyankopɔn*, the *nananom nsamanfo* and the *abosom* and they ask the spiritual beings to guide them with the loom. Peter King Appiah explained that 'the weavers perform rituals to be able to receive weaving patterns from the spirits that are appropriate to the situation' (interview with Peter King Appiah, 38).

A weaver befriended by the *abusua* of the *Saamanhene* had designed a particular *Kente* cloth to cover the body of the deceased. The *Kente* cloth that the *abusua* chose is called 'Ideas Finished' (*Edwina Asa*). The cloth shows that the family of the deceased chief believes him to be ready to depart to the world of the ancestral spirits. In preparation for this journey, the deceased chief also wore traditional leather sandals (*ahenema*) while 'laying-in-state'. In his right hand the *Saamanhene* 'held' a whisk to protect him against evil spirits during his journey to the world of the ancestors, which confirms that the family believed that he would soon start his journey to that world. *Kente* cloths do not only have a variety of meanings, but the quality of different cloths varies as well; therefore, these clothes are also often used by various families to compete and show off their wealth. Generally, the more expensive the *Kente* cloth used for the *ahodae* ceremony of a deceased person, the wealthier a family is believed to be. The *Kente* cloth used thus does not only say something about the status of the deceased but also of his *abusua.* In terms of symbolic meaning, each type of cloth has its own name that is given to the cloth by its weaver. Just as is the case of the *Adinkra* symbols which were accompanied by Akan proverbs, the author will also look at whether there were strips (*ntomaban* or *bankuo*) of *Kente* cloth that were chosen for the design of the *Kente* cloth of Nana Saaman Nantwi II.

In the *Saamahene's Edwina Asa Kente* the author has identified seven different types of strips. The strips of cloth that she found in relation to the invocations of ancestral spirits were:

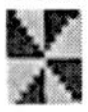 and 2.  'zigzag' (*nkyimkyim)* cloth designs (Smith 1975:38). The angle shapes create staccato rhythms that make the cloth suitable for use in ceremonies, and refer to the synchronised rhythm of a talking drum (*fɔn ntɔnfrɔm, dono* or *atumpan*) that is used for funeral (*adowa*) dances (Thompson 1983:207-222). The chosen colours for the whole *Kente* cloth were yellow, green, gold, black, purple and white. The majority of the colours were dark, which associate the *Kente* cloth used with grief. The symbolic meaning of the colours used is as follows:

Colour	***Symbolic meaning***
Yellow	A reminder of eggs, fruits and gold. Symbolises wealth, fertility, vitality, spirituality and sanctity.
Green	Associated with planting, vegetation and harvesting. Symbol of growth, fertility, life, fruitfulness, rejuvenation.
Gold	Associated with gold–the precious metal, and symbolises wealth, glory, high status, elegance and spiritual purity.
Black	Things get darker as they mature and the Akan people make things darker to make them spiritually more powerful. Symbol of spiritual potency, maturity, energy and communion. 'Generally, the colour black shows recognition of life changes: death, reincarnation, ancestral power, stool power, history, tradition, and memories' (Bartle 1982).
Purple	Associated again with female essence. Symbolises life and healing. Almost always worn by women.
White	Associated with the white of an egg and white clay used in purification ceremonies. Symbol of spirituality and gods. 'Symbol of fertility, joy, purity, victory and cleansing (Bartle 1982).

Scheme 2: symbolic meaning of *Kente* cloth colours. Source: interview with Kwaku Amoako Attah Fosu, 39.

The use of a *Kente* cloth in itself also has a symbolic meaning. In many non-Western societies, cloths are used to sustain relationships with animals, ancestral spirits and divinities, which is why cloth is also often used in shrines. The Asante use *Kente* cloth to venerate the *Tano* deity *Twumpuduo* in a shrine room in Tuobodom (Busia 1998:64). Since the late seventeen century *Tano* is a well-known river deity in the Ashanti Region that originates from Bono and who has various other deities under him. In the nineteenth century, river deities (*atano*) were believed to be significant beneficent tutelary *abosom* that were venerated on one of the bad days (*da bone*), either *fodwo* or *fofie* (Bartle 1978). According to Bonnat in the nineteenth century children were ritually killed on these days. The *atono* are significant spirits, because they are believed to be the children of the twin ancestral serpent spirits *Nyame* and *Ngame*. The more important the deity is, the more important his shrine, and the more expensive the acquired *Kente* cloth. Besides, the Asante also use *Kente* cloth as a medium to communicate the rank and social status of a particular person to both spiritual beings and human beings (Darish 1988:112). An example of *Kente* cloth that clearly refers to an Asante's ancestral lineage is for instance *akyempem*. As mentioned before, *Kente* cloth also has a religious connotation because of the way it is manufactured. It is through the observance of strict taboos, such as the absence of women near the loom during their menstruation period, that *Kente* cloths obtain their religious meaning. The discussion of the *Saamanhene*'s *Kente* cloths and the *ahodae* ceremony demonstrate that locality and the invocation of ancestral spirits are significant for this third of the *Saamanhene*'s pre-burial rite events.

The fourth of these of the *Saamanhene*'s events was the shaking of hands of various groups (militaries, servants and sub-chiefs) who were closely related to him. These groups shake hands in order to severe ties with the family of the deceased, to break the relationship with the deceased as a living person and to establish a relationship with him as a spirit. One of the chiefs that the author spoke to after the pre-burial ritual said: 'When we shake hands with the family of the deceased, we think about the deceased and we wish him good luck on his journey to *asamando*' (interview with Nana Prenhyia, 28).

For the fifth event, the performances of the musicians of the *Manhyia Kete Nnwokorɔ* group and *adowa* dancing, 'locality' and 'the invocation of ancestral spirits' were also significant. In Asante funeral dirges, such as those of the 'Manhyia Kete', much attention is paid to the domicile of both the ancestors and the deceased. In the case of Nana Saaman Nantwi II both his birthplace Sewua, which is a craft village of goldsmiths (Johnson 1979:81; Schneider 1987:414) 'located eight miles southeast of Kumasi' and 'Ashanti Town', a district in the city centre of Kumasi in which the *Saamanhene*'s house was located (near Manhyia palace), were mentioned. In AIR, the domicile of the deceased is mentioned in the dirges, because these places are the bonds between a person and his ancestors. A village and especially its burial grove containing the members of the lineage are regarded as the common habitat of the *nsamanfoɔ* and the living (*asefoɔ*). In these days, many people spend most of their lives outside their birth village and therefore important ancestors of the clan of the deceased who died inside a section of the town (*borɔno*), or in other towns, can also be mentioned in a funeral dirge, depending on the preferences of the singers. A member of the *ɔyokoɔ* clan can, for instance, be associated with *ɔyokoɔ* people in Kumasi, Kokofu, Bɛkwae and Dwaben.

The 'locality' of the deceased's origin is mentioned because his domicile demonstrates how (s) he was related to both the living and the ancestral spirits. The relation to the living is emphasised in the dirges by praising the social qualities of the deceased, such as his benevolence and generosity. By praising the deceased, the clan members do not only emphasise the loss for the community, but also show how (s) he was related. Important praise appellations and by-names were given to the deceased when (s) he was in good relationship with the living. During the observed pre-burial rite, the *Saamanhene* was praised as a 'warrior' (*Barima*), which is a title reserved for royal rulers.

The Asante make reference to the ancestral spirits by making use of a standard set of dirges, which refer to particular common clan ancestors. The clan of the deceased determines which of these dirges will be used. The *ɔyokoɔ* clan, together with the Dako clan is dominant in Kumasi. However, since each deceased is not only a clan member but also an individual, the 'standard' dirges are also adapted here and there to be able to refer to the particular relationships of the deceased to his *abusua,* other living clan members and to the ancestral spirits. Examples of standard *ɔyokoɔ* clan dirges that were sung during the *Saamanhene*'s funeral were a name song (*amankwatiaa*) and a praise song announcing the arrival of the *Akyɛmpimhene* 'Amankwatiaa', who was an Asante war general. Among the many *ɔyokoɔ* clan standard dirges, the clan members mentioned this name song because Nana Saaman Nantwi II had played an important role in the Ghanaian army. This also explains why many soldiers were present during his pre-burial ritual. Particular reference was made to some of Nantwi II's colleagues in the army, which gave the standard dirge a personal note (interview with nana *Maabahene*, 28). The standard praise song for Nana Akyɛmpim was not personalised. The *Akyɛmpimhene* is the title given to the first son of a king, who is symbolically in charge of the sons and daughters of the past and present *Asantehene*. As during many *ɔyokoɔ* pre-burial rites, this paramount chief represented the *Asantehene*. The Manhyia Kete *Nnwokorɔ* group sang a praise song to announce his arrival and informed the audience that 'a grandchild was coming', which refers to the mutual lineage history of the *Saamanhene* and the *Akyɛmpimhene.*

A third standard song, known as 'ancestors' (*nsamanfoɔ*), was adapted to reflect the history of the lineage of the deceased. This song reminds the spirit of the deceased of his father and grandfather. They tell the spirit of the deceased about all his ancestors. They also refer to the specific matrilineal bloodline (*mogya*) and extended family (*abusua*) relationship of a person, which derives through his or her mother and his or her *ntoro,* which is derived from her father. The *abusua* is important for a person because it impacts upon one's individual norms, values, behaviour and social role in society. Membership of an *abusua* requires certain ritual obligations and the observance of taboos. The *ntoro* determines the way people greet each other and what they can and cannot eat. Food taboos are dependent on the deity (*ɔbosom*), and for some, on the totem to which the *ntoro* is linked (Clarke 1930:460).

In dirges, the *ntoro* and *abusua* are honoured because they determine the membership of the deceased to two social groups, both of which have lost a member in the form of the deceased. Although in social life the importance of both family (*abusua*) ties and the membership of an *ntoro* group for individual Asante is declining, in funeral dirges, the Asante make reference to both of these elements of their identity. During funeral rites the relationship of the deceased with both the living and the ancestral spirits is emphasised. The ancestors are mentioned in funeral dirges for at least two reasons. First, the dirges give an opportunity for the family to remember the ancestors and refer to their personality, character, conduct and accomplishments. Secondly, it is believed that during the pre-burial ritual, the spirit of the deceased is still among the living. Therefore, the ritual is seen as a last opportunity for the living to inform the deceased about his ancestors and his origin. The deceased's relatives hope that this information will enable his or her spirit to find the world of the ancestors. Although there is acknowledgement of a break with the deceased in relation to the physical body, the spiritual connection between the deceased and the living is to persist into eternity. Therefore, there must be some guidance from the living and gifts to the deceased to enable him to make the journey to the land of the spirits (Chukwukere, De Mahieu et al. 1981:62-63; Arhin 1994:310-311).

The sixth event consisted of the drinking of palm wine (*nsa fufuo*) and the eating of kola nuts. A big red truck entered the square in front of the house of Nana Saaman Nantwi II and a blue container full of *nsa fufuo* was lifted out of the truck.[65] Male family members of the deceased who were all dressed in *kuntunkuni*, which shows their association with the dead, carried the container to the square. Then, one of those men used half of a plastic bottle to take out some *nsa fufuo* from the container and gave the bottle filled with *nsa fufuo* to one of the male family members of the deceased to drink. After this man drank the *nsa fufuo,* he presented the plastic bottle to one of the other men who wore *kuntunkuni.* This way the men distributed the *nsa fufuo* among themselves. The women who belonged to Nantwi II's *abusua* also drank palm wine, but in a less public venue. They took their share later on that day when they sat together on red plastic chairs at the end of the street that was fenced off for the celebration of the pre-burial ritual. Traditionally, the Asante drank *nsa fufuo*, which is an alcoholic liquid, at funerals to show respect to the ancestral spirits and 'to bridge the gap between the living and the spiritual worlds' (Akyeampong 1995:262). The main purpose of drinking palm wine is the 'invocation of ancestral spirits'. The invocation of ancestors in this way forms another piece of empirical evidence for the

---

[65] *nsa* means 'alcohol', *fita/fufu* means 'white'.

significance of these spirits, who are venerated by Asante during current Asante funeral rituals. Together with the drinking of *nsa fufuo* there was the distribution of kola nuts, which were consumed by men and women. The Asante use kola nuts, which contain caffeine, *theobromine* (Greek for god's spicen – *theos broma*) and *kolanin*, for producing a stronger state of euphoria and well-being. Although the living members of a matrilineage belong to the same group as the ancestral spirits, they are in a different stage of life as those spirits. This thought is expressed by the Akan maxim: 'The one who has kola has life' (interview with Kwaku Amoako-Attah Fosu, 39). 'Locality' also played a role in this event, because palm wine and kola nuts are forest products and stimulants used in indigenous religious rituals that are native to the Ashanti Region.

The seventh event during the pre-burial ritual was 'the giving of gifts' (*adosoa*) and *nsa*. Women wearing *koben* on their forehead, right shoulder and neck carry the *adosoa* and are besmeared with red clay (*kotobirigya*). They chew kola, which shows that they are bereaved and that they belong to the same *abusua* as the deceased. They carry a metal tray on their head containing different types of cloth and *ahenema*. In this case, it also contained bottles of the 'original' schnapps from Holland (J. Henkes Jonge Bols from Schiedam) which the Asante also refer to as *nsa* (van den Bersellaar 2007). There is also a less expensive local version of schnapps, but bringing in the more expensive and foreign one contributes to the social prestige of the *abusua*. It was therefore explicitly mentioned that the schnapps came from Holland. The presentation of *nsa* could be seen as the modern and symbolic version of the drinking of *nsa fufuo*. The donors of both *adosoa* and *nsa* are families connected through marriage (de Witte 2003:536-540). Donating the *adosoa* and the *nsa* symbolise the commodification of the relationship between the families and the deceased. The more *adosoa* and *nsa* are donated to families of the deceased, the better the bond between the families of the donors and the deceased and the more they can count on reciprocity of gifts during forthcoming funerals. The *adosoa* and *nsa* are a symbolic way of maintaining good relationships within the *abusua* and they are often accompanied by an amount of money contributed towards the costs of the funeral. In contrast to members outside the family who contribute to the funeral costs by giving money instead of *adosoa* and/or *nsa*, in-laws are not supposed to give money only. In line with their relationship with the *abusua* of the deceased, they are expected to deliver a more intimate contribution in the form of *nsa* or *adosoa*. 'Giving money' is the standard way for people outside the *abusua* to give their condolences and confirm the relationship with the family of the deceased. The amount of money that is given depends on the value of goods consumed by the guests during the pre-burial ritual, and on the presumed reciprocity of money gifts by the *abusua* of the deceased during forthcoming funerals. To strengthen ties with their *abusua* and disclose the amount of money that the family expects to be reciprocated, 'money gifts' are always publicly announced. The amount of money that the *abusua* receives from its guests reflects its social prestige, because all extra contributions from guests – those who do not cover the actual costs of the funeral should be paid back by the *abusua* at upcoming funerals. Therefore, at the end of a funeral the family announces that there is a debt, which prevents the family from paying back huge amounts on future funerals.

The eighth funeral event was the *akɔm* dancing of an experienced indigenous priest, dressed in white cloth, who frequently gave spiritual advise to the ruling pair and other royal rulers and elders (see 7.6.1 photograph 5) (interview with the *Maabahene*, 28). *Akɔm* is different from normal dancing. It is a religious ritual, but is also admired as art, enjoyed as entertainment and it is a tool to make political statements (Hanna 1979). *Akɔm* dancing is performed at festivals, funerals and other religious rituals. Prior to *akɔm* dancing the indigenous priest or priestess has to request to the deities (*abosom)* to come and enter their body by offering an animal sacrifice, e.g. a chicken. If the chicken dies falling down with his face on his left side it means that the *ɔbosom* has rejected the sacrifice, if it dies with its face on the right side it has accepted the offer. The *ɔkɔmfoɔ* will feel the deity's acceptance of their body by sensing that something rests on his or her shoulder. Then, he or she will enter into a trance, speak in a different language and behave in a way that does not correspond with his or her usual behaviour. Subsequently, the spirit medium will start singing and dancing thereby requesting the musicians to follow the rhythm of the deities. The audience can then ask questions to the *abosom* that manifest themselves through the body of the medium. The medium, whose individuality is suppressed by the *ɔbosom* but who is in control of them, gives meaning and context to the *abosom*'s answers by the use of Asante proverbs, maxims and poetic language. Whereas the *abosom* are thus the *ɔkɔmfoɔ's* source of passive or spiritual knowledge, the myths and proverbs are the symbolic language in which he or she speaks to the audience and/or his clients (interviews with *ɔkɔmfoɔ* Agyei, 2). Two *abosom* are believed to sit upon the shoulders of the spirit medium during trance. These are the nature deities, such as the river and mountain spirits, who they simply call the *abosom* and the *abosom brafo*. Trance by *abosom* is said to bring fertility. The Asante believe that these deities make barren women pregnant and bring rain to the land and that they are important because they are 'a life-sustaining source of water and food' (Silverman 1987:273). Examples of famous Akan *abosom* are the rivers *Prah, Bea* and *Tano*, the lake *Bosomtwe* and the Ocean (*Bosompo*) (Owoahene-Acheampong 1998:91). The function of the executioner deities (*abosom brafo*), such as the famous *Bere-Kunde* and *Aprade-Tongo*, however, is to get rid of evil spirits who are said to be threatening the well-being of the inhabitants of the Asante kingdom and to control witchcraft. Since the 1920s, these deities are held to have manifested themselves in the *akɔm* dance of the *akɔmfoɔ*. The new type of deities entered AIR at the time of an economic crisis among the cocoa farmers, when these farmers were looking for more powerful deities from northern Ghana to help them to overcome their economic problems (Christensen 1959:277; Allman and Parker 2005:143-182). Three *akɔmfoɔ* dressed in white, who were ritually possessed by the *abosom brafo* performed the *akɔm* dance at the square in front of the Manhyia royal palace and were mimicking serpents as part of their dances. One of them wore a skirt (*odoso*) made of raffia; a talisman made of animal skins (*sebe*) and traditional beads (*ahwenee*) and wore twinkling bells (*adoma)* around her ankles. Next to the musicians who rhythmically supported the dancers sat a man holding a pan that contained two whisks (*bodua).* The bodies of the *akɔmfoɔ* were covered with white clay *(hyire)* symbolising the personification of the *abosom,* the essence of which is to cleanse evil spirits (Bartle 1982:82-91). A person on whom *hyire* is placed is believed to be in a heightened state of spiritual grace and is close to the ancestors. *Hyire* is said to be a potent substance that empowers these portions of the body that receive it (interviews with *ɔkɔmfoɔ* Agyei, 2).

Wreaths of a plant (*asuani*) were passed over their shoulders and crossed, passing under the arms. In the past, widows used these plants during their one year period of mourning after the death of their husband (Rattray 1959 [first published in 1927]:172-174). The two other *akɔmfoɔ* were wearing *bata kari kese,* which was introduced by the Mande-Dyula *alim* clerks and traders to the Ashanti Region in the fifteenth century (Hiskett 1984:131-135) (see 7.5 maps 5 and 7). To create a rhythm, two men were drumming with hooked sticks on an *atumpan* and two others were using their bare hands to beat a *dono* drum. Two other men were creating rhythm by using a *dawuro*. A few onlookers were watching the traditional priests and dancers. The majority of the audience gathered behind the railing of the Manhyia palace. In *akɔm* dancing, the *akomfoɔ* communicate with the *abosom brafo* by using their body as their medium of expression. They hold their hands in the sky and dance in circles to chase away evil spirits. Their eyes are red, which is caused by the use of a sap made from special leaves of a local plant, that encourages dissociation. Another characteristic of *akɔmfoɔ* in states of mediumship is that their eyelids twinkle very often. While the *akomfoɔ* are dancing *atumpan* players use the rhythm of their drum to invoke the ancestors and to drive away evil spirits. 'Locality' also plays an important role in present-day pre-burial *akɔm* dancing, as the *abosom brafo* that are invoked are localised spirits. Although imported from northern Ghana in the 1920s, these spirits now belong to the pantheon of indigenous religious deities in the Ashanti Region. Besides being married to an *obosom*, each *ɔkɔmfoɔ* has his own connections with deities in the spiritual world, which means that during *akɔm* dancing (s)he invokes those *abosom* with whom he or she has a personal connection. An important *ɔbosom* that was invoked by the performing *ɔkɔmfoɔ* Adwoa Bona was, for instance, *Aprade Tongo*. *ɔkɔmfoɔ* Tawiah invoked the *ɔbosom* Akonode Asuo Gyebi, which belongs to the locality 'Kronom'. The purpose of pre-burial ritual *akɔm* dancing is to cleanse the environment and to drive away evil local *abosom*. The music on which the spirits make the *akomfoɔ* dance, the types of drums they use, the *akomfoɔ*'s association with the spirits and their knowledge of plants all depend on a local indigenous religious context. Locality is thus a significance characteristic of *akɔm* dancing. Furthermore, the author's conversation with *ɔkɔmfoɔ* Akyei demonstrates that *akɔm* funeral dancing is also of an indigenous religious nature, because of the significance of the invocation of spirits during this ritual. As *ɔkɔmfoɔ* Agyei said: '*Akɔm* dancing is not an act or performance. I am not an actor or a weaver of illusion. I am a trained medium, who deals with the reality of the spirits. It is usually my catching up with the *abosom* and sometimes with the ancestors that make me dance. The deities are like radio waves and it is my two-way connection with them that keeps me moving. I do not act or pretend the spirits to be there, but they come and go. When they are there I catch up with them and I know how to interpret their messages' (interviews with *ɔkɔmfoɔ* Agyei, 2).

The underlying scheme below gives insight into the findings regarding the significance of the invocation of ancestral spirits and locality for the described events during the *Saamanhene*'s pre-burial ritual.

Events during the pre-burial ritual	***Elements of Asante Indigenous Religion***
(1). The announcement of the pre-burial rite by the musketry of fire	Locality
(2). Public mourning and mimic dancing on the rhythm of a gong and various African drums	Invocation of ancestral spirits
(3). A laying-in-state (*ahodae*) ceremony	Locality, invocation of ancestral spirits
(4). The last expression of care and respect for the deceased by shaking hands with the *abusua*.	Invocation of ancestral spirits
(5). Performances of the musicians of the Manhyia Kete *Nnwokorɔ* group and *Adowa* dancing	Locality, invocation of ancestral spirits
(6). The drinking of palm wine (*nsa*) and eating of kola nuts	Invocation of ancestral spirits
(7). A gift giving ritual (*adosoa*)	Invocation of ancestral spirits
(8). The *akɔm* dance of an indigenous priest	Locality

Scheme 3: events during Nana Saaman Nantwi II's pre-burial ritual and the elements of AIR in those events.

The above scheme demonstrates that in four (1,3,5,8) out of eight of the described events that were part of the *Saamanhene*'s preburial ritual, locality was a significant characteristic. For another six (2,3,4,5,6,7) events, the 'invocation of ancestral spirits' was significant. In the next section, the author will demonstrate the connection between the resilience of pre-burial rituals, such as those of the *Saamanhene* and the persistence of Asante chieftaincy.

5.3. The *Saamanhene* II's pre-burial ritual in the context of the persistence of Asante chieftaincy

My findings with regard to the statutory necessary and sufficient connections between the resilience in the performance of Asante indigenous religious rituals, such as the *Saamanhene*'s preburial ritual, and the persistence of chieftaincy are based on fieldwork in the National House of Chiefs (NHC) and the Regional House of Chiefs (RHC) in Kumasi. The NHC is the umbrella organisation of all RHC in Ghana and it represents more than 32,000 recognised traditional rulers who exercise considerable influence throughout Ghana, especially in the countryside. In article 272 of the 1992 Constitution of Ghana the functions of the NHCs are set out. Of great importance with regard to funeral rites is article 272 (c), which shows that traditional authorities are meant to 'undertake an evaluation of traditional customs and usages with a view to eliminating those customs and usages that are outmoded and socially harmful'. Furthermore, article 27 of the Constitution states: 'all customary practices which dehumanise or are injurious to the physical and mental well-being of a person are prohibited'. Additionally, amendments to the Criminal Code have made some of these practices a criminal offence, such as widowhood rites that force a woman to sleep next to the body of her dead husband or force her to appear naked in front of an audience (see: section 88 (a), Section 69 (a) and section 314 (a) of the Criminal Code).

As a product of these laws, the NHCs and all RHCs now have regulations on how traditional rituals should be performed. With regard to funeral rituals, there are generally two practices that are believed to be outmoded and socially harmful by the members of the mentioned HC (including *Asantehene* Osei Tutu II) and the national Ghanaian government. These practices are:

(a) Lavish spending on funeral rituals by poor people.
(b) The performance of widowhood rites after the celebration of funeral rituals, which according to the 1992 Ghanaian Constitution are known to be a criminal offence.

Funeral rituals are not only about the deceased but are also a status symbol of what a family has achieved, celebrated through a display of lavishness and conspicuous consumption. It is therefore tempting for poor families to borrow money to celebrate the death of one of their members. Funeral rituals can be considered as harmful when the celebration costs are an unrealistic reflection of the social status, and thus leaving the financial capital of the *abusua* of the deceased.

To help poor people in the Kumasi metropolis avoid running into serious debt due to funeral celebrations, the Ashanti Regional House of Chiefs (ARHC) has compiled a list of regulations which, among other things, determines the maximum price for material necessities such as a coffin, the various objects used for the *ahodae* ceremony and the number of musical bands invited to the funeral (no more than two).

In Kumasi, which is known as 'Ghana's funeral capital', there are about fifty funerals per weekend. These funerals are important for the economy. In a report on, among other topics, the contribution towards funeral costs by Ghanaian migrants – most of whom were Akan – Mazzucato (2005:13) concludes: 'Funeral ceremonies [LM: in Ghana] sustain a diverse range of business and services adding to economic activities and employment possibilities in Ghana'.[66] For instance, the rent of plastic chairs with *Adinkra* symbols, the creation of coffins by artists, the production of videos, music CDs, photographs and T-shirts with a picture of the deceased are all produced locally. From an economic perspective, funeral rituals per se are thus a contribution to local economic enterprise and are not perceived as harmful. Besides, socially, the funeral spending is the way for the family members of the deceased to demonstrate the social significance of their *abusua*. The video films of the funeral, for instance, are 'not only being produced to remember the deceased, but also to be able to compete with other *abusua* in the social ranking on the basis of the number of VIP guests who attended the funeral in and outside Ghana including Europe' (interview with Nana Ama Serwah Nyarko, 29). Not surprisingly therefore, the author observed that the video filmmakers concentrate on the funeral audience rather than on its ritual. Although funeral spending has thus a clear socio-economic advantage, Major (rtd.) Courage Quashigah, the minister of health, recently made an effort to raise national consciousness against excessively costly funerals. In his opinion, in a country with mortality rates at an average of fifty-seven years for adults and sixty-eight deaths per thousand births for infants, it would make more sense to spend money on the improvement of healthcare than on conspicuous consumption during funeral celebrations (Agency, the 8th of July 2007).

Although there are different points of view on the degree of perniciousness of funeral rituals, what academic authors, such as Mazzucato, on this rituals and the members of the RHCs in Kumasi have in common is that they believe it to be detrimental for poor people to borrow huge amounts of money: figures can be as high as 5,658 pounds for funerals of members of their *abusua*, while Ghana has an annual capital Gross National Income (GNI) of 452 pounds (World Bank 2008:334).[67] A cynical outsider might say this is all about prevent-

---

[66] In Ghana, 6 percent of all remittances are spent on funerals.

[67] Mazzucato, V. 2005. "Ghanaian Migrant's Double Engagement: A Transnational View of Development and Integration Policies," *Global Migration Perspectives* 48: 1-17. This report mentions the example of a female migrant who she interviewed who spent 5,658 pounds on a funeral of a deceased family member, which was four times her income. For further information on the reasons of poor people for borrowing money for funerals see Twum-Barima, S. A. (09-05-2007). Lavish Funerals and Poverty. The Statesman. The 'Gross National Income' (GNI), the broadest measure of national income, measures the total value added from domestic and foreign sources claimed by residents. GNI comprises 'Gross Domestic Product' (GDP) plus net receipts of primary income from foreign sources.

ing commoners from competing with the big men in the lavishness of their funerals. However, the Asante Kwaku Amoako Attah Fosu who wrote a book on Asante funerals, told the author:

> Because the royal rulers are sacred, there is and should be a difference between the celebration of their funerals and those of ordinary people. The burials of Asante royal rulers endure two weeks, whereas the funeral of ordinary people usually is only one day and those of royal rulers should be more expensive, because they are the earthly representatives of the ancestral spirits (interview with Kwaku Amoako Attah Fosu, 39).

In line with AIR, the spending of huge amounts of money on the burial rituals of royal rulers is thus generally accepted.

(b) Widowhood rites are performed as part of AIR. When a woman's husband dies, her soul (*sunsum*) should be separated from that of her deceased husband. If no widowhood rites are performed or they are not performed properly it is believed that her husband's *sunsum* can come back to earth to sleep with her, to make her barren (Rattray 1959 [first published in 1927]:171). Widowhood rites are derived from the Asante belief that ancestral spirits and the living are part of the same spiritual community, 'the living-dead' (1992[first published in 1969]:83-91). The rites prevent the soul of a woman's deceased husband from coming back to disturb her. Among the Asante, such rites are rarely performed for widowers, and if so, the rituals are much shorter and less humiliating than in the case of the rites that are performed for widows. According to the Kumasi State Council (KSC) regulations on funerals 'widowhood rites should be discontinued'.

In conclusion, the statutory regulations of the ARHC that are set out in points (a) and (b) do not support the existence of any relationship between the resilience of AIR and the persistence of Asante chieftaincy. On the contrary, the points demonstrate that officially the traditional authorities are assumed to rather discourage the performance of what they consider outmoded Asante indigenous religious rituals. The 'KSC' regulations of 2006 state that 'chieftaincy in Ghana is a modern institution and its task is to prevent the performance of rituals, which are harmful or outmoded'.

The author found out, however, that with regard to funeral celebrations the traditional authorities do not follow these regulations. According to the KSC regulations there should, for instance, not have been more than two drum bands, whereas at Nana Saaman Nantwi II's funeral, four drum bands were present. The regulations also forbade the serving of drinks and the hiring of gifts, whereas they were part of the *Saamanhene*'s ritual. They further say that 'a person may

---

Data are converted from national currency to current pounds using the 'World Bank Atlas Method' (WBAM). This involves using a three-year average of exchange rates to smooth the effects of transitory exchange rate fluctuations. GNI per capita is GNI divided per midyear population.

not "lay-in-state" with an expensive cloth and gold items during pre-burial rituals'. Nana Prenyia remarked, however, that 'the costs of Nana Saaman Nantwi II's *Kente* cloth were, however, around 260 pounds' (interview with Nana Prenyia, 28). Perhaps needless to say, this is a considerable amount in a country where highly developed or educated people (*abengfo*) earn around a thousand pounds a year. Another of the KSC regulations is that after the funeral only one other funeral ritual should be performed at the fortieth day, which forms part of the *adaduanan* Akan ritual calendar. What actually happened, however, was that both one week and forty days after the post-burial mourning rite (iv.), funeral rituals were still being performed.[68]

Apart from these observances, several respondents informed the author that with regard to the regulations on the performance of traditional rituals, the traditional authorities have a double standard. While their subjects are advised not to spend too much money on funerals, those that the traditional authorities organise for colleagues and other prominent members within the society are lavish. In case of the 'ARHC' it is the House itself that finances the costs for those funerals. In case of the recently deceased *Kumawuhene* 'Barima Asumandu Sakyi II', who is the chief of Kumawu in the Sekyere East District of Ashanti, the Kumasi Traditional Council (KTC) appointed a funeral committee of sixty *Otumfuo* – members to plan the burial and funeral arrangements. With permission of *Asantehene* Osei Tutu II, the KTC funeral committee, which falls under the ARHC, lent 60,000 new Ghana cedis (GHC) [3,070 pounds] for the preparation of the chiefs' burial place, his actual burial ground, the ground for the celebration of the funeral, and schnapps. It is usually the Kumasi Metropolis Assembly (KMA), who 'as protocol demands', donates at the funeral of paramount chiefs. Officially, the KMA has a 'free margin' of 6.5 percent of the total yearly KMA budget to spend on social activities, such as funerals. In practice, however, approximately 33.3 percent of the yearly KMA budget is spent on funerals. The autonomy of District Assemblies (DAs) in all likelihood contributes to an easy misappropriation of resources, particularly where the assembly is not accountable to anyone. The poor are victims of a lack of basic capital, because they normally pay taxes but are not involved in any budget decisions and do not benefit from any city expenditures (King, Inkoom et al. 2001:157,160, 180-184).

With regard to widowhood rites, five of the author's female respondents confirmed that unofficially those rites are being performed. When a woman's husband dies, she needs to take a bath three times a day with cold water, usually under the supervision of an older woman, which means that she does not have any privacy. The rites put these women in an embarrassing situation. A female respondent, who prefers to stay anonymous, lost her husband a few years before,

---

[68] Nketia, J. H. K. 1963. *Drumming in Akan Communities of Ghana*. Edinburgh: Published on Behalf of the University of Ghana by T. Nelson., mentions that in addition to the four mentioned phases to one stretch of funeral celebration there are subsequent periods of mourning on the 8th, 15th, 40th and 80th days and on the first anniversary, though these are officially no longer strictly observed.

and said: 'When I lost my husband, I was not allowed to shake hands with anybody because they were afraid that his spirit would come and disturb them. I had to undergo certain rituals to separate my soul from that of my husband's. For instance, I had to shave my hair, take several ritual baths per day and was forced to stay naked in the presence of others. I needed to stay in a room for days and was not allowed to come out. When I was finally allowed to leave I was being asked to marry my dead husband's brother'. Another of the author's respondents, who is also a widow, remarked: 'When I lost my husband five years ago, I was asked to sleep next to his dead body. My family told me that "one who dies is not really dead" – *onipa wu a na ɔnwuyɛ* – and that if I refused to sleep next to his body, his soul would come back from *asamando* to disturb me or other members of my *abusua*.' Since the Ghanaian constitution of 1992 the performance of widowhood rites has been recognised as a criminal practice. However, the answers demonstrate that unofficially, widowhood rites continue to be performed in the Ashanti Region, including the ones such as 'being forced to be naked in the presence of others' and 'being forced to sleep with one's dead husband'.

Therefore, it can be convincingly argued that there is no official connection between the resilience of AIR and the persistence of Asante chieftaincy. Instead, there are many indigenous religious rituals for which the Asante royal rulers have created customary laws that should prevent harmful indigenous religious rituals from being performed. Unofficially, however, the traditional authorities have continued to perform these rituals, such as pre-burial rites, and have not reduced the recently highly increased commercial costs involved with their performance.[69] Those costs include rent for silk *Kente* cloth, the salary for 'traditional' *Nnwokorɔ* dancing groups,'traditional' drumming bands, ghetto blasters, and photographers and cameramen to record the images of the funerals of prominent people.[70] The Asante institution of chieftaincy is still largely legitimised by AIR. There is therefore a strong correlation between the continuation in the performance of harmful – and/or expensive – indigenous rituals and the persistence of Asante chieftaincy.

The crucial question is, however, whether the reasons of the traditional authorities to perform these and other Asante rituals are of an indigenous religious nature. According to van der Geest, who conducted six and a half months of fieldwork (in 1994, 1995 and 1996) among the Kwahu Akan group, the reason for the performance of indigenous religious rituals is mainly social. Van der Geest remarks: 'My view of the Akan funeral is that it is more social than religious, more *diesseitig* ('this-worldly', lit. 'this-sidedness') than *jenseitig* ('otherworldly', lit. 'other-sidedness'' (van der Geest 2000:107). He also said: 'I will

[69] In the precolonial and colonial period 'traditional' funerals used to be less costly, mainly because the performance of Asante indigenous religious rituals was not as commercialised as today.

[70] The deceased family gave the author of this book permission by to use her video camera to record Nana Saaman Nantwi II's pre-burial ritual for academic purposes. No money has either been received or paid to create the video stream.

argue that the deceased and his or her dead body, though apparently at the centre of the funeral, are primarily symbols, ritual objects that the family needs to perform a ceremony for itself' (van der Geest 2000:107). His main conclusion is that 'the principal gratification does not lie in the glorification of the deceased, contrary to what the words and rituals suggest, but in the self-glorification of the organisers, the *abusua*, and other related groups' (van der Geest 2000). De Witte, an anthropologist who conducted fieldwork in the Ashanti Region, followed in his footsteps and wrote: 'It seems to be family status which is at stake rather than the status of the deceased'. "Respect for the dead" is the framing narrative families use to celebrate their own excellence' (de Witte 2003:535-536) .

Although gaining social prestige is certainly a reason for Asante *abusua* to perform indigenous rituals, the author does not agree with van der Geest's observations that this-worldliness (*diesseitigkeit*) is more significant than the otherworldliness (*jenseitigkeit*). De Witte's conclusion that among the Asante the status of the deceased is less at stake than that of the family is also refuted by the author's data. In her opinion, the status of the deceased and the family is equally important, simply because they are indistinguishable. In AIR, the living and the dead are part of the same family and are in a reciprocal relationship. The higher the social status of the deceased and the living members of the *abusua,* the more they benefit from one another's′ existence. The focus during the funeral rituals is therefore as much on the living members of the *abusua*, as on its deceased members. However, by separating 'the living' from 'the dead', one does not acknowledge the unity or the bond between the two types of members of any given *abusua*.

In a wider context, this means that the author does not agree with the creation of an academic distinction between 'social' and 'religious' aspects of African funeral rituals. In fact, an absolute distinction between these two aspects can only be made when one uses a Eurocentric definition of 'religion', that accepts a binary opposition between *diesseitigkeit* and *jenseitigkeit.* The author is of the opinion that Africanist academics can better use a concept of religion that corresponds to the reality of religious experiences of Africans in Africa. In IRs, one does not clearly distinguish 'the religious' from 'the secular'. The concept of 'Indigenous Religions' emphasises the importance of the ancestral spirits and does not clearly attempt to separate 'the physical' or natural from 'the metaphysical' or supernatural (Cooper 1988). Why are the traditional authorities so keen on the performance of the Asante indigenous rituals, seeing that these very authorities have set the rules on what is permissible and non-permissible at funerals?[71] And why are they, even more so than people poorer than themselves, so eager to break their own rules? From an indigenous religious perspective this

[71] From debate in Ghanaian newspapers on funerals in Ghana, the author understood that most poor people do not have lavish funerals, just like most poor people do not buy expensive houses or cars. See: *The Statesman*, *The Accra Daily Mail*, *The Ghanaian Times*, *GNA*, especially in the period between November 2005 and April 2006.

makes sense, because Asante royal rulers are prominent and powerful persons within the society, which means that when they turn into ancestral spirits they will remain prominent and powerful. And so it is especially important for the family of deceased royal rulers, but also for their subjects, to make sure that in the form of an ancestor (s) he will remember them positively after arrival in the spiritual world, and this can be realised by the celebration of a lavish funeral. As Rattray (1959 [first published in 1927]:104), puts it:

> In the ceremonial for a dead king the differences possibly [LM: in comparison with ordinary deceased individuals] arose from a desire on the part of his people, not only to accentuate the disparity between the king, *Asantehene*, and the common herd, and even the great chiefs, but also to preserve his remains more carefully and reverently in order that these might serve as a medium or shrine for his spirit when it was summoned to return to his people in times of national reunion or national emergencies.

The important function of the Asante royal rulers as major mediators with the spiritual world explains the contradiction between setting and breaking the rules with regard to the performance of Asante indigenous religious rituals; the so-called chieftaincy paradox.

In conclusion, the study of the pre-burial ritual of Nana Saaman Nantwi II demonstrates that the Asante indigenous religious elements, 'locality' and 'the invocation of ancestral spirits', were significant aspects of the *Saamanhene*'s preburial ritual. However, it also reveals that there is, only an official relationship between the presence of Asante indigenous religious elements and the persistence of Asante chieftaincy.

5.4. Two Asante rituals performed by chiefs where libation is poured and the Asante Indigenous Religion is significant

In this section, the author will again examine the statutory and actual relationship between AIR and the persistence of Asante chieftaincy. Traditional authorities perform two types of libation. While they are sitting in state, the pouring of libation is public and is performed by the *ɔkyeame*. Libation is a form of prayer and a form of communication between the living and spiritual beings (the *abosom* and *nsamanfoɔ*) where unifying the living and spirits is attempted.[72] The pouring of libation, which is an act of pouring a liquid, for example from a sacrifice, reminds the Asante that they are not self-sufficient but dependent on spiritual beings who intercede for them in every aspect of life. The function of pouring libation is also to ask spiritual beings for blessings. It is an opportunity for the performer to show off and display his or her knowledge of the Akan culture, especially Akan proverbs and history and important community events that occurred in past and present times. Libations are poured by both Asante men and

[72] *Libare* means to pour an offering.

women, who each have different functions in diverse settings, which are an obligatory part of their position, are private or public, and have a religious and/or political purpose. The purpose of libations is both religious and political. They are performed to invoke blessings for the community, but also to make reference to political leaders and are a subtle way of communicating veiled communal political discontent. At the royal's palace, the *ɔkyeame* performs a private religious libation ritual in the chief's stool room to invoke his family's ancestors on ritual sacred days (*akusidae*). In most cases, the *ɔkyeame* pours libation for the chief. In some exceptional cases, however, when the chief is not in his village, he himself pours libation. In all cases, the one who performs the pouring of libation ritual, whether the chief or the *ɔkyeame*, should have undergone his puberty ritual (*bragro*). Usually, performers are older, since it takes some time for people to gain enough knowledge about Asante history and culture to demonstrate their knowledge during performances.

Since the precolonial period, pouring libation has been an obligatory part of the religious function of the Asante traditional authorities. Every Asante royal ruler is obliged to celebrate the two types of *akusidae*, every six weeks (the *akwasidae* and the *awukudae*). The *akwasidae* are reserved for honouring personal and community ancestors and always fall on a Sunday.[73] *Awukudae*, or 'little *adae*', falls on a Wednesday and is reserved for the veneration of ancestors. It is also a day on which Asante practitioners can make donations towards any good cause and visit those who are ill. In the Kumasi metropolis the *akwasidae* is more popular among traditional authorities than *awukudae,* because, in addition to their chieftaincy duties, most traditional authorities also have to work in town. Therefore, it is not very convenient for them to leave their places of employment during the week to travel back to the village and fulfil their religious obligations. However, those traditional royal rulers who do not pour libation on any of the *awukudae* will be charged and when there are many charges against them, they can easily be destooled. Therefore, the pouring of libation is an art that is performed in both private and public settings on many religious and political occasions by various (religious) leaders, both male and female, in Asante society.

For the following two private libation-pouring rituals, the author will now demonstrate the extent to which the 'invocation of ancestral spirits' and 'locality' were significant for the performance of these rituals. Then, she will enhance understanding of the official and unofficial relationships between the pouring of libation and the persistence of Asante chieftaincy.

Nana Brefo Gydedu Kotowko II, chief of Gyamasi, stated that the libation pouring ritual performed in his stool room – a room that is filled with the stools of former ruling ancestors – is a private, secret and sacred ritual.[74] Nana

[73] *Kwasidae* is Sunday.

[74] Gyamasi is located twenty-five miles north of Kumasi, near Mampong.

Brefo first indicated that for this reason, he could not share everything concerning the ritual he performed. He stated the following:

> On *akwasidae*, my linguist goes with me inside the stool room, where he first calls upon the ancestral spirits. He then fills a whisky glass with schnapps and each time he mentions a spiritual being, he drips some of the liquor on the earth. He starts by 'pouring libation' for *Onyankopɔn* and *nananom*. Then, he calls the rivers and waters that are associated with me, for instance, Lake Bosomtwi and the river Prah. After each river of water, he says *nsa* (liquor) and spills some alcohol. The type of rivers that are mentioned, however, differ each time my *ɔkyeame* performs a pouring of libation ritual. Finally, he calls my family and the ancestors of my community, for instance, Yaw Kotoko I, Adudei, Nana Mensa or Adu Nku. Which ancestors are mentioned depends on the situation. He asks for help for my family and my subjects in whatever situations or challenges which are before me and them (*nsa*). He also asks the ancestors to help to continue to let my family and my community grow (*nsa*). He says, for instance, 'Nananom, I know that you will do this for Nana Brefo Gydedu Kotowko II and our community. And, I thank you for your assistance'. Then, he finishes with the words Yoooooooo and pours out all of the drink that is left from his whisky glass. After the pouring of libation, he remembers the first ancestors by leaving mashed yam (*etɔ*) in front of the stool. He asks them to support the lineage and to bring blessings to his people. After this ceremony, he walks back together with his linguist and a boy who carries my palanquin to the *ahemfi*. Meanwhile, his stool wives have cooked food for all of my subjects and help me feed them. Traditionally, a chief's subjects always bring food to the palace for the stool wives to cook. These days, there are not many people who bring food, but we still cook for everybody who comes to the palace during *awukudae*. Giving food is a way of making a sacrifice on behalf of the people (interview with Nana Brefo Gyededu Kotowko II, 23).

The second chief that the author interviewed on the Asante libation pouring ritual is Nana Yaw Dwubeng, chief of Achiase Nwabiagya.[75] His explanation of the libation ritual he performs during the *akusidae* is as follows:

> My linguist pours libation for my ancestors, who are also venerated by my subjects, to contact the spiritual beings. The libation is meant to create a sacred space on earth and to bring the past alive. It is meant to unify the deceased members of our family with the living. My *ɔkyeame* starts the libation by calling upon God, the Dependable One (*Otwedeampɔn*). Then, he calls the ancestors and pours libation (*nsa*). He invokes local deities and asks them to come and receive their drink. He mentions, for instance, *Tankwasi*, who is a priest-professor deity that came from a very small village and is now venerated in the whole of the Kumasi Metropolis. Then, he mentions the names of all the river spirits and asks them to drink. For example, the Ofin River spirit (*Ofin*, *nsa*) and the Densu river spirit are both invited to drink (*Densu Asuo Yaa, nsa*). Then, he invites all Asante matriclans to come and drink (e.g., ancestors of the *oyoko* clan (*Oyokofoɔ*, *nsa*) and those of the Bretuo clan drink (*Etena ne Bretuo*, *nsa*). He next asks all deities and ancestors again to come and receive a drink and asks them to give us good health and a good temperament. He finishes with the words *Yɛn a yɛahyia nyianaa nkwa so* 'to the health of all of us who gathered here'. Besides the pouring of libation, we add two hard-boiled eggs to propitiate the ancestral spirits, male and female, which are a symbol of life and fertility. During the last *akusidae*, we slaughter a sheep. If we had more money, we could do it more often, but sheep are expensive these days – one sheep is between 600,000-1000, 000 million old cedis – which is why we slaughter them only once a year (interview with Nana Yaw Dwubeng, 3).

The above descriptions demonstrate that during the royal pouring of libation ancestral spirits are invoked. 'Locality' also plays an important role in all rituals,

[75] Achiase Nwabiagya is located north of Kumasi and forms part of the Kumasi metropolis.

since authorities call upon local deities, such as river and water spirits. The ritual of pouring libation shows many similarities with the local hymns that are sung as part of the Manhyia Kete *Nnwokorɔ* group performance. Both religious events are meant to invoke help from ancestral spirits and natural deities for the living. The mentioned hymns for ancestral spirits, who are part of the *abusua* of the living, are sung to qualify the deceased as a good ancestor (*saman-paa)* so that (s) he can depart to the world of *nsamanfoɔ*. Deities are also called upon to reveal the family background of the deceased. If the living neglects to sing such hymns for the deceased, chances are higher that they will end up losing their way while travelling to the land of the ancestors and be classified as vagrant spirits (*ɔsaman twɛn-twɛn*). In that case the *ɔkɔmfoɔ* will have to carry out special rituals to guide the spirit of the deceased to *asamando.* The same applies for deceased individuals who are not qualified as ancestors (*tofo*), due to a violent death that damaged their body so badly that it could not be recovered for the *ahodae* ceremony. The Asante believe that with the help of special rituals, eventually these deceased individuals will be brought to *asamando.* If not, both those deceased – consisting of the living and the dead – who are qualified by the *abusua* as *ɔsaman twɛn-twɛn* and those qualified as *tofo* will end up disturbing the living as wandering souls, either as an ancestor who is lost or as a deceased person.

Instead of helping one deceased individual, who occurs in the case of a chief's ritual pouring of libation, local ancestors and natural deities are invoked to help the entire community.

5.5. The pouring of libation ceremony and the relationship between the Asante Indigenous Religion and the persistence of Asante chieftaincy

Statutorily, there is a strong correlation between the resilience of AIR and 'the persistence of Asante chieftaincy', because the invocation of local spirits including the ancestors during a pouring libation ritual is how the Asante royal rulers continue their relationships with the deceased royal rulers on the basis of whom they legitimate their religious-political power. Without a continuation of the relationship of the Asante royal rulers between their ancestors and the living kin, would Asante chieftaincy as an institution continue to exit? Nana Brefo Gydedu Kotowko II, who believed the answer to this question is positive, stated the following:

> As a chief, I have to establish a liaison between the living and the deceased spirits of my extended family. If I fail to do so, I will not receive the spiritual powers that are necessary to be a ruler, which means that chieftaincy will not persist. The ancestors are the custodians of the laws, customs and traditions of our society and, therefore, we need to abide by their rules. As long as we listen carefully to our ancestors, our community will continue to live in prosperity (interview with Nana Brefo Gydedu Kotowko II, 23).

According to Brefo, the invocation of the ancestors is still a significant factor in the persistence of Asante chieftaincy. However, Brefo also demonstrated that his belief in the significance of the ancestral spirits for chieftaincy is no longer shared by a large number of people. He said:

> Nowadays, there are so many churches around, that few people in the Kumasi metropolis really give serious thought to the idea that by pouring libation you become their spiritual leader. Christianity, the cosmopolitan character of the area and the enhanced education of subjects, have affected the religious authority of chiefs (interview with Nana Brefo Gydedu Kotowko II, 23).

Brefo exemplifies that in actual practice the relationship between AIR and Asante chieftaincy, statutory and non-statutory, is as follows:

> If there is a catastrophe in the village, such as a cholera epidemic, then as a chief, you are responsible for coping with it. It is our religious duty to perform rituals to please the ancestral spirits and failing to do so will be a charge against us. If there are many charges, one can easily be destooled. However, today, there are not many of my subjects who believe that a cholera disaster comes to them because they have angered the spirits. If such an epidemic breaks out today, everybody goes to the hospital, because they know its cause. So, officially, I have to pour libation and sacrifice to the spiritual beings to restore relations with them, but in actuality, nobody will rush to me in Kumasi and beg me to perform those rituals in Gyamasi, which is my village. Education has brought the knowledge to my subjects that cholera is caused by bacteria, rather than the spell of spiritual beings (interview with Nana Brefo Gydedu Kotowko II, 23).

Traditional authorities are thus obliged to perform statutory religious rituals, including libations, and they believe in the reality of the spirits. In actual practice, however, the performance of such rituals is believed to bring prosperity, whereas, its neglect is no longer necessarily believed to bring misfortune. Nana Brefo Gydedu Kotowko II concludes with the following:

> Generally, we believe that ancestral spirits will guide us, but in times of disaster, such as a cholera epidemic, my subjects put more trust in modern medical treatments than the advice of ancestral spirits (interview with Nana Brefo Gydedu Kotowko II, 23).

Nana Brefo's remark demonstrates that indigenous practitioners combine the passive wisdom of their ancestors, which can be derived from introspection with the active wisdom derived from sense data and scientific findings, depending on the nature of their problems. The acceptance of multiple sources of knowledge has been an aspect of Asante culture since the precolonial period, when indigenous practitioners combined the wisdom of the *akomfoɔ* with their traditional authorities and the Asante *Nkramofoɔ*. These days, the point of focus of Asante indigenous practitioners has changed. They now combine their passive intuitive knowledge derived from indigenous religious leaders, such as the royal rulers and the *akomfoɔ*, and their intuitive knowledge derived from Islam and Christianity, with active knowledge derived from North Atlantic science. AIR has thus remained pragmatic and multi-stranded. This explains how despite the mentioned new religious and scientific influences in Asante society, the Asante traditional authorities have been able to continue to fulfil their spiritual mediating role and are still being perceived as sacred in the eyes of their indigenous religious subjects.

5.6. A rite of passage for enstoolments and the presence of indigenous religious elements

The focus of this section will be on a paramount chief's rite of passage for enstoolment. Female paramount Asante rulers undergo a similar enstoolment ritual. After a destoolment or the death of a chief, the traditional authorities have to make a decision in consultation with their elders and subjects about who is going to be enstooled as the new chief. *Offinsohemma* Ama Serwah Nyarko states that after the burial of a chief, the elders of his family announce to all royal rulers that the stool is vacant. Every royal may apply for the position of a chief, but there are certain criteria that make it unlikely that some royal rulers will be chosen. For a candidate to be selected, he needs to have a proven record. He should not chase other men's wives; he should not drink excessively or have a criminal record. He should also not be physically disabled because a chief is supposed to become a good ancestor (*saman-paa*), in order to help the living and it is believed that those royal rulers who have a physical impairment will not be able to reach *asamando*. To make a decision about a prospective chief, the elders and the female ruler need to research his personal history and his moral behaviour. Nana Ababeo said:'The community also researches the prospective chief's knowledge about his connections with the spiritual world (e.g., local natural deities, such as those of the rivers and mountains), because they believe that these connections might spiritually affect them once the prospective chief rules' (interview with Nana Ababeo, 30).

Once a selection of a chief has been made, the invocation of the ancestors plays a role in three phases of the enstoolment rite. First, the ancestors are called upon inside the stool room, where the ancestral spirits choose a traditional ruler. The ritual that is performed inside the stool room by the *ɔkyeame* is a secret ritual overseen by the *abusua panin*. Once the ruler is confined inside the stool room, the *abusua panin* educates him or her on many aspects of chieftaincy. Finally, after the royal has been installed and has been shown to the public, the *ɔkyeame* invokes the ancestral spirits; a ritual that goes together with the slaughtering and offering of a sheep. The royal rulers' first *ɔkyeame* will finish the ritual by performing the first libation pouring ritual and will repeat his performance during every following *akusidae*.

The Asante *rite of passage* of enstoolment can best be understood with the help of the theory of Belgium-born anthropologist van Gennep (1960 (first published in 1908), who made a distinction between three phases: the preliminal phase (separation), the liminal phase (transition) and the postliminal phase (incorporation).[76] During the preliminal phase, the royal spends time in a stool room, which is a physically separate space where ancestors are believed to be present. The room represents the royal's transition from the outside unknown realm to the inside realm. This phase is characterised by his or her symbolic separation from his or her social environment as a sign of respect towards the ancestors. The separation is realised by the performance of religious rituals by an *ɔkɔmfoɔ*, who sprinkles the royal rulers with white clay, which transmits the potent spiritual power of the ancestral stool to the royal rulers, and then pours libation to bless and protect them from bad spirits. During the liminal phase, the royal ruler has no position and is neither an insider nor outsider. Dependent on his behaviour during the period of confinement in the stool room, he or she may become incorporated into chieftaincy and is thus transformed to the position of an insider. In this phase, the royal learns the dos and don'ts of his or her function. He or she is instructed in the history of the stool, the history and social and political structure of his community and chieftaincy in general. The elders point out important landmarks in the history of the community, such as famines, plagues and wars, to him or her, while the taboos and customs of the people are explained. The history of their people includes traditional accounts of ancient homes where they came to settle, the reasons behind emigration and the roles and achievement of their former leaders. Normal rules of behaviour may be suspended or exaggerated and the royal's ritual companions, the *ɔkyeame* and the *abusua panin,* are allowed to humiliate him or her; a practice that can only take place when normal rules are suspended. Body (*honam*) and soul (*sunsum*) need to be transformed so that they can be united and the relationship with the ancestors can be fortified. The royal has to spend seven days on a sheep's skin, and is offered poor food and has poor bedding during the night. Sometimes, the liminal phase is so physically difficult that if the male or female co-ruler of the royal does not properly support him or her, the prospective royal dies. In this case, the ritual companions explain his or her death as a rejection by the ancestral spirits. According to Nana Brefo Gydedu Kotowko II, however, today, the only foods not allowed during the period of confinement are pepper and salt. With regard to physical endurance, he mentions that the testing of strength is only important for certain stools for chiefs in military service. The general rule with regard to installation rituals is that the more important the royal ruler, the more elaborate and demanding the enstoolments rites are. Today, however, a traditional ruler rarely dies or is severely physically harmed as a consequence of these rites (interview with Nana Brefo Gydedu Kotowko II, 23).

[76] The term limen is Latin for 'threshold'. van Gennep uses this term when referring to the symbol or literal change of physical space in which a person resides during the transition phase. In the case of the chief's rite of passage, the physical space literally and symbolically changes.

The function of the post-liminal phase is to reintegrate the royal into the community. The traditional ruler, who is nameless and stateless during the liminal phase, now receives the name of one of his or her forefathers that previously occupied an ancestral stool, which is another way in which ancestral power is symbolically transmitted to them. Nana Brefo Gydedu Kotowko II mentions that in the past, the chiefs had to enter the stool room blindfolded. They then had to pick the name of a stool of a particular ancestor, which they would receive. Nana Brefo Gydedu Kotowko II would be called as such because he pointed to a stool of an ancestor of the same name, which could be of a different lineage. Today, however, a royal may choose what name he or she prefers, so that he or she can be sure of receiving the name of an ancestor of his or her own lineage. Today, the demands of the spirits are manipulated by human intervention to protect the royal's lineage (interview with Nana Brefo Gydedu Kotowko II, 23). In the author's opinion, the ritual change should be interpreted in a diminishment in the authority of the spirit, the fear for his possible wraths in case of disobedience and of the royal's mediatory function.

The royal's rite of passage of enstoolment is a dialectical process that goes from structure (*preliminal*) to anti-structure (*liminal*) back to structure (*post-liminal*) (Turner 1991). During the rite, the social and political structures of the community are first questioned and then re-established (1960 (first published in 1908)), after which, the new chief is accepted within the society. The descriptions in this section of a modern royal enstoolment rite, demonstrate that the locality of spirit and the invocation of ancestors are significant attributes of this rite. The relationship with the resilience of AIR in these types of royal rituals and its relation to the persistence of Asante chieftaincy will be discussed in the next section.

5.7. The relationship between a royal's rite of passage of enstoolment and the persistence of Asante chieftaincy

Statutory, the Asante enstoolment rites reveal that the invocation of ancestral spirits and the connection with local deities continues to be important in the mediatory functions of an Asante ruler, which serve to legitimise Asante chieftaincy. In actual fact, however, the royal's rite of passage of enstoolment has become much easier and the actual belief of the Asante in the authority of the spirits and of the spiritual power of the royal rulers has been diminished. Today, the actual relationship between chiefs and subjects is no longer based on a reciprocal pact with the spiritual beings, which were the source of the royal rulers' passive or intuitive knowledge. Nevertheless, many Asante believe in the reality of the ancestral spirits but as benign guides and healers rather than as fearful bringers of misfortune.

5.8. Asante indigenous religious elements of the *Asanteman Adae Kese* festival

The *Asanteman Adae Kese* festival, which literally means the big (*kese*) burial ground (*adae*) of the Asante state (*Asanteman*) and the extent of its indigeneity, will be the focus of this section. *Asanteman Adae Kese* is the modern version of the *Odwira* festival that was first celebrated in 1717. The festival combines elements that formed a part of the *Odwira* festival in the precolonial period and events that have been added in the colonial or postcolonial periods of the Asante history. The first open celebration of the *Odwira* festival took place in 1985 and was meant to mark the fiftieth anniversary of the restoration of *Asantehene* Prempeh I and the *Amantoonum* in 1935. The here described celebration of *Asanteman Adae Kese* in Kumasi took place between the 15th of March 2004 and the 16th of May 2004 and was celebrated together with the birthday and fifth year reign of *Asantehene* Osei Tutu II. The theme of the festival was '*Asanteman Adae Kese*: promoting traditional leadership for accelerated development', which demonstrates that today the festivals are about more than the legitimation of the institution of chieftaincy by performing religious rituals. Its purpose is also to promote the modern role of the traditional rulers as development workers, to support current development projects and to educate the Asante youth on Asante traditional culture. The most important remnant of the *Odwira* festival that was incorporated in the *Asanteman Adae Kese* celebration is a purification ritual performed at Lake Bosomtwi.

As explained in Chapter III, the purpose of the *Odwira* festival was to legitimate the power of the Asante royal rulers and the supreme council (*Asantemanhyiamu*); its celebration was thus politically motivated. During the colonial period the open celebration of the *Odwira* festival in Kumasi was suppressed, although the *adae* continued to be celebrated in the surrounding villages (Lewin 1978). The return of the traditional ruler Prempeh I to Kumasi in 1925, the restoration of the Asante Confederacy in 1935, and the installation of Prempeh I as *Asantehene* did not led to the open and stately celebration of *Odwira,* which was banned under colonial rule. In 1985, fifty years after the foundation of the Asante Confederacy, the *Odwira* festival was celebrated again. However, this time it was not only celebrated to legitimate the institution of Asante chieftaincy (and especially the Asante Traditional Council) but also to discuss Asante cultural-religious identity politics and to reveal the demands of the Asante people to Ghanaian national politicians. Under *Asantehene* Opoku Ware II, who also celebrated the twenty-fifth year of his office, the *Odwira* festival was again a cultural-religious celebration but was used to install a development chief (*nkosohene*), who was trained to discuss development issues with these politicians, such as the need for more schooling for girls and better health care. The planning of this festival in February clearly demonstrated its detachment from the celebration of the new harvest in September/October and the concomitant invocation of the ancestral spirits. Besides, the indigenous ritual of the cleansing of the *abusua*'s *ntoro* from evil spirits (*akradware*) was interpreted in a modern context and used as an occasion to cleanse the environment from waste. Since 1998, the festival has been organised by the Asante Congress, which is an organisation that was founded by the modern *nkwankwaa* consisting of the Asante Kotoko Society, the Kumasi Youngster Club and the Asante Students Union. Since 1991, the *Odwira* festival has been celebrated every four years, with the exception of 1999, when the Asante Congress was much occupied with the organisation of the enstoolment of *Asantehene*, Osei Tutu II, who is still ruling. In other districts of the Ashanti Region, the *Odwira* festival is celebrated every year on both district and village levels. The national celebration of *Asanteman Adae Kese* in Kumasi is the culmination of a series of yearly-celebrated local *Odwira* festivals in the Ashanti Region (interview with Osei Kwadwo, 26). With regards to the national 2004 *Asanteman Adae Kese*, the author will discuss to what extent the locality and the invoking ancestral spirits were significant aspects of this celebration.

'Locality' plays an important role in the celebration of the *Asanteman Adae Kese* festival. The Asante royal rulers attribute great importance to this festival for the maintenance of good relationships between the local community, the ancestors and the other traditional authorities. To engage in business in the Kumasi metropolis, one needs to have a good relationship with the *Asantehene*, since every person in the metropolis is the kings' guest, as he embodies all ancestral land. For businessmen paying homage to the *Asantehene* is therefore an important event during the festival. Businessmen, market women and other inhabitants of Kumasi give the *Asantehene* gifts, such as a sheep or goat meant for the ancestors, or money. *Kente* cloth weavers in Bonwire usually give some free cloth to the king, whereas the market women in Kumasi give free tomatoes and cassava. The Asante present gifts to the *Asantehene* because he allows them to stay and trade on his land with permission of the spirits. During the festival held on Thursday the 15th of April 2004, many companies brought gifts to the *Asantehene*, including the 'Ghana Telecom Company' (GTC), who presented a cheque of sixty million old Ghana cedis [508,717 pounds], 'Photographs-Riker Pharmaceuticals' (PRP), who presented a cheque of five million old Ghana cedis [35,869 pounds] and 'Unipharma Company Ltd'. (UC), who presented two bottles of aromatic schnapps and one carton [200 bundles] of paper napkins. Apart from companies, many clubs paid homage to *Otumfuo*, such as members of the AKS, the Nkosuo Fan Club of Nkosuo FM Radio Station, both of who presented two bottles of aromatic schnapps meant for the pouring of libation (interview with Kwaku Amoako Attah Fosu, 39). Good relationships must be maintained between Asante family members. Before the start of the *Asanteman Adae Kese* and the local *adae* festivals in the Ashanti Region, Asante families must settle all disputes and resolve issues in order to receive blessings from local deities during the forthcoming year. The idea is that before one can cleanse the whole of *Asanteman* from evil spirits, every Asante should be on good terms with his or her family (interview with Patrick Domfeh, 36). In a material sense, locality has everything to do with gift-giving to maintain harmonious relationships with local spirits (see 7.6.1 photograph 4). Besides, evil spirits from the Asante state (*Asanteman*) should be cleaned. According to the Asante, evil spirits that, for example, cause witchcraft (*bayi*) enter a person through his or her *mogya*, which symbolises the link with their *abusua*. Therefore, it is only through contact with one's family members that one can be bewitched, which implies that evil spirits are always local. Spiritually, locality also played a role during the *Asanteman Adae Kese busumuru* rites held on Monday, the 17th of May 2004 that were meant to protect the *Asantehene*'s *busumuru* sword that the Asante traditional authorities used to swear an oath to the *Asantehene* against attacks *akɔmfoɔ* from local evil spirits.

Besides, the festival is also still an occasion on which the traditional authorities demonstrate their allegiance to the Golden Stool and on which local nature deities are venerated. The Asante believe that each town has its own eternal nature deities, because unlike the ancestors, natural elements like rivers and trees can never die. Important river deities of the Kumasi metropolis include *Sumankwaa* and *Tano-Adwuman*. Other local deities are *Fofie* and *Asuo Aketego* of Bomso-Kumasi, Apumasu of Edwinase Kumasi and Odefour Anyanor of Ayigya Kumasi.[77] Besides these ancient local nature deities, on the 23rd of April 2004, the *akomfoɔ* invoked the executioner deities (*abosom brafo*). To demonstrate their powers to a public audience one *ɔkɔmfoɔ* swallowed an egg whereas another chewed raw charcoal (see 7.6. photographs 6 and 7). After the *abosom brafo* performance, they shook hands with the *Asantehene* and pledged an oath of allegiance to him. In return, the king provided them with schnapps to be used in the future to pour libation and invoke the *abosom brafo* spirits. The first event in which the invocations of ancestral spirits, which are another indigenous religious element, play an important role is *kuntunkunidae*. On the 28th of March 2004, at the venue Dwaberen Manhyia palace at 11:00 a.m., all Asante that participated in the festival put on *kuntunkuni* cloth: a brown cloth that comes from the bark of a tree called *kyenkyen*. Symbolically, the cloth represents bereavement. *Kuntukunidae* marks the start of a forty-day period in which funerals are banned as well as eating *etɔ*, since this staple food needs to be pounded, making

---

[77] For more on the *Fofie* cult in southern Ghana see: Venkatachalam, M. 2012. "Between the Devil and the Cross: Religion, Slavery, and the Making of Anlo-Ewe," *The Journal of African History* 53(1): 45-64., Venkatachalam, M. (2012). Slavery in Memory. Anthropology. London, SOAS. PhD., Venkatachalam, M. 2012. "Between the Umbrella and the Elephant: Elections, Ethnic Negotiations and the Politics of Spirit Possession in Teshi, Accra," *Africa* 81(2): 248-268., Müller, L. and M. Venkatachalam 2013. "African Conversion Revisited: A Comparative Study of Religious Change in Asante and Anlo society, c. 1820 – c. 1940," *International Journal of African Historical Studies*: Forthcoming.

lots of noise. In fact, there is a ban on everything that makes noise, including pounding food, dancing and drumming to remember the ancestors. On Saturday, the 30th of March 2004, there was a cleaning exercise at Asawasi and Amakom, two districts in Kumasi. This event consisted of the cleaning of the environment, the ritual cleaning of shrines and temples and the washing of domestic materials, such as cooking pots. This exercise was perceived as preparing for the invocation of ancestral spirits. Then, on the 12th of April 2004, around 17.00 p.m., ancestral spirits were invoked during a purification rite at Lake Bosomtwi, which is located thirty kilometres south of Kumasi. In precolonial times, Asante warriors who had killed human beings had to purify and release themselves from the dead spirits of their enemies before they were allowed to return to Kumasi by washing themselves in the lake. This purification ritual involved the ritual slaughter of a sheep, cow or fowl. The warriors were obliged to step in the blood (*mogya*) that was poured on the earth before entering Kumasi. During the *Asanteman Adae Kese* celebration in 2004, a bird and a cow were ritually sacrificed. After Nana Saaman Nantwi II, who helped in the financing of the festival, had poured libation and said a prayer, the throat of a living bird was slit and was then set free to swim on the surface of the water. The bird died on its back with the chest facing the sky (*dayaya*), symbolising the Lake's approval of the celebration of the festival. After the fowl, a cow, believed to be a highly prized domestic animal, was also ritually killed. During the rite, the *Asantehene* addressed a prayer to the lake, then cut the cow's throat and quickly removed its heart and some of the lungs, which were cast into the lake. As soon as this was done, the assembled people fell upon the carcass and cut it up, portioning out the meat to everyone.

Another *Asanteman Adae Kese* event that took place on Wednesday, the 14th of April 2004, at 9.00 a.m., was a performance by *atano akomfoɔ* who are connected to *atano abosom*, which are powers that are derived from rivers, including the river *Tano* in northwest Asante. In the Ashanti Region alone, there are about sixty-five *atano-abosom*. Two principal *Tano* deities in the Kumasi metropolis are *Sumankwaa*-deity and *Tano-Adwuman* deity. According to oral tradition *Sumankwaa*, the *Sumankwaa*-deity is believed to be one of the ancient Asante *abosom*. The *Tano-Adwuman* deity is one of the deities that revealed itself through the body of priest (*ɔkɔmfoɔ*) Anokye, and was later used by the Asante as a means of protection during wars. Today, during ceremonies such as *Asanteman Adae Kese*, the priests in which the *Tano-Adwuman* deity reside during trance, walk in front of (*sumankwaa*) and at the back (*adwuman*) of the *Asantehene*, giving him spiritual protection. Each traditional *atano akomfoɔ* has a shrine to use for the veneration of the deities. After the performance of the *atano akomfoɔ*, royal messengers presented Holy water (*atanosuo*) in a brass bowl to the *Asantehene*'s *ɔkyeame*. A *bryophyllum pinta* (*egoro*) plant was put on top to protect the water from spiritual contamination. After removing the plant, the water was used for the ritual washing of the royal black stools for washing the regalia of the *oyoko* clan ruling in the Kumasi metropolis. The entire performance of the *atano akomfoɔ* can be perceived as preparing for the invocation of ancestral spirits in the stool house (*nkonnwafieso som*), which is where the stools of the royal ancestral spirits are kept.

Then, on Thursday, the 22nd of April 2004, a procession began to the *Asantehene*'s *nkonnwafieso som* in Breman, which is a northern district in the city of Kumasi. After a royal dies, they put his white stool on his grave for a week before they take it off to blacken it with the blood of a sheep, a chicken or a cow and with soot and egg yolk. The ritual of blackening a chief's stool is performed in order to convert his throne to a shrine, known as 'blackened stool' (*akonwatumtum*). It is believed that during a royal's lifetime, there is a strong connection between the royal's *sunsum* and the communal *sunsum* inside the stool. Once (s) he dies, this connection continues, which is why the stool is converted into a resting place for the communal *sunsum*. It is believed that *Asanteman* benefits from the invocation of the spirits of the deceased royal rulers inside the *nkonwatumtum*.

On the 26th of April 2004, at 10.00 a.m., the ancestral spirits were actually invoked inside *nkonnnwafieso som* during an event which is known as *banmu som*. While a crowd of *adowa* dancers and drummers waited outside and praised the *Asantehene* by making a V-sign with their hands, the *Asantehene*, his *ɔkyeame* and a few elders went inside *Nkonnnwafieso som* to perform rituals. The royal anthropologist Charles Coffie said that 'the Breman *Nkonnwafieso som* is the most important events of the *Asanteman Adae Kese* festival' (interview with Charles K. Coffie, 4).

Two days later, attention was given to the royal ancestors in a material form. On Thursday the 29th of April 2004 at 11.00 a.m., a statue of the late *Asantehene* Opoku Ware II was unveiled at the Suame Roundabout in Kumasi. The former *Asantehene* was praised for his contribution to the prosperity of the Asante Traditional Council. In a libation pouring prayer, offered by the *Asantehene*'s *ɔkyeame*, Opoku Ware II's good deeds for Asante chieftaincy were summarized and his ancestors were also mentioned.

On Friday the 30th of April 2004 at 11.00 a.m. *esom kese* took place, which is the last *Asanteman Adae Kese* event during which the ancestors were invoked and venerated. The traditional authorities of Sawua, the elders and other prominent members of the Sawua community marched to Manhyia palace accompanied by young women carrying brass pans (*yawa*) on their heads loaded with *etɔ*. The *Sawuahene* presents the *etɔ* to another chief (*Asemhene*), who then presents this staple food to the *Asantehene*. The king's *ɔkyeame* offered the *etɔ* to the ancestors who dwelled inside *nkonwatumtum*. This ritual originates from the Gonja people who also ate yam, with whom the Asante fought an intertribal war in 1744-1745. One of the *Sawuahene*'s soldiers developed the idea of attempting to cook *etɔ* and the *Sawuahene* liked this idea. He asked one of his stool wives to cook the *etɔ* and found out that it was edible. Nana Sawua then encouraged his subjects to look for *etɔ*. He also informed the *Asantehene* of this discovery. Consequently, *Otumfuo* raised the *Sawuahene* to his traditional office and gave him the symbolic title of 'test-yam-see' (*so-adee-hwe*). Since then, each year, during the *Odwira* festival, the *Sawuahene* boils *etɔ* and tastes the food before offering it to *nananom* (interview with Nana Ama Boakyewaa, 9).

In conclusion, the locality of spirits and the invocation of ancestral spirits were significant indigenous religious attributes of the 2004 *Asanteman Adae Kese* celebration. In the next section, the author will therefore explore the statutory and actual relationship between the resilience of AIR as expressed during the *Asanteman Adae Kese* celebration with the persistence of Asante chieftaincy in the Kumasi metropolis.

5.9. The *Asanteman Adae Kese* festival and its relationship to the persistence of Asante chieftaincy

During *Asanteman Adae Kese*, the power of the *Asantehene* and other Asante royal rulers is renewed by their subjects who show allegiance to their traditional authorities by organising and paying for some of the festival events. The subjects also present gifts to their rulers in the form of schnapps meant for the ancestral spirits and/or money. Besides confirming the legitimation of the institution of chieftaincy, the *Asanteman Adae Kese* festival is also an occasion for Asante to demonstrate to surrounding cultural groups, who they are. It is an occasion where Asante traditional dancers demonstrate their skills and where *akomfoɔ* can demonstrate their power. Traditional games are played, such as *oware*, *dame*, *ate sie*, *tayato* and *ampe*. The royal rulers' demonstration of an indigenous Asante identity during the *Asanteman Adae Kese* festival binds the Asante people together in a cultural-religious sense, which contributes to the persistence of Asante chieftaincy.

In actual practice, however, the existence of any relationship between the two mentioned factors is questionable because the *Asanteman Adae Kese* festival is also celebrated for socio-political and economic purposes. Each of these purposes might in their own way threaten the persistence of the 'indigenousness' of the celebration of the *Asanteman Adae Kese* festival. From a socio-political perspective, the festival, like many other state festivals in Ghana, is used to promote Asante culture to the outside world. It is an opportunity for the Asante people as a cultural group to place themselves on the diary of politicians who decide to whom they allocate scarce resources, and to compete for prestige and influence among other cultural groups. When advertising one's culture, each cultural group, including the Asante, incorporates 'invented' traditional elements with the original (precolonial rooted) festival script. The question that arises is to what extent these invented elements have robbed the *Asanteman Adae Kese* festival of its indigenous religious meanings.

In chronological order, 'invented' indigenous religious elements that form part of the *Asanteman Adae Kese* festival celebration are, for instance, the debate between pupils of various secondary schools in Kumasi about the role of traditional leadership for accelerated development held on Thursday the 29th of April 2004. Another example is the dramatic performance shown at the Kumasi cultural centre on Monday the 3rd of May 2004, which was titled 'Asante *nkabom*'. On Tuesday, the 4th of May 2004, a symposium was held at the Kumasi Cultural Centre (KCC) for secondary school teachers and university lecturers focusing, on the role of traditional rulers in accelerated development. On Wednesday, the 5th of May 2004 there was a photograph exhibition on the *Asantehene*'s reign at the Prempeh Assembly Hall, an inauguration of a CD album of *Nnwokorɔ* in honour of the *Asantehene* and the opening of a cultural exposition at the National Cultural Centre (NCC) in Kumasi. On the 6th of May 2004 attention was paid to the celebration of *Otumfuo's* birthday in the Inner Gardens of the Manhyia Palace, followed by the launching of an *Asanteman Adae Kese* Festival brochure by *Otumfuo's* private secretary. On the 7th of May 2004, nationally sponsored dictionaries (e.g., those distributed by the SSB Bank and Anglo Gold) were distributed to select schools in the Ashanti Region to show the *Asantehene* that others were concerned about the improvement of education in his region. On Sunday the 9th of May 2004, a Grand Durbar was held at the Kumasi Sports Stadium in which both the *Asantehene* and President John Agyekum Kufuor delivered a speech to remind the audience that they should forge ahead in unity. The main purpose of this Durbar, which was a British colonial invention, is to renew and reinforce the relationship between the *Asantehene*, a cultural leader, and the national leader, president Kufuor. During these occasions, the ruler counts the number of common people. The importance of the dignitaries who are attending the Durbar determines the importance of the cultural group celebrating the religious festival. The *Asanteman Adae Kese* celebration was very important, as the dignitaries who were present at the Durbar were the president Ahmed Kabba of Sierra Leone, President Gbagbo of La Cote d'Ivoire and there were a number of local significant dignitaries from Ghana. Although the Asante thus invited national and international politicians of significance, the political issues discussed were of a domestic nature and meant to demonstrate the pride and pomp of the Asante as a cultural group. Finally, on the 20th of August 2004, there was a contest between traditional beauty pageants (*ahoɔfehemaa*) at the Prempeh Assembly Hall in Kumasi.

In fact, one third of the activities during the *Asanteman Adae Kese* celebration were 'invented' events, which are not related in any sense to the indigenous religious meaning of the *Odwira* festival that is currently part of the *Asanteman Adae Kese* celebration. Politically, the emphasis of the issues discussed during the festival has also shifted from state politics to domestic cultural-religious identity politics. There are also invented elements within the other two-thirds of the events, but modifications are easily recognisable as forms of the original version of these events, although, the emphasis of *Asanteman Adae Kese* festival events still focuses on AIR. Some of the author's respondents feared that the addition of many non-indigenous religious-related events is threatening the existence of *Asanteman Adae Kese* as an indigenous religious festival. Nana Yaw Dwubeng stated the following:

> One of the main goals of the *Asanteman Adae Kese* festival is to educate our subjects. We teach them the religion and the history of our people and our stools. We also like to give them insight in the traditional customs in and around the royal courts. Today, however, the organisers of this festival add so many extra events to it, such as the *ahoɔhemaa* contest, the many sellers of food and *nsuo*, the omnipresence of ghetto blasters and cameramen, that one might wonder what is left of the main festival goals and might worry about whether we are still carrying out the right religious message (interview with Nana Yaw Dwubeng, 3).

Economically, the question arises to what extent *Asanteman Adae Kese* is celebrated for the promotion of the tourist industry. Generally, the local government in the Kumasi metropolis and the National Ghanaian Government (NGG) are inventing a new conception of culture and spreading local cultural identities nationally and globally by using festival performances for economic development. The local and national tourist boards anticipate national needs, but especially focus on international tourists when reconstructing a local history, religion and culture. In 2000, for instance, as a side effect of the celebration of the *Yaa Asantewaa* festival, the female Asante anti-colonial warrior after whom this festival is named was promoted both nationwide and worldwide, as her image could be found on an extensively used Ghanaian stamp. Thus, the Ghanaian government attempts to create links between local cultures and economic and spiritual needs of national or international tourists, through this so-called 'coming home' industry. Mr. Kwasi Asare Ankomah, the registrar of the ARHC in Kumasi, where the author resided during the completion of her fieldwork, stated the following:

> The *Asanteman Adae Kese* is a classic indigenous religious state festival, which is hardly meant for boosting the tourist industry. Other festivals, such as *Yaa Asantewaa* in Ejisu and *Kente* in Bonwire, however, are primarily there to please African-Americans, who form the majority of the tourists who come to the Ashanti Region. They want to feel at home here in Ghana and are searching for their spiritual roots. We have created festivals that fulfil the needs of these African-Americans in terms of educating, the Asante religion, culture or history. Meanwhile, we hope that these 'coming home' festivals for African-Americans on a pilgrimage, contribute to the development of our region (interview with Kwasi Asare Ankomah, 19).

The 'invention of Asante traditions' is thus a deliberate part of the policies of local and national politicians. Consequently, in the Ashanti Region new festivals are introduced rapidly, including the *Yaa Asantewaa* festival in Ejisu, the *Kente* festival in Bonwire, the *Papa* festival in Kumawu, the *Mmoa etɔnni nketɔ* festival in Offinso and the *Nkyidwo* festival in Essumeja. The question is what the long-term effects will be on the Asante indigenous culture from the creation of these festivals. Will it rob the Asante people of their Indigenous Religion or will it cause 'damage' to that religion? Or will the attention that African-American tourists give to AIR create valuable syncretic forms of that religion?

These questions are not directly applicable to the *Asanteman Adae Kese* festival, because this festival was never geared to the needs of national or international tourists. Kwaku Amoako Attah Fosu, an employee of the NCC in Kumasi, raises the following point:

> *Asanteman Adae Kese* promotes the tourist industry. Roads are constructed because of the festival and hotels are filled with guests. The festival is there for local people; tourism plays a marginal in the decision of the Asante to organise an *Asanteman Adae Kese* festival, which should primarily be understood as a religious experience and an expression of the Asante culture (interview with Kwaku Amoako Attah Fosu, 39).

Economic motives have thus far not had a direct effect on the relationship between Asante Indigenous Religion and the persistence of Asante chieftaincy in the *Asanteman Adae Kese* festival.

The indigenous religious elements, which emphasise 'locality' and celebrate the 'invocation of ancestral spirits' are part of the celebration of *Asanteman Adae Kese*. 'Locality' plays an important role during the gift-giving ritual, the cleaning ritual ridding an environment of evil spirits, the ritual invoking the protection of the *Asantehene*'s sacred swords against evil spirits and a ritual that was meant for the veneration of local natural deities. The ancestral spirits are invoked during *kuntunkunidae*, a cleaning ritual, a purification ritual at Lake Bosomtwi, and during *banmu som*, the unveiling of the statue of the late Opoku Ware II and *esom kese*.

Needless to say, the presence of indigenous religious elements is a *conditio sine qua non* for the relationship between those elements and the persistence of Asante chieftaincy. Statutory, the discovered relationship between 'Indigenous Religion' and 'the chieftaincy's persistence' is mutually reinforcing, since the *Asanteman Adae Kese* festival legitimises *Asanteman*, both by strengthening the relationship between traditional rulers and subjects and the cultural foundation on which the Asante traditional political institution is based.

In actual practice, socio-political and economic reasons might destroy any type of relationship or threaten a positive relationship between indigenous religious elements and the persistence of chieftaincy within the *Asanteman Adae Kese* festival. This research, however, reveals that in a social-political sense, the majority of *Asanteman Adae Kese* events are performed for an indigenous religious purpose. Even though many 'invented' traditional events have been added to the original *Asanteman Adae Kese* program, from an objective point of view there is no direct threat that these events will rob the festival of its original indigenous meaning, even though some traditional authorities might think otherwise. In an economic sense, while some festivals in the Ashanti Region are used mainly for the promotion of the tourist industry, the ancient rooted *Asanteman Adae Kese* festival is only marginally used for this purpose. Interviews with many Asante respondents reveal that economic considerations do not pose a direct serious threat towards the performance of indigenous religious events during the *Asanteman Adae Kese* festival.

To what extent is the *Asanteman Adae Kese* festival crucial to the persistence of Asante chieftaincy, considering the fact that between 1896 and 1985 – an eighty-nine year period – the festival was not openly celebrated? In Chapter IV, the author argues that the decision not to celebrate the festival was made by the British and was politically motivated; it was not the result of a diminishment of the significance of the Asante traditional authorities as indigenous religious mediators.

5.10 Conclusion

In this chapter, the author has discussed to what extent a number of significant rituals that are being performed in today's Kumasi metropolis can be regarded as expressions of AIR. The rituals that contained indigenous religious elements were: (a) the pre-burial ritual of a deceased paramount chief; (b) a chief's libation pouring ceremony; (c) the rite of passage of enstoolment for a chief; and (d) the *Asanteman Adae Kese* festival.

The author's analysis of the above-mentioned rituals demonstrates that in each ritual, there is a statutory and an actual relationship between indigenous religious elements and the persistence of Asante chieftaincy. Nana Saaman Nantwi II's pre-burial ritual led to an actual relationship between Asante Indigenous Religion and the persistence of chieftaincy. In all other rituals this religion is actually the main basis for a statutory relationship between the two. A look at the actual relationship of both factors demonstrates that, apart from the case of the *Saamanhene*'s pre-burial ritual, which formed an exception to the rule, these practices are 'officially' released from statutory indigenous rules. The current Asante belief in ancestral spirits is in actual fact weaker than the impression one gets when one studies the 'official', indigenous religious protocol of the Asante traditional authorities. In comparison to the precolonial and colonial periods, the indigenous religious mediatory function of the Asante royal rulers has changed, as the current AIR is no longer an aspect of an entirely mythopoeic worldview, and it has changed even more in practice than in chieftaincy documents.

Chapter VI: The Asante traditional authorities and their role as indigenous religious peacekeepers in today's Kumasi Metropolis

Ɔpanyin n-tena fie m-ma asadua m-fɔ – 'It is the responsibility of the elderly (chief) to see to it that the loom is not left in the rain to become wet'

Asante proverb

6.1. Introduction

Compared to many other African countries, contemporary Ghana has relatively few religious conflicts. For instance, neighbouring Nigeria is plagued with religious and ethnic strife, especially in the areas in Nigeria previously known as the Sokoto Caliphate. There have been many instances of severe religious conflicts between Muslims and Christians in postcolonial northern Nigeria. The main reason cited by Ghana studies experts for the country's religious stability is its syncretic forms of Islam and Christianity (Downie 11-07-2011). This chapter will focus on the role of the Asante royal rulers in promoting religious syncretism in their function as indigenous religious peacekeepers, which has partially contributed to that stability. The processes of religious syncretism practiced in postcolonial Ghana will be discussed with the help of Ulrich Berner's model (see section 2.4.1). In section 6.2 of this chapter, the author will first focus on the *Asanteman Adae Kese* festival celebration and its meaning for the socio-political and religious relationships between the Asante royal rulers, Christians, and Muslims. In section 6.3 and 6.4, she will concentrate on the socio-political and religious aspects of the relationship of these rulers with Muslims and Christians.

6.2. The *Asanteman Adae Kese* festival celebration of 2004

Since 1985, the *Asanteman Adae Kese* festival has been celebrated to promote the integration of Islam and Christianity with AIR. This is why a 'Muslim Thanksgiving Service' and a 'Special Christian Thanksgiving Service' have been part of every *Asanteman Adae Kese*.[78] During the Muslim and Christian thanksgiving services, the *Asantehene*'s personal imam (*Imam al-bilad*) and the religious leaders of the Christian Council Churches (consisting of Roman Catholics and PCCs), offered their prayer to the Asante king. The Dagomba, the Mossi, the Mamprusi headmen, and Peter Kwasi Sarpong (the Roman Catholic bishop of Kumasi), also attended the 1985, 1991 and 1999 celebrations (interview with Charles Kingsley Coffie, 4). The 2004 *Asanteman Adae Kese* celebration attracted a lot of important Muslim heads: the National Chief-Imam Sheikh

[78] The Muslim Thanksgiving Service was held on Friday the 28th of May 2004 at 13.00 p.m. at Manhyia (Dwaberem). The Special Christian Thanksgiving Service was held on Sunday, the 30th of May 2004 at 2.15 p.m. at Manhyia (Dwaberem).

Usumanu Nuhu Sharabutu; the Regional Chief Imam Sheikh Imurana Musa; Council members of Ulama, and the Imams Ameer and Mauvi A. Wahab Adam, the missionary in charge of the Ahmadiyya Muslim Mission and the Ghana Ahmadiyya Community. The Regional Chief-Imam opened the service with a prayer, distributed extracts from the Qur'an to all Muslims, and then prayed for the *Asantehene*. The Ahmadiyya Muslim Mission leader Mauvi A. Wahab Adam preached the first sermon, in which he advised his audience to show respect for Asante royal rulers since they are the agents of Allah, who appointed them to lead the nation. He ended by assuring the *Asantehene* that Muslims would always support him with their prayers. Sheikh Sharabutu, who preached the second sermon, said that the institutions of chieftaincy in Ghana should be used to foster unity, peace, and development of the country. On behalf of his Mission, he then presented a Qur'an (along with a Twi commentary, and a big ram to the *Asantehene*. The *Asantehene*'s *ɔkyeame* Baffour Kwaku Amoaten II received gifts on his majesty's behalf, and the *Offinsohene* Wiafe Akenten III was delegated to render thanks to the Muslim community. He told them to come to the palace in case of trouble and thanked the Muslims for their ceaseless prayers for the Asante community. Important guests at the Special Christian Thanksgiving Service were the Presiding Elder, Rev. Ben Mills of the Ame Zion Church, who did 'Call to Venerate', and the Regional Head of the Church of Pentecost, Apostle J. Essel, who prayed at the beginning of the programme. Rev. Dr. Mensah Otabil of the 'International Central Gospel Church', a PCC in Accra, preached the sermon. The Catholic Bishop of Cape Coast, Peter K. Appiah Turkson, the Anglican Bishop of Kumasi, Rt. Rev. Daniel Yinka Sarfo, the Moderator of the Presbyterian Church of Ghana, Rt. Rev. Dr. Sam Prempeh, and others prayed for the *Asantehene* and *Asanteman*, which is the nation as a whole. They all mentioned the need for unity and peace and the importance of the institution of chieftaincy in reaching and maintaining these goals. With permission of the traditional authorities, the Christians referred to Christ as Nana the Great Ancestor, and the Muslims offered animals for the ancestral spirits as a form of alms giving (*sadaqa*) (interviews with S. F. Adjei 41, Charles Kingsley Coffie, 4, Al-Hajj Abdul Karim Sina, 14, Al-Hajj Sheikh Zakuruka, 17) (see 7.6. photographs 8 and 9).

6.3. The relations of the Asante traditional authorities with Muslims

To understand how the Asante relate to Muslims in the Kumasi metropolis and vice versa, it is important to know a little more about the Muslims, their living area, their religion, and their lifestyle. Statistics from the Kumasi Statistical Service (KSS) demonstrate that in the year 2000, 56.9 percent (665,884 people) of the total population of 1,170,270 people in the Kumasi metropolis were Asante, 20.8 percent were other Akan groups, 5.8 percent were non-Akan groups (the majority are Ewe), and 16.5 percent were Mole-Dagbani, Ga-Dangme and others.[79] Muslims of various cultural groups made up 16 percent (187,243 people) of the population. In 2005, 16 percent of the then 1.16 million inhabitants of the metropolis were still Muslims, 8.5 percent were indigenous practitioners, 69 percent were Christians, and 6.5 percent had no religion (U.S. Department 2005). The majority of Muslims live either in low-income areas in the metropolis, such as Aboabo No. 1 and 2, and in Muslim settlements (Post, Inkoom et al. 2003). Muslims outside the settlements mostly come from the so-called first group of Asante *Nkramofoɔ*, the descendants of the Muslim scholars (*ulama*) (e.g. Uthman Kamagatay of Guipe and Daboya and Muhammad al Ghama from Gonja, who worked at the royal court in Kumasi in the eighteenth and nineteenth centuries). These Asante *Nkramofoɔ* are scattered all over the Kumasi metropolis with a concentration in the district area Suame. Non-Asante Muslims, who also live outside the settlements, adhere to a form of Islam that was brought into Ghana in the colonial period, such as that of the Tijaniyya, the Ahmadiyya, the Alhus-Sunnah wal-Jama'ah body, and Wahhabi organisations.

Muslim settlements are areas that the Islamic Mande-Dyula traders originally set up in the nineteenth century in the larger cities in Ghana to provide Muslims with a place to stay and live. Today, these settlements house Muslims of various cultural groups, some who live there permanently and some who stay there with their family for a limited period. The latter come from outside the area to do seasonal work, mostly performing low-income jobs such as loading and unloading vehicles. In the settlements, they are looking for a place to sleep in houses rented or owned by members of the same cultural group. In its literal meaning, Muslim *zongos* (settlements) are 'motels' (interview with Hane Harune, 37). The present Kumasi metropolis counts five Muslim settlements that form separate communities, but which are also somehow integrated in the wider population of the city and its adjacent villages: (see 7.5 map 6) (1) the *zongo* near Manhyia palace (the original Kumasi settlement, which is referred to as *zongo*); (2) the North settlement (the Sabon or New *Zongo*); (3) the Mossi (Moshie) settlement that dates back to 1958 (interview with Ustaz Ali Adam Al-

[79] This specification comes from the report Langer, A. (2007). Ethnicity, Religion and the State in Ghana and Nigeria: Perceptions from the Street. Crise Working Paper. Oxford, Centre for Research on Inequality, Human Security and Ethnicity (CRIHSE), Department of International Development (CRISE). 34., Aboabo No.1 is a sub-community within Aboabo, located within the transitional zone of Kumasi. Dichemso, bound it to the north to the south by Aboabo No. 2, to the west by Asawasi, and to the east by the Eastern By-Pass. Aboabo No. 2 is another sub-community within Aboabo with characteristics very much like that of Aboabo No. 1. It is bounded to the north by Aboabo No. 1, to the south by the Kumasi-Accra railway line, to the west by Asawasi, and to the east by the Eastern By-Pass Post, J., D. Inkoom, et al. (2003). Local Governance, Civil Society, and Partnerships: Community Action in Neighbourhoods Service Upgrading in Kumasi, Ghana. Amsterdam, Amsterdam Research Institute for Global Issues and Development Studies: 1-35.

Ameer, 27); (4) the *Suame* settlement; and (5) the Ayigya settlement (Post, Inkoom et al. 2003:13).[80]

6.3.1. The socio-political relations

To gain an understanding of the socio-political relations between the Asante traditional authorities and Muslims in the Kumasi metropolis, it is necessary to describe the leadership structure in the Muslim settlements where the majority of all of Kumasi's Muslims live. These settlements can be regarded as separate Islamic communities, though they are also integrated within the metropolis. The aspects of separation and integration of these settlements provide insight into the relation of its predominantly Muslim inhabitants with the wider Asante community. The settlements are separate Islamic communities in the sense that within them, the Muslims live on parcels of land that the *Asantehene* has allocated to them. The Asante king and other Asante royal rulers are the custodians of the ancestral land, whereas the Muslims are sojourners who borrow land from the Asante royal rulers who manage land issues on the *Asantehene*'s behalf. The Asante tolerate the Muslims as a cultural and religious minority as long as they obey the *Asantehene* and other royal rulers who are the custodians of almost all the land in the metropolis. Small pieces of this land belong to individuals or to the state, but the latter can also compulsorily acquire land. An example of a parcel of land in the Kumasi settlement that belongs to Muslims is that on which the central Friday Mosque is built (Maier 1997:323-325).

Another example of land that belongs to Muslims is that of the Mossi settlement in Kumasi. In the beginning of the colonial phase, Dawuda Mossi David, who was the first Mossi headman to leave Burkina Faso to settle in this town, received a plot of land from the *Asantehene*. However, this plot gets flooded during the rainy season, which is in all likelihood why the *Asantehene* gave it away (interview with Mossi headman Al-Hajj Ibrahim Abdul Achman Adam the III, 18). The gratefulness of the Mossi chief for this less valuable piece of land demonstrates that 'strangers' in Kumasi are dependent on the goodwill of the *Asantehene*, which is why they are happy with every little gift they receive. The majority of the land in Kumasi, however, belongs to the *Asantehene*'s stool, and through him it belongs to other Asante traditional authorities. Due to the authorities' link with the ancestors, members who belong to the ruling lineages may use stool-land without payment ('usufruct'). Strangers are instead obliged to lease land that belongs to the stools, which enables the Asante royal rulers to be rich and powerful.

The land issue creates a clear inequality between the Muslim headmen and the Asante traditional authorities. For instance, the inequality in the relationship

[80] On map 5 Suame is referred to as Suame *zongo*, but whether this area should be called a *zongo* is debatable.

between the two became evident during the author's interview with Nana Ama Serwah Nyarko. This Asante *omanhemma* from Offinso explained that she had the Islamic *Nkosohemma*, a Mossi female royal ruler, under her division and revealed that she regarded her as a royal equal to herself. The *Nkosohemma* is the co-ruler of the *Nkosohene*; a paramount position that had been 'enskinned' in Northern Ghana, where one uses skins instead of stools to enthrone a chief. As Ama Serwah Nyarko and the *Nkosohemma* are both *omanhemma*, they are equal in rank on the social ladder. Ama Serwah Nyarko emphasised that the only difference between her and the *Nkosohemma* was that the latter had a different religion, though this did not affect her perception of the *Nkosohemma* in terms of social status, unlike the issue of power over land. With regard to land issues, the *Offinsohemma* said:

> Some time ago a northerner cursed a neighbour. I called the *Nkosohemma* to the palace, but she said that she did not have money to go and perform a ceremony to settle the case. I then gave her money from my own pocket, because I wanted peace. But then, after the settlement, instead of saying 'nana I will go back to give you the money', the *Nkosohemma* said that she did not want to give back my money because she did not ask me to pay for her. I just stood there and looked at her and then asked somebody to bring her to the police and arrest her. I asked for the clan. She was a Mossi and I went to the head of that clan to tell him that this Mossi female ruler was misbehaving. Then, the Mossi headman came with a delegation to my house. They gave me a sheep, plantain, and money and begged for mercy. So, whenever I call the Muslims to my palace they will come. If the Muslim headmen are equal in rank, I normally treat them as equal. The fact that they are staying on my land does not mean that I should bully them, but they should do the right thing (interview with Nana Ama Serwah Nyarko, 29).

The quotation demonstrates that the *Offinsohemma* treats strangers on her land as 'equals' if they are equal in rank with her out of respect for their institution of chieftaincy. In case of misbehaviour on the part of Muslims, however, the Asante female ruler uses her power, which she derives from the inequality in land issues, to 'correct' them. The majority of the population in the settlements still consists of Muslims because it is easier for them to live together in one place. There are a lot of duties that come with the Islamic religion that are easier to fulfil when it is the social norm, for example, the fasting during *Ramadan* and the prayers that are performed five times a day.[81] When one is outside the Muslim community, it is more difficult to sustain one's Islamic religious duties. Additionally, Muslims within the community might think that those outside are not good Muslims because they do not see them praying. Apart from the religious bond between multiple families, members of the settlements are bonded by 'lineage', mainly through marriage. According to Islamic (*Sunni*) law, Muslim men can have a maximum of four wives. Although schooling and housing are currently so expensive that most male settlement inhabitants do not reach the maximum, most of them have more than one wife, regardless of their cultural

[81] *Ramadan* is a Muslim religious observance that takes place during the ninth month of the Islamic calendar. It is believed to be the month in which the Qur'an began to be revealed.

background (interview with Hane Harune, 37). Most of the inhabitants are extended family members of one another and this creates a bond between them.

The settlement areas can also be distinguished from all other areas in Kumasi by the shape of the houses. Muslims live in square family compounds, whereas those of the Asante are rectangular. Muslim men and women live in separate houses, whereas members of each core family occupy one room in most Asante extended-family houses.[82] Most Asante houses belong to an *abusua* (Tipple 1987). Hausa families instead own the majority of the Muslim houses, which is why they are powerful in the settlements, even though the position of the Hausa headman is not recognised by all members of the various settlements. Muslim members of other cultural groups and Akan Christians are often lodgers in the houses of the Hausa families (interview with Al-Hajj Sheikh Zakuruka, 17).

The Muslim settlements should also be viewed as a separate area in town because they receive their main funding from outside of the local and national Ghanaian government. Unlike the majority of the Asante paramount traditional authorities, the leaders of the various communities in these settlements do not receive a government allowance because by law they are not 'chiefs' but 'headmen'. They can therefore never aim for the position of becoming a 'Gazetted chief', or 'chief by law', unlike all Asante chiefs who are non-Muslim. The Gazetted chiefs, who are recognised by the state, receive an allowance to exercise their function. Because the headmen can never be Gazetted, they have to find other ways of earning an income and are often rewarded by (international) Islamic organisations, NGOs, international agencies, and foreign governments with whom they maintain personal and institutional links. Examples of such foreign governments to which they are linked are those of Libya, Saudi Arabia, Kuwait, Egypt, Iran, and more recently Pakistan. Additionally, they uphold links with other organisations, agencies, and governments who seek allies among Muslims in West Africa in order to 'win souls' for the Islamic religion (Weiss 2007:44-47).

Some headmen have been very successful in receiving an allowance from one of these Islamic funding bodies. The *zongo* headman Al-Hajj Sheikh Zakuruka, for instance, received financial help from Kaddafi, the yet former president of Libya to build an Islamic school in his Muslim settlement. However, other Islamic leaders such as the Mamprusi headman Ibrahim Abdullah do not receive any income from anybody but their own people, who pay a small sum of money for their service. The differences in wealth among the various cultural groups in these Muslim settlements are therefore huge, and according to the Mamprusi headman, this causes tension between those groups (interview with the Mamprusi headman: Ibrahim Abdullah, 15).

[82] Of all households in Kumasi, 74 percent occupy only one room, despite a mean household size of 4.8 persons and 55 percent of households having 6 or more members.

These headmen also swear allegiance to the *Asantehene* by reading from the Qur'an in place of swearing an oath as a sign of respect to the political head of the wider community. The Asante *ɔkramoni* is the only headman who both swears allegiance to the *Asantehene* and takes an oath to him. Due to their historically unique position at the Asante royal court, the Asante *nkramo* are both headmen and paramount chiefs. This is why the ritual behaviour of the Asante *Nkramofoɔ* is similar to that of the Asante chiefs.

Besides being separate communities, there are at least four reasons why the settlements are also part of the Kumasi metropolis. As geographical spaces, they are not bounded, and anyone can walk in and out of these areas. Besides, their inhabitants do not have any separate institutions, such as a police force or guardians, and they are secured by their social network and by the governmental police force of the Kumasi metropolis.[83] The inhabitants of the Muslim settlements pay taxes to the Kumasi Traditional Council (KTC) like any other inhabitants of the Kumasi metropolis. There are no separate hospitals for Muslims in the Kumasi settlements or in the rest of the metropolis. The majority of primary schools that are attended by Islamic children are also public schools that the local government owns (interview with Al-Hajj Hamidu Usman Madugu, 16).[84]

The Muslim settlements are thus permeable spaces, which enable Muslims to create a Muslim sphere of life in separated areas of the metropolis without being isolated from the rest of the population. The remaining part of this section will be devoted to enhance understanding of the attitude of that population towards the Muslims within the settlements, as this demonstrates the socio-political relationship between the Asante royal rulers and Muslims.

The Asante acknowledge the need for Muslims in the settlements to create their own Muslim way of life, and the *Asantehene* has allocated land to them that was not yet occupied by other inhabitants of the metropolis. Generally, the Asante do not interfere with the lives and religious practices of the inhabitants of the Muslims settlements because they believe that each cultural group should run its own affairs. *Zongo* inhabitants are free to go to any imam and school they like, and there is no censorship on what they teach. The Asante traditional authorities are by law not allowed to restrict the religious freedom of Muslims, and they are free to build mosques anywhere in the Kumasi metropolis. Most mosques, however, are located in the Muslim settlements, and the great central mosque that the Asante royal rulers visit is located in the Kumasi settlement (see

---

[83] The Kumasi *zongo* has its own police station that deals with specific *zongo* problems, but this station is part of the local police force in the Kumasi metropolis.

[84] There are, however, at least two Muslim secondary schools in Kumasi: (a) T.I. Ahmadiyya Secondary School and the Sakafiyya Islamic Senior High School. Weiss, H. (2007). Begging and Almsgiving in Ghana: Muslim Positions Towards Poverty and Distress. Uppsala, Nordiska Afrikainstitutet. 133. These schools are meant for Muslims in and outside the Kumasi settlements, which means that they are also part of the wider Kumasi community rather than contributing to the separate Muslim sphere of life.

map 6 where it is referred to as *zongo*). Since precolonial times, every Friday at 10.00 am, the *Asantehene* and his *Imam al-bilad,* the Asante *ɔkramoni* Al-Hajj Abdel Momen Haruna II, who is the second in command of the deputy chief-imam of the Ashanti Region, go together to this mosque for prayers (interview with Asante *ɔkramoni* Al-Hajj Abdul Karim Sina, 14). The *Asantehene's* beliefs are to be spiritually strengthened by these prayers, but his visits to the mosque are also a sign of respect to the Islamic community of these Suwarian Muslims in Kumasi. The Asante royal rulers are obliged to take into account the Islamic religion when setting the requirements of Muslim behaviour towards them. For instance, according to Islam, Muslims are only allowed to bow down to Allah, and the Asante royal rulers respect this aspect of the Islamic religion. The Ghanaian law requires the Asante traditional authorities to demonstrate religious tolerance towards these and any other non-Asante indigenous practitioners, but without that law the *Asantehene* would, in the absence of these laws and as part of AIR, also demonstrate his respect to Muslims. For instance, he would send two or three of his delegates to attend important Islamic festivals, such as *Eid-al-fitr* and *Eid-al-adha* (interview with Al-Hajji Sheikh Zakuruka, 17).[85] To sum up, the Asante royal rulers are tolerant towards the separate religious space of Muslims in the Kumasi metropolis and do not interfere with their religious affairs unless these affairs also affect the Asante people.

When there are internal problems within the Muslim settlements, its inhabitants should first report them to the Council of *Zongo* Chiefs (CZC). In most Muslim settlements, all headmen are members of this council, which works together with the local police. In fact, the Asante royal rulers only interfere in the religious affairs of Muslims in case of problems between the Asante people and the Muslims within the settlements, but most Asante live outside these settlements. In case of interreligious Asante-Muslim conflicts, the Asante traditional authorities turn to most important headmen of the settlements. The Hausa rule three of the five Muslim settlements in the metropolis. It is therefore the headman of the Hausa – the so-called Sarkin *Zongo* – who is the most significant Islamic ruler within these settlements. The Sarkin *Zongo Malam* Kardi, who was ruling the Kumasi Muslim settlement, was the first Muslim headman who the British recognised (interview with Al-Hajji Sheikh Zakuruka, 17). In 1920, the British officially approved three other headmen (Mossi, Yoruba and Wangara) in this settlement, but they especially acknowledged the political-religious power of the Sarkin *Zongos*.

Because of this colonial history, the Hausa are still acknowledged as the highest authority in almost all Muslim settlements in the Kumasi metropolis. The Sarkin *Zongo,* who represents all settlement headmen in delegations to the royal

---

[85] *Eid-al-fitr* is a feast that starts on the last day of *Ramadan*, once the sun has set. *Eid-al-adha* is a religious festival of sacrifice celebrated by Muslims worldwide as a commemoration of God's mercy to Ibrahim (Abraham) releasing him from his vow to sacrifice his son, as commanded by Allah.

palace (*ahemfi*) of the *Asantehene*, heads the Council of *Zongo* Chiefs (CZC). In case of Asante-Muslim conflicts, the Sarkin *Zongo* usually goes to Manhyia to communicate with the *Asantehene* for conflict resolution. For this purpose, the Asante traditional authorities relate directly to the *primus-inter-pares* among all *zongo* headmen. A Hausa occupies this position in three of the five settlements in the metropolis. In the Kumasi settlement, however, this strategy is more difficult because historically it has more than one leading Muslim headman. By 1900, the British recruited many more Hausa and Mossi, who the Asante mistakenly took for Hausa, to join the West African Frontier Force (WAFF) of the Gold Coast to fight for them against the Asante in the last *Yaa Asantewaa* uprising.

Since 1904, many of the Hausa and Mossi Muslims have occupied the same area as the old Kumasi settlement that dates back to at least 1817, and they have also occupied the new Muslim settlement (see 7.5 map 5).[86] Among the first of its new inhabitants were Islamic traders who came from centralised states long influenced by Islam, such as the Hausa, Fulani, Mossi, Wangara, and Dagomba (Schildkrout 1970:256-258; Skinner 2010). In the 1950s, the spread and intensification of mining activities and cocoa farming led other groups from northern areas to migrate to the south for work, such as the Kusasi, Frafra, and Grunshi labourers. Some of these immigrants converted to Islam within the new settlement (Sabon *Zongo*) located north of the old Kumasi settlement (Allman 1991:3-4; 2008; Skinner 2009).[87]

Thus, in today's Kumasi metropolis, the Asante traditional authorities have to maintain relationships with six different Muslim groups:

(1) The descendants of the Mande-Dyula traders, who came from Bighu (Begho) in 1400, whose medieval trade route brought them to Tafo, and since 1701 to the capital of the new Kumasi state (see 7.5 map 5) (Wilks 1961:27; Skinner 2010).
(2) The Asante *Nkramofoɔ*, who the *Asantehene* Osei Kwadwo (1764-1777) invited to work at the royal palace in Kumasi.
(3) A group of Muslims and Asante, who converted to Islam and who were equally known as the Asante *Nkramofoɔ*.
(4) The descendants of Hausa Muslims, who came to Kumasi in the early nineteenth century from the Sokoto Caliphate (currently northern Nigeria) (Lovejoy 1982:252) (see7.5 map 7).
(5) Other cultural groups who are Muslims inside the settlements, such as the Mossi, Frafra, Dagomba and the Grunshi people.

---

[86] Both Mossi and Hausa traded with the Asante in the nineteenth century. Since 1904 the number of immigrants of these two cultural groups who came to Kumasi has increased. Lovejoy, P. E. 1982. "Polanyi's 'Port of Trade': Salaga and Kano in the Nineteenth Century," *Canadian Journal of African Studies/ Revue Canadienne des Études Africaines* 16(2): 245-277.

[87] The New Settlement is situated in the core of the Kumasi metropolis; Manhyia, bound it to the north to the south it is bound by the Kumasi central market, to the west by the old Kumasi settlement, and on the east by the Asawasi neighbourhood. The area is dominated by government-built housing estates. These housing units were built to house veterans of the Ghana army after World War II; Adarkwa, K. A. and J. Post 2001. *The Fate of the Tree, Planning and Managing the Development of Kumasi, Ghana*. Amsterdam and Accra: Thela Thesis and Woeli Publications.

(6) Muslims from new Islamic movements who live outside the settlements, which were more recently imported and have their historical roots outside Ghana (e.g. the Ahmadiyya, Tijaniyya, Alhus-Sunnah wal-Jama'ah and the Wahhabi movements).

From this historical background, one can say it is remarkable that in three of the five settlements the ultimate leadership of the *zongo* is clear: Hausa headmen or Sarkin *Zongos*, who the British had appointed, are still ruling them. The recognition of a supreme leader in the old Kumasi settlement is, however, more problematic, because since 1924 the members of the Muslim movements (1, 2 and 3) in these settlements do not all recognise the Hausa headmen as their leader. In 1927, the British therefore recognised another six Muslim headmen, and in 1990, there were even thirty-three headmen who sat on a council headed by the Sarkin *Zongo*, who the *Asantehene* recognised (interview with Hane Harune, 37).[88] Only if the Sarkin *Zongo* could not resolve a dispute in the Muslim settlements did they go to the *Asantehene* via the *nsumankwahene,* who is the head of all Asante *Nkramofoɔ* (Schildkrout 2006:593). These types of disputes of position occur often in the Muslim settlements. The *Asantehene* has attempted to reinforce the Sarkin *Zongo*'s position because it is the easiest way for him to rule and to maintain a peaceful relationship with all the inhabitants of the settlements. Today, many Muslims do not recognise the Sarkin *Zongo* as the supreme headman of the old Kumasi settlement. The Asante *ɔkramoni* Al-Hajji Abdul Karim Sina is a member of the council of settlement chiefs, and he recognises the Sarkin *Zongo.* However, when he wanted to bring or receive news from the *ahemfi,* he told it to or heard it directly from the *nsumankwahene.* The Asante *Nkramofoɔ* thus sometimes bypassed the Sarkin *Zongo* and used his own information channel (interview with Asante *ɔkramoni* Al-Hajji Abdul Karim Sina, 14). But despite the Hausa dominance in the Kumasi settlement, other Muslim headmen also preferred to communicate with the *Asantehene* via a direct link with the *nsumankwahene.* To solve these issues, the ruling pair Opoku Ware II and Ama Serwaa Nyaako introduced a regulation in the 1990s that the deputy chief-imam can never be from the same cultural group as the second-in-command of the deputy chief-imam. If the deputy chief-imam is, for instance, an Asante *Nkramofoɔ,* then the second in command should be chosen from another cultural group. This way, the *Asantehene* attempts to stay in a cordial relationship with the members of those movements in the settlements that do not recognise the Sarkin *Zongo* as their ultimate leader. At the moment, however, both the deputy chief-imam and the second in command of this chief-imam are Asante *Nkramofoɔ.* This probably means that since the 1990s, the Asante *Nkramofoɔ*

[88] In settlements such as 'the old Kumasi settlement', each cultural group has its own headman. Examples of cultural groups in this settlement are the Yoruba, the Gau from Timbuktu, the Wangara, the Kusasi, the Sisala, the Grunshi, the Dagomba from Tamale, the Frafra, the Gonja, the Mossi, the Mamprusi, the Hausa, and Asante *nkramo* (interview with Hane Harune, 37).

has gained power inside the old Kumasi settlement and/or that criticism towards the Sarkin *Zongo* has increased.

I have honed in on the authority crises in the old Kumasi settlement because it provides information on how the Asante royal rulers understand and apply the concept of 'religious tolerance' towards the religious space of Muslims of the Kumasi metropolis. Religious tolerance is the condition of accepting or permitting other's religious beliefs and practices that disagree with one's own. The Asante traditional authorities demonstrate tolerance by the fact that they remain religiously neutral toward the religious background of leaders of these settlements. Asante royal rulers regard the authority conflicts within the settlements as internal issues and do not interfere. In case of problems that concern both Muslim and Asante, the Asante royal rulers wait for the Muslim leader(s) to come to *ahemfi.* In cases that involve more than one Muslim authority, the focus of the Asante royal rulers is on the creation of regulations that prevent further conflicts between the Islamic movements. Religion is left out from the laws created by the Asante royal rulers, which they believe to be essential for the maintenance of the established order. In the case of Asante-Islamic religious conflicts, laws for the purpose of religious peacekeeping are the only restrictions on the religious freedom of Muslims.

'Tolerance' is a form of behaviour where people mutually recognise everybody's religious freedom. Today's Asante royal rulers are tolerant because they perceive religious freedom as a fundamental right, and they demonstrate full respect for the adherents of all religious beliefs, who they treat as equals. Unlike in the precolonial and colonial periods, the Asante royal rulers are no longer significantly more tolerant towards the Asante *Nkramofoɔ* and other adherents of moderate forms of Islam than to the orthodox Muslims in Kumasi, such as the Hausa people. The Asante traditional authorities perceive religion as a private matter, and restrictions on forms of Islamic religion are only imposed on Muslims if these practices do not fall under a range of behaviour that is acceptable in the Kumasi metropolis. When it comes to religious tolerance, there cannot be an inclusion of religious practices and beliefs by a community without excluding other beliefs and practices. All religious tolerance has its boundaries, since it should enable people with different beliefs to live together. In many cases, it is sufficient for the Asante royal rulers to use their power to regulate the community. For instance, they regularly request the chief-imam and the imams of the cultural groups in the settlements to come to the palace to discuss religious issues that create tension within the community (interview with chief-imam Imrana Musah, 40). However, the Asante royal rulers use a police force to keep order with regard to some issues. The ARHC has the task of collecting information about religious customs that may impinge on others and therefore need to be restricted in a byelaw. Chieftaincy byelaws locally regulate religious behaviour. Each community creates its own byelaws, which means that those in the Ashanti

Region may differ from town to town. In the Kumasi metropolis, with regard to religion, the following three byelaws are significant:

(1) Between 21.00 p.m. and 04.00 a.m., religious practitioners are not allowed to disturb the public peace with any of their religious practices.
(2) For a major religious performance, such as a festival, one should seek permission of the Town Development Committee (TDC).
(3) Out of respect for the deceased, nobody in the Kumasi metropolis is allowed to organise a funeral before the burial of a deceased Asante paramount chief.

None of these three byelaws were created to avoid trouble that Muslim practitioners might cause. Francis Mark Domenya, employee of the ARHC, informed the author that in the Kumasi metropolis religious byelaws are usually created to warn or penalise Christian members of PCCs who sing and dance and make a lot of noise for long periods of time. Muslims, in contrast, do not cause many disturbances by praying. The five-daily calls for prayer are usually very short, and prayers are held in silence (interview with Francis Mark Domenya, 5).[89]

Due to the *Asantehene*'s policy of non-interference, most of the Asante-Muslim conflicts are of a non-religious nature. Conflicts with Muslims are due to the disobedience of Muslim youth towards the constitutional laws by stealing or fighting, for instance. Problems internal to the Muslim community that also affect the non-Muslim community of the metropolis and are reported to the *Asantehene*: these problems typically involve the use of weapons. Succession disputes between headmen, and conflicts over the authority of the central Friday mosque in the Kumasi settlement, are examples of such severe conflicts (Schildkrout 1974 ; 2006). The focus of the next subsections will be on the specific socio-political relationship of the Asante royal rulers with a few of the many Muslim headmen that the author interviewed during her fieldwork in the years of 2006 and 2007.

The Asante Nkramofoɔ

Al-Hajji Abdul Karim Sinam, who is the current Asante *Nkramofoɔ,* maintains his relationship with the Asante ruling pair by responding to invitations that he receives from them to go to Manhyia palace to meet with all other Asante royal rulers lower in the social hierarch and the Muslim headmen of the Council of *Zongo* Chiefs (CZC). Occasionally, the Asante *Nkramofoɔ* receives letters from the *Asantehene* when the latter wants to know what is happening in the settlement. In normal circumstances, the job of sending letters is preserved for the *nsumankwahene*. According to Al-Hajji Abdul Karim Sinam, 'the *Asantehene* sometimes calls me to his palace to help to solve Asante-Muslim con-

[89] In the Kumasi metropolis, some pastors of Pentecostal-Charismatic churches have been sent to court, and some have even been imprisoned after disobedience of bye-law 1.

flicts. Moreover, I visit the *Asantehene* every Friday to pray for him and to read from the Qur'an' (interview with Asante *ɔkramoni* Al-Hajji Abdul Karim Sina, 14).

The Mossi headmen

The author interviewed two Mossi headmen in the Mossi settlement: the ruling Al-Hajji Ibrahim Abdul Achman Adam III and his predecessor Ustaz Ali Adam Al-Ameer. In the opinion of Al-Hajji Ibrahim Abdul Achman Adam III, the relationship between the Mossi and the Asante royal rulers has generally been good. In 1902, David Dawuda, who was the first Mossi headman, travelled from Burkina Faso to settle in Kumasi. The Mossi and the Asante share so many cultural-religious similarities that many Mossi refer to themselves as Mossi-Asante. For instance, the *Asantehene* and the Mossi headman both ride in a palanquin and both believe in the reality of spirits that can determine one's destiny. One of the few problems that the Mossi experience with AIR is the ritual of the pouring of libation. Islam does not allow the Mossi to perform AIR rituals, which is why they cannot swear an oath to the Asante king (interview with Al-Hajji Ibrahim Abdul Achman Adam III, 18). The *Asantehene* demonstrates his respect to this and other religious differences between the Mossi and the Asante people. The Chief-Imam of the Ashanti Region said: 'The Muslims do not need to swear an oath to the *Asantehene* but those who wish to 'enskin' their headman, should first introduce him to the king' (interview with Imrana Musah, 40). This compromise was clearly a crucial point for the Mossi headman, who said: 'If *Otumfuo* would not demonstrate his respect to our religion that does not allow us to worship the floor, we would leave because even though we are born on this land, our religion is most important for us. I am therefore very grateful that *Asantehene* Osei Tutu II respects this difference between the Asante and Islam' (interview with Al-Hajji Ibrahim Abdul Achman Adam III, 18). The Mossi demonstrate a great respect for the *Asantehene* because he is the custodian of the land on which they live. Due to his position of land custodian, the Mossi perceive the *Asantehene* as an elder, and the Qur'an says that one should demonstrate one's respect to the elders. The current Mossi headman further mentioned that when there is an intra-cultural group problem among the Mossi people, they normally do not involve the *Asantehene* unless the problem is so serious that they need to seek the king's permission to send the troublemaker to prison. He said: 'Unlike the *Asantehene*, I do not have my own prison to lock people away. That is also why the Mossi cooperate with the Asante'. If there is an intercultural group problem between the Asante people and the Mossi, the *Asantehene* calls the Mossi headman to the palace to discuss it. These days, what usually happens is that in cases where the Mossi are clearly at fault, the *Asantehene* asks them to pay a fine. Unlike in the colonial period when all Muslims were regarded as strangers, the *Asantehene* cannot send any Muslims away from his land. Besides, in times of problems, the *Asantehene* and the Mossi headmen also meet when the former has foreign guests. The Muslim headmen of the home country of the visitor are then asked to meet up with them and the *Asantehene* at the palace. If the visitor is from the Mossi area, the Mossi headman is also present. For the *Asantehene*, this is an occasion where he can demonstrate to the outside world that he maintains a cordial relationship with the Asante headmen in the Kumasi metropolis (interview with Al-Hajji Ibrahim Abdul Achman Adam III, 18).

The former Mossi headman, Ustaz Ali Adam Al-Ameer, who was also the head of all Mossi in the Ashanti Region, also told the author that the Mossi have a cordial relationship with the Asante royal rulers. They respect the *Asantehene* and the Asante people, including those who are Muslim, because the Asante royal rulers have treated the Mossi people well from the start. When the Mossi first came to Kumasi, they received a place to sleep, a plot of land on which to build houses, and the *Asantehene* even gave them Asante wives, including some of his own daughters. With this custom, the *Asantehene* aimed to establish a good relationship between the Asante and the Mossi people. The custom of giving away of wives as a way of establishing relationships with neighbouring cultural groups has been part of the Asante diplomacy since the precolonial period (Smith 1989). Ali Adam Al-meer also said: 'I find it important to be in a good relationship with the Asante people, because unlike the situation back home in Burkina Faso, in Kumasi we are dependent on the goodwill of the *Asantehene* on whose land we stay' (interview with Ustaz Ali Adam Al-Ameer, 27). The land custodianship of the *Asantehene* thus creates an element of power on the side of the Asante. However, in order to solve community problems, the Mossi do not only have to collaborate with the Asante traditional rulers but also with other cultural groups. The institutions such as police and prisoners are local-and state-owned, and most laws are national. All cultural groups are therefore dependent on one another to build a peaceful community (interview with Ustaz Ali Adam Al-Ameer, 27).

The Mamprusi headman

The Mamprusi in Kumasi are closely related to the Mossi because David Dawuda, the first Mossi headman, married a Mamprusi wife. The current Mamprusi headman, Ibrahim Abdullah, mentioned that his community is very poor and that they would like to receive help from outside. Neither the *Asantehene* nor the Ghanaian government were, however, in a position to help them. Also, on behalf of the Mamprusi, Imrana Musa (the chief-imam of the Ashanti Region) prays for the *Asantehene* and the prosperity of Asante society. In return, the *Asantehene* demonstrates his respect for the Muslims, and on official occasions he calls them to the palace to advertise the peaceful relationships with Muslims in the Ashanti Region. Besides this, he does not interfere in the lives of the Muslims, and likewise his help to the communities in the Muslim settlements is minimal. In line with the colonial period, his policy towards Muslims is one of non-interference except in the case of an escalation of intercultural and interreligious violence. In fact, there is more a policy of the Asante royal rulers of toleration of Muslims in the Kumasi metropolis than one of actual tolerance.

The positive answers of above-mentioned headmen should be partly understood with regard to the fact that in Kumasi, it is not permissible to openly criticise the *Asantehene*. The Muslims are also in a subordinate position since they live as guests on the *Asantehene*'s land.

6.3.2. The religious relations

'Syncretism', as a strategy to prevent conflicts and to stimulate dialogue, is a reciprocal process, which means that it needs the cooperation of two parties in order to work. It is therefore important to research the opinion of Muslim headmen in Kumasi on the desirability of syncretism as related to the form of Islam to which they adhere. In the following three sub-sections, the author will give an overview of the five main forms of Islam in the Muslim settlements of the Kumasi metropolis.

The Suwarian tradition

Al-Hajj Salim Suwari (1523/24-1594), the creator of the Suwarian tradition, was a Muslim scholar (*ulama*) from Soninke who believed, among other points, that God would bring non-Muslims to convert in His own time. To actively proselytise Muslims who lived as guests in a mainly non-Muslim area and to attempt to transform their hosts' environment from a *Dar-al-Kufr* into a *Dar-al-Islam* would be interfering with God's will (Robinson 2004:124-139).[90] According to the Suwarian tradition, Muslims may accept the authority of non-Muslim rulers and indeed support it insofar as this enables them to follow their own way of life in accordance with the *Sunna* of the Prophet.[91] The Suwarian tradition is adhered to by the aforementioned groups one, two and four – the Mande-Dyula traders and scholars and the Asante *Nkramofoɔ* in the meaning of 'Muslims who belong to the cultural group of the Asante people' – in the Kumasi metropolis. Important issues of the Suwarian tradition mentioned in relation to syncretism are its 'non-proselytising character' and the limitations set on following the authority of the 'pagan' ruler in order to follow the *Sunna* of the Prophet. These attributes of the Suwarian tradition imply that its followers are religiously syncretic (Wilks 2000:98). In spite of this, there is no stimulation of

[90] *Dar-al-Kufr*: the territory of Infidelity. *Dar-al-Islam:* the territory of Islam.

[91] *Sunna* is a normative custom of the Prophet or of the early Muslim community, as set forth in the hadith (q.v.).

dialogue in this Islamic tradition, and the characteristic of waiting for Allah to pull the infidels (*kufr*) out of the state of ignorance (*jahiliyya*) promotes more an attitude of indifference of Islamic practitioners towards their hosts than one of religious tolerance.

The Asante history shows, however, that there has been a clear difference between the theory of the Suwarian tradition and its practical use by its practitioners. In theory, for instance, Suwarians believe infidelity to be caused by ignorance rather than wickedness, but in the obituary of the *Kitabal-Ghanja* a mid-eighteenth century Arabic document, the *Asantehene* Opoku Ware I was portrayed as a wicked ruler. The imam Sidi Umar wrote: '[M]ay Allah curse him and put his soul into hell. It was he who harmed the people of Ghanja [Gonja], oppressing and robbing them of their property at his will' (Kitabal-Ghanja) (Wilks, Levtzion et al. 1986: 86, 104). The *Asantehene* Osei Tutu Kwame and his successors, on the other hand, were regarded as more than just 'infidels' with whom some Muslims living in *Dar-al-Islam* did not even wish to be in physical touch. The Muslim community in Kumasi regarded *Asantehene* Osei Tutu Kwame as a friend, and the Muslim scholar (*ulama*) Kamagate (*Karamo Togma*) called him a 'misguided infidel' who was superior to the king of Dahomey; an infidel of infidels (*Kaffar ben al Kufr*) (Wilks 2000:104-105). During the colonial and the postcolonial periods, the attitude of the adherents of the Suwarian tradition towards the *Asantehene* was also often more cordial than this tradition prescribes. Since the colonial period, the intensity of cooperation of the Mande-Dyula traders and the Asante *Nkramofoɔ* with the *Asantehene* has been diminished. By then, the importance of the medieval Mande-Dyula trade-route from the Niger to the gulf of Guinea had decreased due to the rivalry with European trade, and the production of charms by Muslim scholars (*ulama*) at the royal court also had gone out of fashion. Consequently, Asante *Nkramofoɔ* switched their attention to the state leaders to whom they showed more loyalty than to the *Asantehene* at times. Despite this development, in a religious sense, one could say that in practice the Asante *Nkramofoɔ* have remained syncretic in their attitude towards the Asante royal rulers since the death of the *Asantehene* Opoku Ware II. The attitude of the current Asante *Nkramofoɔ* and of other Muslims in the Kumasi settlements or other Muslim camps will be discussed in the next subsections.

The Asante Nkramo chief

Al-Hajj Abdul Karim Sina, the current leader of the Asante *Nkramofoɔ* perceives himself as both a stimulator of religious dialogue and someone who justifies his position as both an Islamic Asante *Nkramo* headman and as an Asante paramount chief. Just like any other Asante paramount chief, the Asante *Nkramo* chief has to swear an oath to the ruling pair to swear allegiance to the owner of the land. The Asante *Nkramo* chief should promise the Asante royal rulers that if he calls him, he would always come to *ahemfi*, except for when he falls ill or is fulfilling his religious duties as a Muslim. Unlike all other paramount chiefs, however, there are some religious duties that come with the swearing of an oath that the Asante *Nkramo* chief cannot fulfil, because it is against his Islamic religious tradition. An example is the ritual of the 'pouring of libation' to venerate the ancestral spirits. Al-Hajj Abdul Karim Sina said the following about the syncretic religious solution that he had found for his religious dualism:

> I have sworn an oath to the *Asantehene* like any other paramount chief. Unlike those chiefs, however, I did not pour libation because my grandparents never did this, and it is not part of our religion. After *Otumfuo* invited me for the oath swearing ceremony, I informed Al-Hajj Abdel Momen Haruna II, the chief-imam of all Asante *Nkramofoɔ* and the personal imam of the *Asantehene,* that he should pray for *Otumfuo*. This chief-imam then bought a sheep for the purpose of sacrifice, cut its throat, and gave it to *Otumfuo*'s *ɔkyeame* Baffour Kwaku Amoaten II who on behalf of him received a gift, which is part of our tradition of alms giving (*sadaqa*).[92] Then Al-Hajj Abdel Momen told to Baffour that *Otumfuo* should send our gift, the sacrificed sheep, to a children's home and to prisoners (interview with Asante *ɔkramoni* Al-Hajj Abdul Karim Sina, 14).

The Asante *Nkramo* chief has thus found a point of similarity between AIR and Islam, which he uses to justify his position as both an Asante paramount chief and a Muslim headman. According to his Islamic religion, he cannot give drinks in the form of pouring libation to the ancestral spirits, which is normally part of the oath swearing ceremony. However, what the Asante *Nkramo* has in common with the Asante indigenous believer is that he brings food as a form of sacrifice and presents this as voluntary alms giving (*sadaqa*). During the reign of *Asantehene* Osei Tutu Kwame, the Asante king was requested to give *sadaqa* to the Muslim community. The phenomenon of *sadaqa* at the royal court thus has a long history, and the present-day Asante *Nkramo* chief makes creative use of an old tradition.

In a religious sense, the idea behind the indigenous religious ritual and the Islamic ritual of slaughtering an animal is completely different. Whereas Asante indigenous religious practitioners slaughter animals to cool down the ancestral spirits with their blood to establish or maintain a harmonious relationship with them, for the Islamic believer, giving alms such as slaughtered animals is a form of alms giving (*sadaqa*). This is a private contribution made by a Muslim as a result of individual choice (Weiss 2007:78). Despite these religious differences, the practical ritual of slaughtering the animal is the same in AIR and the Suwarian tradition (interview with Asante *ɔkramoni* Al-Hajj Abdul Karim Sina, 14). The Asante *Nkramo* chief therefore uses this ritual to negotiate his position

[92] The Muslims in Ghana distinguish two forms of almsgiving: (a) obligatory almsgiving (*zakat*) and (b) voluntary alms giving (*sadaqa*). *Zakat* is a public contribution that consists of two and a half percent of one's income and wealth and between two and ten percent of one's harvest. It purifies legally acquired wealth in order to purify the soul of a Muslim from greed and miserliness. The giver is promised a reward in heaven.

in both religious worlds, and a side effect of his behaviour is the promotion of religious dialogue.

The Mossi headman

The Mossi originally come from Burkina Faso, the Upper Volta. The majority of the Mossi are indigenous religious believers, even though Islam was introduced in the area as early as 1328 after a Yatenga Mossi sacked Timbuktu. Because of the Mossi's strong African indigenous religious roots, most of the intermarriages between the Mossi Muslims and Mossi non-Muslims in Kumasi are mostly unproblematic. The Mossi indigenous religious believers have faith in the efficacy of the ancestral spirits and frequently visit earth shrines. In most of these cases Mossi Muslims marry non-Muslim Mossi wives, who are allowed to venerate the ancestors as long as their children are raised as Muslims. The same religious pattern can be found among Mossi Muslims who marry non-Muslim Asante wives (interview with Al-Hajj Ibrahim Abdul Achman Adam III, 18).

The Mamprusi headman

Ibrahim Abdullah, who is the current Mamprusi headman, practices a form of African Islam. He wears a Muslim cloth (*fugi*) that he believes protects the community against evil spirits, and he wears a necklace that he believes enhances his spiritual powers. He sits on a skin (*alagalami*) and carries a stone with him that he believes cures wounds. Abdullah clearly feels that he is a sacred leader who receives powers from spirits. In this aspect, his belief is similar to that of the Asante indigenous religious believers. However, as a religious leader, the Mamprusi headman felt that he received less appreciation of the Asante than his predecessor, and he said:

> The *Asantehene* maintains a good relationship with the *Nsumankwahene*, but Muslims are not being welcomed at the royal court as much as they used to be. Muslim healers do not live any longer at the Manhyia palace, and since the precolonial and colonial periods their position has waned (interview with Ibrahim Abdullah, 15).

The Methodist Joice Boakye shared this insight and said:

> If I have a problem, I go to either my pastor of the Methodist Church or to the *ɔkɔmfoɔ*. I know that there are Muslim healers in the Mossi settlement, who can heal you with a boiled egg (*mugi*) or pieces of wood (*dawa*) if you have stomach pains. However, I never go to the Muslim healers because I don't believe they can cure me (interview with Joice Boakye, 6).

In conclusion, the Suwarian tradition that the Muslim headmen and their subjects adhere to is not religiously syncretic, in theory. It includes great reservations towards the religion of the host community on account of fear of losing sight of the true Islamic religion. There is no process of proselytising or assimilation, which is the opposite of religious tolerance, but the adherents of this moderate form of Islam have demonstrated their willingness to coexist. They have demonstrated their loyalty to the political authority of the host community but not by compromising in the field of religion.

Uthman dan Fodio's and the Qadiriyya brotherhood reform movements

In the colonial period, the descendants of Hausa Muslims in the Kumasi metropolis were members of the 'Qadiriyya Brotherhood Reform Movement' (QBRM) that was founded by Uthman dan Fodio, a Hausa who was born in the 1750s in the city-state Gobir. This Islamic teacher (*ulama*) heavily criticised the rulers from the sultanate of Gobir for being corrupt. In the opinion of Uthman dan Fodio, the government of Gobir was encouraging an Africanised form of Islam that did not support the development of a good distribution system for the income generated by alms giving (*sadaqa*). It imposed unlawful taxes on the peasantry and pastoralists, and it twisted the law of Islam for its own purpose. Consequently, in 1804, Uthman immigrated to the south of present day Nigeria to start a reform movement. In 1808, he and the other members of his movement gained victory over Gobir and established the Sokoto Caliphate on its southern confines. The main task Uthman set himself after his victory was to reinvent the *Dar-al-Islam* in the Sahel as an 'imitation of Muhammad' during the founding days of the religion. Uthman's movement has, until today, been very important for Islamising Hausa land (presently northern Nigeria) (Robinson 2004:139-152).

Contrary to the Muslims of the Suwarian tradition, the Hausa did not share any religious practices with the Asante indigenous believers. The Islamic teaching of Uthman dan Fodio was radically opposed to religious syncretism and did not tolerate moderate forms of Islam. Uthman's reform movement was based on an assimilation model and encouraged conversion of the infidels (*kuffr*), which included even less-stringent Muslims such as the Asante *Nkramo* chief, instead of stimulating the peaceful coexistence of religious beliefs. If the Sarkin *Zongos,* whom the British first appointed in 1900, were loyal followers of Uthman dan Fodio, their main interest in relation to the *Asantehene* should have been to attempt to convert the Asante king to Islam. Later on, the whole of the Asante kingdom could then easily be transformed from an area in the stage of *Dar-al-Kufr* to one of *Dar-al-Islam.* The only two steps in saving the Asante from living in a 'Territory of Infidelity' were in imitation of Uthman dan Fodio; first to flee (*al-hijra*) to a neighbouring area, and then to start an Islamic Holy war (*jihad*). The leading of *alhijra* and *jihad* were perceived to be the obligation of an orthodox Muslim to prevent apostasy among fellow Muslims. *Was the carrying out of Uthman's plans a historical reality?* In 1818, Shaikh Baba, a Hausa from Kassina, did affect a limited and revocable sort of *alhijra*. In general, however, the Kumasi Muslims seem to have been too deeply involved in

Asante affairs to be able to regard the pronouncement of the reformers as indicative of any practical course of action. Due to the intertwining of economics and politics, as well as the Asante *Nkramo* chief, the Hausa Muslim traders were also involved and acted in support of Asante politics. They did so even when this caused an authority and religious conflict among their members, such as in the case of 1818 when Muslims were obliged to fight against their own people at the launching of the Asante invasion of Gyaman. Despite being deeply involved in Asante affairs, the Hausa people did not hold a model of religious syncretism, and they attempted and succeeded to proselytise a small number of Asante to orthodox Islam (Wilks 1966:152).

In the colonial period, several Sarkin *Zongos* maintained the relations between the Hausa and the *Asantehene*. The Sarkin *Zongo* was an office introduced by the British in 1900, though it had already been abolished in 1932. Kwame Nkrumah, the first president of Ghana, reintroduced the function of Sarkin *Zongo* in 1958 (interview with Al-Hajj Sheikh Zakuruka, 17). Between 1932 and 1958, the *nsumankwahene* was a key figure and the first person to talk to in the relation between the *Asantehene* and the Kumasi *zongo*. Until the 1940s, the *Asantehene* Osei Agyeman Prempeh II and his female co-rulers followed a policy of non-interference with *zongo* affairs, which enabled him to maintain a peaceful relationship with all the Muslim headmen of the settlement (Schildkrout 1974).

There was a clear indigenisation of the Hausa religion after Ghana gained independence, which contributed to a more syncretic attitude of Hausa headmen towards the Asante royal rulers and their religion. Since the government of President Busia (1969-72) under the Aliens Compliance Order, many Muslims were deported from Ghana. At the time, the Kumasi *zongo* leadership was divided. The Hausa headman Ahmadu Baba supported the *Asantehene* and was a member of the same party as the *Asantehene*, the UP, which was a fusion of the MAP and NLM. His rival, the Hausa Mutawakulu, attempted to become headman and joined forces with the government party CPP. The CPP attempted to diminish the power of the *Asantehene*-supported Mutawakulu, and in 1958, they appointed him as the new Sarkin *Zongo*. Mutawakulu encouraged the deportation of Hausa and other 'alien' Muslims and imams, such as Al-Hajj Amadu Baba and his friend Alfai Othman. In the 1970s, however, Al-Hajj Amadu Baba and Alfai Othman came back from exile in Nigeria, and these Ghanaian Muslims replaced the powerful Hausa Muslims whose Islamic religion had then already been indigenised (Schildkrout 1974; Weiss 2007).

Another reason for the indigenisation of the Hausa religion was the increase in the number of intermarriages between the Asante and Hausa Muslims in the Muslim settlements. When Hausa men marry Asante women, they do not force them to abandon their own Indigenous Religion or Christian faith, but they ask them whether they can raise their children as Muslims. The children of these couples are usually educated in more than one religious tradition, and this has also stimulated the indigenisation of the Hausa belief (interview with Hane Harune, 37). A third factor in the 'indigenisation' of Hausa Islam, and all other forms of Islam in the Kumasi metropolis, was the change in the education they received. In the precolonial and the colonial periods, many settlement Muslims who had money sent their children to Qur'anic schools (*Marakantas*) where they learned Arabic, or in some cases to state schools.[93] An example of the latter is the director of radio station Zuria 88.7 FM, who spent his youth together with the current *Asantehene* at the Assim-Government Boys School in Kumasi (interview with Hane Harune, 37). Since the postcolonial period, more children of Muslims go to Arabic-English schools, where they learn English, Arabic, and Twi.

The Hausa headman: the Sarkin Zongo

Al-Hajj Sheikh Zakuruka, who is the ruling Sarkin *Zongo*, praised the Asante ruling pairs Opoku Ware II and Ama Serwaa Nyaako and Osei Tutu II and Afia Kobi Serwaa Ampem II for their stewardship of peaceful coexistence between people of different faiths. Since the postcolonial period, these Asante ruling pairs have put in an effort to avoid further violent clashes between religious movements in Kumasi, such as those between Muslims and Christians in 1995. *Asantehene* Osei Tutu II said to the sarkin *Zongo,* 'There cannot be unity without prayers'. Every Friday, the *Asantehene* therefore goes to the mosque with his chief-imam, who prays for him. The *Asantehene* and other Asante people also acknowledge Islam by attending Muslim festivals and the funerals of Muslim headmen. In return, Al-Hajj Sheikh Zakuruka and other Muslim headmen observe the *Asanteman Adae Kese*. As the successor of the *Odwira* festival, this is still the most significant indigenous religious celebration of the Asante. When *Asantehene* Opoku Ware II passed away, Sheikh Zakuruka's predecessor Al-Hajji Abu-Bakr Ali III gave his condolences to the Asante royal rulers (interview with Al-Hajj Sheikh Zakuruka, 17). During important national days such as Independence Day and Republic Day, and during official occasions, e.g. when the Asante king has Muslim VIP visitors from abroad, the *Asantehene* also always invites the Muslim headmen to the palace (interview with Al-Hajj Ibrahim Abdul Achman Adam III, 18).

Al-Hajj Sheikh Zakuruka did not mention any negative aspects of his relationship with the Asante ruling pairs or other Asante people. All Muslim headmen, and also Hane Haruna, the Director of Zuria 88.7 FM, have a photo of

[93] According to Weiss, this was the only type of education for Muslims during the colonial period. Recent research of D. Skinner shows, however, that in this period Muslim children also went to state schools and schools that were sponsored by the Ahmadyyia. Weiss, H. (2007). Begging and Almsgiving in Ghana: Muslim Positions Towards Poverty and Distress. Uppsala, Nordiska Afrikainstitutet. **133**. v.s. Skinner, D. E. 2009. "The Incorporation of Muslim Elites into the Colonial Administrative System of Sierra Leone, Gambia and the Gold Coast," *Journal of Muslim Minority Affairs* 29(1): 91-108.

themselves with the present *Asantehene* hanging in their palaces or office. They all emphasised the positive qualities of the current *Asantehene*, such as being a wise and understanding person. They also greatly appreciated that to their mind, *Asantehene* Osei Tutu II, does not discriminate against Muslims in the distribution of scholarships of the *Otumfuo* Educational Fund (OEF), which both Asante in the diaspora and in the Ashanti Region set up to help brilliant and needy students.

In their legal treatment of the Hausa, the Asante royal rulers follow the current regulations of the Ghanaian state, which regards them as Ghanaians and not as foreigners. In 1969, Ghanaian citizenship was still not provided on the basis of the place of birth but of ethnicity. Due to some inaccuracies in the ongoing population and housing census, the Hausa language is currently regarded as a foreign language. Despite their Ghanaian citizenship, the Hausa in Ghana are therefore still somehow regarded as foreigners, which is a matter of great concern for them. The Hausa feel that they are foreigners in name only and because most of them are born in Ghana, they have adjusted many of their customs to Ghanaian indigenous customs, and they speak Twi. To their mind, there is therefore no reason at all not to recognise Hausa as an indigenous Ghanaian language, and they are currently taking juridical steps to make this happen (Alhassan, the 22nd February 2012). In terms of the job market, the Hausa do not compete much with the Asante because most of them are not well educated and tend to fulfil the lower paid jobs, like loading and unloading goods (interview with Hane Harune, 37). The Hausa in Nigeria are for the majority Muslims, but some of them are Christians, and others are practitioners of African indigenous religious movements such as *bori,* which is a form of spirit mediumship. The Hausa in Kumasi, however, are all Muslims, and they have remained adherents of the form that originates from the Uthman dan Fodio. Orthodox Islam does not share many attributes with AIR but nevertheless the Hausa headmen strive for a harmonious relationship with the Asante royal rulers. They regard Allah and *Nyame*, who was originally the male Asante ancestor, as one and the same God, who is omnipotent and omniscient. In terms of the Berner model, AIR and Hausa Islam are in an A1 process of religious syncretism.

New Islamic movements

As is evident, the Asante-Muslim tensions occur in cases of severe violent intrareligious conflicts. In 2003, for instance, the head of the Tijaniyya movement Sheikh Abdulai Maikano and the Al-Sunnah leader Alfa Ajua had a disagreement of an intrareligious nature. In the violence that followed between their followers, a teenage boy was accidentally murdered.[94] More incidents of

---

[94] For tensions among Kumasi Muslims see: Accra Daily Mail, the 9th of December 2003, http://www.accra-mail.com/mailnews. asp? ID=8581.

this nature in the Kumasi metropolis may take place in future, as there have been a series of on-going violent clashes between the two mentioned Islamic movements in the Ashanti Region.[95] On the 16th of April 2007, in Ejura north of the Ashanti Region, ten members of the Alhus-Sunnah wal-Jama'ah body sustained gunshot wounds in a clash with members of the Tijaniyya movement who accused their opponents of preaching against them. Four of these members were hospitalised in critical conditions and sent over from the Ejura hospital to the *ɔkɔmfoɔ* Anokye Hospital in Kumasi.[96] The members of the Tijaniyya movement and the Al-Sunnah sect are also members of the United Front for Islamic Affairs (UFIA); an umbrella organisation of several Islamic movements in Ghana. The leading members of UFIA occasionally meet at Manhyia palace, together with the Asante ruling pair and Christian Church leaders of various Christian denominations in Kumasi, to discuss religious matters (interview with Mohammed Braimah Joseph and Zedan Rashid, 13). One of UFIA's aims is to incorporate the various postcolonial rooted Muslim organisations in Ghana to make it easier to maintain peaceful relationships between them.

One can also distinguish between orthodox and indigenised forms of Islam in the new Islamic movements. The Alhus-Sunnah movement was established in 1997 as an umbrella organisation for all Wahhabi organisations in Ghana, of which most have connections with Saudi Arabia. It is the Sunni orthodox Islamic movements whose members only believe what the holy prophet Mohammed told them and follow the Qur'an strictly. They preach against Africanised forms of Islam and are opposed to any form of religious syncretism. From their perspective, the adherents of Sufi movements, such as the Tijaniyya, also practice an Africanised form of Islam. The members of the Tijaniyya movements indeed adhere to a more moderate form of Islam, which includes the veneration of saints, but they do not perceive their own Islamic religion to be Africanised. The Ahmadiyya movement, which receives funding from the Islamic Republic of Iran, was introduced in Ghana in 1921 by a section of coastal (Fante) Muslim converts. The membership of this movement remains in the hands of Fante and Asante cultural groups, which is why the Ahmadiyya is also known as 'Fante or Asante Islam'. Their supreme head was Bashir ud-Din Mahmud Ahmad I from Rabwa, which is the name for the Indian subcontinent. By 1927 they had established forty stations along the coast and in Asante with an estimated number of 3,000 members. The Ahmadyyia movement led by Pakistani missionaries spread rapidly in southern Ghana and used both the Bible and the Qur'an in their teaching. The Ahmadiyya movement is tolerant towards AIR and promotes religious syncretism (Azumah 2012: Mohammed Bramah Joseph and Zedan Rashid, 53).

---

[95] http://religion.info/english/articles/article_327.shtml.

[96] The Ghanaian Times, the 16th of April 2007.

6.4. The relations of the Asante traditional authorities with Christians

The Christian Church leaders in the Kumasi metropolis have more in common with the Asante royal rulers than the Muslim headmen because many of these royal rulers and their subjects are both indigenous religious practitioners and Christians. There are no examples of Muslims in the Ashanti Region who occupy the position of traditional authority. This is because Muslims are usually circumcised, which is perceived as a disfiguring of the body that excludes them from occupying a stool. In AIR, the wholeness of the body is as a prerequisite for one's capabilities as a spiritual medium and of becoming an ancestral spirit in *asamando*. One of the few similarities between AIR and Islam is their approval of polygamy. However, although there are fewer religious and cultural distinctions between Asante and Christians, not all churches in the Ashanti Region allow Asante royal rulers to be members of their Christian Church denominations. The Mainline Churches (MCs) generally accept the Asante royal rulers as their members, but several of the PCC leaders request that these rulers should refrain from further involvement with AIR after their enstoolment (interview with Nana Brefo Gydedu Kotowko II, 23).

6.4.1. The socio-political relations

In this section, the focus will be on the socio-political relationship between the Asante traditional authorities and the Christian religious leaders of the MCs (the Methodists, the Roman Catholics, the Presbyterians and the Anglicans), the New African Indigenous Religious Movements (NAIRMs) and the New Religious Movements (NRMs) in today's Kumasi metropolis.[97]

The Mainline Churches

From the sixteenth century, European Christian missionaries (ECMs) transmitted the Christian faith as part of the political process of creating and extending the right of European sovereignty over 'newly discovered lands'. They accompanied European colonialists on their divine mission to conquer the world and to take all land that was in the hands of the indigenous people who they perceived as the inhabitants of a *terra nullius*. As written in the Book of Psalms, the Christians or chosen people were destined to inherit the earth and rule over it. The title of the lands encountered by the Europeans was held by the Christian king, whose explorers 'discovered' it (McSloy 1996). The initial aim of the ma-

[97] To be consistent in the use of IRs, the author refers to New African Indigenous Religious Movements (NAIRM) as those movements that previous scholars have referred to as New African Traditional Religious Movements (NATRM).

jority of the ECMs was to destroy the societies of the indigenous people and to replace them with new Christian European societies that were built according to the laws of the Christian God. The ECMs did not intend to go into dialogue with the natives but to refute their IRs and to portray the indigenous religious deities as the helpers of Satan in order to wipe out the existence of these religions (Mudimbe 1988). Due to a change in the power relations between ECMs and most of the former European colonies in Africa, the leaders of the Mainline Churches have changed their strategies in bringing the gospel. They have become more tolerant to African Indigenous Religions, and as a result, many practitioners of mainstream Christianity in these former colonies believe in a form of Christianity that also contains elements of the local IRs (Kaplan 1995). In the postcolonial period, most of the (ex) Missionary Churches in Asante society became more tolerant towards AIR and Mainstream Christianity grew enormously in terms of numbers, church buildings, and schools (Committee 1989). The focus of the next section will be on the postcolonial history of the MCs in the Kumasi metropolis.

The Methodist Church, Ghana

Like most MCs in Ghana, the Methodist Church has become more open to African religious influences since independence. In the 1990s, the Methodist Church in Kumasi organised a charismatic renewal for the whole church. Charismatic renewal movements, such as the Methodist Prayer fellowship in Kumasi, organise regular prayer meetings on Fridays, which easily attract over five hundred people a day. The Methodist Renewal Movement bridges the gap between African Indigenous Religions in Ghana and the Methodist Church teachings. Like the PCCs, this movement perceives the Bible as major source of power to overcome evil and to gain material welfare. Their Christian belief corresponds with IRs that power dwells in religious objects and that those who are in contact with these objects will often also be economically advanced (Müller 2012). The Pentecostal-Charismatics also believe that the blood of Jesus cleanses people's sins, which affiliates to the offering of animal blood as part of African indigenous religious rituals (Omenyo 2005). Since the postcolonial period, the Methodist Church in Ghana also places more emphasis on prayers during marriage ceremonies meant to bless the bride with a big womb to bear children, to come to meet the significance that many African put on childbearing as a sign of a successful marriage (Edusa-Eyison 2011).

The Presbyterian Church of Ghana

In 1918, the British colonial government of the Gold Coast had arrested and deported the Basel missionaries. Since most of these missionaries were of German origin, the British distrusted them and preventively closed down their schools. In 1927, the Scottish missionaries who had taken over the Presbyterian mission in the country a year earlier founded the Presbyterian Church of Ghana (Arhin 1985). Since then, the Presbyterian Church leaders had a problematic relationship with the Asante royal rulers because of the centrality of the ritual of sacrifice of animals for the veneration of the royal ancestors (Gilbert 1988).

The Anglican Church

The Church of the province of West Africa was formed in 1951 out of five Dioceses, including that of Accra, and was meant to service the whole of Ghana. In 1973, the Ghana diocese was split between Accra and Kumasi (Pobee 2009). The main clash between the Anglican Church and the Asante royal rulers is in the field of the appreciation of material wealth. Whereas the Anglican Church preaches soberness in the spending of money, in AIR material wealth is perceived as a blessing of *Nyame* and *Asase Ya*. Today, the Anglican Church in Ghana is highly influenced by the High Church tradition, which has resulted in an Anglo-Catholic Church tradition. The latter are more tolerant towards the Asante indigenous believers' attitude towards the accumulation of material wealth. The Anglican Church is eager to develop an authentic Ghanaian African Anglican identity and not be a clone of the Church of England. These days, various provinces of the Church have their own prayer books and liturgies.

The Roman Catholic Church

Like any of the other ECMs, the Roman Catholic missionaries in Ghana did not initially acknowledge the indigenous belief of the Asante people as a religion. Instead they regarded it as a set of superstitious ideas of barbarians who could only be civilised by being converted to Roman Catholicism. Nevertheless, the Roman Catholic missionaries believed that they could better succeed in bringing the Gospel by studying the African superstitions, and for this reason they learned Twi and translated the Bible into the language. They also allowed the influence of Asante music into the church and Asante architecture into the church building. In terms of processes of religious syncretism in the Berner model, the colonial period was in a phase of transition from an A1 process to a C2 process of systematic religious syncretism, as explained in Chapter IV.

In the postcolonial phase, the Christian Churches, including the Roman Catholic Church, increased the adoption of Asante indigenous religious attributes into their belief. Nkrumah, who became the first president of Ghana after the country gained independence, encouraged Black Nationalism and therefore pushed for Ghanaian leadership in the church and educational institutions. At the time, scholars like Mbiti, Idowu, and Sarpong re-emphasised the significance of interreligious dialogue between African Indigenous Religions, Islam, and Christianity. The transition from Vatican I (1869-1960) to Vatican II (1962-1965) was a development in the history of the Roman Catholic Church that stimulated interreligious dialogue. In comparison with the period of Vatican I, Vatican II was much more tolerant towards the incorporation of elements of IRs in Catholicism. By then the Roman Catholic Church acknowledged the African Indigenous Religions as religions. Since 1964, Pope Paul VI established a council for Interreligious Dialogues with the non-western world, including the African continent. Both independence and Post-Vatican II were historical developments that encouraged the Roman Catholic Church to maintain a positive relationship with the Asante royal rulers by being tolerant towards the incorporation of aspects of AIR in Roman Catholicism.

The Neo-Indigenous Religious Movements (NIRMs)

Especially in the 1940s of the colonial period, the neo-indigenous religious movements that first date from 1879 evolved into two forms of Christianised neo-indigenous religious movements: the New African Indigenous Religious Movements (NAIRMs) and the Spiritual Churches (SCs) (*sunsum nsore*). The author will elaborate on both movements in the coming sub-sections.

New African Indigenous Religious Movements (NAIRMs)

The NAIRMs in Ghana arose within the matrix of African Indigenous Religions. In 1982, Osofo *ɔkɔmfoɔ* Vincent Damuah, who was a former Catholic priest (*osofɔ*), founded the *Afrikania* Mission Church (AMC). This church belongs to the so-called contemporary NAIRMs (Gyanfosu 2002; de Witte 2008).

The AMC emerged out of the encounter of African indigenous religious believers with Christianity. Its founders and adherents borrowed selected elements from Christianity but remain essentially indigenous religious believers (Dovlo 1998:53-54). The AMC, since 2004 under the leadership of Atsu Kove, has three branches in the Ashanti Region, including one in Kumasi, and is still opening new branches throughout Ghana. It has not only adopted elements of Christianity but also challenges this world religion since it perceives God as the first ancestor and believes the pouring of libation to be the climax of community veneration. AMC church leaders are tolerant towards the Asante traditional authorities and their IRs. For this reason, however, they have a problematic relationship with fundamental mainline Christians who are not tolerant towards the latter religion (Gyanfosu 2002). Most problematic, however, is not the relationship of the NAIRMs with the adherents of Mainline Christianity but with the SCs that form part of the New Religious Movements (NRMs), which are the second form of movements in which AIR evolved. *Asantehemma* Ama Serwah Nyarko describes an example of tensions between the AMC and the SCs. The *Offinsohemma* said that what attracts her to the AMC is that, similarly to the Asante chieftaincy institution, its church leaders do not discriminate against people on e.g., the grounds of their colour, creed, national origin, or income. She especially emphasised equality towards the 'income' of her members as a positive point that made her utter criticism towards the leaders of some SCs in Offinso, such as the 'Adorn Samaria Healing Church of Grace'. Nana Nyarko said:

> The Spiritual Churches are in there for money, money and nothing else. If you get a post in the church it means you have money. The church excludes people without money, while in my place of traditional veneration; people can come without paying anything. [....] When I was young my mother told me that there was a Spiritual Church in Offinso where they asked money for prayers. They had two million cedis prayers, one million cedis prayers, and five hundred thousand cedis prayers. But my mother could not afford to spend this amount of money. She could only afford a 5000 cedis prayer, and she though that this type of prayer would not be that strong, so she stopped attending the church services. God came for the needy ones, but money in the churches is ruling and if you do not have money, the church does not recognise you. While in my AMC, my peace palace, if you do not have money you will still get sympathy (interview with nana Ama Serwah Nyarko, 29).

The *Offinsohemma*'s quotation demonstrates that she felt that as a traditional authority, she is and should be there for all religious practitioners, and like AIR, she does not discriminate against those of her subjects who are not wealthy but who come to her for help. According to her, the SCs are very money driven. After the interview, Nana Nyarko showed the author her branch of the AMC, located near the road from Offinso to Kumasi, and she referred to it as her 'peace palace'. There was no altar in the church. Instead there was a podium on which a stool was placed, and the whole entourage was very similar to the ones that the author saw in several of the palaces of the Asante royal rulers that she visited. In the middle of the *Offinsohemma*'s peace palace was a square on which an *ɔkɔmfoɔ* was dancing circles accompanied by a large crowd. From the inside the palace was much closer in outlook to a religious space for indigenous religious practitioners, a combination of both *akomfoɔ* and royal rulers, than to the inside of a Ghanaian Church. Royal insignia were all over the place, whereas Bibles or biblical statues were missing. From the outside, the building of this AMC resembled any other church buildings in Ghana. However, it distinguished itself from those church buildings by the statue of *Kwaman,* a hunter with bow and arrow, at the front. The *Offinsohemma* told the author that she received spiritual protection from this ancient Asante hunter god, after whom the capital of the Kwaman state was named. She believed that this was the reason why members of the spiritual Christian denominations in the Kumasi metropolis had not burnt down her church yet. She told the author that the Spiritual Church denominations were afraid of losing members to the AMC, which is why they had destroyed some of the churches of these movements.

New Religions Movements (NRMs)

Besides the MCs in contemporary Ghana, there is also a fast growing amount of New Religious Movements (NRMs), which includes the Pentecostal

Charismatic Churches (CCs) and the Spiritual Churches (SCs). In the postcolonial period, the Ex-Missionary Churches in the Ashanti Region grew modestly, but the African Independent Churches (AIC) and the PCCs grew most rapidly (Committee 1989). The leaders of the PCCs in Africa condemn the African Indigenous Religions, and they portray *Asase Ya,* the indigenous female spirit of the land, as a devilish Goddess (interview with *Oboguhene* Owusu Asiama II, 12). They are also very intolerant towards any attempt to convert Muslims, who they regard as being part of the empire of Satan (Gifford 1994; Dovlo 2004). The PCC leaders frequently organise deliverance sessions in church, which are occasions for their members to be healed from the evil ancestral female energies that dwell inside their bodies and manifest themselves by vomiting and crawling on the floor.[98] They believe that once the pastor drives out one's evil spirits, the reception of the Holy Spirit is within reach of all people, regardless of their ethnicity. The Pentecostal-Charismatics also believe that under the guidance of the Holy Spirit, prosperity in the global economy becomes within reach for ordinary Africans: wealth and success are perceived as the natural signs of God's blessings in Africa (van Dijk 1999).

The SCs, such as the Nube Divine Healing Church founded in 1944 and the Church of Light Mission founding in 1956 in Kumasi, bridge the gap between AIR and Christianity. In Ghana, they affirm the population's belief in ancestors and perform rituals that are in many aspects similar to those of Asante indigenous religious believers. Like the aforementioned neo-indigenous religious movements of the late precolonial and colonial periods, these churches have copied the structures of Akan chieftaincy institutions. As a result, their religious leaders are referred to as traditional authorities, whereas their organisation has the same hierarchical structure as those of the Akan states or regions. These churches have contributed to the enculturation of AIR in Christian practices (Dovlo 2004).

The SCs are syncretic in character, but this does not always contribute to a harmonious relationship between their church leaders and the Asante traditional authorities. Just like as with the neo-indigenous religious movements, the Spiritual Church leaders sometimes collaborate with these authorities, but at other times they regard themselves as rivals on the religious market because the content of their religious practice shows several similarities with AIR. The relationship of the SCs with the Asante royal rulers is also problematic because they offer the same type of services to believers. Both religious leaders deal with all aspects of indigenous religious life, e.g. puberty rites, naming ceremonies, and

[98] These deliverance sessions are the topic of many New Ghanaian Pentecostal films. See: Müller, L. F. 2011b. "Spirits of Migration Meet the Migration of Spirits Among the Akan Diaspora in Amsterdam in the Netherlands," *African and Black Diaspora: An International Journal* 4(1): 75-97., Müller, L. F. 2012. "Ghanaian Films as Indicators of Religious Change Among the Akan people of Kumasi and Southeast Amsterdam," in R. Heffner and J. Hutchinson. *Religions in Movement: The Local and the Global in Contemporary Faith Traditions*. London: Routledge: 467-503.

marriages, and attempt to cater to the total well-being of their members by providing a range of services, including 'job-services, kindergartens, discussion groups, and marriage counselling' (Dovlo 1998:63). Equally problematic in the relationship between the two is that intellectually, socially, spiritually, and in terms of leadership, the SCs challenge the MCs (Dovlo 1998:58-64). Among the NRMs, the leaders of 'Charismatic Ministries' especially draw the youth and the educated status group away from the MCs. The behavior of these leaders causes problems in the relationship of the SCs with the Asante traditional authorities, who for the most part enjoy a cordial relationship with the MCs. The Asante traditional authorities do, for instance, share members with the MCs: there is an organised body that calls itself the Asante Christian Chiefs and Queen Mothers Association (ACCQA). Finally, the SCs are also rivals of the new PCC, which perceive the former as demonic because of their incorporation of traditional elements, and the copy of organisational structures of AIR and culture. The PCC attempt 'to make a complete break with their [LM indigenous religious] past', and therefore they condemn both AIR and the SCs (Meyer 1998:316; Dovlo 2004). This is not surprising because both of these churches not only venerate the ancestral spirit (*Nyame*) as an omnipotent and omniscient god but also the indigenous Earth spirit (*Asase Ya*) as a Goddess, who under influence of Christianity, replaced the ancestral spirit (*Ngame*).

Chief Brefo Gydedu Kotowko II opinions on Pentecostal Christianity are as follows:

> The Pentecostals make a lot of noise with their veneration services, which disturbs other people. Their church leaders make long hours, but they do not have much knowledge and are not well trained unlike most church leaders of the Mainline Churches, who preach short and to the point and are not that arrogant in their attitude towards our traditional belief (interview with chief Brefo Gyededu Kotowko II, 23).

The case of Nana Brefo Gydedu Kotowko II makes clear that what he appreciates in the Mainline Churches is the attention that their leaders pay to schooling, the short length of their preaching, and their appreciation of AIR. These elements seem to be lacking in the PCC services, which for this chief are therefore less favourable. The Seventh Day Adventist Patrick Domfeh also took note of a negative attitude among the PCC leaders in Kumasi for indigenous religious practices when he said:

> Before the start of the *Asanteman Adae Kese*, the Pentecostal Church leaders entered the Kumasi market to preach to the audience that one should not go to this festival. The 'pentas' said that if we go to the festival, evil spirits would easily attack us. Some of my friends therefore did not go to the festival at all, whereas some did not go to any of the events during this festival that contained traditional religious practices (interview with Patrick Domfeh, 36).

The above interviews with inhabitants of Kumasi demonstrate that the different forms in which the Asante Neo-Indigenous Religious Movements have been transformed share their foundation in AIR but differ in their portrayal of the indigenous female spirits as either 'good and malevolence' or only as 'evil'. These religious differences cause a major source of tension between the religious movements who are one another's rivals at the religious market.

6.4.2. The religious relations

In this section, the author will look at the process of religious syncretism between AIR and Christianity of the Mainline Churches, and the NAIRMs or the NRMs, in the Kumasi metropolis. The processes of religious syncretism in relation to the myth of the *Sika Dwa Kofi* and the Asante indigenous ritual of pouring libation will be the focus of the following discussions.

The Methodist Church, Ghana

Dr. Charles Kingsley Coffie is both an Asante indigenous religious believer and a Methodist priest who feels that both are significant for his religious identity. Coffie believes that there is power dwelling inside the Golden Stool and that the Asante royal rulers who regulate that power can receive help from the spiritual world for the benefit of the community. He perceives himself as a dual believer, whose religions are compatible and comply with his needs in different ways. According to Coffie, the ancestors, of whom the spiritual power in the royal stools derives, are deceased Asante people who have offered their lives for the good of the community; they are more knowledgeable than human beings and can be asked for help. An example of a significant Asante ancestor is *Tweneboa Kodua*, for instance, who offered himself during the war between the Asante and the Dɛnkyira in 1701. In Methodist Christianity, the saints, like Peter, have also offered their lives for the good of the community and can be asked for help. In Coffie's Methodist Church, he preaches that the 'Church Militant' or those who are still struggling in their faith can seek help from 'the Church Triumphant', the one who has already been honoured. In Coffie's eyes, an aspect of both AIR and Christianity is that there are ancestors that the believers can seek help from in times of need. Coffie also remarked, however, that many young Asante people are not familiar with the fact that the royal stools are inspirited. They are also not so concerned with the traditional rituals of the Asante royal rulers. The young ones, for instance, do not go to the *Asanteman Adae Kese* festival for its many traditional rituals that are performed but for relaxation and personal enjoyment. Charles Coffie also said, 'Some Pentecostal Christians do not go to the festival at all because they believe that the chieftaincy rituals such as the pouring of libation are against their Christian religion. Most Asante Methodists, however, do not neglect their traditional religious belief, because they feel that it is also part of their identity' (interview with Charles Kingsley Coffie, 4).

The *Oboguhene* Owusu Asiama II is both a Presbyterian and a chief who preaches to his congregation and gives them moral advice. He said: 'As a leader, one needs to give a sign and to teach people in one's religious tradition, otherwise nobody will follow you. Because I aligned myself to Jesus Christ since childhood, my people follow me in my Christian faith. I already worshipped God in church before I was enstooled as a chief and after my enstoolment I could not stop going to church, because Christianity is part and parcel of me. However, on the *adae,* every chief has to go to the stool room to pour libation to bring unity and peace and on those days one cannot go to church. Times have changed, and Christianity is now very important to us, but nevertheless many of our religious traditions have remained.'

According to the Presbyterian R. Aboagye, the purpose of the ritual of pouring libation during *Asanteman Adae Kese* is to invoke the ancestral spirits and to cleanse the society from evil spirits. Before going to the festival, the individuals in each village cleanse themselves, and the traditional authorities should cleanse their own villages, so it is a bottom-up construction. The *Asanteman Adae Kese* festival is then the coming together of at least the majority of the Asante traditional authorities and the cleansing of the whole Asante society. The invocation of the spirits in order to remove the evil spirits is one of the reasons that some Presbyterians do not want to go to the Durbar ground of the festival, because of their fear of being attacked by the evil spirits. Many Christians, however, do take part of the festival because they feel that it is beneficial to the society, and they just do not take part in the indigenous religious events, such as the pouring of libation (interview with R. Aboagye, 33).

R. Aboagye is a Presbyterian Christian, but his discussion of the topic of the pouring of libation demonstrates that this does not exclude his or other members of his congregation's fear for evil spirits, which includes those of an indigenous religious nature. As *Oboguhene* Owusu Asiama II explained to the author: 'Denying these traditions is very dangerous, because according to the traditional religion, if you do not respect the stool and obey the morals that come with the function of chief, the spirit of the stool can kill you. You die instantly!' (interview with *Oboguhene* Owusu Asiama II, 12).

The Anglican Church

Nana Serwaah Amponssaa, the *omanhemma* of Kumawu, regularly visits the Anglican Church that was built by her grandfather, who was the *Kumawuhene* in the 1930s. She is both an Asante indigenous religious believer and an Anglican Christian. On the question of how she feels by being a dual believer, she said:

> My belief is rooted in Christianity. I cannot define being a Christian, but I am a liberal person who believes both in the power of the ancestors who dwell inside our stools and in that of the saints. I do not see any problem in receiving powers from the ancestors inside my stool and from venerating the saints when I go to church. This is my personal opinion. If other female rulers see this differently, I respect them for that (interview with Nana Serwaah Amponssaa, 43).

The *Kumawuhemma* has a crucifix on top of her bed, but also pours libations, and she feels that both are part of her religious life. She has her own counselling group and helps people on the basis of AIR. If there are conflicts between her subjects, for instance, they go to the village shrine and slaughter a sheep to pacify the spirits. She also works together with the pastor, who has his own counselling group, and she feels that she and the pastor have similar tasks and goals. They both preach for peace, either in the palace or in the Anglican Church, and are both leaders and servants of their community (interview with Nana Serwaah Amponssaa, 43).

The Roman Catholic Church

Peter Sarpong has been a significant promoter of integrating AIR and Roman Catholicism from 1970 by measures such as preaching of the gospel into the context of Asante social life, for example. In 1969, he was consecrated as Bishop in the St. Peter's Cathedral in Kumasi, and in the period between 2002-2008, he was the Archbishop of this metropolis. Sarpong was the first to say the mass in Twi rather than Latin and to preach in Twi rather than English (interview with Peter Sarpong, 11). He also took the initiative to establish the Asante Chiefs and Queen Mothers Association (ACCQA). All MCs in the Ashanti Region are members who have set up regulations in order to maintain a good relationship between the Asante royal rulers and mainline Christians (Asante 2006). Significant for the maintenance of a good relationship is also the celebration of 'Corpus Christi'. This is a day for the commemoration of the supreme gift of the institution by Jesus Christ. During this celebration, the body of Christ is shown in a monstrance, which is an open or transparent receptacle in which the consecrated Host is exposed, for the venerators to renew their allegiance to Him – King Jesus Christ – *ɔhene Yesu Kristo* – at the *Manhyia* palace Durbar ground.[99] Traditionally, each royal has his or her own place at the Durbar ground, which enabled the Asante to organise themselves efficiently during wars. The closer a royal sits to the *Asantehene* at the Durbar, the more important is his or her position (interview with Nana Brefo Gyededu Kotowko II, 23). Now, during the 'Corpus Christian' celebration, the 'body of Christ' is placed at the spot that the *Asantehemma* normally occupies. *Adowa* dancers, who during funerals and other Asante indigenous ceremonies point to the chest to refer to the *Asantehene*, now

[99] A 'monstrance' is an open or transparent receptacle in which the consecrated Host is exposed for veneration.

point to Christ's feet to show that the Asante state belongs to Him (*Yesu Kristo*). Singers of the *Nnwokorɔ* group refer to the *ɔhene Yesu Kristo* as their king.

One would imagine that since the celebration of 'Corpus Christi' in *Asanteman*, the Asante ruling duo Osei Agyeman Prempeh II and Ama Serwaa Nyaako, and the current ruling pair Osei Tutu II, and Afia Kobi Sewaa Ampem II should have been furious about the occupation of their place by Sarpong's indigenous Catholics, since they refer to *Yesu Kristo* as their leader rather than the Asante king. On the contrary, both mentioned that the Asante royal rulers were very positive towards Sarpong's mission of selective implementation of indigenous elements in Roman Catholicism and his promotion of the *Asantenisation* of the liturgy of the Roman Catholic Church. In fact, in 1967 when Sarpong, who at the time was an assistant priest at St. Peter's Cathedral in Kumasi, asked *Asantehene* Prempeh II for the royal regalia to be used during 'Corpus Christi', the Asante king answered: *Adae yede hoahoa me Asantehene, no wode ko ako woahoe Nyame. Fa ko fa ko hey Nyame anomonyam.* – 'I am honoured that regalia used in honouring me, as king of Asante, are considered fitting to honour God. I freely allow you to borrow them for this great purpose' (Obeng 1996:187). Instead of perceiving Roman Catholic Church leaders and *Yesu Kristo* as rivals, Asante royal rulers have thus encouraged them to make use of Asante indigenous religious symbols during Christian ceremonies. When Thomas Mensah was appointed as the successor of Sarpong as bishop of the Kumasi diocese in March, 2008, the current *Asantehene* Osei Tutu II and Afia Kobi Serwaa Ampem II confirmed that he would continue collaboration in line with Sarpong's visions on the development of the Roman Catholic Church in the Ashanti Region (Unknown author, the 4th of May 2008).

According to the Roman Catholic respondents, most of the Roman Catholics in this region are also adherents of AIR. An example is Osei Kwaku, an elder of a village chief from Heman Buoɔho. Kwaku believes that there is only one God (*Nyame*), who he honours by both venerating the ancestors and by attending Roman Catholic Church services. With regards to the royal stool, he believes that as long as the chief lives, his stool will not be permanently inspirited, but at times the ancestral spirits will come to him to empower him. This happens during the *adae,* which are those days in which the chief is obliged to visit the stool room and to pour libation and slaughter a sheep to propitiate the ancestral spirits. If the chief does not respect this part of AIR, as Osei Kwaku explains, the spirits in the stool will kill them. However, when the chief dies a natural death, and after his family has blackened the stool, his spirit will dwell permanently inside this royal seat and join the ancestral spirits of his royal predecessors (interview with Osei Kwaku, 44). Remarkably, the Roman Catholic Osei Kwaku and the Presbyterian *Oboguhene* Owusu Asiama II both believe that the stool can kill those royal rulers who occupy this royal seat and do not respect the religious obligations that come with their function.

The Roman Catholic *Asantehemma* Nana Nyarko believes that the one who sits on a stool is in connection with the ancestors. Her idea about the collective *sunsum* that dwells inside stools becomes clear from the answer she gave to a woman who came to her for consultation on spiritual matters. Nana Nyarko said:

> I told this woman, who goes to the same church, that there are two ways in which she is spiritually protected. First my family stool, because of the power of the blood (*mogya*) of a fowl or chicken that is used to blacken this stool gives ancestral spiritual protection to all my subjects. Secondly, the blood of Jesus protects her, because she goes to church (interview with Nana Nyarko, 29).

In her Roman Catholic belief, Nana Nyarko has thus added a second source of spiritual power (the blood of Jesus) to the source that she is familiar with as an Asante indigenous religious believer (the blood of an animal, such as a chicken or a goat).

New African Indigenous Religious Movements (NAIRMs)

The *omanhemma* of Offinso is the religious leader of an *Afrikania* Mission Church, and she calls herself a 'traditional Christian' because she already worshipped God before the Christians did. Her forefathers used a tree with many branches and put an egg in the middle of that tree. She said: 'My forefathers woke up early in the morning; they kneeled down and prayed to the Almighty God. I am continuing this tradition and I call it Christianity because like other Christians I am also praying to God' (interview with Nana Ama Serwah Nyarko, 29).

Like many Asante of today, the *Offinsohemma* came to meet both religions in her youth. At home she was brought up traditionally, and she regularly pours libation for the ancestral spirits, but at school and at work they were brought up in the Christian tradition. It is therefore self-evident for many Asante to refer to themselves as traditional Christians and to feel that both AIR and Christianity make up their religious identity. For many Asante, this means that they go to one of the churches that the European missionaries brought, such as the Methodist Church or the Roman Catholic Church, and also pay a visit to an *akomfoɔ* to venerate the ancestors. Others go to the SCs or the Pentecostal Churches. The *Offinsohemma* said:

> In my *Afrikania* Mission Church, we use the Bible as a source of inspiration, but we venerate God in the traditional way. We, for instance, pour libation to honour *Nyame* through the ancestral spirits. We also believe that one should not kill another person because the Bible says that "thou shall not kill", and in the traditional religion it is also forbidden for subjects to kill. However, we find that Christians in the Missionary Churches are worshipping God in the wrong way. Many members of those churches all curse one another, which means that they do not do what the Bible says, whereas in the *Afrikania* Mission Church this is not a practice. Another problem in these churches is that people steal one another's properties, such as mobile phones. The Bible says that thou shall not steal, and in the AMC this is not a practice. A final problem with these churches is that they are money driven. One can only buy a good prayer if one has money, which means that poor people are left out, whereas in

> the traditional religion and according to the Bible God is there to help those in need regardless of their financial situation (interview with Nana Ama Serwah Nyarko, 29).

The *Offinsohemma* also said that she works together with a Christian NGO from Kenya to finance projects such as the paying of school fees for sixty-five orphans in the Ashanti Region. The *Offinsohemma* said: 'I believe that God is good and he created heaven and earth, and he brings power to all things and beings, including royal stools and to people. It is through Him that I received the spiritual power to rule, and it is because of Him that I should use that power to help all of my subjects.' In 1988, the *Offinsohemma* founded the 'Ashanti Queen Mother Association' (AQMA), which takes charge of the interests of women in the Ashanti Region. Currently, the association has about forty-four female Asante rulers. They regulate communal labour and settle disputes between married couples. Furthermore, their aims are especially to protect young girls, by the re-introduction of *bragro* puberty rituals for instance. This gives all girls who turn eighteen an opportunity to marry a good husband and to get counselling in preparation for the marriage. It also prevents them from having sex outside marriage, with all the risks of getting pregnant and/or of getting sexual transmittable illnesses like HIV/AIDS. The *Offinsohemma* is an example of one of the many Asante female royal rulers who combines their indigenous religious functions with those of a modern female development worker (*nkosohemma*) in collaboration with a Christian development organisation.

New Religions Movements (NRMs)

One of the significance aspects of the Christian members of the NRMs is that they do not believe that there is ancestral power dwelling inside the Golden Stool. Ernestina Ama Brenya is a member of a Spiritual Church who believes that the Golden Stool is not occupied by a communal *sunsum* but by an indigenous evil force (*sasa bonsam*). Ernestina Brenya said:

> The spirits or *sunsum* inside the stools, which the Asante traditional authorities occupy, are not derived from God but from *sasa bonsam*. It is therefore better for everybody to stop being in connection with those spirits (interview with Ernestina Ama Brenya, 8).

Osei Hyiaman, a Christian of the Assemblies of God, a Pentecostal denomination, warned the author that she should not believe what the people in the villages tell her in terms of the existence of spirits that affect the leadership of the Asante chiefs. He explained that the chiefs are political leaders who only have political authority but who do, however, help to solve conflicts of a religious nature that cannot be solved by the religious leaders. He said:

> If I have a religious problem, I first go to my pastor because church matters are primarily settled within the church. If he is not able to solve the problems, then the chief and his elders can come to solve the problem, and if he does not succeed then he invites all the pastors of different churches to

come to the palace to help solve the problem. The chief and the pastor collaborate, and they show a great respect for one another (interview with Osei Hyiaman, 32).

The quotation demonstrates that Osei Hyiaman thinks of his chiefs more as political leaders and councillors in religious affairs; he does not believe that they use spiritual power to rule. He also said that he respects the chiefs because they are authorities, and it is written in the Bible that one should honour those who deserve honour because they are higher in social ranking. Hyiaman thus clearly showed a great respect for hierarchy and the authority of the chiefs, but he does not believe that this authority has a religious source. The Pentecostals-Charismatics do not venerate the ancestors, but they portray indigenous female spirits as devils (Müller 2012).

6.5 Conclusion

The aim of this chapter was to provide insight into the meaning of the indigenous religious peacekeeping function of the Asante royal rulers in contemporary Ghana. The author aimed to increase insight in these functions by describing the socio-political and religious relations between these rulers and the Christians and Muslims in the Kumasi metropolis.

In the field of socio-political relationships, the Asante royal rulers maintain a policy of non-interference with the affairs of Muslims and Christians. The Islamic and Christian religious leaders in the first instance solve all intra-religious conflicts without consulting with the Asante traditional authorities. In cases of inter-religious Asante-Muslim or Asante-Christian conflicts these authorities meet with either the Islamic or Christian religious leaders. When there are persisting conflicts in Asante society of an inter-religious Asante-Christian-Muslim nature, the Asante royal rulers meet with the Islamic and Christian religious leaders and fulfil a religious mediatory role. Politically, the Asante royal rulers who are the custodians of the land are superior to Muslims in the settlements who merely have a guest status. In terms of religious organisation, however, the Asante traditional rulers and Muslims maintain a relationship of respect and regard of one another as different but equal in the eyes of God. Unlike in the precolonial period, and to a lesser extent in the colonial period, the Asante royal rulers no longer make a clear distinction in their attitude towards Muslims that adhere to the Suwarian tradition and orthodox Islam. The *Asantehene* respects all Muslims on equal footing, and they regard the decision of who represents the settlement Muslims at the royal palace as an intra-religious Islamic affair. The Asante traditional rulers tolerate the wishes of the Muslims to maintain and build a semi-autonomous Muslim space inside the settlements, which includes their own hospitals and schools. The relationship of the Asante royal rulers with Christian religious leaders of the Mainline Churches has generally improved since the colonial period. All of these churches have become more tolerant towards indigenous religious practices, and these practices have also adjusted to the norms and values of these churches. The various forms of Mainline Church Christianity and AIR have become more intertwined since their foundation at the end of the precolonial and the colonial periods. The New African Indigenous Religious Movements (NAIRMs) are also closely interlinked with AIR of the Asante *akomfoɔ* and royal rulers, and many adherents of the latter are also members of one of these movements, such as the AMC. In terms of religious organisation, the two are very similar, and in many aspects the NAIRMs are syncretised successors of the neo-indigenous religious movements of the colonial period, such as *Tigare* and *Nana Tongo*. The relationship between the Asante royal rulers and adherents of the NRMs is most problematic. The SCs are at times in conflict with the Asante traditional rulers because they offer the same kind of services and are therefore rivals in the religious market. However, the main problems occur between the Asante traditional rulers and the leaders of the PCCs, whose members attempt to free themselves from their Asante indigenous religious roots by condemning the female indigenous (ancestral) spirits. They believe that calling upon the Holy Spirit in church during sessions of deliverance can destroy these spirits. Not surprisingly, the Asante royal rulers and the Pentecostal-Charismatic Church leaders are often in conflict about the content of the traditional (bye) laws that regulate religious life and the lack of one another's obedience towards these laws.

For the religious relations between the Asante traditional rulers and the Islamic and Christian religious leaders and their followers, one can conclude that in terms of levels of religious syncretism (as explained in the Berner model), the postcolonial phase in the history of the Asante is characterised by an A1 determination of relations on the systemic level. In AIR, there is a realisation of unity with either Christianity or Islam but not to such an extent that there is an attempt to turn AIR and one of these religions into one unifying whole. In the A1 process of religious syncretism as described in the Berner model, the competitive relationship between the religions is eliminated as all religions are placed on the same level, but the boundaries between them remain intact. The extent to which the Asante royal rulers have succeeded in harmonising the relationship with the Islamic and Christian leaders also depends on the attitude of these leaders towards the Asante traditional rulers and their IRs. That attitude will now be analysed using the Berner model and its processes of religious syncretism. The Suwarian tradition places unity in the practice of its belief and that of AIR rather than in its religious theories. Many of the religious practices are similar, but their meaning is different for Asante indigenous religious believers than it is for adherents of the Suwarian tradition of the Asante *Nkramo* chief in Kumasi. The Hausa in Kumasi are all adherents of the orthodox form of Islam that originates from Uthman dan Fodio, the nineteenth century *jihadist* from the Sokoto Caliphate in contemporary northern Nigeria. AIR does not share many attributes with the Orthodox Islam, but nevertheless the Hausa strive for a harmonious relationship between the two religions (the A1 process of the Berner model). Allah and the original male ancestral spirit of the Asante, who under the influence of Islam and Christianity became the Supreme Being (*Nyame*), are perceived as one and the same God. The members of the MCs all believe in a melding of AIR and various forms of Christianity. Several of the author's Methodist respondents stressed the similarity between belief in the ancestors and the saints. The Presbyterians and the Roman Catholics emphasised the parallels in the power of Jesus Christ and that of the spirits inside the royal stools. The Anglican *omanhemma* of Kumawu demonstrated that in terms of counselling, she and the pastor of the Anglican Church had similar goals that derive from a context of religious compatibility of AIR and Anglican Christianity. All of the MCs in Kumasi are thus clearly in a process of levelling AIR and Christianity (the A1 process of the Berner model), and its leaders are actively searching for religious similarities. The religion of the NAIRMs is very much in line with AIR. In many aspects, the NAIRMs continue the indigenous religious practices, but they actively do look for similarities in the Bible between AIR and Christianity. Their main reason for regarding themselves as traditional Christians is that, in theory, the Christian religion and AIR are not so different. Its objects such as the Bible and God can be incorporated in AIR. In terms of religious practices, however, the NAIRMs very much rely on AIR. They especially criticise the SCs for being money driven, for not helping the poor and the needy, and for cursing their neighbours. Nevertheless, the NAIRMs generally have a cordial relationship with the Asante royal rulers. The main difficulties in this relationship, not only socio-politically but also on a religious basis, occur between these authorities and the adherents of the NRMs, such as the PCCs and the SCs. The members of these movements regard the indigenous religious spirits as devilish powers that can also negatively affect the traditional authorities, or they believe that the rulers are not at all in connection with spirits and that they should be regarded as secular leaders that operate next to religious leaders. In terms of the Berner model of religious syncretism, one can speak of (A3) a distancing relationship where the boundary and the competitive relationship between systems are preserved, and the very existential value of the competing systems is thrown into doubt. A hypothetical example, given by Berner, is that of the early Christian apologists, such as Justin, who condemned the Mithraic religion in its entirety as expressed in particular with claims that 'central elements of the Mysteries of Mithras can be traced back to the influence of the devil or evil demons' (Berner 2004:304). Similarly to this, the Pentecostal-Charismatic churchgoers condemn the Asante indigenous religious spirits, who can be either good or evil depending on the situation, as forces that are devilish by nature and act in an evil way regardless of the situation. In conclusion, except for the NRMs and their A3 process of religious syncretism in the Berner model, both the Islamic and the Christian religious leaders strive for a harmonising of both their socio-political and religious relationships with the Asante traditional rulers (Berner's A1 process).

Final Conclusion

The aim of this book was first to enhance understanding of the religious bond between Asante royal rulers and their subjects, and secondly, between these royal rulers and the spiritual beings in Asante history. On the basis of these insights, the author aims to demonstrate how belief in the Indigenous Religion of the Asante accounts for the persistence of Asante chieftaincy in Ghana, alongside economic, juridical and political factors. The author therefore focussed on the indigenous religious function of the Asante traditional rulers within their society as mediators between human beings and non-human entities and between human beings with distinct religious beliefs and preferences in the social world. It is only by exploring and understanding the nature of the Asante Indigenous Religion and the deeply rooted basic religious values of the Asante that we can grasp the mystery behind the bond between Asante royal rulers and their subjects, and their interwovenness of interests not only in Asante history, but also in the contemporary period.

With regards to the differences between the theoretical insights into the nature of Indigenous Religions and Asante Indigenous Religion and the actual historical and empirical reality of the latter the author's final conclusions are as follows.

With reference to the first mentioned characteristic of IRs one can conclude from this study that locality is indeed a significant aspect of these religions. The spirits that are being invoked used to be and are still local. From the description and analysis of the indigenous religious rituals in Chapter V one can conclude that those spirits who fly in or out of the region e.g. through the medium of video films of indigenous religious rituals are added to a local pantheon of spirits and are thereby localised. A main characteristic of IRs as mentioned by MacDonald in point two is indeed that those who adhere to those religions believe in the existence of a local creator God. The Asante's concept of *Onyankopɔng*, which represents the star Sirius B, is native to them and predates the influences of Christianity and Islam. The absence of the concept of a creator God in ter Haar's theory of IRs and the denial of the existence of such a God in IRs by Cox is remarkable, since to the knowledge of the author most of the African Indigenous Religions (e.g. the Asante, the Fon, the Yoruba and the Anlo-Ewe) have a creator God that predates the encounter of those who adhered to these religions with either Christianity and/or Islam. It might not be the case that all IRs had or have a creator God. However, the existence of such a God in AIR should be the topic of debate rather than that of denial. The point three, four and five of the attributes of IRs mentioned in section 1.3 can also be applied to AIR. An aspect that is lacking from the theory of African Indigenous Religions of ter Haar, MacDonald, Alola, Fisher and Cox but not from the actual historical-anthropological social reality of AIR is that it is not only local discourses that transform the tales on the relationship between the spirits, people and their environment but also the encounter of indigenous people with world religious discourse. The significance of that encounter for the transformations of IRs becomes, however, crucial for the history of AIR. In summary, the relation to the ancestral spirits in this history is as follows.

In the early precolonial period the Asante believed in the male ancestral serpent spirit (*Nyame*) and the female ancestral serpent spirit (*Ngame*) who lived on Earth in a separate sacred space that was accessible by spiritual specialists. Since the second half of the eighteenth century, however, under influence of Islam *Nyame* transformed into an omnipotent and omniscient monotheistic Islamic God, whose attributes were universal and abstract. Then, in the nineteenth century, both Asante indigenous believers, Asante Muslims and Asante Christians venerated *Nyame* as a monotheistic God with these abstract attributes. *Asase Ya* was originally the spirit of the Earth that, in line with the indigenous priest Anokye's customary laws, was venerated on a Thursday (*Yaa*) to prevent the Asante from going to the farm on this day so as not to disturb the earth thereby protecting agricultural land from exploitation. In the colonial period, as a result of the encounter with Christianity, *Asase Ya* became known as the female Earth Goddess. Whereas Rattray still referred to *Asase Ya* as a local spirit of the Earth, in the postcolonial period a large number of academic missionary-oriented scholars started to refer to *Asase Ya* as 'Mother Earth' thereby implicitly also providing her with abstract and universal attributes (Pobee 1976; Pobee and Mends 1977). Both in the meaning of Earth Goddess and Mother Earth, *Asase Ya* replaced the precolonial rooted female ancestral spirit *Ngame*. Under influence of Islam and Christianity the power and influence of both of the Asante royal ancestral serpent spirits (*anini nananom nsamanfo*) thus diminished and since then the Asante indigenous believers, Asante Muslims and Asante Christians have simply referred to these spirits as sexless 'ancestors'. They thereby significantly diminished the power of *Ngame* and the female ancestral ruler and in the hierarchy of the spirits they placed the ancestors (*anini nsamanfo*) under the Supreme Being *Nyame* and the Earth Goddess or Mother Goddess *Asase Ya*, who eventually all received universal attributes. Whereas in the colonial period *Nyame* and *Asase Ya* were still equal in ranking, under the increasing Christian influence in postcolonial Ghana *Nyame* became higher in ranking than *Asase Ya*; a process that further undermined the religious-political influence of the female Asante rulers. The study of AIR demonstrates that the politics of the representation of the spirits has clear implications for the position of the traditional rulers, who legitimate their religious-political power on the basis of their relationship with those spirits. The influences of the world religions, Islam and Christianity, have had a devastating effect on the position of the female Asante rulers, whose position has become increasingly less significant under influence of these world religions that, unlike the African Indigenous Religions do not promote the harmonious living together of the sexes but promote the curtailment of the social and intellectual development of women and economic dependency on men. Remarkably, these effects of Christianity and Islam on women, which are frequently discussed in the academic fields of gender studies and differential thinking in philosophy, are completely left out from the field of the academic study of (African) Indigenous Religions. A major characteristic of these religions is that they are about the veneration of male and female ancestors, but the gender of these spirits is not mentioned in any of the books on theories of African Indigenous Religions or Indigenous Religions. With this book the author hopes to have contributed to the start of an academic debate on the (mis) representations of (African) Indigenous Religions in terms of their (deliberate) omission of the history of the female spirits and the concomitant female rulers. Unlike in most other works on chieftaincy, these female spirits and rulers are included in the author's historical anthropology of the Asante people.

With regards to the theory of African Indigenous Religions, as observed by ter Haar observed in (1), this book on AIR demonstrates that these religions are indeed the religions of kinship-based communities who venerate the ancestral spirits. The Asante are multi-kinship based, because they do not only venerate the ancestors of their own *abusua* but also those of the *abusua* of their royal rulers, who can belong to a different matriclan. In the precolonial and colonial history Asante royal rulers often presented their subjects or whole villages as a gift to other royal rulers during important occasions. Royal rulers also sold portions of their territory to defray stool debt, which saw the development of a multi-kinship society. The notion, as mentioned in (2), that African Indigenous Religions are the religions of small-scale communities with food gathering (hunting and gatherers) and food producing (agrarian-metropolitan) societies demands further scrutiny. African Indigenous Religions indeed originate from small-scale communities with these modes of production, but today, as mentioned in Chapter VI, African diaspora communities in North Atlantic societies also adhere to IRs (even though they refer to the attributes of these religions as 'culture' rather than 'religion'), whereas these small-scale communities are capitalistic by nature. One can therefore conclude that African Indigenous Religions came into being in societies with a non-capitalist mode of production, but that they have survived the introduction of capitalism. (African) Indigenous Religions are thus resilient towards both the encounter with world religious systems of belief and world economic modes of production. In relation to the transfer of African Indigenous Religions to the rest of the world, e.g. through video images and previously through the transatlantic slave trade, (3) the mentioned attributes of African Indigenous Religions are also debatable. In today's Kumasi metropolis, the author met some Asante who were born outside of Ghana, in Europe, who were Christians, but who now lived in the Metropolis and decided to become dual believers and adhere to AIR and Christianity. As these Asante were thus not born into the community of Asante believers, it seems that also this characteristic of African Indigenous Religions is no longer applicable to the situation in the many and growing urban areas in Africa. Point (4) also seems outmoded, because today anthropologists also write down the traditions of many African Indigenous Religions. Perhaps one could better say that African Indigenous Religions initially had no written scriptures and the current scriptures are less central to the religious experience of the believers than in at least most if not all of the World Religions. Taking point (5), the notion that African Indigenous Religions would be invisible because they are embedded in all other aspects of life is also debatable. This book demonstrates that Asante indigenous religious rituals can clearly be distinguished from other rituals that are being performed to boost the tourist industry and are also boundered in space and time. In comparison to the religious expressions of believers of the world religions, those of indigenous religious believers are, however, indeed less visible and distinct from other aspects of life. The author agrees with the points 6,7,8,9 and 11 as attributes of African Indigenous Religions. A clear difference between the theory of African Indigenous Religions and the historical and anthropological reality of at least AIR is, however, that presumed 'lack of belief in life after death' among African indigenous religious believers. The Asante have a strong belief in life after death and, as discussed in Chapter I, they believe that their eternal soul (*ɔkra*) will return in a different body (*honam*) after one passes away. The historical anthropology of AIR in this book demonstrates that the royal ancestors were believed to be spirits of deceased royal rulers who presumably lived in a universe parallel to that of the living, with whom they lived together on Earth as 'living-dead' as part of the same extended family (the *abusua*).

These findings about the difference between the theory of IRs and African Indigenous Religions, and the actuality of AIR have brought new insights into the indigenous religious roles of the Asante traditional rulers in historical and contemporary Ghana as an explanatory factor in the persistence of Asante chieftaincy. The remaining part of this conclusion will address these royal rulers' indigenous religious roles throughout their history: those of mediation between the spiritual and human beings and those of socio-religious peacekeepers.

In the precolonial period, AIR enabled the Asante traditional authorities to ritually mediate between the beings of the spiritual and the social worlds and so to receive consent among their subject to ritually control their life and death. The royal rulers organised 'naming ceremonies,' *bragro*, and funeral rituals to provide meaning in the life of the Asante by invoking the spirits, and, to maintain stability within the Asante kingdom. The royal rulers were the only ones authorised to carry out executions, often taking the form of the ritual killing of human beings, which was part of their strategy to rule by fear. T.C.McCaskie uses Gramsci's historical materialist conception of 'cultural hegemony' to explain that the religious-political power of the Asante traditional rulers was also based on the dominance of their elitist ideas, and the spread of these ideas among their subjects that enabled them to be in control. This book, however, centralises around the Asante indigenous religions derived notion that the Asante traditional authorities were themselves not *in control* but were trained as religious specialists who had learned how to get *out of control;* a process that allowed the spiritual forces to take control of them first, and then to get back into a form of ritual control. The book demonstrates that the Asante royal rulers themselves were spiritual mediators. Their religious-political power was derived from their religious relationships with the more powerful spiritual beings. This striving for harmony between humans, spirits and the Earth resulted from the equality in the appreciation of the – in Jungian terms – *anima* or female principle and the *animus* or male principle in the Asante psyche. Unlike the attributes of the monotheistic religions, it was not an aspect of AIR to control nature by suppressing the *anima* but instead to live in harmony with nature. To maintain these relationships and to legitimise their position, the Asante royal rulers used the *Odwira* festival, and the custom of swearing an oath to the *Asantehene* and the myth of the Golden Stool to re-enact, re-interpret, and transmit Asante history, and to renew communication between the living and the dead. The *Odwira* festival was an occasion to remember the ancestral spirits by giving them yam of the new harvest and so to renew the relationship with them, thereby being ensured of their blessings in the year to come. The Asante royal rulers are thus not portrayed in this book as Gramsci's secular political agents, but also as religious-political leaders, whose source of power came from the spiritual world. In their roles as indigenous religious peacekeepers, the Asante royal rulers maintained the social connection between Islamic and Christian religious leaders, and they incorporated those into their religious landscape who adhered to the moderate forms of Islam and Christianity to maintain a good relationship with the Asante hinterland and the European traders at the Gold Coast. In terms of religion, the Asante rulers only took elements of the moderate forms of Islam and Christianity to add them to their pantheon of existing Asante indigenous religious state deities (*tete abosom*) and material objects. This phase in the Asante history corresponds with the Berner C2 model of religious syncretic processes. Those Muslims and Christians who adhered to the more orthodox forms of Christianity and Islam were in general not welcome in Kumasi, because they were believed to cause a threat to the persistence of the Asante state and as a result religious syncretism did not occur between AIR and these forms of religion.

In the colonial period, the Asante traditional authorities continued their indigenous religious mediatory role. Despite the British colonisation and their support for CPP chiefs, the Asante royal rulers still needed to be ritually enstooled and were destooled in case of discontent of their subjects. They continued to swear oaths to demonstrate their loyalty towards the *Asante* ruling pair and their subjects (e.g. the *nhenkwaa*, the *akonkofoɔ* and the *nkwankwaa*) who continued to venerate the Golden Stool as an indigenous religious shrine. Also, they continued to celebrate the *Odwira* festival although not openly and on a state level, as the British deemed this too much of a threat to the persistence of the Asante state. However, in comparison to the precolonial period, the attitude of the Asante subjects towards their royal rulers became more complicated and less self-evident. The *nhenkwaa,* a status group that served the Asante traditional rulers, who would not exist without their support, became dual believers. This means that besides AIR they also adhered to a form of Christianity or Islam. The *akonkofoɔ* and the *nkwankwaa* kept loyal to the stool and contributed financially to the organisation of the *Odwira* festival but also developed alternative readings of AIR that were more in line with their own interests. The *akonkofoɔ* wished to accumulate more private wealth and were therefore against the privileges of the Asante traditional rulers in the custodianship of the ancestral land and the high taxes on private capital. The *nkwankwaa* played an important role in the foundation of Neo-Indigenous Religious Movements, which were female friendly movements that demonstrated resistance against the Christianisation and Modernisation of Asante society in the colonial period at the cost of women. The NIRMs increased the importance of the witch-catching deities (*abosommerafoo*) and diminished the significance of the old Asante state deities (*tete abosom*) and of their mediators: the *akyeame* of the Asante royal rulers and the *akomfoɔ* which became less significant due to the high popularity of the *nsuman* of the Suwarian Asante *Nkramo* chief, which formed an alternative source of healing power with a divine origin in Asante society. The indigenous religious mediatory function of the Asante royal rulers themselves also became less significant due to the ban on the performance of the *Odwira* festival and the political superstructure of colonial ruler, which made the royal rulers subordinate to the British, who emphasised the secular function of chieftaincy. However, in this same period, the indigenous religious peacekeeping function of the Asante traditional rulers increased in significance, due to the increase in numbers of Christians and Muslims in Asante society also among their own subjects and the location of Christianity and Islam within AIR, which modified the latter religion. The Asante ruling duo Prempeh I and Konadu Yaadom II and the royal rulers Prempeh II and Konadu Yaadom II, succeeded by Ama Serwaa Nyaako encouraged the existence of a dual belief system. *Kumasihene* Prempeh I adhered to the Anglican belief and restored the *nsumanfiesu* of the *nsumankwahene,* who was the leader of the Asante *Nkramofoɔ,* Muslim healers and the physician of the *Asantehene.* King Prempeh II and his female co-ruler Ama Serwaa Nyaako were Roman Catholics and fused their political party (the NLM) with the Muslim Association Party (MAP) to form the United Party (UP). The general attitude of the Asante royal rulers was to tolerate the activities of the missionary Christians and not to interfere with the internal affairs of the Muslims in Asante society. Orthodox Christians and Muslims were still treated with great caution and were generally less welcome than the Christians and Muslims who adhered to a moderate form of their beliefs. In terms of religious syncretism and the incorporation of Christianity and Islam into AIR, the colonial period was a transitional phase between the precolonial and the postcolonial periods.

In the postcolonial period, the Asante traditional authorities have persistent to be significant in the lives of their subjects, who have continued to celebrate the *Odwira* festival on all hierarchical traditional political and spatial levels. The research results presented in this book demonstrate that unlike some other festivals in Ghana, the *Odwira* festival celebration has kept its Asante indigenous religious nature despite its transformation in form and content since the precolonial period and it has merged with the *adae* celebrations that became more prominent during the colonial period in the *Odwira*'s absence. The celebrations of the *Odwira* festival in postcolonial Ghana are based on the interpretation of historical texts about past *Odwira* celebrations and of the belief of the continuation of that past in the present in the parallel universe and sacred space of the spiritual beings. The *Odwira* festival discussed in Chapter V demonstrates that locality, which is an important aspect of AIR, is also a significant characteristic of this festival. Besides the celebration of the *Odwira* festival, the Asante subjects have continued to venerate the Golden Stool that plays a role in the enstoolment of their royal rulers who still need to swear an oath to the *Asantehene*. Nevertheless, the indigenous religious mediatory function of the Asante traditional rulers have continued to be diminished in significance in comparison to the precolonial and colonial periods in the Asante history.

Even more apparent than in the colonial period, the majority of Asante commoners of today are dual believers. They have continued to demonstrate their loyalty towards the Asante royal rulers by adhering to AIR but are also as frequent visitors of one of the Mainline Christian Churches or one of the New African Indigenous Religious Movements such as the AMC. However, the members of the Anglican Church or one of the New Religious Movements, such as the PCCs or the SCs are most often not in favour of the dual belief system of the Asante royal rulers and often refuse to adhere to AIR, which is against customary law. The role of the Asante traditional rulers as indigenous religious peacekeepers has therefore again increased in significance in the postcolonial period in comparison to the previous historical periods, as they perform the increasingly difficult task to maintain harmonious relationships with the dual believers and world religious believers in Asante society. The attitude of the Anglican Christians and the adherents of the Christian New Religious Movements also make clear that the self-perception of 'peacekeepers' is not shared among mainline Christians and Muslims, of whom some feel that AIR is legally forced upon them and infringes their right to freely choose their religion. Nevertheless, the Asante traditional rulers have continued to monitor the way in which AIR can be and should be merged with the various forms of Islam and Christianity in Asante society. In terms of the Berner model of processes of religious syncretism in postcolonial Ghana, the model that corresponds with the religious attitude and activities of the Asante royal rulers is A1, which refers to religious syncretism on a system level. Regarding the processes of religious systematic syncretism in the Berner model, Asante society has thus undergone a transition since the precolonial period, from a C2 to an A1 of these processes.

In conclusion, finally, the indigenous religious function of the Asante traditional rulers has continuously changed in meaning and importance throughout Asante history, whereas their peacekeeping function has remained similar and has become more and more significant. This book has enhanced the insight of what IRs are and demonstrates that due to the flexibility of AIR in various fields, it has continued to exist alongside the increasing influence of other Neo-Indigenous Religious Movements, Islam and Christianity and neo-Islamic and Christian movements in Asante society. AIR has not survived due to the incorporation of Islam and Christianity on an increasing level of religious syncretism, but also because of the openness towards and adaptability of written versions of indigenous religious celebrations. The Asante belief has been successful in adjusting the past to the preferences of the current adherents of AIR, who are most often dual believers. Additionally, AIR has survived the transformation of the economy to a capitalist mode of production, which is a development that Weber did overlook as a possibility for IRs. Above all, this book demonstrates that AIR and its traditional political institutions that have been legitimated by that religion have survived all the transformations of Asante society, because of its capacity to incorporate world religions and to adjust itself to the wishes of its adherents that have changed over time. It also shows that earlier explanations for the persistence of chieftaincy by scholars who emphasised the political, juridical, and economic factors are not only complemented, but also have to be seen as being preceded by prevailing basic religious values and assumptions.

Bibliography

Abarry, A.S. 1991. "The Significance of Names in Ghanaian Drama," *Journal of Black Studies* 22: 157-167.

Adarkwa, K.A. and J. Post 2001. *The Fate of the Tree, Planning and Managing the Development of Kumasi, Ghana.* Amsterdam and Accra: Thela Thesis and Woeli Publications.

Adjaye, J.K. 1985. "Indigenous African Diplomacy," *The International Journal of African Historical Studies* 18(3): 487-503.

Adjaye, J.K. 1989. "Asantehene Agyeman Prempe I and British Colonisation of Asante: A Reassessment," *The International Journal of African Historical Studies* 22(2): 223-249.

Adjaye, J.K. 1990. "Asantehene Agyeman Prempe I, Asante History, and the Historian," *History in Africa* 17: 1-29.

Adjaye, J.K. 1996. *Diplomacy and Diplomats in Nineteenth Century Asante.* Trenton and New York: Africa World Press.

Agency, G.N. (the 8th of July 2007). Funeral: Most Productive Industry in Ghana ? *Daily Graphic.*

Agyekum, K. 2006. "The Sociolinguistic of Akan Personal Names," *Nordic Journal of African Studies* 15(2): 206-235.

Agyeman, F. 1978. *We Presbyterians.* Accra: Select Publications and Promotions.

Akuamoah, O. 2007. *The History of the Presbyterian Church in Abetifi.* Accra: Quick Service Book Limited.

Akutsu, S. 1992. "The Demise and Enthronement of the Asantehene: Political Aspects of Asante Kingship," *Ethnological Studies* 31: 503-534.

Akyeampong, E. 1995. "Alcoholism in Ghana: A Socio-Cultural Exploration," *Culture, Medicine and Psychiatry* 19(2): 261-280.

Akyeampong, E. 1999. "Christianity, Modernity and the Weight of Tradition in the life of Asantehene Agyeman Prempeh I, c. 1888-1931," *Africa: Journal of the International African Institute* 69(2): 279-311.

Akyeampong, E. 2003. "Agyeman Prempeh's Return from Exile," in E. Akyeampong, A.A. Boahen, N. Lawler, T.C. McCaskie and I. Wilks. *The History of Ashanti Kings and the Whole Country Itself and Other Writings by Otumfuo, Nana Agyeman Prempeh I.* Oxford: Oxford University Press: 43-55.

Alhassan, I. (the 22nd of February 2012). Hausa Community Raises Alarm. *The Chronicle.*

Allman, J.M. 1990. "The Youngmen and the Porcupine – Class, Nationalism and Asante's Struggle for Self-Determination, 1954-1957 " *The Journal of African History* 31(2): 263-279.

Allman, J.M. 1991. "Hewers of Wood, Carriers of Water: Islam, Class and Politics on the Eve of Ghana's Independence " *African Studies Review* 34(2): 1-26.

Allman, J.M. 1993. *The Quills of the Porcupine: Asante Nationalism in an Emergent Ghana.* Madison: University of Wisconsin Press.

Allman, J.M. 1996. "Rounding up Spinsters: Gender Chaos and Unmarried Women in Colonial Asante," *The Journal of African History* 37(2): 195-214

Allman, J.M. and J. Parker 2005. *Tongnaab: The History of a West African God.* Bloomington: Indiana University Press.

Alolo, N.A. (2007). *Religion and Development: Research Programme: African Traditional Religion and Concept of Development – A Background Paper.* Birmingham, Africa Development Bank, Department for International Development. Working paper 17.

Amanor, J.D. (2011) Pentecostalism in Ghana: An African Reformation. *Cyberjournal for Pentecostal-Charismatic Research.*

Aning, B.A. 1968. "Factors that Shape and Maintain Folk Music in Ghana," *Journal of the International Folk Music Council* 20: 13-17.

Anti, A.A. 1996. *Kumasi in the Eighteenth and Nineteenth Centuries, 1700-1900.* Accra: Damage Control Limited.

Anyinam, C. (1987). *Persistence with Change: A Rural-Urban Study of Ethnomedical Practices in Contemporary Ghana.* Department of Geography Kingston, Queens University. PhD.

Anyinam, C. 1989. "Traditional Medical Practice in Contemporary Ghana: a Dying or Growing 'Profession' ?," *Canadian Journal of African Studies/ Revue Canadienne des Études Africaines* 21(3): 315-336.

Appiah, J. 1990. *Joe Appiah: The Autobiography of an African Patriot.* New York and London: Westport CT and Praeger Publishers.

Appiah-Poku, J., R. Laugharne, et al. 2004. "Previous Help Sought by Patients Presenting to Mental Health Services in Kumasi, Ghana," *Social Psychiatry and Psychiatric Epidemiology* 39: 208-211.

Arhin, K. 1978. "Gold-Mining and Trading Among the Ashanti of Ghana," *Journal des Africanistes* 48(1): 89-90.

Arhin, K. 1985. "The Role of the Presbyterian Church in the Economic Development of Ghana," *Journal Institute of African Studies: Research Review* 1(2): 152-165.

Arhin, K. 1986. "A Note On the Asante *Akonkofoɔ*: A Non-Literate Sub-Elite, 1900-1930," *Africa: Journal of the International African Institute* 56(1): 25-31.

Arhin, K. 1994. "Economic Implications of Transformations in Akan Funeral Rites," *Africa: Journal of the International African Institute* 64(3): 307-322.

Arhin, K., K. Afari-Gyan, et al. 1992. *The City of Kumasi: Handbook Past, Present, Future.* Legon: The Institute of African Studies, University of Ghana.

Asante, E. 2006. "The Relationship Between the Chieftaincy Institution and Christianity in Ghana," in I. Odotei and A. K. Awedoba. *Chieftaincy in Ghana: Culture, Governance and Development.* Legon: Sub-Saharan Publishers: 231-246.

Austin, G. 1987. "The Emergence of Capitalist Relations in South Asante Cocoa-Farming, c. 1916-1933," *Journal of African History* 28(2): 259-279.

Austin, G. 1988. "Capitalists and Chiefs in the Cocoa Hold-Ups in South Asante, 1927-1938," *The International Journal of African Historical Studies* 21(1): 63-95.

Austin, G. 1995. "Between Abolition and Jihad: The Asante Response to the Ending of the Atlantic Slave Trade, 1807-1896," in R. Law. *From Slave Trade to Legitimate Commerce: The Commercial Transition in Nineteenth Century West Africa.* Cambridge: Cambridge University Press: 93-119.

Austin, G. 1996. "'No Elders Were Present': Commoners and Private Ownership in Asante, 1807-1896," *Journal of African History* 37(1): 1-30.

Austin, G. 2007. "Labour and Land in Ghana, 1874-1939: A Shifting Ratio and an Institutional Revolution," *Australian Economic History Review* 47(1): 95-119.

Azumah, J. (2012) *Muslim-Christian Relations in Ghana: 'Too Much Meat Does not Spoil the Soup'*. World Council of Churches. http://www.wcc-coe.org/wcc/what/interreligious/cd36-01.html.

Bacon, F. 1905 [original 1609]. *Sapienta Veterum xxvi [The Wisdom of the Ancients]* London: Cassell National Library.

Baesjou, R. 1979. *An Asante Embassy on the Gold Coast: the Mission of Akyempon Yaw to Elmina, 1869-1872*. Leiden: African Studies Centre.

Baffoe, E.Y. (1954). *Cocoa Price Agitation*. Kumasi.

Bamfo, N. 2000. "The Hidden Elements of Democracy among Akyem Chieftaincy: Enstoolment, Destoolment, and other Limitations of Power," *Journal of Black Studies* 31(2): 149-173.

Bartels, F.L. 1965. *The Roots of Ghana Methodism*. New York: Cambridge University Press.

Bartle, P.F.W. 1978. "Forty Days: The Akan Calendar," *Africa: Journal of the International African Institute* 48(1): 80-84.

Bartle, P.F.W. 1982. "The Universe Has Three Souls. Notes on Translating Akan Culture," *Journal of Religion in Africa* 14(2): 85-114.

Bell, C. 1992. *Ritual Theory, Ritual Practice*. New York: Oxford University Press.

Benewick, R. and P. Green 1992. *The Routledge Dictionary of Twentieth-Century Political Thinkers*. London and New York: Routledge.

Berner, U. 2001. "Historical Reflections/Réflexions Historiques," *The Notion of Syncretism in Historical and/or Empirical Research* 27(3): 499-509.

Berner, U. 2004. "The Concept of 'Syncretism': An Instrument of Historical Insight/ discovery ?," in A. M. Leopold and J. S. Jensen. *Syncretism in Religion: A Reader*. London: Equinox: 295-316.

Berry, S. 1997. "Tomatoes, Land and Hearsay: Property and History in Asante in the Time of Structural Adjustment," *World Development* 25(8): 1225-1241.

Berry, S. 2009. "Property, Authority and Citizenship: Land Claims, Politics and the Dynamics of Social Division in West Africa," *Development and Change* 40(1): 23-45.

Blume, H. (1998). An interview with Daniel Dennett. *Atlantic Monthly.*

Blumenthal, M. 2000. "Cola nut. I," in A. Goldberg, M. Blumenthal, S. Foster and J. Brinckmann. *Herbal Medicine: Expanded Commission E Reviews. Integrative Medicine Communications*. Newton: MA: 72-73.

Boahen, A.A. 1966. "The Origins of the Akan," *Ghana Notes and Queries* 9: 3-23.

Boahen, A.A. 1975. *Ghana: Evolution and Change in the Nineteenth and Twentieth Centuries*. London: Longman.

Boddy, J.P. 1989. *Wombs and Alien Spirits*. London: University of Wisconsin Press.

Boddy, J.P. 1994. "Spirit Possession Revisited: Beyond Instrumentality," *Annual Review of Anthropology* 23: 407-434.

Bosman, W. 1704 (translation 1705). *Naauwkeurige Beschryving van de Guinese Goud-, Tand- en Slave-Kust [New and Accurate Descriptions of the Coast of Guinea]*. London: J. Knapton.

Bourguignon, E. 1976. *Possession*. San Francisco: Chandler and Sharp.

Bowdich, T.E. 1819. *Mission from Cape Coast Castle to Ashantee: With a Descriptive Statistical Account of that Kingdom and Geographical Notices of Other Parts of the Interior of Africa*. London: John Murray.

Braffi, E.K. 1992. *The Akan Clans: Totemism and 'Nton'*. Kumasi: Kumasi University Press.

Braffi, E.K. 2002. *Akwasidae and the Odwira Festival*. Krofrom-Kumasi: Bayoba Limited.

Brempong, N.A. 2000. "Elite Succession Among the Matrilineal Akan of Ghana," in J. de Pina-Cabral and A. Pedroso de Lima. *Elite, Choice, Leadership and Succesion*. Oxford and New York: Berg Publishers: 75-91.

Brookins, C. 2003. "Anansi and How the Moon Got Put in the Sky," *American Journal of Community Psychology* 32(3-4): 283-284.

Bryman, A. 1988. *Quantity and Quality in Social Research*. London: Unwin Hyman.

Buah, F.K. 1980. *A History of Ghana*. London: Macmillan.

Busia, A.P.A. 1998. "Maternal Legacies: A Weave of Stories," in D.H. Ross. *Wrapped in Pride: Ghanaian Kente and African American Identity*. Los Angeles University of California (UCLA Fowler Museum of Cultural History Textile Series): 61-64.

Busia, K.A. 1951. *The Position of the Chief in the Modern Political System of Ashanti*. London: Frank Cass Publishers.

Busia, K.A. 1954. "The Ashanti of the Gold Coast," in D. Forde. *African Worlds: Studies in the Cosmological Ideas and Social Values of African People*. London: Oxford University Press: 197-200.

Chapman, G. 1844. "Journal of the Rev. George Chapman, 1843-1857, entry dd Kumasi 24 January 1844."

Chazan, N., P. Lewis, et al. 1999. *Politics and Society in Contemporary Africa*. Boulder: Lynne Rienner Publishers.

Chidester, D. 2004. "'Classify and Conquer': Friedrich Max Müller, Indigenous Religious Traditions, and Imperial Comparative Religion " in J. K. Olupona. *Beyond Primitivism: Indigenous Religious Traditions and Modernity*. London and New York: Routledge: 71-89.

Chidester, D. (2000). *Christianity: A Global History.* New York, Harper Collins.

Christaller, J.G. 1881. *A Dictionary of the Asante and Fante Language Called Tshi (Chwee,Twi), With a Grammatical Introduction and Appendices on the Geography of the Gold Coast and other Subjects*. Basel: Published for the Evangelical Missionary Society by Trüner and Co.

Christensen, J.B. 1959. "The Adaptive Functions of Fanti Priesthood," in W.R. Bascom and M.J. Herskovits. *Continuity and Change in African Cultures*. Chicago: University of Chicago Press: 257-278.

Chukwukere, I., W. De Mahieu, et al. 1981. "A Coffin for 'The Loved One': The Structure of Fante Death Rituals," *Current Anthropology* 22(1): 61-68.

Clarke, E. 1930. "The Sociological Significance of Ancestor-Worship in Ashanti," *The International Journal of African Historical Studies* 3(4): 431-471.

Committee, G.E. 1989. *National Church Survey: Facing the Unfinished Task of The Church in Ghana.*

Cooper, G. 1988. "North American Traditional Religion," in S. Sutherland and P. Clarke. *The World's Religions: The Study of Religion, Traditional and New Religion*. London: Routledge: 115-124.

Cortesão, A. and A. Teixeira da Mota 1962. *Portugaliae Monumenta Cartographica* Lisbon: Comissão Executiva Das Comemorações do V Centenario da Morte do Infante D. Henrique.

Coulson, S., S. Staurset, et al. 2011. "Ritualised Behavior in the Middle Stone Age: Evidence from Rhino Cave, Tsodilo Hills, Botswana," *PaleoAnthropology*: 18-61.

Cox, J.L. (1998). Rational Ancestors: Scientific Rationality and African Indigenous Religions: Including Field Descriptions of Zimbabwean Myths and Rituals by University of Zimbabwe Students Cardiff, Cardiff Academic Press.

Cox, J.L. 2007. *From Primitive to Indigenous: The Academic Study of Indigenous Religions*. Aldershot: Ashgate.

Cox, J.L. 2012. *The Invention of God in Indigenous Societies*. London: Continuum.

Crook, R.C. 1986. "Decolonisation, the Colonial State, and Chieftaincy in the Gold Coast," *African Affairs* 85(338): 75-105.

Crowder, D. 1977. *West Africa: An Introduction To Its History*. London: Longman Group.

Cruickshank, B. 1966 [1853]. *Eighteen Years on the Gold Coast of Africa*. London: Hurst and Blackett Publishers.

Daaku, K.Y. 1970. *Trade and Politics on the Gold Coast 1600-1720: a Study of the African Reaction to European Trade*. Oxford: Oxford University Press.

Daaku, K.Y. 1972. "Aspects of Precolonial Akan Economy," *The International Journal of African Historical Studies* 5(2): 235-247.

Danquah, J.B. 1952. "Autopsy on Old Ashanti," *African Affairs* 51(203): 134-143.

Dapper, O. 1668. *Nauwkeuringe Beschrijvinge der Afrikaense Gewesten van Egypten, Barbaryen, Libyen, Biledulgerid, Negroslant, Guinea, Ethiopiën, Abyssinie*. Amsterdam: Jacob van Meurs.

Darish, P.J. 1988. "Dressing for the Next Life: A Reconsideration of Raffia Textile Fabrication and Display Among Kuba Peoples of South-Central Zaire," in A. B. Weiner and J. Schneider. *Cloth and Human Experience*. Washington DC: Smithsonian Institution Press: 117-140.

de Marees, P. 1912 [original edition 1602]. *Beschrijvinghe ende Historische Verhael van het Gout Koninekrijck van Gunea, Anders de Gout-Custe de Mina Genaemt Liggende in het Deel van Africa*. 's-Gravenhage: Nijhoff (Published by the Linschoten Society).

de Witte, M. 2003. "Money and Death: Funeral Business in Asante, Ghana," *Africa: Journal of the International African Institute* 73(4): 531-559.

de Witte, M. (2008). *Spirit Media: Charismatics, Traditionalists, and Mediation Practices in Ghana. Anthropology*. Amsterdam, University of Amsterdam. PhD.

Debrunner, H., W. 1959. *Witchcraft in Ghana: A Study on the Belief in Destructive Witches and its Effects on the Akan Tribes*. Accra: Waterville Publishing House.

Debrunner, H.W. 1967. *A History of Christianity in Ghana*. Accra: Waterville Publishing House.

Dennett, D.C. 1991. *Consciousness Explained.* Boston and New York and London: Back Bay Books.

Dovlo, E. 1998. "The Church in African and Religious Pluralism: the Challenge of New Religious Movements and Charismatic Churches," *Exchange: Bulletin of Third World Christian Literature* 27(1): 52-69.

Dovlo, E. 2004. "African Culture and Emergent Church Forms in Ghana," *Exchange: Bulletin of Third World Christian Literature* 33(1): 28-53.

Downie, R. (11-07-2011). *Stress Testing Ghana*, CSIS: Center for Strategic and International Studies.

Dumett, R.E. 2009. "African Merchants of the Gold Coast, 1860-1905: Dynamics of Indigenous Entrepreneurship," *Comparative Studies in Society and History* 25(4): 661-693.

Dupuis, J. 1824. *Journal of a Residence in Ashantee*. London: H. Colburn.

Edusa-Eyison, J.M.Y. (2011). "*The History of the Methodist Church Ghana.*" from http://hdl.handle.net/10516/1318.

Ellis, A.B. 1893. *A History of the Gold Coast of West Africa*. London: Chapman and Hall.

Femia, J. 1975. "Hegemony and Consciousness in the Thought of Antonio Gramsci," *Political Studies* 23(1): 29-48.

Fernandes, V. 1507. *Description of the West Coast of Africa*. Unknown: Unknown.

Field, M.J. 1940. "Some New Shrines of the Gold Coast and Their Significance," *Africa: Journal of the International African Institute* 13(2): 138-149.

Findlay, G. G. and W. W. Holdsworth 1921. *The History of the Wesleyan Methodist Missionary Society*. London: Epworth.

Fisher, M.P. 1997. *Living Religions*. London: I.B. Taurus and Co Ltd.

Fisher, R.B. 1998. *West African Religious Traditions: Focus on the Akan of Ghana*. Maryknoll and New York: Orbis Books.

Forster, P.G. 1994. "Culture, Nationalism, and the Invention of Tradition in Malawi," *The Journal of Modern African Studies* 32(3): 477-497.

Fortes, M. 1950. "Kinship and Marriage among the Ashanti," in A. R. Radcliffe-Brown and C. D. Forde. *African Systems of Kinship and Marriage.* London: Oxford University Press: 252-284.

Fortescue, D. 1990. "The Accra Crowd, the *Asafo*, and the Opposition to the Municipal Corporations Ordinance, 1924-1925," *Canadian Journal of African Studies/ Revue Canadienne des Études Africaines* 24(3): 348-375.

Frazer, J.G. 1913. *The Belief in Immortality*. London: Macmillan and Co.

Freeman, T.B. 1844. *Journal of Various Visits to the Kingdoms of Ashanti, Aku, and Dahomi in Western Africa*. The Hague: Archive of the Ministry of Colonies, 1813-1850.

Freeman, T.B. (1886). the 24th of March 1886. *The Western Echo*. I,13.

Friedson, S.M. 2009. *Remains of Ritual: Northern Gods in a Southern Land*. Chicago: University of Chicago Press.

Fynn, J.K. 1971. *Asante and Its Neighbours,1700-1807*.Evanston: Northwestern University Press.

Gailey Jr., H.A. 1971. *The History of Africa in Maps*. Chicago:Denoyer-Geppert Company.

Geschiere, P. 1997 [originally published in French in 1995]. *The Modernity of Witchcraft:Politics and the Occult in Postcolonial Africa [Sorcellerie et Politique en Afrique-la Viande des Autres]*. Charlottesville and London: University Press of Virginia.

Ghana, S.S. 2002. *2000 Population and Housing Census. Summary/Report of Final Results: 22: Table 4 - Ethnic Groups of Ghanaians by Birth and by Region*. Accra: Ghana, Ministry of Finance and Economic Planning Head Office.

Ghana, S.S. 2002. *2000 Population and Housing Census. Summary/Report of Final Results: Table 1 - Ethnic Groups in the Kumasi metropolis and Table 2: Detailed Akan Cultural Groups in the Kumasi metropolis*. Accra: Ghana, Ministry of Finance and Economic Planning Head Office.

Ghana, S.S. 2002. *2000 Population and Housing Census. Summary/Report of Final Results: Table 3 - Religious Affiliation in Kumasi Metro*. Accra: Ghana, Ministry of Finance and Economic Planning Head Office.

Ghana, S.S. 2002. *2000 Population and Housing Census. Summary/Report of Final Results: Table 23 - Population by District, by Sex and Type of Locality of Enumeration, Ashanti Region*. Accra: Ghana, Ministry of Finance and Economic Planning Head Office.

Gifford, P. 1994. "Some Recent Developments in African Christianity," *African Affairs* 93(373): 513-534.

Gifford, P. 1998. *African Christianity: Its Public Role*. London: Hurst.

Gilbert, M. 1988. "The Sudden Death of a Millionaire: Conversion and Consensus in a Ghanaian Kingdom," *Africa: Journal of the International African Institute* 58(3): 291-314.

Gilbert, M. 1994. "Aesthetic Strategies: The Politics of a Royal Ritual," *Africa: Journal of the International African Institute* 64(1): 99-125.

Gocking, R.S. 1994. "Indirect Rule in the Gold Coast: Competition for Office and the Invention of Tradition," *Canadian Journal of African Studies* 28(3): 421-446.

Graves, R. 1992. *The Greek Myths*. London: Penguin Books.

Groves, C.P. 1955. *The Planting of Christianity in Africa*. London: Lutterworth Press.

Guttenplan, S. 1996. *A Companion to the Philosophy of Mind*. Oxford: Blackwell

Gyanfosu, S. 2002. "A Traditional Religion Reformed: Vincent Kwabena Damuah and the *Afrikania* Movement, 1982-2000," in D. Maxwell and I. Lawrie. *Christianity and the African Imagination: Essays in Honour of Adrian Hastings*. Leiden: Brill Academic Publishers: 271-294.

Gyekye, K. 1995. *An Essay on African Philosophical Thought: the Akan Conceptual Scheme*. Philadelphia: Temple University Press.

Hammond, D.N.A. 2001. "Land Tenure and Land Policy," in K.A. Adarkwa and J. Post. *The Fate of the Tree, Planning and Managing the Development of Kumasi, Ghana*. Amsterdam and Accra: Thela Thesis and Woeli Publications: 79-101.

Hanna, J.L. 1979. *To dance is Human. A Theory of Non-Verbal Communication*. Austin: University of Texas Press.

Harper, M. 1921. *Harper Papers. Harper to Colonial Secretary (Accra)*. Oxford: Rodes House.

Hart, G. 1990. *The Egyptian Myth*. London: British Museum Press.

Harvey, G. and C.D. Thompson Jr. 2005. "Introduction," in G. Harvey and C.D. Thompson Jr. *Indigenous Diasporas and Dislocations*. Aldershot and Burlington: Ashgate: 1-12.

Hertz, C. 1885. *Le Paradis des Noirs: Excursion Sur la Côte de Guinée, 1877-1878* Paris: Librairie C. Delagrave.

Hiskett, M. 1984. *The Development of Islam in West Africa*. London: Longman.

Holm, N.G. 1982. *Religious Ecstasy*. Uppsala: Almqvist and Wiksell.

Hunt, A. 1990. "Rights and Social Movements: Counter-Hegemonic Strategies," *Journal of Law and Society* 17(3): 309-328.

Huppenbauer, D. 1905 [4th edition]. *Von Kyebi nach Kumasi*. Basel.

Insoll, T. 2003. *The Archaeology of Islam in Sub-Saharan Africa*. Cambridge: Cambridge University Press.

Jacquemot, P. 2007. "Chefferies et Decentralisation au Ghana," *Afrique Contemporaine* 1(221): 55-74.

Jeffries, R. 1984. "The Image of Women in African Cave Art," in I. v. Sertima. *Black Women in Antiquity*. London: Transaction Books: 98-122.

Jenkins, P. 1974. "The Anglican Church in Ghana, 1905-1924 (I)," *Transactions of the Historical Society of Ghana* 15(1): 23-39.

Jenkins, P. 1974. "The Anglican Church in Ghana, 1905-1924 (II)," *Transactions of the Historical Society of Ghana* 15(2): 177-200.

Johnson, M. 1979. "Ashanti Craft Organisation," *African Arts* 13(1): 60-63+78+80-82+97.

Jones, A. 1986. "Semper Aliquid Veteris: Printed Sources for the History of the Ivory and Gold Coasts, 1500-1750," *The Journal of African History* 27(2 Special Issue in Honour of J.D. Fage): 215-235.

Jones, A. 1991. "'Four years in Asante': One Source or Several?," *History in Africa* 18: 173-203.

Jung, C. 1982. *Aspects of the Feminine*. Princeton: Princeton University Press.

Kankpeyeng, B.W. 2009. "The Slave Trade in Northern Ghana: Landmarks, Legacies and Connections," *Slavery and Abolition* 30(2): 209-221.

Kaplan, S. 1995. "The Africanisation of Missionary Christianity: History and Typology," in S. Kaplan. *Indigenous Responses to Western Christianity*. New York and London: New York University Press: 9-28.

Kea, R.A. 1971. "Firearms and Warfare on the Gold and Slave Coasts from the Sixteenth to the Nineteenth Centuries," *The Journal of African History* 12(2): 185-213.

Kimble, D. 1963. *A Political History of Ghana: the Rise of Gold Coast Nationalism, 1850-1928*. Oxford: Clarendon Press.

King, R., D. Inkoom, et al. (2001). *Urban Governance in Kumasi: Poverty and Exclusion. Urban Poverty and Governance* Birmingham, University of Birmingham. WP 23.

Kirby, J.P. 1986. *God, Shrines, and Problem-Solving Among the Anufo of Northern Ghana*. Berlin: Dietrich Reimer Verlag.

Kirby, J.P. 1993. "The Islamic Dialogue with African Traditional Religion: Divination and Health Care," *Social Science Medicine* 36(3): 237-247.

Klein, A.N. 1996. "Toward a New Understanding of Akan Origins," *Africa: Journal of the International African Institute* 66(2): 248-273.

Konadu, K. 2010. *The Akan Diaspora in the Americas*. Oxford: Oxford University Press.

Korang, K.L. 2004. *Writing Ghana, Imagining Africa: Nation and African Modernity*. New York: University of Rochester Press.

Korboe, D. and A.G. Tipple 1995. "City Profile Kumasi," *Cities* 12(4): 267-274.

Kwadwo, O. 2000, 2nd edition. *An Outline of Asante History, part I*. Wiamoase-Ashanti: O. Kwadwo Enterprise.

Kwamena Poh, M.A. (1974). *The Reverend F. A. Ramseyer and the Foundation of the Presbyterian Church in Kumasi.* Kumasi, Ramseyer Centenary Committee.

Kwamena-Poh, M. A. 1973. *Government and Politics in the Akuapem State, 1730-1850*. London and Evanston, Illinois: Longman and Northwestern University Press.

Kyerematen, A. 1969. "The royal Stools of Ashanti," *Africa: Journal of the International African Institute* 39(1): 1-10.

Lamb, V. 1975. *West African Weaving*. London: Duckworth.

Lambek, M. 2007. "Sacrifice and The Problem of Beginning: Meditations from Sakalava Mythopraxis," *Journal of the Royal Anthropological Institute* 13: 19-38.

Lane, E. 2010 [first published in 1836]. *Manners and Customs of the Modern Egyptians*. New York: Cosimo Classics.

Langer, A. (2007). *Ethnicity, Religion and the State in Ghana and Nigeria: Perceptions from the Street. Crise Working Paper. Oxford, Centre for Research on Inequality*, Human Security and Ethnicity (CRIHSE), Department of International Development (CRISE). 34.

Law, R. 1985. "Human Sacrifices in Pre-Colonial West-Africa," *African Affairs* 84(334): 53-87.

Lawrence, C. 1978. "The Healing Serpent; the Snake in Medical Iconography," *The Ulster Medical Journal* 47(2): 134-140.

Lemon, M.C. 2003. *Philosophy of History*. London and New York: Routledge.

Lentz, C. 2000. "Of Hunters, Goats and Earths-Shrines: Settlement Histories and the Politics of Oral Tradition in Northern Ghana," *History in Africa* 27: 193-214.

Lévi-Strauss, C. 1958. *Anthropologie Structurale*. Paris: Agora.

Levtzion, N. 1968. *Muslims and Chiefs in West Africa: A Study of Islam in the Middle Volta Basin in the Pre-Colonial Period*. Oxford: Clarendon Press.

Lewin, T.J. 1978. *Asante Before the British: The Prempean Years, 1875-1900*. Lawrence: Regents Press of Kansas.

Lewis, I.M. 1989. *Ecstatic Religion: A study of Shamanism and Spirit Possesion*. London and New York: Routledge.

Lonsdale, R.L.T. (1882). *Report by Captain Rupert La Trobe Lonsdae on His Mission to Coomassi, Salagha and Yendi*, British Parliamentary Papers Comd. 3386.

Lovejoy, P.E. 1971. "Long-Distance Trade and Islam: The Case of the Nineteenth Century Hausa Kola Trade," *Journal of the Historical Society of Nigeria* 5(4): 537-547.

Lovejoy, P.E. 1982. "Polanyi's 'Port of Trade': Salaga and Kano in the Nineteenth Century," *Canadian Journal of African Studies/ Revue Canadienne des Études Africaines* 16(2): 245-277.

Lugard, L. 1965. *The Dual Mandate in Tropical Africa*. London: Frank Cass Publishers.

MacDonald, M.N. 2004. "Thinking and Teaching with the Indigenous Traditions of Melanesia," in J. O. K. Olupona. *Beyond Primitivism. Indigenous Religious Traditions and Modernity*. London and New York: Routledge: 314-324.

Macfarlane, A. 1970. *Witchcraft in Tudor and Stuart England: A Regional and Comparative Study*. London and New York: Routledge.

Magee, C. 2005. "Forever in *Kente*: Ghanaian Barbie and the Fashioning of Identity," *Social Identities* 11(6): 589-607.

Maier, D., J.E 1981. "The Dente Oracle, the Bron Confederation, and Asante: Religion and the Politics of Secession," *The Journal of African History* 22(2): 229-243.

Maier, D., J.E. 1997. "Islam and the Idea of Asylum in Asante," in J. Hunwick and N. E. Lawler. *The Cloth of Many Colored Silks: Papers on History and Society, Ghanaian and Islamic in Honour of Ivor Wilks*. Evanston, Illinois: Northwestern University Press: 319-338.

Malinowski, B. (2006). *Tales from the Jungle: Bronislaw Malinowski*, BBC Four Documentary.

Martin, K. and A. Ronnberg 2011. *The Book of Symbols* (*Het Boek Der Symbolen*). Köln: Taschen.

Marx, K. E. u. B. v. G. M. u. M. v. E. G. n. S. (1841 (1964)). *Differenz der Demokritischen und Epikureischen Naturphilosophie* (*Difference Between the Democritean and Epicurean Philosophy of Nature*). Jena, Friedrich-Schiller-Universität Jena.

Mazzucato, V. 2005. "Ghanaian Migrant's Double Engagement: A Transnational View of Development and Integration Policies," *Global Migration Perspectives* 48: 1-17.

Mbiti, J.S. 1992 (First Published in 1969). *African Religions and Philosophy.* Nairobi: Heinemann.

McCaskie, T.C. 1972. "Innovational Eclecticism: The Asante Empire and Europe in the Nineteenth Century," *Comparative Studies in Society and History* 14(1): 30-45.

McCaskie, T.C. 1981. "Anti-Witchcraft Cults in Asante: an Essay in the Social History of an African People," *History in Africa* 8: 125-154.

McCaskie, T.C. 1983. "Accumulation, Wealth and Belief in Asante History. I. To the Close of the Nineteenth Century," *Africa: Journal of the International African Institute* 53(1): 23-43+79.

McCaskie, T.C. 1986a. "Accumulation: Wealth and Belief in Asante History: II the Twentieth Century," *Africa: Journal of the International African Institute* 56(1): 3-23.

McCaskie, T.C. 1986b. "Komfo Anokye of Asante: Meaning, History and Philosophy in an African Society," *The Journal of African History* 27(2 Special Issue in Honour of J.D. Fage): 315-339.

McCaskie, T.C. 1989. "Death and the Asantehene: A Historical Meditation," *The Journal of African History* 30(3): 417-444.

McCaskie, T.C. 1992. "Empire State: Asante and the Historians," *The Journal of African History* 33(3): 467-476.

McCaskie, T.C. 1995. *State and Society in Pre-Colonial Asante*. Cambridge: Cambridge University Press.

McCaskie, T.C. 1999. *Custom, Tradition and Law in Precolonial Asante*. Münster and London and Piscataway: Lit Verlag.

McCaskie, T.C. 2001. *Asante Identities: History and Modernity in an African Village, 1850-1950*. Edinburgh: Edinburgh University Press.

McLeod, M.D. 1981. *The Asante*. London: The British Museum Press.

McSloy, S.P. 1996. "Because the Bible Tells Me So: Manifest Destiny and American Indians," *St Thomas Law Review* 9: 37-47.

Medupe, R.T., B. Warner, et al. 2008. "The Timbuktu Astronomy Project: A Scientific Exploration of the Secrets of the Archives of Timbuktu," *African Cultural Astronomy*: 179-188.

Meyer, B. 1998. "Make a Complete Break with the Past. Memory and Post-Colonial modernity in Ghanaian Pentecostal Discourse," *Journal of Religion in Africa* 28(3): 316-349.

Meyerowitz, E.L.R. 1960. *The Divine Kingship in Ghana and in Ancient Egypt*. London: Faber and Faber.

Middleton, J. 1983. "One Hundred and Fifty Years of Christianity in a Ghanaian Town," *Africa: Journal of the International African Institute* 53(3): 2-19.

Miller, J. 1990. "Class Collaboration for the Sake of Religion: Elite Control and Social Mobility in Nineteenth-Century Colonial Mission," *Journal for the Scientific Study of Religion* 29(1): 35-53.

Miller, N.N. and E.P. Skinner 1968. "The Political Survival of Traditional Leadership: the 'Paradox' of Rural Leadership: a Comment," *The Journal of Modern African Studies* 6(2): 183-201.

Minkus, H.K. 1980. "The Concept of Spirit in Akwapim Akan Philosophy," *Africa: Journal of the International African Institute* 50(2): 182-192.

Mittermaier, A. 2011. *Dreams that Matter: Egyptian Landscapes of the Imagination*. London: University of California Press.

Mohr, A. 2009. "Missionary Medicine and Akan Therapeutics: Illness, Health and Healing in Southern Ghana's Basel Mission, 1828-1918," *Journal of Religion in Africa* 39: 429-461.

Molendijk, A.L. 2005. *The Emergence of the Science of Religion in the Netherlands*. Leiden: Brill Academic Publishers.

Morgan, P.D. 2009. "Africa and the Atlantic, c.1450 to c.1820," in J. P. Greene and P. D. Morgan. *Atlantic History: A Critical Appraisal* Oxford: Oxford University Press: 223-248.

Mudimbe, V.Y. 1988. *The Invention of Tradition: Gnosis, Philosophy and the Order of Knowledge*. Bloomington and Indianapolis and London: Indiana University Press and James Curry.

Müller, L.F. 2004. "A Thematic Comparison between Four African Scholars: Idowu, Mbiti, Okot p'Bitek, Appiah: What Do They Tell Us About the Existence of 'Truth' and a 'High God', And Why Is Their Work Significant?" *Quest: An African Journal of Philosophy/ Revue Africaine de Philosophie* **18**(1-2): 109-125.

Müller, L.F. 2008. "The Reality of Spirits: A Historiography of the Akan Concept of Mind." *Quest: An African Journal of Philosophy* **XXII**(1-2): 163-185.

Müller, L.F. 2010. "Dancing Golden Stools," *Fieldwork in Religion* 5(1): 31-54.

Müller, L.F. 2011a. "Spirits of Migration Meet the Migration of Spirits Among the Akan Diaspora in Amsterdam in the Netherlands," *African and Black Diaspora: An International Journal* 4(1): 75-97.

Müller, L.F. 2011b. "The Persistence of Asante Chieftaincy in the Colonial Period (1896-1957): Explanations For An Enigma." *Africana Studia* **14**(2): 61-85.

Müller, L.F. 2012. "Ghanaian Films and Chiefs as Indicators of Religious Change Among the Akan people of Kumasi and Southeast Amsterdam," in R. Heffner and J. Hutchinson. *Religions in Movement: The Local and the Global in Contemporary Faith Traditions*. London and New York: Routledge: 467-503.

Mundkur, B. 1983. *The Cult of the Serpent: An Interdisciplinary Survey of its Manifestations and Origins*. Albany: State University of New York Press.

Nathan, M. 1904. "Historical Chart of the Gold Coast and Ashanti," *Journal of the Royal African Society* 4(13): 33-43.

Nketia, J.H.K. 1955. *Funeral Dirges of the Akan People*. Achimota: James Towns end for University College of the Gold Coast.

Nketia, J.H.K. 1963. *Drumming in Akan Communities of Ghana*. Edinburgh: Published on Behalf of the University of Ghana by T. Nelson.

Nugent, P. 2004. *Africa Since Independence*. New York: Palgrave Macmillan.

Obeng, J.P. 1996. *Asante Catholicism: Religious and Cultural Reproduction Among the Akan of Ghana*. Leiden: Brill Academic Publishers.

Odotei, I.K. and G.P. Hagan 2002. *The King Returns: Enstoolment of Asantehene Otumfuo Osei Tutu II and the Ayikesee (great funeral) of Otumfuo Opuku Ware II*. Legon: University of Ghana, Institute of African Studies.

Ogot, B.A. 1992. *General History of Africa: V Africa from the Sixteenth to the Eighteenth Century*. London: James Curry. California. Unesco.

Okot p'Bitek. 2011. *Decolonising African Religion: A Short History of African Religions*. New York: Diaspora Africa Press.

Olsen, W.C. 2003. "The Empire Strikes Back: Colonial 'Discipline' and the Creation of Civil Society in Asante, 1906-1940," *History in Africa* 30: 223-251.

Omenyo, C.N. 2005. "From the Fringes to the Centre: Pentecostalisation of the Mainline Churches in Ghana," *Exchange: Bulletin of Third World Christian Literature* 34(1): 39-60.

Opoku, K.A. 1970. *Festivals of Ghana*. Accra: Ghana Publishing Corporation.

Opoku, K.A. 1978. *West African Traditional Religion*. Accra: Ghana: FEP International Private Limited.

Owoahene-Acheampong, S. 1998. *Inculturation and African Religion: Indigenous and Western Approaches to Medical Practice*. New York and Bern and Berlin and Frankfurt and Paris and Wien: Peter Lang – International Academic Publishers.

Owusu-Ansah, D. 1987. "Power and Prestige? Muslims in Nineteenth Century Kumasi," in E. Schildkrout. *The Golden Stool: Studies of the Asante Center and Periphery*. New York: Anthropological Papers of the American Museum of Natural History. 65: 80-92.

Owusu-Ansah, D. 1991. *Islamic Talismanic Tradition in Nineteenth Century Asante*. Lewiston and Lampeter: Edwin Mellen Press.

Owusu-Mensa, K. (1974). Prince Owusu-Ansa and Asante-British Diplomacy, 1841-1884 Wisconsin-Madison, University of Wisconsin.

Pacheco Pereira, D. 1937 (1505). *Esmeraldo de Silu Orbis*. London: Hakluyt Society.

Pals, D.L. 1996. "Religion as Alienation,". *Seven Theories of Religion*. New York: Oxford University Press: 124-157.

Parrinder, G. 1954. *African Traditional Religion*. London: Hutchinson's University Library.

Peel, J.D.Y. 1987. "History, Culture and Comparative Method," in L. Holy. *Comparative Anthropology*. Oxford: Oxford University Press.

Perbi, A. 1991. "Mobility in Pre-colonial Asante from a Historical Perspective," *Research Review* 7(1 and 2): 72-86.

Perrot, C. and A. van Dantzig 1994. *Marie-Joseph Bonnat et les Ashanti. Journal (1869-1874)*. Paris: Société des Africanistes.

Platvoet, J.G. 1979. "The Akan Believer and His Religions," in P. H. Vrijhoff and J. D. J. Waardenburg. *Official and Popular Religion: Analysis of a Theme for Religious Studies*. The Hague and Paris, and New York: Mouton Publishers: 544-606.

Platvoet, J.G. 1982. *Comparing Religions, A Limitative Approach: An Analysis of Akan, Para-Creole, and IFO-Sananda Rites and Prayers*. The Hague and Paris, and New York: Mouton Publishers.

Platvoet, J.G. 1985. "Cool Shade, Peace and Power: the *Gyadua* (Three of Reception) as an Ideological Instrument of Identity Management Among the Akan People of Sourthern Ghana," *Journal of Religion in Africa* 15(3): 174-200.

Platvoet, J.G. 1992. "African Traditional Religions in the Religious History of Humankind," in G. ter Haar, A. Moyo and S. J. e. Nondo. *African Traditional Religions in Religious Education: A Resource Book With Special Reference to Zimbabwe*. Utrecht: Utrecht: Theologische Faculteit Universiteit Utrecht: 11-28.

Pobee, J.S. 1976. "Aspects of African Traditional Religions," *Sociological Analysis* 37(1): 1-18.

Pobee, J.S. 2009. *The Anglican Story in Ghana: From Mission Beginnings to Province of Ghana*. Kaneshi-Accra, Ghana: Amanza Limited.

Pobee, J.S. and E. H. Mends 1977. "Social Change and African Traditional Religion," *Sociological Analysis* 38(1): 1-12.

Polakoff, C. 1982. *African Textiles and Dyeing Techniques*. London: Routledge and Kegan Paul

Posnansky, M. 1977. "Archeology and the Orgins of Akan Society in Ghana," in G. de Sieveking, I. M. Longworth and K. E. Wilson. *Problems in Economic and Social Archaeology*. London: Westview Press: 49-59.

Post, J., D. Inkoom, et al. (2003). *Local Governance, Civil Society, and Partnerships: Community Action in Neighbourhoods Service Upgrading in Kumasi, Ghana. Amsterdam*, Amsterdam Research Institute for Global Issues and Development Studies: 1-35.

Prabhupada, A. C. B. S. 1984. *Bhagavad-Gita As It Is: His Divine Grace* Los Angeles: The Bhaktivedanta Book Trust.

Priestly, M. and I. Wilks 1960. "The Ashanti Kings in the Eighteenth Century: a Revised Chronology," *The Journal of African History* 1: 83-96.

Quartey, S. 2007. *Missionary Practices on the Gold Coast, 1832-1895: Discourser, Gaze and Gender in the Basel Mission in Pre-Colonial West Africa.* New York: Cambria Press.

Ramseyer, F.A., J. Kühne, et al. 1875. *Four Years in Ashantee*. London: James Nisbet and Co.

Ranger, T.O. 2002. "The Invention of Tradition in Colonial Africa," in E. J. Hobsbawm and T. O. Ranger. *The Invention of Tradition*. Cambridge: Cambridge University Press: 211-263.

Rathbone, R. 2000. *Nkrumah and The Chiefs: The Politics of Chieftaincy in Ghana, 1951-60*. Oxford: James Currey.

Rathbone, R. 2006. "From Kingdom to Nation: Changing African Constructions of Identity," in I. Odotei and A. K. Awedoba. *Chieftaincy in Ghana: Culture, Governance and Development* Legon: Sub-Saharan Publishers: 43-54.

Rattray, R.S. 1955 (first published in 1923). *Ashanti*. Oxford: Clarendon Press.

Rattray, R.S. 1956 (first published in 1929). *Ashanti Law and Constitution.* London: Oxford University Press.

Rattray, R.S. 1959 (first published in 1927). *Religion and Art in Ashanti.* Oxford: Clarendon Press.

Ray, D.I. 1996. "Divided Sovereignty: Traditional Authority and the State in Ghana," *Journal of Legal Pluralism and Unofficlal Law* 181: 181-202.

Ray, D.I. and P.S. Reddy 2003. *Grassroots Governance? Chiefs in Africa and the Afro-Caribbean*. Alberta: University of Calgary Press.

Recorded by Agyeman-Duah, J. 1972. *Ashanti Stool Histories*. Accra: University of Accra, Institution of African Studies.

Reindorf, C.C. 1966. *The History of the Gold Coast and Asante. Based on Traditions and Historical Facts Comprising a Period of More than Three Centuries from about 1500-1860*. Accra: Ghana University Press.

Ringwald, W. 1952. *Die Religion der Akanstamme und Das Problem Ihrer Bekehrung*. Stuttgard: Evangelischer Missionsverlag.

Robinson, D. 2004. *Muslim Societies in African History*. Cambridge: Cambridge University Press.

Ross, D.H. 1998. "Fashioned Heritage," in D.H. Ross. *Wrapped in Pride: Ghanaian Kente and African American Identity*. Los Angeles University of California 273-290.

Russell-Wood 2009. "The Portuguese Atlantic, 1415-1808," in J.P. Greene and P. D. Morgan. *Atlantic History: a Critical Appraisal*. Oxford: Oxford University Press.

Saad, E.N. 1983. *Social History of Timbuktu: The Role of Muslim Scholars and Notables, 1400-1900*. Cambridge: Cambridge University Press.

Sarbah, J.M. 1968 (first published in 1904). *Fanti Customary Laws: A Brief Introduction to the Principles of the Native Laws and Customs of the Fanti and Akan Districts of the Gold Coast with a Report of Some Cases thereon Decided in the Law Courts*. London: Frank Cass Publishers.

Sargent, t. R. R. N. C. (April 1960). A Peep into the Past: Exile of An Asante King". *The Golden Shore*. XV, No 2: 352-354.

Sarpong, P.K. (1971). *The Sacred Stools of the Akan*. Accra-Tema, Ghana Publishing Corporation.

Schildkrout, E. 1970. "Stranger and Local Government in Kumasi," *The Journal of Modern African Studies* 8(2): 251-269.

Schildkrout, E. 1974. "Islam and Politics in Kumasi: An Analysis of Disputes over the Kumasi Central Mosque," in E. Schildkrout. *The Golden Stool: Studies of the Asante Center and Periphery*. New York: Anthropological Papers of the American Museum of Natural History. 52: 111-138.

Schildkrout, E. 1978. *People of the Zongo: The Transformation of Ethnic Identities in Ghana*. Cambridge and New York: Cambridge University Press.

Schildkrout, E. 2006. "Chieftaincy and Emerging Identities: Establishing Legitimacy in Immigrant Communities in Ghana and the Diaspora," in I. Odotei and A. K. Awedoba. *Chieftaincy in Ghana: Culture, Governance and Development*. Legon: Sub-Saharan Publishers: 587-601.

Schneider, J. 1987. "The Anthropology of Cloth," *Annual Review of Anthropology* 16: 409-448.

Schofield, J.W. 1993. "Increasing the Generalisability of Qualitative Research," in M. Hammersley. *Social Research: Philosophy, Politics and Practice*. London: Sage: 200-225.

Schwarzmantel, J. 2009. "Gramsci and The Problem of Political Agency," in M. McNally and J. Schwarzmantel. *Gramsci and Global Politics: Hegemony and Resistance*. London and New York: Routledge: 79-92.

Seligman, E.G. 1934. *Egypt and Negro Africa. A Study in Divine Kingship*. London and New York: Routledge.

Shank, D. (1980). *A Prophet of Modern Times: The Thought of William Wade Harris, West African Percursor of the Reign of Christ*. Aberdeen, Aberdeen. PhD.

Shinnie, P.L. and A. Shinnie 1995. *Early Asante*. Calgary: Calgary University Press.

Shott, M.J. 1992. "Radiocarbon Dating as a Probabilistic Technique: the Childers Site and Late Woodland Occupation in the Ohio Valley," *American Antiquity* 57(2): 202-230.

Silverman, R.A. 1987. "Historical Dimensions of Tano Worship Among the Asante and Bono," in E. Schildkrout. *The Golden Stool: Studies of the Asante Center and Periphery*. New York: Anthropological Papers of the American Museum of Natural History. 65: 272-288.

Silverman, R.A. and D. Owusu-Ansah 1989. "The Presence of Islam Among the Akan of Ghana: A Bibliographic Essay," *History in Africa* 16: 325-339.

Skinner, D.E. (2010). Da'wah and Politics in West Africa: Muslim *Jama'at* and Non-Governmental Organizations in Ghana, Sierra Leone and the Gambia. *Development and Politics from Below: Exploring Religious Spaces in the African State*. B. Bompani and M. Frahm-Arp. London, Palgrave Macmillan: 99-130.

Skinner, D.E. 2009. "The Incorporation of Muslim Elites into the Colonial Administrative System of Sierra Leone, Gambia and the Gold Coast," *Journal of Muslim Minority Affairs* 29(1): 91-108.

Smith, R.S. 1989. *Warfare and Diplomacy in Pre-Colonial Africa*. Madison: University of Wisconsin Press.

Smith, S.C. 1975. "Kente Cloth Motifs," *African Arts* 9(1): 36-39.

Southall, R.J. 1978. "Farmers, Traders and Brokers in the Gold Coast Cocoa Economy," *Canadian Journal of African Studies* 12(2): 185-211.

Spencer, A. 1998. "Samuel Cophie, Master Weaver," in D. H. Ross. *Wrapped in Pride: Ghanaian Kente and African American Identity*. Los Angeles University of California 97-101.

Steegstra, M. 2008. "Development Encounters: Westerners and Chieftaincy in Southern Ghana," in J. Abbink and A. Van Dokkum. *Dilemmas of Development: Conflicts of Interest and their Solutions in Modernising Africa*. Leiden: African Studies Centre: 228-241.

Stocking, G.W. 1992. *Paradigmatic Traditions in the History of Anthropology*. University of Wisconsin Press: Madison.

Stoeltje, B.J. 2003. "Asante Queen Mothers: Precolonial Authority in a Postcolonial Society," *Research Review* 19(2): 1-19.

Stoeltje, B.J. 2006. "The Performance of Litigation: Asante Custom and the Juaben Court," *Research Review* 21(1): 47-61.

Sullivan, L. 1991. "Dissonant Human Histories and the Vulnerability of Understanding," in S. Friesen. *Local knowledge, Ancient Wisdom: Challenges in Contemporary Spirituality*. Honolulu: Institute of Culture and Communication, East-West Center: 26-33.

Swaab, D. 2011. *We Are Our Brain (We Zijn Ons Brein)*. Amsterdam: Contact.

ter Haar, G., A. Moyo, et al. 1992. *African Traditional Religions in Religious Education. A Resource Book with Special Reference to Zimbabwe*. Utrecht: Utrecht University.

Terray, E. 1987. "Asante Imperialism and Gyaman Resistance: Forms, Motivations, Trends," in E. Schildkrout. *The Golden Stool: Studies of the Asante Center and Periphery* New York: Anthropological Papers of the American Museum of Natural History. 65: 245-251.

Thomas, N. 1996. *Encyclopedia of Social and Cultural Anthropology*. London and New York: Routledge.

Thompson, P.R. 2000. *The Voices of the Past: Oral History*. Oxford: Oxford University Press.

Thompson, R.F. 1983. *Flash of the Spirit: African and Afro-American Art and Philosophy*. New York: Random House.

Thompson, T. 1937 (first edition 1758). *An Account of Two Missionary Voyages* London: Benj. Dod, rpt. by the Society for Promoting Christian Knowledge.

Tipple, G.A. 1987. "Housing Policy and Culture in Kumasi, Ghana: A Study of Constraints and Resources," *Environment and Behavior* 19(3): 331-352.

Tordoff, W. 1962. "The Ashanti Confederacy," *The Journal of African History* 3(3): 399-417.

Tordoff, W. 1965. *Ashanti under the Prempehs, 1888-1935*. London: Oxford University Press.

Tordoff, W. 1968. "The Dismemberment and Revival of the Ashanti Confederacy," *The Journal of British Studies* 7(2): 151-168.

Turner, V. 1991. "Liminality and Communitas," in V. Turner, V. Abrahams and A. Harris. *The Ritual Process: Structure and Anti-Structure*. Ithaca and New York: Cornell University Press: 94-130.

Twum-Barima, S. A. (09-05-2007). Lavish Funerals and Poverty. *The Statesman*,http://www.thestatesmanonline.com/pages/news_detail.php?newsid=3378andsection=11.

U.S. Department, o. S. 2005. *Background Note: Ghana*. Washington, DC: Bureau of African Affairs.

Unknown (4 May 2008). Kumasi Catholic Archdiocese Gets New Archbishop. *Ghana News Agency.*

Unknown author (the 25th of November 1961). *The Guardian*. London.

van Binsbergen, W.M.J. 2003. *Intercultural Encounters: African and Anthropological Lessons Towards a Philosophy of Interculturality*. Münster: Lit Verlag.

van Binsbergen, W.M.J. (2012). *The Relevance of Buddhism and Hinduism for the Study of Asian-African Transcontinental Continuities*. International Conference, African Studies Centre. Leiden.

van den Bersellaar, D. 2007. *The King of Drinks: Schnapps Gin from Modernity to Tradition*. Leiden: Brill Academic Publishers.

van den Braembussche, A.A. 1985. *Theory of History of Societies (Theorie van de Maatschappijgeschiedenis)*. Baarn: Ambon.

van den Heuvel, A. 1981. *Willem Bosman in Gold and Slaves [Willem Bosman in Goud en Slaven]*. Amsterdam: Meulenhoff.

van der Geest, S. 2000. "Funerals for the Living: Conversations with Elderly People in Kwahu, Ghana," *African Studies Review* 43(3): 103-129.

van Dijk, R. 1999. "The Pentecostal Gift: Ghanaian Charismatic Churches and the Moral Innocence of the Global Economy," in R. Fardon, W. van Binbergen and R. van Dijk. *Modernity on a Shoestring: Dimensions of Globalisation, Consumption and Development in Africa and Beyond*. Leiden: Eidos.

van Gennep, A. and M. V. a. G. C. trans. 1960 (first published in 1908). *The Rites of Passage*. Chicago: University of Chicago Press.

van Rouveroy van Nieuwaal, E.A.B. and R. van Dijk 1999. *African Chieftaincy in a New Socio-Political Landscape*. Münster and London and Piscataway, N.J.: Lit Verlag.

Venkatachalam, M. 2012. "Between the Devil and the Cross: Religion, Slavery, and the Making of Anlo-Ewe," *The Journal of African History* 53(1): 45-64.

Venkatachalam, M. 2012. "Between the Umbrella and the Elephant: Elections, Ethnic Negotiations and the Politics of Spirit Possession in Teshi, Accra," *Africa* 81(2): 248-268.

Venkatachalam, M. (2012). *Slavery in Memory*. Anthropology. London, SOAS. PhD.

Vries, P. 1991. "The Triumphal March of the Annales (De Zegetocht van de Annales)," in H. Beliën and G. J. Van Setten. *History in the Twentieth Century: an Endless Discussion (Geschiedenis in de Twintigste Eeuw: Discussie zonder Eind)*. Amsterdam: Agon: 181-223.

Waardenburg, J. 1999. *Classical Approach to the Study of Religion: Aims, Methods and Theories of Research Introduction and Anthology*. Berlin and New York: de Gruyter.

Wachtel, N. 1992. *The Vision of the Vanquished: the Spanish Conquest of Peru through Indian Eyes, 1530-1570 (La Vision des Vaincus; Les Indiens du Pérou devant la Conquête Espagnole, 1530-1570)*. Paris: Gaillimard.

Wainwright, G.A. 1949. "Pharaonic Survivals, Lake Chad to the West Coast," *Journal of Egyptian Archaeology* 35: 167-175.

Wallace-Johnson, I. T. A. 1935. *Minutes of the Ashanti Confederacy Council*. Accra: Unknown.

Wallace-Johnson, I. T. A. 1935. *The Restauration of the Ashanti Confederacy*. Accra: Unknown.

Walls, A.F. 2004. "Geoffrey Parrinder (1910) and the Study of Religion in West Africa," in F. Ludwig and A. Adogame. *European Traditions in the Study of Religion in Africa*. Wiesbaden: Harrassowitz Verlag: 207-215.

Warren, D.M. (1974). *Disease, Medicine, and Religion among the Techiman Bono of Ghana: a Study in Cultural Change*. Bloomington, University of Indiana. PhD. dissertation.

Weiss, H. (2007). *Begging and Almsgiving in Ghana: Muslim Positions Towards Poverty and Distress*. Uppsala, Nordiska Afrikainstitutet. 133.

Wilks, I. 1961. "The Northern Factor in Ashanti History: Begho and the Mande," *The Journal of African History* 2(1): 25-34.

Wilks, I. 1966. "The Position of Muslims in Metropolitan Ashanti in the Early Nineteenth Century," in I. M. Lewis. *Islam in Tropical Africa* London: Oxford University Press for the International African Institute: 144-166.

Wilks, I. 1979. "The Golden Stool and The Elephant Tail: An Essay on Wealth in Asante," *Research in Economic Anthropology* 2: 1-36.

Wilks, I. 1982. "Wangara, Akan and Portuguese in the Fifteenth and Sixteenth Centuries. II. The Struggle for Trade," *The Journal of African History* 23(4): 463-472.

Wilks, I. 1988. "Asante: Human Sacrifice or Capital Punishment ? A Rejoinder," *The International Journal of African Historical Studies* 21(3): 443-452.

Wilks, I. 1989 (first published in 1975). *Asante in the Nineteenth Century: The Structure and Evolution of a Political Order*. Cambridge: Cambridge University Press.

Wilks, I. 1995. "State and Society in Precolonial Asante," *The Journal of African History* 37(1): 138-140.

Wilks, I. 1999. "Unity and Progress: Asante Politics Revisted,". *Akan Worlds: Identity and Power in West Africa*. Paris: L'Harmattan: 43-69.

Wilks, I. 2000. "The Juula and the Expansion of Islam into the Forest," in N. Levtzion and R. L. Pouwels. *The History of Islam in Africa*. Oxford: James Currey: 93-115.

Wilks, I.,N. Levtzion, et al. 1986. *Chronicles from Gonja: a Tradition of West Africa Muslim Historiography*. Cambridge: Cambridge University Press.

Williamson, S.G. and J. Bardsley 1953. *The Gold Coast: What of the Church?* London: Edinburgh House Press.

Willis, W.B. 1998. *The Adinkra Dictionary: A Visual Primer on the Language of Adinkra*. Washington DC: The Pyramid Complex.

Wiredu, K. 1996. *Cultural Universals and Particulars: An African Perspective*. Bloomington: Indiana University Press.

Wiredu, K. 1998. "The Moral Foundations of an African Culture," in P. H. Coetzee and A. P. J. Roux. *The African Philosophy Reader*. London and New York: Routledge: 306-317.

Wolf, E.R. 1982. *Europe and the People without History*. Los Angeles and Berkely: University of California Press.

World Bank, T. (2008). *The World Development Report: Agriculture for Development*. Washington DC: 1-386.

Wright, B.E. 2004. *Mate Masie*. Unknown: Kwesi Ra Nehem Ptah Akhan.

Wright, J. 1987. "Desire's Design, Vision's Resonance: Black Poetry's Ritual and Historical Voice," *Callaloo* 30: 13-28.

Wyllie, R.W. 1980. *Spiritism in Ghana: a Study of New Religious Movements*. Missoula, Montana: American Academy of Religion. Studies in Religion and Scholars Press.

Yankah, K. 1995. *Speaking for The Chief: Okyeame and the Politics of Akan Royal Oratory*. Bloomington: Indiana University Press.

Yarak, L.W. 1986. "Elmina and Greater Asante in the Nineteenth Century," *Africa: Journal of the International African Institute* 56(1): 33-52.

Yarak, L.W. 1987. "Kwasi Boakye and Kwame Poku: Dutch-Educated Asante Princes," in E. Schildkrout. *The Golden Stool: Studies of the Asante Center and Periphery*. New York: Anthropological Papers of the American Museum of Natural History. 65: 131-145.

Yarak, L.W. and D.M. Graves 1997. "A Dutch Embassy to Asante in 1857: the Journal of David Mill Graves," *History in Africa* 24: 363-380.

Chapter VII: Appendices

7.1. Archives

7.1.1. (ARC): Public Records and Archives Administration Department (PRAAD) at the Kumasi National Cultural Centre (NCC)

1/2/30/2/12a: Asante customs.

1.—1/30/1/1-21: 1902-1946.
1/30/1/1— Forwarding statement of king of Atebubu. Having reference to certain woman went to Kratchi to serve fetish (14/08) 1902-1908.
1/30/1/3 — Native fetish in Offin River requesting 1906.
1/30/1/6 — Chief fetish Priest Aberewa (2/07) 1907-1908.
1/30/1/7 — 'Aberewa fetish 1907-1912.
1/30/1/10 — Sikaman Fetish (n 60/12) 1912-1913.
1/30/1/11 — Fetish custom which necessitates the murder of the ninth child (11/12) 1912.
1/30/1/12 — Ejura Fetish Kune 1914-1916.
1/30/1/14 — Deteh Fetish 9N83/1918 1918.
1/30/1/18 — Fetishes and native customs-General 1931-1939.

6 —1919-1959.
6/1/12 — Fetishes (28/1929) 1929-41.
6/1/14 — Lunatics (25/32) 1932-49.
6/1/40 — Fetishes (0014) 1944-1948.

2:2/2/11 — Nine Fetishes and Native Customs General 1944-1969 J 265/2.
2/30/1 — Organisation of the Spiritual cult 1 1967 (6/re/3).
2/10/13 — Ghana Psychic and Traditional Healing Association 1962-1969 (134118) vols.
2/1/21 — Ashanti history.
2/1/50 — Legalisation of locally distilled spirits (*akpeteshie*).

7.1.2 Other Archives

Minute of the 8th of June 1876, by A.W.L. Hemming; CO/96/118.
Letter of the 18th of Dec. 1877, from the Rev. F. Ramseyer to Freeling, referring to the journey to Kumasi in 1839 by the Rev. A. Riis; CO/96/122.
Letter to Fr. Planque, the 23rd of May 1880, in *AMA* 15/802.02 19.180.
Letter to Fr. Planque, the 10th of September 1880, in *AMA* 15/802.02 19.184.
Letter to Fr. Planque, the 10th of September 1880, in *AMA* 15/802.02 19.184.
Report, the 16th of June 1882, in *AMA* 15/802.02 19.222.

Governor Sir Shenton, letters 1924.
Eastern Provincial Commissioner's Diary, April 1928, NAG, Accra.
District Minutes 1961, Synod Letter.
Manhyia Archives Group 1/15/2 1929-1947
Harper Mss. Brit. Emp. S. 344. Box 2/5. 1920. Colonial Reports: Ashanti 905

7.1.3 Abbreviations

ACC: Asante Confederacy Council
ACCQA: Asante Christian Chiefs and Queen mothers Association
AIC: African Independent Churches
AIR: Asante Indigenous Religion
AKS: Asante Kotoko Society
AQMA: Ashanti Queen Mother Association
ARHC: Ashanti Regional House of Chiefs
BG: British Governor
BMS: Basel Missionary Society
CC: Chief Commissioner
CCA: Chief Commissioner of Ashanti
CEM: Church of England Mission
CPP: Convention People's Party
CS: Colonial Secretary
CZC: Council of the *Zongo* Chiefs
DA: District Assemblies
ECM: European Christian missionaries
ERAC: English Royal African Company
FAFS: Friends of Asante Freedom Society
HC: Houses of Chiefs
IR: Indigenous Religion
KNUST: The Kwame Nkrumah University of Kumasi University
MC: Mainline Church
MAP: Muslim Association Party
NAG: National Archives of Ghana
NAIRM: New African Indigenous Religious Movement
NIRM: Neo-Indigenous Religions Movement
NCCQA: National Christian Chief and Queen Mother Association
NGMS: North German Missionary Society
NHC: National House of Chiefs
NLM: National Liberation Movement
NRC: National Redemption Council
NRM: New Religious Movement
PCC: Pentecostal-Charismatic Church
PPTAP: Promoting Partnership for Traditional Authorities Project
RHC: Regional House of Chiefs

SAM: Society of the African Mission
SC: Spiritual Church
SPG: Society for the Propagation of the Gospel
TC: Traditional Council
TDC: Town Development Committee
UFIA: United Front for Islamic Affairs
UC: Urban Council
UG: University of Ghana
UP: United Party
WAFF: West African Frontier Force
WB: World Bank
WBAM: World Bank Atlas Method (WBAM)
WIC: West Indian Company
WMMS: Wesleyan Methodist Missionary Society (currently the Methodist Church)

7.2. Glossary of Asante indigenous religious (Twi) term

TWI WORD	MEANING[100]
ABEREWA	Old woman.
ABOWMUBODEƐ	Singl. Knocking fee.
ABUSUA	Pl. *mimosa.* Matrilineage, descent and kinship reckoned by matrifiliation: maximal matrilineage: family, kin, relatives on the mother's side: the der. of this fundamental word is obscure: the most common traditional explanation is that it means lit. 'Imitating Abu', i.e. *Abu.,* a proper name and *sue*, to imitate, to learn: cu *usual,* the act of learning by imitation: i.e. an Asantehene (a ruler of the pre-Asante Akan polity of Adams) had an *ɔkyeame* called Abu: asked his children (his heirs) to help to pay his fine, but they refused and went to live with their mothers' relatives: but Abu's sister's children helped him to pay his debt: so, when Abu died he left all of his property to his sister's children: other people began to imitate him, hence *abusua.* This account is clearly aetiological. But it shows (a) the bedrock antiquity of the institution, (b) the Asante understanding that other peoples trace descent in the paternal line, and (c) awareness of the abiding tensions in Asante social structure between the claims of matriclans and patrolling: cf. *obusuani* syn. *oni,* plural. *Abusuafoɔ*, a kinsman, a relative: *abusuapanin,* pl. *abusua mpanifoɔ*, the senior member (s) of a matrilineage: *obaapanin*, the senior female in an *abusua,* the holder of the 'royal' stool.
ABUASUA PANIN	Pl. *Abusua mpaninfo* Heads of families (mother's lineage only).
ADADUANAN	Forty days (*da* means 'day', *aduanan* means 'forty'). The forty-two named day cycle of the ritual Asante calendar combined the *nanson* cycle of six days with the *nawotwe* cycle seven days: alt. *adaduana*: der. *eda*, a day and *aduanan/aduanan*, forty: cf. the common-but erroneous-

[100] The sources for these meanings are: (a) the English-Twi translations of Benedict Asante Kyei, linguist at the language centre of the University of Ghana, (b) McCaskie, T. C. 1995. *State and Society in Pre-Colonial Asante.* Cambridge: Cambridge University Press.

	rendering 'forty days'. In the oral tradition the *adaduanan* was known as forty days.
ADAE	Lit. a lying down, resting or burial place: der *da*, to lie down, to sleep, to remain, to rest: cf. also *eda*, a day: *oda*, a tomb, a grave: *adae* were festival days upon which offerings were made to the ancestors: there were two *adae* in every *adaduanan* cycle: these were *awukudae* (the 'small' or Wednesday *adae*) which took place on day fifteen: *kurudapaawukuo* and *akwasidae* the 'big' or Sunday *adae* which took place on day thirty-three: *kurukwasie*. It is sometimes said that the distinction between *awukudae* and *akwasidae* is that it is only on the latter that the ancestral stools are actually taken out of the stool house and carried in procession to the burial ground (*baamu*): certainly, people 'petitioned' the ancestral stools on the *akwasidae*, on the grounds that they were temporarily 'occupied': on both of the *adae*, the reigning *Asantehene* made offerings to his ancestors, processed to the *bantama baamu*, and held a public reception in the afternoon.
ADAE KESE	The *Odwira* festival was also known as the *adae kese* or 'big *adae*' as it refers to the ninth unit of the *adaduanan* cycle of the Akan ritual calendar.
ADINKRA	*Di nkra* means to part, to be separated, to leave one another or say goodbye. It usually refers to a symbol in cloth.
ADOSOA	Gift giving.
ADOMA	Twinkling bells.
ADOWA	Symbolic dance of the Akan people usually performed at funerals and festivals.
ADURO	Pl. *Nnuru* Medicine.
ADWUMAN	At the back.
AFONA	State ceremonial swords.
AFONASOAFO	Pl. *Afonasoani*. The *Asantehene*'s and *Asantehemma*'s war shield bearers.
AGYI	Locally made incense.
AGYINA	Inner Council.
AHEMFO	More than one *Asantehene* or *Asantehemma*, senate of royal rulers
AHENEMA	Traditional leather sandals.
AHEMFI	(*passim*) syn. *Ahemfi*. der *ɔhene* and *ofie*, a house: lit. 'the house of an *ɔhene*': used her of the palace of the Asantehene in Kumasi.
AHENKWAA	Pl. *nhenkwaa*. Der. *ɔhene (*pl. *ahene)* and *akoa (*pl. *nkoa),* in the sense of servant and subject: lit. 'the servant of an *ɔhene*': used here of those who served in the status of *nhenkwaa* to the *Asantehene: ɔsomfo*; plural *asomfoɔ*: der. *som,* to serve a master (human or supernatural) : Christaller gives three glosses: (a) the servant of a king; (b) a courtier (which is good, very suggestive reading); (c) (in another context), a type of performance with singing and dancing: recruitment to the status of *ahenkwaa* to the Asantehene was a somewhat haphazard business that might involve a number of factors: residence in Kumasi, the chance to be noticed and/or demonstrate talent, personal liking on the part of the Asantehene and/or a senior office holder, finding oneself delivered up to the Asantehene in settlement of a debt or fine, etc. : number of Asante informants emphasise the *personal* link in this pattern of recruitment: by

	contrast , a minority of the royal *nhenkwaa* were recruited on a hereditary basis (but the son appears only to have succeeded the father as *ahenkwaa* if the mother herself was an *akoa* in direct service to the 'Golden Stool'): the nature of the relationship between the two categories of *nhenkwaa* remains uncertain: *nhenkwaa* formed the base or bottom tier of officialdom, but, crucially, this status bespoke *inclusion* within the state: a variety of factors, in determining whether or not someone who achieved or inherited the rank of *ahenkwaa* might rise to any higher office: the central idea of *personal* service is also evidenced in the case of those *nhenkwaa* who served an *ɔbosom* in the status of *ɔbosomkwaa* 'a servant of an *ɔbosom*': both the *abosom* and the Asantehene were legal heirs to the property left by their respective *nhenkwaa*.
AHODAE	Laying-in-state.
AHOƆFEHEMAA	Beauty pageants.
AKAN	The academic fields of religious studies and political sciences have different ways of referring to the Akan. The Akan is the umbrella name of culturally and linguistically connected Niger-Congo groups in Ghana, the Côte d'Ivoire and a very small minority in Northern Togo. The Akan cultural groups all speak Kwa languages and dialects and have linguistically been connected to the Ewe, the Fon, and other groups that live to the east. They number over eight million (8,562,748) and make up to 49.1 percent of the Ghanaian population (Ghana 2002). The Akan cultural groups share the same cultural customs such as naming ceremonies, rite of passages and festivals and they are also linguistically related. Scholars of religion usually focus on 'the Akan'. Historians, however, refer to 'the Asante' as the unit of analysis. Historically Akan has namely been a problematic term. The concept was first used in 1602 by Portuguese map makers, who drew the first map of Guinea, which was based on details of the Gold Coast that they collected during a Portuguese mission to the interior in 1573 (Cortesão and Teixeira da Mota 1962:6769, plate 362).[101] The Portuguese mapmakers commented on two interior states known as 'Acanes grande' and 'Acanes pequenos', which in actual fact never existed. Portuguese traders on the Gold Coast used 'Akan' to refer to Asante traders from the interior. The Portuguese myth of the existence of two 'Acanes' states and of the 'Acanes' people became widespread and on the maps of Guinea of 1606, 1616 and 1729 cartographers in different countries referred to these imaginary states as 'Akkany'. Only in 1819 Akkany was removed from maps of Guinea. By then, however, the term 'Akan' was widespread. In 1875 the Danish missionary J.G. Christaller contributed to the popularity of the term Akan by including an entry in his dictionary regarding this cultural group (singl. *ɔkànni*, pl. *Akanfo*). The name *ɔkànni* in Christaller's dictionary refers to inhabitants of Akem, Akwam, Akuapem, Asen, Asante, Dɛnkyira, Twuforo and Wasa, but does not include the Fantefo, the Nnonkofo, the Ntafo, and other *potofo* (Christaller 1881:220). By excluding the Fante (*Fantefo*), the term *ɔkànni* became known as a more limited term than 'Twi', which referred to the language of various cultural groups in the Gold Coast, including that of the Fante. Currently, the term 'Akan' still exists although the meaning of Akan and Twi has been turned around. These days 'Akan' refers to various cultural groups in

[101] See: kaartencollectie Universiteit van Amsterdam: http://dpc.uba.uva.nl.

	Ghana including the Fante, whereas Twi refers to various subgroups of Akan dialects, such as the Akuapem and the Asante, but not the Fante.[102] Historically, the *Akanfo* were thus never real, but Portuguese mapmakers and a Danish Missionary spread the myth of their existence. Most historians who work on Ghana, such as Wilks, McCaskie, Allman, Parker, Yarak, Adjaye and Lewin, seem to be aware of this history. Most often they prefer to refer to the emic terms Asante and the Fante instead of using the historically inaccurate term 'Akan'. Most scholars of religion, such as Platvoet, Parrinder, Danquah and philosophers from Ghana, such as Gyekye and Wiredu, however, seem to be influenced by Christaller's dictionary entry on the *ɔkànni* people. As a result, they refer to 'the Akan' as a cultural-linguistic term. The author uses the term 'Asante' rather than 'Akan', because she writes on the Asante in particular and not on the Akan in general. More accurate descriptions can be derived from reference to the Asante only than to all Akan in mentioned countries, which is why 'Asante' is the best term to use in the context of this book.
AKƆM	This is a bodily movement, which has many functions. It is a religious ritual, but is also admired as art, enjoyed as entertainment and a tool to make political statements. *Abɔbom* dancing is performed at festivals, funerals and other religious rituals.
AKOA	(pl. *nkoa*) 'Subject', a term of wide connotation. An *akoa* is the subject or servant of a chief, but a slave is also an *akoa* of his or her master.
AKONKOFOƆ	Syn. *akonkofoɔ.* Der. *Konko.* To retail, to broker: cf. *konkosifoɔ,* a retailer, pl. the same: this term was used to describe the prominent *Asante* 'businessmen' of the early colonial period; no exact translation is adequate, but the term carried clear implications of wealth (initially rooted in retailing goods between the Gold Coast and Asante), of capital 'individualism'', and of 'modernity' in consumption patterns and attitudes: *akonkofoɔ* were themselves often illiterate, but they commonly funded the education of junior relatives and/or dependants: the origin of this group lay in those *nhenkwaa* and others who rebelled against the fisc al policies of the Asante state in the 1880s/90s who fled into the Gold Coast Colony and prospered there, and who returned to Kumasi after the deportation of the Asantehene Agyeman Prempeh (1896) and the annexation of Asante by the British Crown (1901): the *akonkofoɔ* were arrivistes, and something of this suggested by the (twentieth-century) meaning of *konkɔm* (der *konkoɔ*), to flaunt oneself, to be haughty, to strut, to 'look big'.
AKONWATUMTUM	Pl. *Nkonwatumtum* Blackened stools.
AKRADWARE	Cleansing ritual.
ANYANSATO	Wise person
AKUSIDAE	Ritual sacred days that are celebrated every six weeks.
AKWASIDAE	(The 'big' or Sunday *adae*) which took place on day thirty-three of the *adaduanan* cycle, also named *kurukwasie.*
AKYEAME POMA	The spokesmen´s staff.
AMAN MMU	Immemorial custom.
AMAN BRE	Jural custom.

[102] http://www.akan.org/akan_cd/ALIAKAN/course/U-References-p01.html.

AMANKWATIAA	Name song.
AMANTOO	States of the Asante Confederacy.
AMANTOONUM	The Asante Confederacy or union.
AMPE	A game played mainly by girls by clapping and jumping using legs. Each of the contestants selects the leg that she will draw to get a point.
ASAFƆHENE	Pl. *Nsafohene.* Titled military commanders.
ASAMANDO	The realm of the ancestral spirits.
ASANTEFOƆ	The Asante people.
ASANTEHEMMA	Female Asante state ruler. The *Asantehemma*, who is the senior of the *Asantehene* and first ruler, was a co-ruler of the *Asantehene* with a well-defined constitutional and political role.
ASANTEHENE	Pl. Asante *ahemfo*. Singl. The Asante king.
ASANTEMAN	*Asanteman* refers both to the Asante nation (or 'union' means *amantoo-num*) as well as the gathering of all paramount chiefs (*amanhene*) and paramount queen mothers (*omanhemma*) and all other Asante chiefs (*ɔhene*) and queen mothers (*nhemma*) to discuss chieftaincy matters.
ASANTEMANHY-IAMU	The gathering of all chiefs and queen mothers
ASANTEMAN ADAE KESE	The current name for the eighteenth century rooted *Odwira* festival.
ASANTEMANHY-IAMU/ASANTEMAN KOTOKO	Pl. *oman-ahemfo.* The council or assembly of the Asante nation. The highest legislative council and court.
ASANTEMANSO	The Asante oral history makes notice of seven ancestors (five women and two men) who had crawled out of a hole in the ground in a place known as *Asantemanso* currently a village twenty miles south of Kumasi in the territorial division of Asumegya.
ASANTENESS	The nature of human culture.
ASASAMDO	Court personnel.
ASASE YA	The 'spirit' of the earth or Earth goddess: der. *(asɔ ase*), that beneath or below, the ground, the soil, the earth and *yaa*, name day of a female born on 'Thursday' (cf. *yawo* in the *nawotwe* cycle): the earth was anthropo-morphised and personalized as female, and no 'disturbance' (i.e. agricultural work) of 'her' was permitted on her 'name day', i.e. every recurrent Thursday in the *adaduanan* cycle. Under Christian influences *Asase Ya* was also wrongly translated as Mother Earth and She replaced the ancestral spirit *Ngame*.
ASUANI	Wreaths of a plant.
ATANO ƆBOSOM	Pl. *Atano abomsom* Water deities (name derived from the river *Tano*).
ATANOSUO	Holy water
ATE SIE	A game in which there are two or more sides. A marble is thrown to hit a collection on the opposite side.
ATEASEFOƆ	The living.
ATUDURO	Gun powder.
ATUO	Pl. *Otuo*. Singl. Local gun.

ATUMPAN	Pl. *Ntumpane.* Talking drums: usually people who play these drums can skilfully sound appellations or titles of notable people in the community.
AWOAMEFIA	The Bate clan among the Anlo – Ewe, was composed of priests, soothsayers and magicians. Their leader (*awoamefia*) also performed secular functions but leadership was based on religious and ritual ascendancy.
AWUKUDAE	The 'small' or Wednesday *adae,* which took place on day fifteen of the *adaduanan* cycle, also termed *kurudapaawukuo.*
AWUNNYADEƐ	Death duties levied by the state on an individual's self-acquired movable property: root der *wu,* to die + *nnya,* with the sense of leaving, loosening one's grip (imp. Of something) and *ade,* things, possessions, movable property: hence, 'heritage' (*ade a obi awu de agyaa wo*), the things left behind: cf. *owunnyafo,* pl. *awuunyafoɔ.* A survivor, an heir ('someone left behind'): ant, *anikanne,* property given (to a son) in a father's lifetime.
AYA KESEE	A huge brass pan used for indigenous religious rituals.
BANKUO	Pl. Strips of cloth.
BANMU SOM	A veneration of non-Muslim, non-Christian origin.
BARIMA	Warrior
BATA KARI KESE	Islamic warrior cloth.
BAYI	Witchcraft. *Oba* (child) and *yi* (to remove, take away): lit. 'to take away a child', encapsulating the belief that witchcraft operated most potently within the *abusua.:* cf. *bayi yɛ abusaude,* 'witchcraft is inborn among or hereditary between members of an *abusua*: syn. *bayi, abayigoru, abayide:* cf. *obayifoɔ* (pl. *abayifoɔ*), a witch or wizard): syn. ay*ɛn, kaberɛ, obansoam:* the word ayɛn (cf. y*ɛnn,* a fiery red; y*ɛn,* to foster, to breed; *ye,* to have the condition of, to manifest or display) gives some insight into the conceptualisation of woman (a hag), and that *mberewa* (old women) were widely regarded as adepts of witchcraft (being ideally placed in *abusua* terms, and 'jealous' of those who could still bear children): the Asante distinguished between the practices of *bayi boro* ('hot' or maleficent witchcraft: cf. *aboro,* injury, hurt, malevolence) and *bayi papaa* ('cool' or beneficent witchcraft: cf. *papa,* moral good, benefit, welfare: impl. Prosperity).
BEREMPON-DOMS	Little states. *Birɛmpɔn, pl. Abirɛmpɔn)* means literally, 'big man' *(edom* means army, *odom* means favour*).* A hereditary title held by the heads of territorial chiefdoms, but also attainable by achievement by the very wealthy.
BIRIBI WO HO	'Something is there', 'something is' or 'being there'.
BODUA	Whisk, usually used by the indigenous priest during the performance of rituals.
BORƆNO	A section of a town.
BRAGRO	Puberty rite ceremony.
DA BONE	Pl. *nnabɔne*: a 'bad' or unlucky'day: i.e. a day that was ritually important and devoted to some ritual observance: der. ɛda (pl. *nna*), a day and *bɔne*, bad, evil, wicked; impl. Powerful, fraught, demanding due attention: sometimes used of those days upon which no farm work might be done, but only domestic or household tasks: in this sens syn. *fo fida;* der. *afo fi*, refraining from farm work, staying at home resting or doing domestic chores: cf. *obene,* a bad man: ant. *dapaa.*

DAME	Draughts (US) checkers. A game for two people using twenty-four round pieces of wood that is moved on a board with black and white squares.
DAWA	Pieces of wood.
DAWURO	Gong-gong.
DAYAYA	Sky. Literal: supine position, lying flat on the back.
DONO	Singl. An African talking drum, meant to invoke the spirits, usually with the skin that is played at both ends and has cords that can be modulated to change the sound.
DUA	Pl. *Nnua*. Tree
DWO	Coolness.
DWETE	Silver stool. Syn. *ɔhemma adwa*
EGORO	*Bryophyllum pinta* (name of a plant).
ESƐN	Singl. Town crier.
ESOM KESE	Great veneration of the ancestral spirits
ETƆ	Mashed yam.
FƆNTƆNFRƆM	An African drum usually big and high that is used to invoke spirits
FODWO	Bad day.
FOFIE ADAE	Bad day.
HONAM	Body.
HYIRE	White clay.
JAMI	Friday mosque.
KENTE	These are silk and cotton traditional cloths that are locally woven by the Asante and originate from Bonwire; a village in the Ashanti Region or possible Tekyiman.
KOBEN	Red cloth.
KOKOKYIANAKA	A dark blue bird.
KOKOSESENI	Pl. *Kokosesefoo.* Fan carriers
KOTOBIRIGYA	Red clay.
KROKOWA	Footrest.
KUMASI	The *Asante* capital. der. *ɔkum*, inflected to produce a pair of linked meanings: (a) the name of a type of tree; (b) to kill, to execute, the act of killing *+ase,* under, underneath: i.e. the place under the *ɔkum* tree/ the place where executions to place.
KUMASIFOƆ	The inhabitants of Kumasi.
KUNTUNKUNI	Black cloth.
KUROTWIAMANSA	Leopard.
KWASAFOMANHY-IAMU	Interim government.
KYINIƐ	A huge umbrella.
MMOATIA	Dwarfs.
MMRA/MENA	Alt. *mmara, mmana.* The elephant tail: (a) the 'heraldic badge' of the

	ɔbirɛmpɔn; (b) the whisk (Christaller gives 'broom, fan' used by the *ahoprafoɔ* in a sweeping or fanning motion around the person of the Asantehene: the root der, is *pra/para,* to sweep, imp. to sweep away, to disperse (enemies, annoyances, etc.): the basic symbolism is of the Asantehene or the *ɔbirɛmpɔn* in the manner of the huge, lordly elephant- 'sweeping away' all irritants and distractions (these being defined, like flies around elephants, as petty, minor and inconsequential): implicated in this are ideas about volume, mutable substances (gold, excrement) , and of status of loftily 'presiding' over affairs: there is a clearly calculated signal in all of this pertaining to social 'distancing'' : i.e. the possession of the *mena/mmra* is a mark of those (the Asantehene and the *abirɛmpɔn* who are above and beyond concern with the mundane traffic of life: thus, the *mena/mmra* is a symbol of 'completion'-by definition in the case of the Asantehene, by accumulation and manifest achievement at the highest national level in the case of the *abirɛmpɔn*: it should be noted that the word *mena/mmra* is one that describes action, impl. Function, purpose: i.e. the standard term for any quadruped's tail is *dua/edua* (der *edua,* a stick or stalk), hence *bodua* (*aboa,* animal and *dua*), an animal's tail; thus, *nantwi dua,* a cow's tail; *pɔnkɔdua*, a horse's tail; *ɔsono dua* an elephant's tail: only the elephant's tail has a syn. (*mena/mmra*) of function, purpose, impl. Symbolic value: that said, other (lesser) animal's tails were used as signs of rank and/or were held to have 'powers': thus, *pɔnko dua* was the insignia of generals and warriors (and, clearly, ranked below the *mena/mmra*); it was also regarded as a potent 'war charm', and military causalities were 'fanned' with a horse's tail to affect their recovery.
MPONPONSUO	Ceremonial sword used by the Asantehene in oath swearing rituals.
MOGYA	Syn. *Bogya.* Blood, both physiologically as substance and philosophically as concept: most importantly, *mogya* was one of the four essential elements composing a human being: the importance of *mogya* in descent (in etc.) was reflected in the complex of attitudes towards blood as substance: the shedding of blood (*mogya gu*) by execution, accident, menstruation, etc was in all circumstances hedged about with rituals (of performance, avoidance, management, atonement, etc.): the *deliberate* shedding of blood was at once an *attribute* of power and an involvement in or *dialogue with* another, larger autonomous power that was a property in belief: thus, the right to kill (to 'take 'blood' in *extremis*, 'to hold the knife; as the *Asante* said) was a prerogative of the Asantehene: the root der. is (ultimately) *bo,* in the sense of creation.
MUGI	A boiled egg.
NANA	A title for royal rulers
NANSON	A cycle of six days in a week, originating from the Guan.
NAWOTWE	A cycle of seven days in a week.
NHWENE	Pl. *Ahwenee* Traditional beads.
NKONNWAFIESO SOM	Veneration in the stool house.
NKOM-MU	Specialised training of the *akomfoɔ*.
NKOSUƆHENE KOKO	White development chief *Nkosuo* means 'progress', or 'development' (-*hene* is the designation for a chief).
NKOSUƆHEMMA KOKO	White development queen mother *Nkosuo* means 'progresses, or 'development' (*hemaa* for a queen mother).

NKRABEA	Destiny.
NKURO	Pl *nkuro*. Towns.
NKYIMKYIM	Zigzag.
NKWANKAA	Non office holders
NSA FUFUO	Palm wine.
NSUMANKWAHENE	Pl. *Nsumankwaafoɔ*. The king's physician (s) and religious adviser (s) (from *nsuman,* 'protective medicine').
NSUMANFIESU	College of physicians.
NTOMABAN	Strips of cloth.
NTIAMU NTOMA	Cloth.
NTAM KESE	Oath of allegiance.
NTORO	The *ntoro* or totem determines the way people greet each other and what they cannot eat, which is dependent on the *ɔbosom*, and for some of them also the totem to which the *ntoro* is linked.
NUNYA	Active (empirical) or passive (divine) knowledge gained by experience.
NYAME	The Asante male ancestral serpent spirit or the Islamic or Christian omnipotent and omniscient God.
NYAME DAN	Small mosque.
NYAME FRE	To pray to the Islamic of Christian God.
OBAA PANIN	Grandmother.
OBENGFO	Pl. *Abengfo*. This refers to a person, who is highly developed such as rulers and *akomfoɔ,* but is also used with regards to those Asante who have become immortal.
OBONSAM KUROM	The hell fire.
OBURONI	Pl. *aborofo* White men.
ODIKRO	Pl. *Odikra*. Village chief.
ODOSO	A raffia skirt used by indigenous priests when they are possessed.
ODWIRA	*Dwira* means 'to cleanse', 'to purify'. The major annual festival, of religious and political significance, at which attendance was obligatory.
OGYE	Wealth appropriation.
OGYEDUA	A tree with great leaves and many branches, tree of reception, associated with the royal rulers and the ancestors.
OGYEFO	A title of some Asantehene's; meaning 'the taking one'.
OKURASENI	Pl. *Nkuraasefoɔ* Rural dwellers.
OMAN	P. *aman*. 'Nation', 'state', 'polity'.
OMANHENE	Pl. *Amanhene*. A paramount chief or the *primus-inter-pares* among all Asante chiefs (the Asante king).
ONINI	Pl *anini* snakes, e.g. pythons. Female pythos were believed to be prophets with oracular power, which were therefore kept near a shrine.
ONINI NANANOM NSAMANFO	The first or most ancient royal ancestral egg eating snake spirits.
ONIPA	Human.

ONIPAPA	Human-human (a man of great merits).
ONYANSAFO	Pl. *Anyansafo.* Wise persons.
ONYANKOPƆNG	The creator God or High God of the Asante people.
ONYANKOPƆNG KUROM	Heaven.
OPANIN	Gender-neutral term for an elderly person, male-*abusuapanin* or female *obaapanin.*
OSAGYEFOO	Singl. Warrior.
OSIKANI	Pl *asikafo* Big men, wealthy persons.
OTUMFUO	The powerful one.
OTUMI	Power, loyalty. The highest level at which political authority could be exercised, symbolised by the *Sika Dwa Kofi*, and personified in its custodian the Asantehene: der. *tumi*, to be able (to do something), imp. Ability, influence, power: cf. *atumisɛn,* 'things of power' i. e. the externalised display of strength, authority: cf. *Otumfuo,* 'one who has great power', i.e. the Asantehene.
OTWEDEAMPƆN	The Dependable One (reference to the Supreme Being).
OWARE	A game for two people using marbles four each in six holes. The marbles are collected and one is put in each hole until the person comes to an empty hole.
OYOKO	The clan name of the Asantehene's royal family.
ƆBAYIFOƆ	Pl. *Abayifoɔ* Witches.
ƆBOSOM	Pl. *abosom*, *som-bo* means something valuable or precious, such as gold or diamond) Natural deity or the lesser gods. The ultimate der. of this basic word remains unclear: cf. *ɔbo* a stone, a rock/ b), generically a verb of action or movement, specifically (in one aspect) imp. originating or creating and som, to serve, to be a servant of (a master, including *Nyame*): but cf. also so, in the sense of attaining to, being able to: *ɛso*, over, above, up on high: soa, to thrive, to flourish: som, suggesting a continuance: the abosom have been variously rendered as gods, tutelary spirits and 'fetishes': they were in fact powers of supernatural origin, anthropomorphised as the 'children' or as the 'servants' of *Nyame*: the essence of an *ɔbosom* was *tumi* (power) that emanated from *Nyame* and *Ngame*: many classifications of *abosom* assign them an identity by dedicated use-i.e. state, town, lineage, family or a particular *ɔkomfoɔ*: but underlying this is the classification, used here, that orders the *abosom* by the '(super) natural' point of origin of their powers. See *atano*, wesim, *obo*.
ƆBOSOM BRAFO	Pl. *Abosom brafo*. The executioner deities.
ƆBRAFOƆ	Pl. *Abrafoɔ* The kings' executioners.
ƆDEHYE	Pl. *Adehye*. Royal rulers.
ƆDONKƆ	An *ɔdonkɔ* (pl. *nnɔnkofoɔ*) was an enslaved person in the northern Asante hinterlands.
ƆDOMANKOMA	The Almighty.
ƆHEMMA	Pl. *nhemma* or *nhemmaanom*. Female Asante ruler.
ƆHEMMA ADWA	Silver stool.

ƆHENE	Pl. *ahene.* Male Asante ruler.
ƆHENE ADWA	Singl. The king's stool.
ƆHENE KOMFO	Priest-chief
ƆKRA	Eternal soul and spark of the sun. The name of the boy, who protected the Asante king against spiritual evilness.
ƆKYEAME	Pl. *akyeame.* Linguist, diplomat, a person who translates and presents matters that come to the parties before the chief's or queen mother's courts, bearer of wisdom of the Akan culture, protocol and customary laws.
PAPA	The name of a festival in Ghana, e.g. Kumawu. It is an ambiguous word. Depending on the tone and context, it refers to father, good quality material or fan.
PEREDWANS	The Asante currency.
SAMAN-PA	A good ancestor.
SASA	Individual spiritual powers of animals and humans.
SASA BONSAM	A hybrid (human/non-human) predatory 'creature' of the deep forest, servant of the *abosom,* and hostile to human order: it expressed antipathy by preying directly upon individuals and/or by fostering witchcraft: der. *sasa,* is used here in the meaning of being 'occupied' and *abonsam* means wizard, sorcerer or witch.
SEBE	Animal skins.
SIKA DWA KOFI	Golden Stool (*dwa*) means a 'stool', the symbolic throne and the symbol of office and *sika* means gold and *kofi,* the day name of a male person born on a 'Friday' (i.e. *fie* in the *nawotwe* cycle): it is said that, with the enabling mediation of Komfo Anokye, the *sika dwa* descended from the skies and settled on the knees of the seated Osei Tutu on a particular *fie* (Friday): an incumbent Asantehene was the living custodian of the *Sika Dwa Kofi*, and was responsible for exercising and discharging that political authority at the highest level that was embodied in it: the *Sika Dwa Kofi* was held to contain within the collective *sunsum* of the *Asanteman* (as ordained and reinforced by prescriptive ritual measures 'dictated' by Priest Anokye).
SIKA MMRA	The Golden Elephant Tail that stood for the highest level at which wealth was appropriated. 'The Golden Elephant Tail' der. *sika* and *mena/mmra,* an elephant's tail (see *mena/mmra*): the *sika mena* was a crucial item of regalia of The Asante *ahemfo*: it symbolised the very highest level at which wealth was appropriated, and as such it was conceptualised as being the indispensable 'helper' or 'supporter' of the very highest level of political authority (embodied in the *Sika Dwa Kofi* (with the sense of 'assisting' it., (b) to 'preside' as the most senior (as a 'parent') over the lesser elephant tails of the *abirempɔn:* each Asantehene 'made' his own *sika mena*, but detailed information concerning this most potent ritual object is difficult to recover: in part this is because the *sika mena* was a property of the reticent 'mystery' that surrounded power at its highest levels (i.e. its ideological articulation was pervasive, but by corollary its ritual quiddity – its 'being' – was opaque): it is also because the *sika mena* 'vanished' with the Asantehene from 1896 to 1935, and when the Asantehene Osei Agyeman Prempeh II had one 'made' for himself (to commemorate the British 'restoration' of the 'Asante Confederacy') the precolonial systems of accumulation and appropriation of

	wealth had eroded and effectively vanished: it would appear that the appointed head of the *ahoprafɔ* was charged with responsibility for the *sika mena* of the first Asantehene Osei Tutu (and this was kept in the *bantama baamu):* each successive ruler consigned his *sika mena* to the care of a trusted and greatly honoured individual (Kwasi Brantuo) in the case of the *Asantehene* Kwaku Dua Panin) but the person thereby selected was not always or necessarily the *Ahoprafo ɔhene* (that office itself undergoing a formal 'revival' after 1935, when it was (re) assigned to the mid-nineteenth century created *Manwere fekuoɔ*: current readings of the 'passing' of the *sika mena* in its original formulation/ meaning are associated, significantly, enough, with the avaricious Mensa Bonsu's *sika mena:* (a) 'disintegrated' and 'vanished' because it was the product of non-licit accumulation; (b) was appropriated by the people of Saawua; (c) drove its custodians 'mad' and then 'vanished'; (d) was interred with its creator's bones in Kumasi or otherwise 'became lost' during the funeral obsequies.
SUMAN	Pl. *nsuman* protective medicine.
SUNSUM	*Asunsum.* An intangible constituent of the person: non-human in origin, the *sunsum* determined an individual character, but might also be construed as a collective or group 'essence' (e.g. the *sunsum* of the *Asanteman* was contained within the *Sika Dwa Kofi*: the *sunsum* could be 'cultivated' in a variety of ways, chiefly dedicated to defending its host against hostility and 'illness' (witchcraft, etc.): der. *(e) sum (a),* shadow, dark, shade, impl. mysteriousness, hiding: cf. *sunsum*, a shade, a shadow (sometimes used as syn. *sunsum).*
TETE ƆBOSOM	Pl. *Tete abosom* ancient or state deities.
WIASE	The world of the living.
YAWA	Brass pan.

7.3. Glossary of Muslim terms (Arabic, Hausa and Mande)

TERM	MEANING
AL HAJJI	Arabic: haj·is or haj·jis also hadj·is Islam 1. One who has made a pilgrimage to Mecca. 2. Often used as a form of address for one who has made such a pilgrimage.
AL-HIJRA	Arabic: flee.
ALIM	Pl. *Ulama.* Arabic: scholars.
BORI	A gift from Allah that is received through sickness.
DAR-AL-KUFR OR DAR-AL-HARB	Arabic: the territory of Infidelity.
DAR-AL-ISLAM	Arabic: the territory of Islam.
EID-AL-ADHA	Hausa: (in Arabic 'id-ul-adha'). This is a festival of sacrifice. It is a religious festival celebrated by Muslims and Druze worldwide as a commemoration of God's forgiveness of Ibrahim (Abraham) from his vow to sacrifice his son, as commanded by Allah.
EID-AL-FITR	Hausa: (in Arabic 'id-ul-fitr'). This is a feast that starts on the last day of Ramadan, once the sun has set.

IMAM	Arabic: an imam is an Islamic leader, often the leader of a mosque and/or community. Similarly to spiritual leaders, the imam is the person who leads the prayer during Islamic gatherings. More often the community turns to the mosque imam, if they have an Islamic question. In smaller communities an imam could be the community leader based on the community setting.
IMAM AL-BILAD	Arabic: personal imam.
JAHILIYYA	Arabic: the state of ignorance.
JIHAD	Arabic: holy war.
KAFFAR BEN AL KUFR	Arabic: infidels of infidels.
KITABAL-GHANJA	Arabic: a mid-eighteenth century Arabic document written by Muhammed ibn al-Mustafa Kamaghatay and Umar Kunandi ibn Umar Kamaghatay.
KUFR	Arabic: infidels.
MALAM	Arabic: *malam* (Maal-amm) means One Who Has Knowledge of Directions. The word first came to use when people from west India's coast went fishing or travelled across oceans to other countries. The captain was called *malam* as he knew the right direction and took the vessel in that direction. Now *malam* is also used as the Surname/Last Name, in west India, in the Veraval city of Gujarat. There are no written records of when this word was first used and where, but it is believed to have started to be used after people from Rajasthan came to Veraval city of Gujarat for fishing around two hundred years ago.
MARAKANTAS	Arabic: Qur'anic schools.
NASSI-JI	Holy water (Mande).
NKRAMOFOƆ	Malinke (Mande): Asante Muslims. The Malinke (Mande) word 'karamoko' originates from the Arabic term 'qurā'a' which means 'great scholar' or 'one who is able to recite the Qur'an'. Because of the Arabic origin of the word karamoko or Muslims (*Nkramofoɔ*) it is no wonder that the Asante do not know the orginal meaning of the word *nkramo* and gave it the same meaning as to the word Muslims. In the Asante perception Muslims were people who prayed five times a day and practiced divination.
ƆKRAMONI	Pl. *Nkramofoɔ*. Follower of the Suwarian tradition; a moderate form of Islam that was founded by Al-Hajj Salim Suwari, a learned cleric from the core Mali area who lived around 1500.
RAMADAN	Arabic: The name 'Ramadan' is taken from the name of this month; the word itself derived from an Arabic word for intense heat, scorched ground, and shortness of rations. It is considered the most venerated and blessed month of the Islamic year. Prayers, sawm (fasting), charity, and self-accountability are especially stressed at this time; religious observances associated with Ramadan are kept throughout the month.
SADAQA	Arabic: voluntary almsgiving.
SUNNA	Arabic: A normative custom of the Prophet or of the early Muslim community, as set forth in the hadith (q.v.), which is the prophetic tradition; an account of what the Prophet said or did; second in authority to the Qur'an.
SHEIKH	Arabic: sheikh, also rendered as Sheik, Cheikh, Shaikh, and other variants (Arabic: شيخ, shaykh; pl. شيوخ shuyūkh), is a word or honorific term in the Arabic language that literally means 'elder'. It is commonly used to

	designate an elder of a tribe, a lord, a revered wise man, or an Islamic scholar. Although the title generally refers to a male person, there existed in history also a very small number of female sheikhs. It also refers to a man over 40 or 50 years old generally or a Muslim who is a student of knowledge. Whilst even a new Muslim can be called a Sheikh if he is diligent in seeking the knowledge of Islam based upon the Quran and authentic *Sunna*, he can be referred to as such to those he can teach. And usually a person is known as a Sheikh when they have completed their undergraduate university studies in Islamic studies and are trained in giving lectures. The word *Sheikh* is not to be confused with an *Alim*, pl. *Ulema*, (a learned person in Islam, a scholar), Mawlawi, Mawlana, Muhaddith, Faqih, Qadi, Mufti, Hadhrat or Hafiz.
SUMAN	Arabic: pl. *nsuman*. Charms, amulets, talismans (all dedicated to prescribed, circumscribed functions: all aspects or derivations of a much larger embodiment of power: all – unlike the *abosom* – man-made): *nsuman* were the most evident/apparent feature of Asante belief practices, and so Europeans erroneously accorder these 'fetishes'/ 'saphies' a central (sometimes an exclusive) role as 'Asante religion': der. *suma*, to hide, to be hidden: *osumanni* was a maker, owner and/or wearer of *nsuman* (cf. b) *suman*, to make or wear a *suman*; *tu suman*, to make or introduce a *suman* ; *gye suman*, to produce or buy a *suman: nsuman* were commonly worn round the neck or limbs, and might be composed of virtually anything that 'held 'an efficacious aspect of power (s) (e.g. hair, beads, teeth, feathers, leather, scraps of paper with Qur'anic writing/ Islamic cabalistic formulae, etc.): *nsuman* were owned by individuals, and might be protective (against malice, witchcraft, disease, etc.) or aggressively intended (to been known by generic names; e.g. *gyabom*, the 'helpers', der. *gya* , to help, assist, save, *dwenfa*, worn to assist in acquiring property, lit á thing or person found or seized': *ayera*, syn. *otuo suman*, 'the gun *suman*'.
SUNNA	Arabic: *sunna* is a normative custom of the Prophet or of the early Muslim community, as set forth in the hadith (q.v.).
ZAR	The *zar* is performed for the purpose of healing by Muslis, Christians and Jews in Egypt, the Sudan and Ethiopia.
ZONGO	Hausa: the term *zongo* originally derives from *zango*, which is a Hausa term for 'a settlement of Hausa and Hausa speaking traders' (Hiskett 1984). After the colonisation of Asante and the creation of the 'Crown Colony of Asante', the British, however, used the word *zongo* to refer to a squatter for strangers. It was their administrative policy to designate specific areas for the 'strangers'. In terms of the original meaning of *zongo,* these areas are indeed *zongos,* meaning 'settlements of Hausa and Hausa speaking traders', because even among all non-Hausa inhabitants, Hausa is the lingua franca in all Kumasi *zongos.* In terms of the British concept of *zongo,* however, the mentioned areas are not real *zongos*, since there are many Akan of whom the majority in all likelihood are Christians who live inside these *zongos.* The old Kumasi *zongo* (on map 6 referred to as *zongo*), for instance, has an estimated population of 12,400 people, of whom 40 percent are Akan and 60 percent consist of Northerners of whom the majority are Muslims. The 'New *Zongo*', which has an estimated population of 11,830, consists of 30 percent Akan, 5 percent Ewes and 65 percent of them are Northerners. In terms of the religion of the people, 40 percent of them are Christians, whereas 60 percent are Muslims (Post, Inkoom et al. 2003:16). One could thus say that the present day areas that are referred to as *zongos* are indeed *zangos,* but in the British sense of the word they are not real *zongos.* Instead of *zongo*, the author of this book

	therefore uses the Asante indigenous term settler communities or settlements.

7.4. List of respondents

Gender:
01=Male
02=Female

Age:

01=— 16 years old	05=45-54
02=16-24	06=55-59
03= 25-34	07=60 years +
04= 35-44	

Religion:
01= No religion
02= African Indigenous Religion
03= Christian (Mainline Church)
04= Indigenous Christian
05= New African Indigenous Religious Movement (NAIRM)
06= New Religious Movement (NRM)
07=Muslim
08=other (please state)

Nr:	1
Date:	07/04/2008
Name:	Bishop Daniel Yinka Sarfo
Gender:	01
Location:	Email contact

Nr:	2
Date:	5/03/2001 and 23/03/2006
Name:	*ɔkɔmfoɔ* Agyei
Gender:	01
Age:	05:39
Religion:	06: the Asante Indigenous Religion
Town:	Kumasi
Starting time:	13:05:53
End time:	15:08:09
Location:	Kumasi

Nr:	3
Date:	20/11/2005
Name:	Nana Yaw Dwubeng
Gender:	01
Age:	07: 70
Religion:	04: Libito Church God wonderful
Town:	Achiase Nwabiagya
Starting time:	14:07:50
End time:	18:10:05
Location:	Achiase Nwabiagya: inside the respondents' palace

Nr:	4
Date:	16/11/2005
Name:	Rev Dr. Charles Kingsley Coffie (royal anthropologist)
Gender:	01
Age:	05: 50
Religion:	03: Methodist
Town:	Kumasi, formally Sefwa (western region)
Starting time:	13:57:09
End time:	16:58:23
Location:	Kumasi: RHC

Nr:	5
Date:	08/11/2005
Name:	Francis Mark Domenya
Gender:	01
Age:	04: 43
Religion:	03: Presbyterian
Town:	Kumasi
Starting time:	10:59:28
End time:	12:59:41
Location:	Kumasi: RHC

Nr:	6
Date:	10/11/2005
Name:	Joice Boakye
Gender:	02
Age:	05
Religion:	03: Methodist
Town:	Kumasi
Starting time:	13:04:13
End time:	15:12:27
Location:	Kumasi: RHC

Nr:	7
Date:	11/11/2005
Name:	Beatrice Agyeman Dua Prempeh
Gender:	02
Age:	05: 52
Religion:	03: Anglican
Town:	Mampong
Starting time:	10:05:08
End time:	12:07:28
Location:	Kumasi: RHC

Nr:	8
Date:	25/11/2005
Name:	Ernestina Ama Brenya /Abrewa Dokono
Gender:	02
Age:	07: 85
Religion:	06: Spiritual Church
Town:	Achiase Nwabiagya
Starting time:	9:16:29
End time:	12:18:42

Location:	Achiase Nwabiagya: inside the respondents' house

Nr:	9
Date:	23/11/2005
Name:	Nana Ama Boakyewaa
Gender:	02
Age:	07: 126
Religion:	02
Town:	Adomako Abuohoo Krobo
Starting time:	9:10:04
End time:	12:10:22
Location:	Adomako Abuohoo Krobo: inside the respondents' house

Nr:	10
Date:	31/1/2001 and additional questions asked in 22/04/2006
Name:	Nana Osei Bonsu II
Gender:	01
Age:	61
Religion:	N.A.
Town:	Mampong
Starting time:	13:16:05
End time:	15:12:10
Location:	The respondent's house in Kumasi

Nr:	11
Picture:	N.A.
Date:	04/04/2008
Name:	Bishop Peter Sarpong and Nana Arhin Brempong
Gender:	01
Location:	Email interview

Nr:	12
Date:	21/04/2006
Name:	Oboguhene Owusu Asiama II
Gender:	01
Age:	06:57
Religion:	05
Town:	Kumasi
Starting time:	15:11:53
End time:	17:12:04
Location:	Kumasi: RHC

Nr:	13
Date:	20/04/2006
Name:	United Front for Islamic Affairs (UFIA): Mohammed Braimah Joseph and Zedan Rashid
Gender:	01
Age:	05: M: 46 and 04: Z: 40
Religion:	07
Town:	Kumasi
Starting time:	14:11:03
End time:	16:18:34
Location:	Kumasi: UFIA office

Nr:	14
Date:	22/03/2006
Name:	Asante *nkramo* headman: Al-Hajji Abdul Karim Sina
Gender:	01
Age:	06: 56
Religion:	07
Town:	Kumasi: old *zongo,* inside the respondents' palace
Starting time:	12:09:54
End time:	15:10:28
Location:	Kumasi: inside the respondents' palace

Nr:	15
Date:	21/03/2006
Name:	Mamprusi headman: Ibrahim Abdullah
Gender:	01
Age:	07: 62
Religion:	07
Town:	Kumasi
Starting time:	17:11:13
End time:	19:09:38
Location:	Kumasi: old *zongo,* inside the respondents' palace

Nr:	16
Date:	18/04/2006
Name:	Gurunshi and Sisala headman: Al-Hajji Hamidu Usman Madugu
Gender:	01
Age:	07: 67
Religion:	07
Town:	Kumasi
Starting time:	14:08:16
End time:	16:10:26
Location:	Kumasi: Tummu station

Nr:	17
Date:	16/04/2006
Name:	Sarkin *Zongo*: Al-Hajji Sheikh Zakuruka
Gender:	01
Age:	07: 72
Religion:	07
Town:	Kumasi
Starting time:	12:07:07
End time:	14:40:48
Location:	Kumasi: old *zongo*: inside the respondents' palace

Nr:	18
Date:	20/03/2006
Name:	Mossi headman; Al-Hajji Ibrahim Abdul Achman Adam the III
Gender:	01
Age:	07: 60
Religion:	07
Town:	Kumasi: Mossi *zongo*-ash town
Starting time:	18:11:15
End time:	19:40: 20

Location:	Kumasi: inside the respondents' palace

Nr:	19
Date:	05/03/2006
Name:	Kwasi Asare Ankomah
Gender:	01
Age:	N.A.
Religion:	N.A.
Town:	Kumasi
Starting time:	N.A
End time:	N.A
Location:	ARHC

Nr:	20
Date:	05/12/2005
Name:	Paramount queen mother Yaa Asantewaa II
Gender:	02
Age:	04:38
Religion:	03: Roman Catholic
Town:	Ejisu
Starting time:	10:01:45
End time:	12:29:00
Location:	Ejisu: inside the palace

Nr:	21
Date:	05/12/2005
Name:	Afua Tweneboa Kodua: the great grandchild of the late female warrior Nana Yaa Asantewaa
Gender:	02
Age:	07
Religion:	02
Town:	Ejisu
Starting time:	13:17:24
End time:	14:22:33
Location:	Ejisu: inside the Yaa Asantewaa House

Nr:	22
Date:	06/12/2005
Name:	Patricia Kwakye Manu
Gender:	02
Age:	05:54
Religion:	03:Methodist
Town:	Ejisu
Starting time:	10:33:19
End time:	12:01:41
Location:	Ejisu: inside the school of the respondent

Nr:	23
Date:	13/03/2006
Name:	Nana Brefo Gyededu Kotowko II
Gender:	01
Age:	05: 52
Religion:	03: Anglican
Town:	Kumasi

Starting time:	13:06:09
End time:	15:39:48
Location:	Kumasi: the respondent's office in Snitt house

Nr:	24
Date:	08/12/2005
Name:	Sandra Owusu Ansah
Gender:	02
Age:	03: 30
Religion:	03: Roman Catholic
Town:	Kumasi
Starting time:	11:14:58
End time:	13:42:14
Location:	Kumasi: CNC

Nr:	25
Date:	08/12/2005
Name:	Daniel Adjei Junior
Gender:	01
Age:	05
Religion:	03: Methodist
Town:	Kumasi (originally from Achease)
Starting time:	14:31:07
End time:	16:52:27
Location:	Kumasi: CNC

Nr:	26
Date:	09/12/2005
Name:	Osei Kwadwo
Gender:	01
Age:	07: 69
Religion:	08: Seventh Day Adventist
Town:	Kumasi
Starting time:	11:04:58
End time:	12:25:49
Location:	Kumasi: CNC

Nr:	27
Date:	17/03/2006
Name:	Mossi headman- imam Ustaz Ali Adam Al-Ameer
Gender:	01
Age:	05: 55
Religion:	07
Town:	Kumasi
Starting time:	16:19:26
End time:	18:36:26
Location:	Kumasi: Mossi *zongo*-Ash town

Nr:	28
Date:	06/03/2006
Name:	Maabahene and Nana Prenyia-Besease
Gender:	01
Age:	05: 45 and 04: 42
Religion:	02

Town:	Kumasi
Starting time:	10:05:27
End time:	11:05:45
Location:	Kumasi: outside Manhyia's palace

Nr:	29
Date:	10/03/2006
Name:	Paramount queen mother Ama Serwah Nyarko
Gender:	02
Age:	06: 57
Religion:	05: *Afrikania*
Town:	Kumasi
Status:	02
Employment:	02
Level of education:	03: four year A certificate
Starting time:	11:16:52
End time:	12:45:58
Location:	Offinso: in the respondents' palace

Nr:	30
Date:	05/03/2006
Name:	Nana Ababeo (chief of Adiebeba)
Age:	01
Gender:	05: 45
Religion:	03: Methodist
Town:	Kumasi
Starting time:	13:02:00
End time:	14:34:42
Location:	Kumasi: outside Manhyia palace

Nr:	31
Date:	24/11/2005
Name:	Ama Framponee
Gender:	02
Age:	07: 65
Religion:	08: Seventh Day Adventist
Town:	Achiase Nwabiagya
Starting time:	9:14:27
End time:	12:14:42
Location:	Achiase Nwabiagya: outside the respondent's house

Nr:	32
Date:	10/02/2006
Name:	Osei Hyiaman
Gender:	01
Age:	04: 44
Religion:	Assemblies of God
Town:	Kumasi, originally Offinso
Starting time:	13:25:54
End time:	14:21:47
Location:	Kumasi: Faith Assemblies of God-Methodist education unit

Nr:	33
Date:	16/02/2006
Name:	R.Aboagye
Gender:	01
Age:	06: 58
Religion:	03: Presbyterian
Town:	Kumasi
Starting time:	09:29:05
End time:	10:46:41
Location:	Kumasi: inside the respondents office (Metro Education office)

Nr:	34
Date:	16/02/2006
Name:	Margaret Arhin
Gender:	02
Age:	04: 41
Religion:	03: Methodist
Town:	Kumasi
Starting time:	11:51:13
End time:	15:04:19
Location:	Inside the resource centre

Nr:	35
Date:	14/02/2006
Name:	Josef Agyeman
Gender:	01
Age:	05: 54
Religion:	03: Presbyterian
Town:	Kumasi
Starting time:	11:51:25
End time:	13:44:22
Location:	Kumasi: inside the resource centre

Nr:	36
Date:	14/02/2006
Name:	Patrick Domfeh
Gender:	01
Age:	04: 42
Religion:	08: Seventh Day Adventist
Town:	Kumasi
Starting time:	14:51:25
End time:	16:20:20
Location:	Kumasi: inside the resource centre

Nr:	37
Date:	24/02/2006
Name:	Hane Harune
Gender:	01
Age:	07: 63
Religion:	07: Sunni
Town:	Kumasi
Starting time:	14:53:32
End time:	17:20:39
Location:	Kumasi: *Zongo* 88.7 FM radio station

Nr:	38
Date:	02/03/2006
Name:	Peter King Appiah
Gender:	01
Age:	04: 38
Religion:	04
Town:	Kumasi
Starting time:	14:53:48
End time:	16:16:34
Location:	Kumasi: CNC

Nr:	39
Date:	08/03/2006
Name:	Kwaku Amoako Attah Fosu (research officer and publisher of small books on AIR).
Gender:	01
Age:	04:37
Religion:	03 (Protestant: Seventh Day Adventist)
Town:	Kumasi
Starting time:	15:29:55
End time:	16:35:33
Location:	Kumasi: CNC

Nr:	40
Date:	07/03/2006
Name:	Imurana Musah (chief-imam of the whole Ashanti Region)
Gender:	01
Age:	07: 61
Religion:	07
Town:	Kumasi
Starting time:	16:39:54
End time:	17:46:17
Location:	Kumasi *zongo:* inside the respondents' house

Nr:	41
Date:	08/03/2006
Name:	S. F. Adjei
Gender:	01
Age:	05: 49
Religion:	03: Presbyterian
Town:	Kumasi
Starting time:	10:07:14
End time:	11:28:30
Location:	Kumasi: CNC

Nr:	42
Date:	23/1/2001 (course 2)
Name:	Dr. Osei Agyeman
Gender:	01
Age:	05: unknown
Religion:	03: unknown
Town:	Kumasi
Starting time:	N.A.
End time:	N.A.

Location:	Kumasi: KNUST: course (10 weeks) on Akan cosmology

Nr:	43
Date:	11/12/2005
Name:	Paramount queen mother Nana Serwaah Amponssaa
Gender:	02
Age:	04: 40
Religion:	01: Indigenous Religion and Anglican
Town:	Kumawu
Starting time:	N.A.
End time:	N.A.
Location:	Kumasi: KNUST: course (10 weeks) on Akan cosmology

Nr:	44
Date:	24/11/2005
Name:	Osei Kwaku
Gender:	01
Age:	07:70
Religion:	03: Roman Catholic
Town:	Heman Buoɔho
Starting time:	13:15:22
End time:	16:16:34
Location:	Heman Buoɔho: outside the respondents' house

7.5. Maps

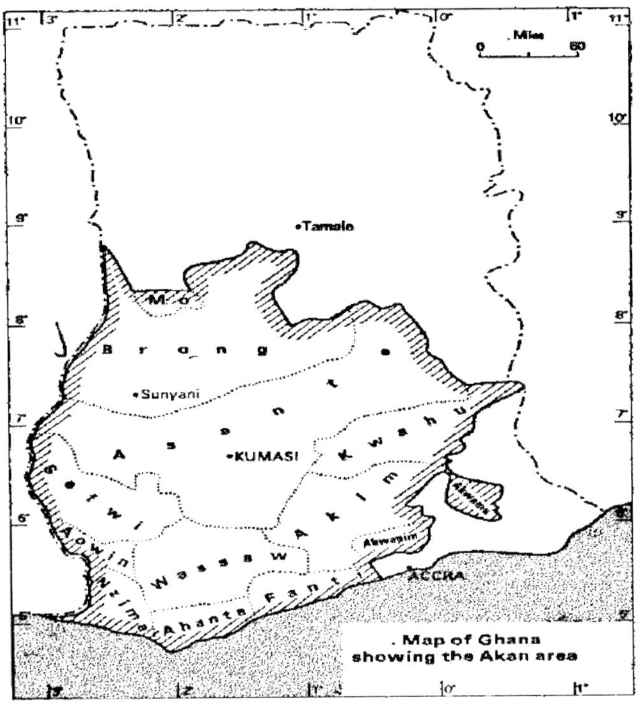

. Map of Ghana showing the Akan area

Map 1: the regions of the Gold Coast in Guinea.

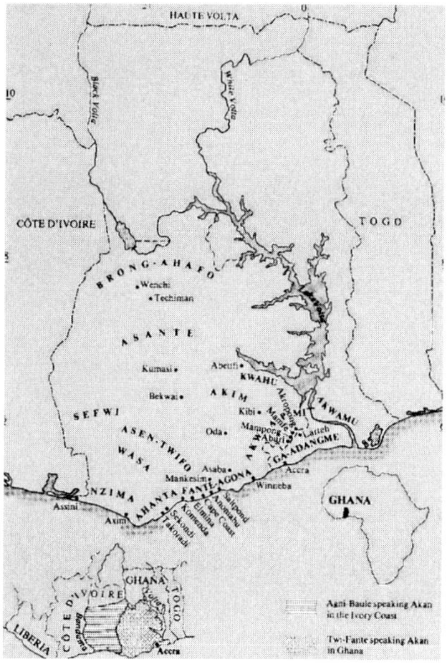

Map 2: the Akan in the Ivory Coast and Ghana.

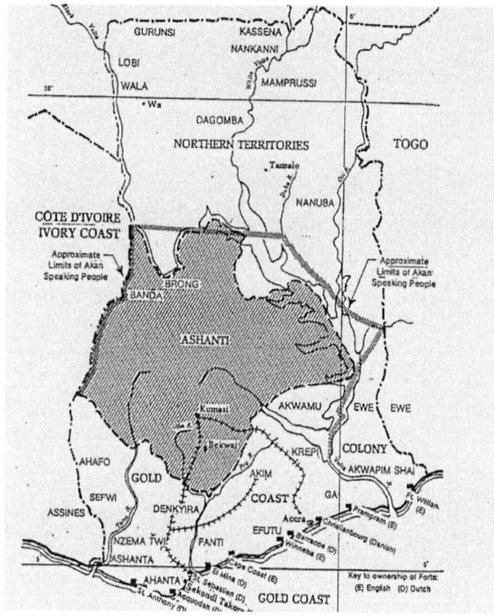

Map 3: the Northern Territories, the Gold Coast Colony and the Crown colony of Asante.

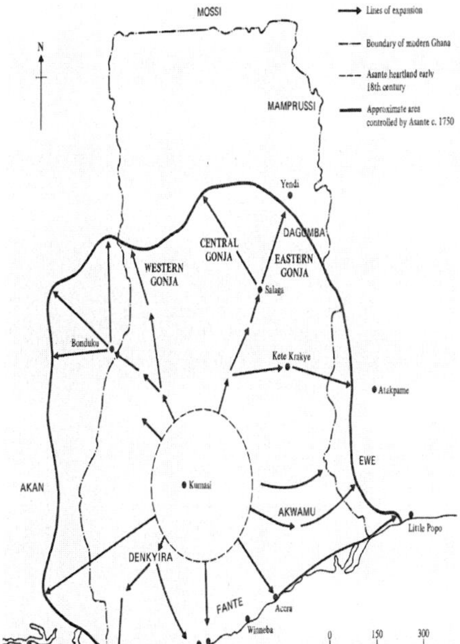

Map 4: the Asante kingdom around 1750.

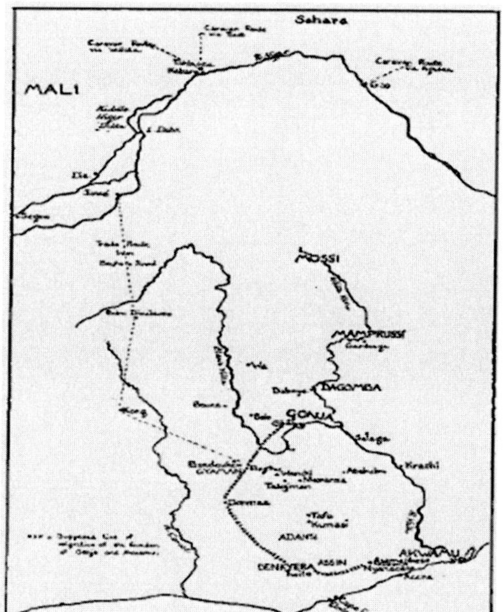

Map 5: the Southern penetration of the Mande.

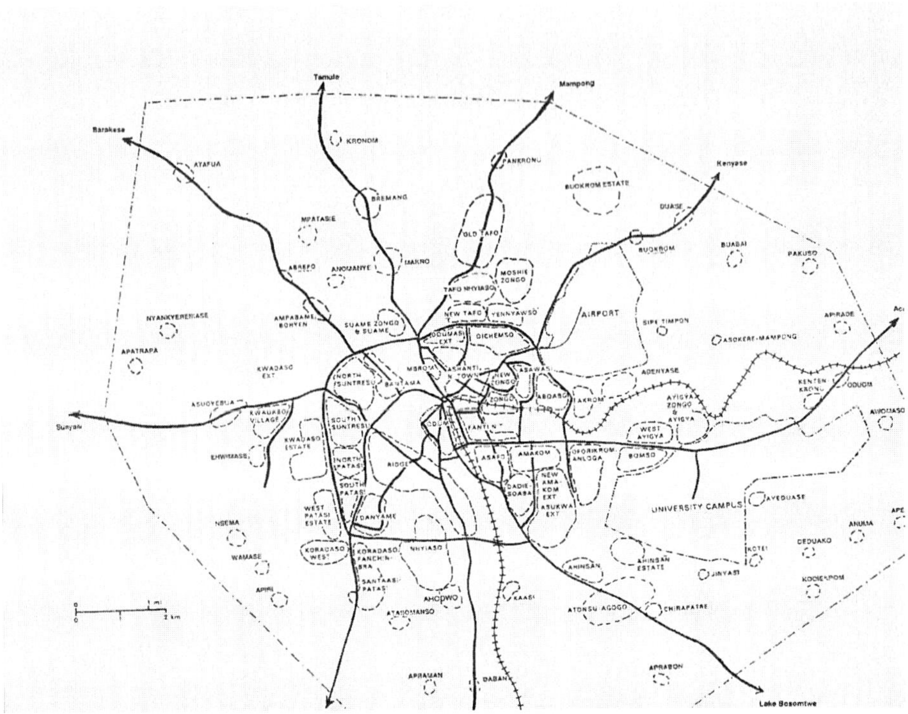

Map 6: the city of Kumasi, showing residential areas.

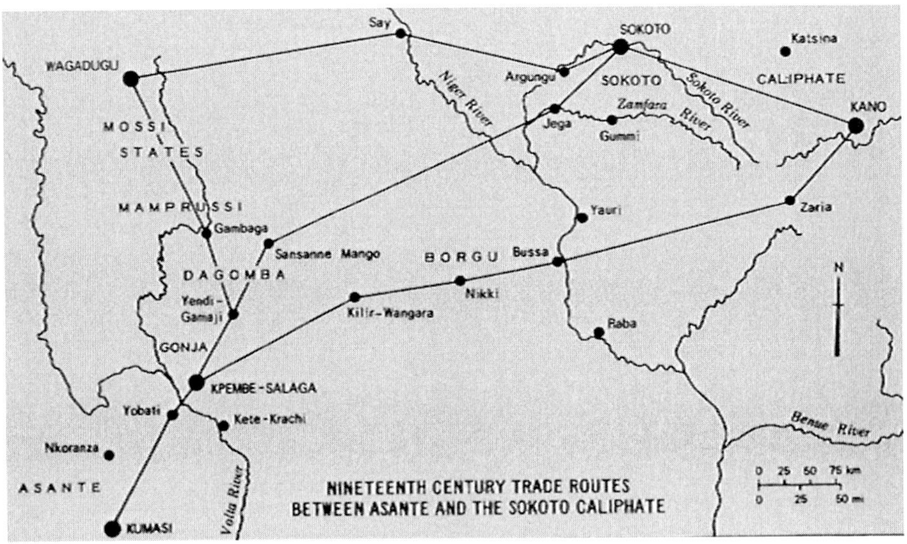

Map 7: the nineteenth century trade routes between Asante and the Sokoto Caliphate.

7.6. Photographs[103]

Photograph 1: *ayakeseho*. The place of the great brass vessel (1896) (Rattray 1959 [first published in 1927]).

Photograph 2: the *ahodae* ceremony of Nana Saaman Nantwi II.

[103] The author took the photographs, unless specified otherwise.

Photograph 3: the public mourning of female family members of the deceased and women.

Photograph 4: a gift giving ceremony.

Photograph 5: the indigenous priest during an *abosom brafo* dancing ceremony.

Photograph 6: an *abosom brafo* dancing ceremony of an indigenous priest.

Photograph 7: *abosom brafo* chews raw charcoal. Source: Dr. Charles Kingsley Coffie.

Photograph 8: (Left) Maulvi Abdul, (in the Middle) *Asantehene* Osei Tutu II, (Right), his eminence Sheikh Wahab Adam Usmanu Sharubutu. Source: Dr. Charles Kingsley Coffie.

Photograph 9: the Asantehene receives blessings. Source: Dr. Charles Kingsley Coffie.

7.7. Symbols

Symbol 1: *Odenkyem da nsuo mu nso ohome nsuo ne mframa* – The crocodile *(odenkyem)* lives under water, but he breathes air.

Index

A

H

I

K

L

M

N

O

Ɔ

P

Q

R

S